TREK

The Encyclopedia

D1287765

HAL SCHUSTER and WENDY RATHBONE

PIONEER BOOKSINC

(800)444-2524 Ext 67

PIONEER BOOKS

MTV: MUSIC YOU CAN SEE   ISBN#1-55698-355-7

TREK: THE NEXT GENERATION CREW BOOK   ISBN#1-55698-363-8

TREK: THE PRINTED ADVENTURES   ISBN#1-55698-365-5

THE CLASSIC TREK CREW BOOK   ISBN#1-55698-368-9

TREK VS THE NEXT GENERATION   ISBN#1-55698-370-0

TREK: THE NEXT GENERATION TRIBUTE BOOK   ISBN#1-55698-366-2

THE HOLLYWOOD CELEBRITY DEATH BOOK   ISBN#1-55698-369-7

LET'S TALK: AMERICA'S FAVORITE TV TALK SHOW HOSTS ISBN#1-55698-364-6

HOT-BLOODED DINOSAUR MOVIES ISBN#1-55698~365-4

BONANZA: THE UNOFFICIAL STORY OF THE PONDEROSA ISBN#1-55698-359-X

THE KUNG FU BOOK ISBN#1-55698-328-X

TREK: THE DEEP SPACE CELEBRATION   ISBN#1-55698 330-1

TREK: THE DEEP SPACE CREW BOOK ISBN#1-55698-335-2

TREK: THE NEXT GENERATION TRIBUTE BOOK TWO   ISBN#1-55698-329-8

COVER BY BRUCE WOOD

Library of Congress Cataloging-in-Publication Data
Hal Schuster, 1955 and Wendy Rathbone—

Trek: The Encyclopedia

1. Trek: The Encyclopedia (television, popular culture)
I. Title

Published by Pioneer Books, Inc., 5715 N. Balsam Rd., Las Vegas, NV, 89130.

First Printing, 1994

ACKNOWLEDGMENTS

I want to thank Andy Rathbone for assisting me in computer format, which often eludes me. Also, James Van Hise was of great assistance with research material. Also thanks to: Della Van Hise, Tina Rathbone, Rhett Rathbone, Alice Rathbone, Alayne Gelfand, Marge Simon, Ann Schwader, Kym Hansen, Linda Berez, Taerie Bryant for assistance and support above and beyond the call of duty.

Publisher and Designer: Hal Schuster   *Editor: Mira Schwirtz*

Interior Color Photos ©1994 Albert L. Ortega

DEDICATED

TO

Dreamers

FOREWARD

This encyclopedia covers all the Star Trek series: classic, The Next Generation, Deep Space 9, the films, and the animated series. Included are not only the names of actors, writers and other people involved with Star Trek, but characters, ships, events, locations and terminology. Since the TNG series is still ongoing, material is covered through the sixth season, but not beyond. DS9 is covered for its first short season only.

As I did the research for this book, I encountered numerous ways to spell certain lesser known terms, planets, races, characters. Without any 'official' guide, I was forced to choose the spellings I thought best described the word. Often, I used spellings from *Starlog* magazine, when that information was available. I also used many different fan encyclopedias, as well as books by James Van Hise, John Peel, and Ed Gross to locate specialized information, spelling, and relevant details. With the amount of information I had to go through, I'm sure there will be mistakes. I have attempted, with the materials on hand, to make this as complete a reference manual as possible, including entries for everything I could find in every source at hand. A bibliography at the end of this book gives credit to those sources which were invaluable. Future editions will correct mistakes as they are spotted, and you, the reader, are invaluable in correcting these mistakes. Please send any detected errors by mail to **THE TREK ENCYCLOPEDIA, 5715 N. Balsam Rd., Las Vegas, NV 89130**

or vial electronic mail through Compuserve to 72160, 151. Assistance is not only appreciated but necessary for this to become a more accurate volume.

Names of episodes and people (both real and fictional) appear in caps. Other references appear in small case. One appendix gives an episode guide to each series, which I hope will be helpful for quickly locating an exact title to look up. A second appendix gives a list of Star Trek novels through summer of '93, of note for those who collect the books.

This is an A to Z guide. Everything is alphabetized for your convenience, and nothing is set off in any special category to confuse you.

Live long and prosper,

—Wendy Rathbone

Additional Note:

Star Trek has become a phenomenon unprecedented in the history of the electronic media. The only universes to even begin to approach that of Trek in sheer size and dedication of following are those of Sherlock Holmes, Ulysses and the Ramayana— and perhaps that is because there is a bit of each in its magic! Trek will endure long after television of the Twentieth Century has passed into memory. It offers hope and a future to a world much in need. As long as we continue to try to understand the beauty of Infinite Diversity in Infinite Combination, our humble world indeed has a chance to shine and reach out to the larger universe.

—Hal Schuster

"I'll Take You Home Again, Kathleen"

the song Kevin Riley sings in Classic episode "The Naked Time" after he has commandeered Engineering.

"Let Me Help"

Kirk tells Edith these three words are revered over "I love you" as suggested by a novelist who lived on a planet orbiting a star in Orion's belt in Classic episode "The City On The Edge Of Forever."

"Maiden Wine"

a song Spock sings in Classic episode "Plato's Stepchildren." It was written by Leonard Nimoy.

"Nightengale Woman"

a poem Gary Mitchell quotes from in Classic episode "Where No Man Has Gone Before." It was written in 1996 by Phineas Tarbolde on Canopus and is considered one of the most passionate sonnets ever written. The excerpt Gary quotes reads: "My love has wings, slender feathered things with grace and upswept curve and tapered tip."

Aucdet IX

a Federation Medical Collection Station mentioned in TNG episode "The Child."

"Old Ones"

referred to in Classic episode "What Are Little Girls Made Of?" as being the long-dead creators of the androids found on Exo III.

11001001

This first season TNG episode was written by Maurice Hurley and Bob Lewin and directed by Paul Lynch. In this episode, Bynars working on repairing the computer on the *Enterprise* steal the ship with Picard and Riker on board trapped on the holodeck. Guest stars: Carolyn McCormick, Gene Dynarski, Ron Brown, Abdul Salaam el Razzac, Jack Sheldon, Alexandra Johnson, Katy Boyer, Iva Lane, Kelly Ann McNally.

498th Air Base Group

where Colonel Fellini interrogates Kirk and Sulu in Classic episode "Tomorrow Is Yesterday." It is located on the Omaha Air Force Base.

829-IV

world that has evolved a culture that looks like a 20th century Rome in Classic episode "Bread and Circuses."

A PIECE OF THE ACTION

Written by David P. Harmon and Gene L. Coon, directed by James Komack, this second season Classic Trek episode aired 1/12/68. On the planet Iotia, mobs run the cities. Years ago, the *U.S.S. Horizon* inadvertently influenced the natives by leaving behind a book called *Chicago Mobs of the Twenties*. The Enterprise is sent to study the effects of this 'infection' and become embroiled in the plots of some mobsters to take over the planet. Guest stars: William Blackburn, Anthony Caruso, Victor Tayback, Lee Delano, Steve Marlo, John Harmon, Sheldon Collins. Of note: Kirk invents a complicated and ingenius card game called Fizzbin.

A PRIVATE LITTLE WAR

Written by Gene Roddenberry and Judd Crucis, directed by Marc Daniels, this second season Classic Trek episode aired 2/2/68. Spock is shot by a native on Neural, and the Enterprise discovers that this peaceful society, first explored 13 years before, is being interfered with by Klingons. Kirk, who was part of the initial exploration team years before, goes back to meet the people he knows and tries to help them. Guest stars: Michael Whitney, Nancy Kovak, Booker Marshall, Arthur Bernard, Ned Romero, Gary Pillar, Janos Prohaska. Of note: Dr. M'Benga makes an appearance, and we learn about Vulcan healing trances.

A TASTE OF ARMAGEDDON

Written by Robert Hamner and Gene L. Coon, directed by Joseph Pevney, this first season Classic Trek episode aired 2/23/67. The Enterprise gets caught between two warring planets, Eminiar VII and Vendikar, who are using computers to fight their battles. Guest stars: Gene Lyons, David Opatoshu, Robert Samson, Barbara Babcock, Miko Mayama, Sean Kenney.

A&P Parisian Grand Premier

alcoholic drink in TNG episode "Datalore" that Lore gave Data to knock him out.

A-7 Computer Rating

Spock has an A-7 computer rating, which means he's an expert in computer science.

AARON, ADMIRAL

character in the TNG episode "Conspiracy" played by Ray Reinhardt. He was controlled by parasites.

ABATEMARCO, FRANK

scriptwriter of TNG episodes "Chain of Command Part I and II," and "Man of the People."

ABBOTT, JOHN

the actor who played Ayleborne in Classic Trek episode "Errand of Mercy." Born 1905 in London, England, he moved to Hollywood in 1941. He has appeared in the films "Mrs. Miniver" ('42), "Gigi" ('58), "The Black Bird" ('75).

ABROM

character played by William Wintersole on Classic Trek episode "Patterns of Force." He is a native of Zeon, and the elder brother of Isak.

Absorbed

term used on Classic Trek episode "The Return Of The Archons" for placing a person under the mental control of the computer, Landru, that runs the society. When a person is "absorbed," s/he becomes

of the 'body', and possesses almost zombie-like qualities. They have no free will of their own.

Academy of Sciences
mentioned in the animated episode "The Pirates of Orion." The school is located on Deneb V and is associated with Star Fleet.

Acadian Star System
mentioned on the animated episode "Mudd's Passion." This region contains the mining planet Motherlode.

Acamar III
Picard visits Acamar III in TNG episode "The Vengeance Factor" in order to reunite the Acamarians with the Gatherers. Acamar III is ruled by Sovereign Marouk.

Acamarian Brandy
served in TNG episode "The Vengeance Factor."

Acamarians
inhabitants of Acamar III, they are encountered in TNG episode "The Vengeance Factor." They have iron-copper composite blood. They are related to the Gatherers who split off from them a century before.

ACCOLAN
character in TNG episode "When The Bough Breaks" played by Dan Mason. He is Harry Bernard's adopted father.

Aceton Assimilators
referred to in TNG episode "Booby Trap," they are used by the Menthars as

booby traps to catch ships. They feed on raw power, convert the power to radiation, then throw it back to the source.

Acetylcholine Test
in the Classic Trek episode "The Immunity Syndrome," Spock gives the amoebae creature this test while he is on the shuttle-craft.

ACHILLES
he is a gladiator in the Classic Trek episode "Bread and Circuses." McCoy fights him almost beating him down, though he is saved ultimately by Spock who gives Achilles the neck pinch.

Achrady VII
referred to in TNG episode "Captain's Holiday," this is the world where Lwaxana Troi was visiting for a conference before meeting the *Enterprise* at Starbase 12.

ACKER, SHARON
actress who appeared in "The Mark of Gideon" as Odona. Born 1936 in England, she has had roles in the series "The Senator," "The New Perry Mason," and "Executive Suite." Films: "Lucky Jim" ('57), "Point Blank" ('67), "Threshold" ('83.)

ACOST, JARED
in TNG episode "Devil's Due," he is the leader of Ventax II. He was played by Marcelo Tubert.

Actos IV
referred to in TNG episode "Manhunt," this world is an oligarchy.

Acts of Cumberland
referred to in TNG episode "The Measure of a Man," this is the Starfleet precedent that makes Data 'owned' by Starfleet.

ADAM
character from the Classic Trek episode "The Way To Eden." Played by Charles Napier, Adam is a follower of Dr. Sevrin looking for the mythical planet Eden. He is the son of an admiral.

ADAMS, MARC
the actor who played Hamlet in Classic Trek episode "The Conscience of the King."

ADAMS, PHIL
a stunt man who was Kirk's double in Classic Trek episode "Amok Time." He's done stunt work on "The Wackiest Ship In The Army", and "The Christmas Coal Mine Miracle" ('77.)

ADAMS, STANLEY
scriptwriter and actor, 1915-1977. Wrote, with George F. Slavin, Classic Trek episode "The Mark of Gideon," and performed as Cyrano Jones in Classic Trek episode "The Trouble With Tribbles," and as the voice of Cyrano in the animated episode "More Tribbles, More Troubles." He also appeared in the sf series "Lost In Space" and "The Atomic Kid" ('54), as well as in "Nevada Smith" ('66). He commited suicide in 1977.

ADAMS, DR. TRISTAN
character from Classic Trek episode "Dagger of the Mind." He is the head doc-

tor of the Tantalus penal colony. He invents a machine called a neural neutralizer with which he can brainwash and control his patients. The machine empties the mind. Adams eventually dies of loneliness under the ray of the neutralizer. He is played by James Gregory.

ADELE, AUNT
mentioned in TNG episode "Cause and Effect" as being Picard's aunt who served him steamed milk to combat insomnia.

Adelphi, U.S.S.
ship in TNG episode "Tin Man" commanded by Captain Darson.

Adelphous IV
destination of the *Enterprise* at the end of TNG episode "Data's Day."

Adini Star Cluster
in TNG episode "Too Short A Season," the *Enterprise* passes through here on her way to Mordan IV.

ADLER, ALAN J.
scriptwriter who penned TNG episode "The Loss."

Agamemnon, U.S.S.
one of the ships being led in an attack against the Borg in TNG episode "Descent."

Age of Ascension
a Klingon term referring to a rite of manhood. It is referred to in TNG episode "Sins of the Fathers."

Age of Inclusion
mentioned in TNG episode "Heart Of Glory," it

is a Klingon term referring to age. Worf had not yet reached the age of inclusion when he was orphaned.

AGMAR
character on the animated episode "The Infinite Vulcan." He is a plant being. His voice is the voice of James Doohan.

Agonizer
a weapon used in the Classic Trek "Mirror, Mirror" episode. In the 'mirror' universe, the device is used for punishment. When it is attached to a person's body, it gives great pain. The Klingons also have a device called the agonizer, which is slightly different.

Agony Booth
used in the Classic Trek episode "Mirror, Mirror," it is a booth about the size of a phone booth in which a person is placed for punishment. When the controls are turned on, great pain is experienced by the victim. One of the victims is Chekov who when placed in the booth, naturally, screams.

AHART, KATHY
actress who appeared as an elite crew woman in Classic Trek episode "Space Seed."

Ahn-woon
a Vulcan weapon that is like a long band used to trip, strangle or tie up an opponent. Spock uses the ahn-woon to strangle Kirk in Classic Trek episode

"Amok Time" and believes he has killed him.

Air Police Sergeant
character played by Hal Lynch in Classic Trek episode "Tomorrow Is Yesterday." He is the one who gets to taste chicken soup in the transporter room.

Ajax, U.S.S.
ship referred to in TNG episode "Where No One Has Gone Before" as being a part of the Kosinski experiments.

AJUR
character from TNG episode "Captain's Holiday" and played by Karen Landry. She is a Vorgon security agent from the 27th century.

AKAAR, LEONARD JAMES
in Classic Trek episode "Friday's Child," Eleen has a baby boy. Because Kirk and McCoy helped deliver him, he is named after them. The child becomes the new ruler of Capella IV.

AKAAR
character played by Ben Gage in Classic Trek episode "Friday's Child." He is the teer, the leader on Capella IV. He has a wife, Eleen, and is killed by Maab.

Akagi, U.S.S.
one of the ship's mentioned as being used in a blockage in the Klingon civil war in TNG episode "Reunion."

AKHARIN
the original name of Flint (played by James Daly) from the Classic Trek episode "Requiem For Methuselah." Akharin was a soldier born on Earth in 3834 B.C. in Mesopotamia who fell in a battle with an arrow through the heart and did not die. He found his tissues regenerated every time he was injured or killed. He took on other personas as he enjoyed a life of immortality, until he met the Enterprise crew in the 23rd century. (See entry for Flint.)

AKUTA
character in Classic Trek episode "The Apple" played by Keith Andes. He is the leader on Gamma Trianguli VI, also known as "the eyes of Vaal." Vaal is a ruling computer, and only Akuta can interpret its demands and orders through a set of antennae behind his ears.

ALAIMO, MARC
actor who played Commander T'Bok in the TNG episode "The Neutral Zone," guest starred in TNG "The Wounded," "Time's Arrow," and guest starred in DS9 "Emissary."

ALANS
a specialist in Vulcanology and geomechanics, he is a member of Wesley's Selcundi Drema team in TNG episode "Pen Pals." He is married to Hildebrandt, and is played by Whitney Rydbeck.

ALAR
a character referred to in the animated episode "Jihad." He was a religious teacher of the Skorr.

Alaynan Singerstone
a gift that Data leaves with the memory-erased Sarjenka at the end of TNG episode "Pen Pals." She finds it in Pulaski's office and plays with it. It sings a different song for every person, but will not sing for Data.

ALBATROSS
written by Dario Finelli, this animated Classic Trek episode aired 9/28/74. McCoy is accused of infecting a planetful of people with a virus that killed most of them nineteen years before. When the Enterprise visits the planet, McCoy is jailed. Meanwhile, when a senility plague hits the Enterprise crew, McCoy must be released to find an antidote. They find out an aurora and not McCoy is responsible for the plague, and McCoy discovers the cure. Guest voices: James Doohan (Kol-tai, Supreme Prefect)

Albeni
Meditation Crystal
in TNG episode "Angel One," Riker gives this item to Beate as a gift.

ALBERT, EDWARD LAWRENCE
actor who guest starred in DS9 episode "A Man Alone."

ALBERT, CADET JOSHUA

the cadet who was killed in the Kolvoord Starburst performed by Wesley and his classmates in TNG episode "The First Duty."

ALBERT, LIEUTENANT COMMANDER

father of Cadet Joshua Albert who was killed in an illegal Academy ship maneuver in TNG episode "The First Duty."

ALBRIGHT, BUDD

actor who played Rayburn in Classic Trek episode "What Are Little Girls Made Of?"

Alcyone

referred to in TNG episode "Haven." The inhabitants killed the plague-carrying Tarellian refugees.

Aldea

planet mentioned in TNG episode "When The Bough Breaks." It is located in the Epsilon Mynos system.

Aldebaran Colony

planet where Dr. Elizabeth Dehner from Classic Trek episode "Where No Man Has Gone Before" has lived.

Aldebaran Exchange

a chess move Riker makes to win against Nibor in TNG episode "Menage A Troi."

Aldebaran III

planet mentioned in Classic Trek episode "The Deadly Years" where Dr. Janet Wallace and her husband Dr. Theodore Wallace experiment on plants to slow their aging process.

Aldebaran Serpent

in TNG episode "Hide and Q," Q assumes this form in front of Picard and the crew.

Aldebaran Whiskey

Mr. Scott and Picard share some in TNG episode "Relics." It is green. Guinan gives it to Picard.

ALDRICH, RHONDA

actress who played the secretary Madeline in the TNG episodes "The Big Goodbye," "Manhunt," and "Clues."

Aldron IV

referred to in TNG episode "Coming of Age" as the *Enterprise*'s destination after leaving Relva.

Alert B-2

Kirk gives this order in Classic Trek episode "The Naked Time" signifying that main sections of the ship should be sealed off.

ALEXANDER, DAVID

director of the Classic Trek episodes "The Way To Eden" and "Plato's Stepchildren." He also directed episodes of "The Man From U.N.C.L.E."

ALEXANDER

character on Classic Trek episode "Plato's Stepchildren" played by Michael Dunn. He is a dwarf who is also the only person on Platonius who does not have the power of psychokinesis. He eventually leaves Platonius with Kirk, Spock and McCoy.

ALEXANDER

Worf's son played by Brian Bonsall. He has a recurring role on "The Next Generation." His last name is Rozhenko. His mother was K'Ehleyr. He was born on the 23rd day of Maktag, on the Klingon calendar.

ALEXANDRA

girl who was kidnapped in TNG episode "When The Bough Breaks" played by twins Jessica and Vanessa Bova.

Alfa 177

planet in Classic Trek episode "The Enemy Within" that contains a strange ore that causes the transporter to malfunction and split Kirk into two people. The rest of the landing party is marooned on Alfa 177 during its long, freezing night while the *Enterprise* crew tries to fix the transporter.

Algeron, Treaty of

established 180 years before, it created the Neutral Zone between the Federation and the Romulans. It is mentioned in TNG episode "The Defector."

Algeron IV

in TNG episode "Coming of Age," this is the *Enterprise*' destination after leaving Relva VII.

Algolian Ceremonial Rhythms

in TNG episode "Menage A Troi," these are chimes played to signal the end to a Trade Agreements Conference held on board the *Enterprise*.

ALICE

character in Classic Trek episode "Shore Leave." Played by Marcia Brown, she is a little blonde girl that only McCoy sees. She is dressed like Alice in Wonderland and is chasing a large white rabbit. Alice is also the name of a character in the Classic Trek episode "I, Mudd," played by twins Rhae and Alyce Andrece. She is an android, and there are 500 of her, all identical.

ALL OUR YESTERDAYS

written by Jean Lisette Aroeste, directed by Marvin Chomsky, this third season Classic Trek episode aired 3/14/69. On the planet Sarpeidon, Kirk, Spock and McCoy discover a library where there is a doorway which is a time machine called an atavachron. The inhabitants sun is about to go nova, and all have escaped to the past except Mr. Atoz, the librarian. He thinks Kirk, Spock and McCoy are there to escape, and pushes them through the doorway. Spock and McCoy end up in a snowy ice age, while Kirk is deposited in a society obsessed with witch-hunting. Spock falls in love with a lonely woman named Zarabeth as he mentally reverts 5000 years into the past when Vulcans were emotional, barbaric creatures. Guest stars: Mariette Hartley, Ian Wolfe, Anna Karen, Johnny Haymer, Ed Bakey, Kermit Murdock, Al Cavens, Stan Barrett. Of note: This episode prompted a sequel by novel writer Ann

Crispin, who wrote *Yesterday's Son* based on this episode, as well as the sequel to it, *Time For Yesterday.*

Allasomorph

a shapeshifter. The Daledi of TNG episode "The Dauphin" are allasomorphs. Odo of DS9 is a shapeshifter, but he is very different in his natural state and so seems unrelated to the Daledi.

ALLEGIANCE

this third season TNG episode was written by Hans Beimler and Richard Manning, and directed by Winrich Kolbe. Aliens replace Captain Picard in the *Enterprise* with a duplicate, and the real Picard is held with three other hostages who face various problems from hunger to mistrust when they believe one among them is involved in the kidnapping itself. Guest stars: Stephen Markle, Reiner Schone, Joycelyn O'Brien, Jerry Rector, Jeff Rector.

ALLEN, CHAD

actor who played Jono/Jeremiah Rossa in TNG episode "Suddenly Human." He was a regular in the tv series "Our House," and is currently a regular on "Dr. Quinn, Medicine Woman." He has a twin sister.

ALLEN, COREY

director of TNG episodes "Encounter At Farpoint," "Homesoil," "Final Mission," and "The Game," and DS9 episode "Captive Pursuit."

ALLEN, GEORGE E.

actor who played the Engineer in Classic Trek episode "Devil in the Dark."

ALLEN, RICHARD

actor who played Kentor in TNG episodes "The Ensigns of Command," and "Darmok."

ALLEN, PHILIP RICHARD

actor who played Captain Esteban in the Classic Trek movie "The Search For Spock." He also appeared in the film "Mommie Dearest" and the series "Get Christie Love!"

ALLENBY, ENSIGN TESS

conn officer on the *Enterprise* in TNG episode "Final Mission." She is played by Mary Kohnert.

ALLEY, KIRSTIE

born 1955 in Wichita, Kansas, Alley is the actress who played Saavik in the movie "The Wrath of Khan," her first feature film role. Another actress, Robin Curtis, took up the role in "The Search For Spock" and "The Voyage Home" after Alley asked for too much money. This didn't hurt her career, however. Known for her character of Rebecca on "Cheers," she's won an Emmy award for best actress in a comedy series. Her other film credits are numerous. She is married to actor Parker Stevenson, and is a Scientologist.

ALLIN, JEFF

actor who guest-starred in TNG episode "Imaginary Friend."

Alondra

a planet mentioned in the animated episode "One Of Our Planets Is Missing." This world is uninhabited, and is eaten by a cosmic cloud creature.

Alpha Carinae V

mentioned in Classic Trek episode "Wolf in the Fold," it is where the Drella comes from.

Alpha Carinea II

mentioned in Classic Trek episode "The Ultimate Computer," this planet is approached by the *Enterprise* and analyzed by the M-5 computer, which notes it is a class M planet and then begins making landing party recommendations.

Alpha Centauri

mentioned in the Classic Trek episodes "Tomorrow Is Yesterday" and "Metamorphosis." In the first, Kirk tells his captors that Alpha Centauri "is a beautiful place, you ought to see it." In the second, Zefrem Cochrane is said to be a native of that world. Also mentioned by Geordi in TNG episode "Elementary, Dear Data."

Alpha Cygnus IX, Treaty of

something Sarek helped create, mentioned in TNG episode "Sarek."

Alpha Cygnus IX

referred to in TNG episode "Sarek" as the location of a treaty negotiation which Sarek attended in the past.

Alpha Leonis

in TNG episode "The Vengeance Factor," this is the *Enterprise* destination after they seal the Gatherer treaty.

Alpha Leonis System

where the *Enterprise* is headed in TNG episode "The Vengeance Factor." They are bringing much needed drugs to this sector.

Alpha Majoris I

mentioned in Classic Trek episode "Wolf in the Fold." It is said the cloud creature, the Mellitus, is from that world.

Alpha Omicron System

where the Galaxy's Child is found in the TNG episode of the same name.

Alpha Onias III

in TNG episode "Future Imperfect," this is the world where Riker supposedly contracted Altairian encephalitus while on an Away Team mission. He didn't. An alien boy lives there.

Alpha Proxima II

mentioned in Classic Trek episode "Wolf in the Fold." On this planet, there were a series of murders similar to the Jack The Ripper murders on Earth.

Alpha Quadrant

the quadrant of the galaxy that is most known and explored by the Federation and Starfleet. The Gamma Quadrant is the unknown section of the galaxy that can be reached through the wormhole near where DS9 is located.

Alpha VI

a known dead world, where Kirk reencounters Khan in the second Classic Trek feature film, "The Wrath of Khan." How he missed the fact that Ceti Alpha V wasn't where it was supposed to be is a mystery.

ALRIK

in TNG episode "The Perfect Mate," he is the Chancellor of Valt Minor, betrothed to Kamala. He is played by Mickey Cottrell.

Altair III

referred to in "Encounter At Farpoint" by Riker who visited this world when he was stationed on the *U.S.S. Hood.*

Altair VI

this planet is mentioned over and over again in Classic Trek episode "Amok Time." The *Enterprise* is headed there for a presidential inaugural dedication, but is diverted to Vulcan when Spock goes into pon farr.

Altairian Encephalitus

Riker supposedly contracted this while on an Away Team to Alpha Onias III in TNG episode "Future Imperfect."

Altar of Tomorrow

in Classic Trek episode "Devil In The Dark," the horta refers to her nest as the 'altar of tomorrow' and the 'chamber of ages.'

Altec

mentioned in TNG episode "The Outrageous

Okona" as being a planet in the Medina system.

ALTERNATIVE FACTOR, The

written by Don Ingalls, directed by Gerd Oswald, this first season Classic Trek episode aired 3/30/67. A traveler from a parallel universe threatens the Enterprise and the entire universe when his ship rips a hole in the fabric of existence. Guest stars: Robert Brown, Janet MacLachlen, Richard Derr, Eddie Paskey.

Alternative Warp

mentioned in Classic Trek episode "The Alternative Factor," it is a negative magnetic corridor where universes come together. In order to avert annihilation, the corridor is not supposed to be breached.

Altine Conference

where the alien scientists aboard the *Enterprise* in TNG episode "Suspicions" are going.

Altor VII

mentioned in TNG episode "Birthright," it is the world Beverly says she is looking forward to recreating on a DS9 holosuite.

ALVA

in the TNG episode "Manhunt," she is a murder victim found in a river. The character is never seen.

ALVIN

old man's dead body which Chekov finds in Classic Trek episode "The Deadly Years."

Alwanna Nebula

in TNG episode "Rightful Heir," the *Enterprise* passes and scans this phenomenon.

AMANDA

character played by Jane Wyatt in Classic Trek episode "Journey To Babel," and the fourth movie "The Voyage Home." Her full name is Amanda Grayson. The character reappears in the animated episode "Yesteryear," but the voice is that of Majel Barrett. She is Spock's human mother, the wife of Ambassador Sarek. She met Sarek on Earth when she was a teacher and he was visiting in his role of ambassador from Vulcan. She is the person from whom Spock learned compassion and a love for the arts. She is not a little perturbed by the fact that Spock seems to have turned his back on his human heritage and she confronts him about it in "Journey To Babel."

AMARIE

character in TNG episode "Unification Part II" who has multiple arms and plays a keyboard. Riker encounters her at the Qualor II bar. She is played by Harriet Leider.

Ambassador Class ship

the *Enterprise-* C from TNG episode "Yesterday's Enterprise" is of this class. *Enterprise* D is Galaxy Class. The first *Enterprise* starship was a Constitution Class ship.

AMBASSADOR SAREK

see entry for SAREK.

Ambergris

referred to in the animated "The Ambergris Element," this substance is produced by sperm whales. A similar chemical is used to make Kirk and Spock water-breathers on the planet Argo.

AMBERGRIS ELEMENT, The

Written by Margaret Armen, this animated Classic Trek episode aired 12/1/73. Kirk and Spock become water-breathers on the water planet Argo, and when rescued cannot survive in the air.

American Continent Institute

referred to in Classic Trek pilot "The Cage," it is the agency which sent the original expedition to Talos IV.

AMICK, MADCHEN

actress who played the teenage girl in TNG "The Dauphin." She is best known for her role in "Twin Peaks," and also appeared in the film "Sleepwalkers."

Amigosa Diaspora

a globular cluster the *Enterprise* charts in TNG episode "Schisms"

Amoebae

a single-celled creature. In Classic Trek episode "The Immunity Syndrome," a giant galactic amoebae which is eleven thousand miles in length is encountered by the *Enterprise.* The optical special effects for this creature were created by Frank Van Der Veer (see separate entry.) The all-

Vulcan manned starship *Intrepid* is destroyed by this creature before the *Enterprise* kills it. The amoebae looks exactly like the Amoebae dubia variety, now known as Polychaos Dubia, with the exception of its size.

AMOK TIME

Written by award-winning science fiction author Theodore Sturgeon (who also wrote the episode "Shore Leave") and directed by Joseph Pevney, this Classic Trek episode began the second season and aired 9/15/67. Spock must return to Vulcan as he enters pon farr, a shameful Vulcan physiological condition which forces him to mate or die. This episode is famous for addressing the delicate subject of Vulcan sexuality. Guest stars: Arlene Martel, Celia Lovsky, Lawrence Montaigne, Byron Morrow. Of note: Here we are first introduced to the Vulcan salute invented by Leonard Nimoy, pon farr, plomeek soup, and Finagle's law. It is the only episode in which Spock's home planet is shown, though the first, third and fourth Classic Trek movies give us further glimpses of this 'desert' world. Also, this episode marks Walter Koenig's first appearance as Ensign Pavel Chekov. This episode was nominated for a Hugo Award for Best Dramatic Presentation of 1967.

AMOS, GREGORY

scriptwriter who penned TNG script "A Matter of Honor."

Ampheon

referred to in the animated episode "The Counter-Clock Incident," it is the term used for a dead star in an antimatter universe.

ANAN 7

character from Classic Trek episode "A Taste Of Armageddon" played by David Opatoshu. He is the first councilman of Eminiar VII.

Anastazine

in TNG episode "The Hunted," this is a gas used to flood the cargo bays on the *Enterprise* in order to put Danar to sleep.

Anbo-jyutsu

a martial art practiced with armor and long sticks. Riker fights in the anbo-jyutsu ring in the *Enterprise* gymnasium on deck 12 with his father, Kyle, in TNG episode "The Icarus Factor."

Anchilles Fever

in TNG episode "Code of Honor," Anchilles Fever sweeps planet Styris Four.

AND THE CHILDREN SHALL LEAD

written by Edward J. Lakso, directed by Marvin Chomsky, this third season Classic Trek episode aired 10/11/68. On the planet Triacus, an evil entity called Gorgan controls five children whose parents he killed. The children use their alien powers to take over the Enterprise. Guest stars: Melvin Belli, Craig Hundley, James Wellman, Pamelyn Ferdin, Brian Tochi, Caesar Belli, Mark

Robert Brown. Of note: Famous attorney Melvin Belli got the role because he was a Star Trek fan. He also managed to get the role of one of the kids, Stevie, for his son, Caesar.

ANDERSON, BARBARA

actress who played Lenore Karidian in "Conscience of the King." She also played Ironside's assistant, Eve, in the "Ironside" series from 1967 to 1971, and won an Emmy for it. She's been in "Mission: Impossible," "The Six Million Dollar Man" and other tv series.

ANDERSON, ERICH

actor in TNG episode "Conundrum."

ANDERSON, JOHN

actor who played Kevin Uxbridge in TNG episode "The Survivors."

ANDERSON, JUDITH

actress (1898-1992) who played the Vulcan High Priestess in the second Classic Trek film "The Search For Spock." Dame Judith Anderson was born in Australia, and has appeared on stage and screen numerous times. She was given the title Dame Commander of the British Empire in 1960 for her excellent work. She won an Emmy award, and appeared in films including "The Ten Commandments" ('56) and "A Man Called Horse" ('70). She also appeared on the soap opera "Santa Barbara."

ANDERSON, SAM

actor who played the assistant manager of the Hotel

Royale in the TNG episode "The Royale."

ANDERSON, STEVE

actor who guest starred in TNG episode "First Contact."

ANDES, KEITH

actor who played Akuta in "The Apple." Born in New Jersey in 1920, Andes has done radio, stage, movie and tv work. He is in the films: "Clash By Night" ('52), "Tora! Tora! Tora!" ('70), and the tv series "Glynis" and "Search."

Andonesian Encephalitis

a non-contagious disease in TNG episode "The Dauphin."

Andonian Tea

in TNG episode "Conspiracy," Picard drinks Andonian tea while on Earth.

Andor

home of the Andorian race and mentioned in Classic episode "Journey To Babel."

Andorian

an Andorian is a being with blue skin, white hair and antennae. They are traditionally warriors with a somewhat violent nature. Andorians are first encountered in Classic Trek episode "Journey To Babel," though the character Thelev (William O'Connell) turns out to be an Orion in Andorian disguise. Shras (Reggie Nalder) is an Andorian in that episode. There is an Andorian (Dick Crockett) in "The Gamesters of

Triskelion." An Andorian (Richard Geary) also appears in "Whom Gods Destroy" as a patient in the penal colony on Elba II. In the animated episode "Yesteryear," an Andorian, Thelin, (voice provided by James Doohan) is first officer of the *Enterprise* when Vulcan history is changed and Spock died as a young boy. Andorians also appear in the animated episode "Time Trap." They are mentioned in TNG, but not seen.

Andorian Sivalthu
a horse.

ANDREA
character from Classic Trek episode "What Are Little Girls Made Of?" played by Sherry Jackson. She is an android created by Dr. Korby on Exo III. While trying to learn of emotion, she falls in love with Dr. Korby and he destroys himself and her with a single, suicidal phaser blast as they embrace.

ANDRECE, ALYCE & RHAE
twin actresses who appeared as the Alices in "I, Mudd." They also appeared in "Batman." They were hired when the Trek casting director saw them walking down the street and asked them if they wanted to be on tv.

ANDREWS, BUNNY
music editor of the Trek Classic film "The Undiscovered Country."

ANDREWS, TIGE
actor who played Kras in Classic Trek episode "Friday's Child." He was the star of "The Mod Squad" (1968-73). Other credits: "The Detectives" (1959-62), "Mr. Roberts" ('55), "The Last Tycoon" ('76), "Raid on Entebbe" ('77), "The Return of the Mod Squad" ('79).

Android
androids are mechanical beings who are made in human form. They are first encountered in Classic Trek episode "What Are Little Girls Made Of?" Andrea, Ruk, Brown, and Dr. Korby are all advanced forms of androids made from a thousand years old superior technology left by an alien race. Androids also appear in "I, Mudd," another race of machines created by a long-dead (1,743,912 years dead), technologically-advanced race called 'the makers.' In "Return To Tomorrow," Sargon, Thalessa and Henoch unsuccessfully work to create android bodies for their energies to inhabit. In "Requiem For Methuselah," Flint created Reena (a.k.a. Rayna) to be his perfect mate. Due to his immortality all his other brides had too-brief lifespans, which made it hard for him to form relationships. Reena was supposed to live forever with him on the planet Holberg 917G. However, when she experienced conflicting emotions by falling in love with both Kirk and Flint at the same time, the power of her feelings destroyed her. Mr. Atoz has android replicants which

help him tend the library on Sarpeidon in "All Our Yesterdays." On "The Next Generation," Data and Lore are androids created by Dr. Noonian Soong, as seen in the episode "Brothers." Data (see entry), one of the most popular main characters in the series, is always trying to learn more about the nature of humans. Although it often gets him into deep trouble, at other times it is a positive experience, and he seems on the verge of becoming human, of evolving. He is, as stated in "The Naked Now," a fully functional male android who can, if he chooses, be sexually compatible with a human. In the episode "The Offspring," Data creates his child, a female android named Lal, whose emotions ultimately destroy her. In the Classic Trek film "Star Trek: The Motion Picture," the Ilia probe sent to the *Enterprise* by Vejur is an android. Her curiosity of humans and desire to seek emotion sends her and Decker to another plane of existence.

Andromeda
referred to in Classic Trek episode "By Any Other Name," it is the galaxy from which the invaders, the Kelvans, come. It is the galaxy closest to our galaxy, The Milky Way. It is also referred to in "I, Mudd" as the galaxy where the 'makers' of the androids are from.

Angel One
in the TNG episode "Angel One," this world is seen as a

matriarchal planet where men are inferior.

ANGEL ONE
This first season TNG episode was written by Patrick Barry and directed by Michael Rhodes. The *Enterprise* finds survivors of the missing *Odin* on Angel One where they are fugitives. On this world, women rule and men are subservient. Guest stars: Karen Montgomery, Sam Hennings, Patricia McPherrson, Leonard John Crowfoot.

ANGELA
character played by Barbara Baldavin (see entry). Her full name is Angela Martinez, and appears in the Classic Trek episodes "Balance of Terror" (wherein she loses her husband whom she marries in that episode) and "Shore Leave."

Angosia
in TNG episode "The Hunted," this world is up for Federation membership. Prime Minister Nayrok tells the *Enterprise* crew that they have dedicated themselves to developing intellectual interests for centuries. However, they have imprisoned veterans from the recent Tarsian War, and when the veterans escape and take over, the government is threatened. The *Enterprise* leaves them behind, as the Prime Directive stipulates, to sort out their differences and we never find out what happens to the world.

Angosian Alteration

used in TNG episode "The Hunted" to turn ordinary men into perfect killing machines for war. The process alters cell structure using cryptobiolin, triclenidil, macrospentol, and other substances which are unrecognized by the *Enterprise* crew.

Angosian Transport

in TNG episode "The Hunted," this ship is captured by Roga Danar, a war veteran. He uses it to escape Lunar V.

ANKA

character on Classic Trek episode "The Cloud Minders" played by Fred Williamson. He is a Troglyte, and also a 'disruptor', or terrorist.

ANSARA, MICHAEL

actor who played Kang in Classic Trek episode "The Day of the Dove." Born in Lowell, Mass. in 1922, his credits are numerous, including "Broken Arrow" (1956-58), "The Law of the Plainsman" (1959-62), "Buck Rogers in the 25th Century" (1979-80), "Voyage To The Bottom Of The Sea" ('60), "Guns of the Magnificent Seven" ('69), and "The Manitou" ('78).

Ansata

in TNG episode "The High Ground," the Ansata are terrorist separatists fighting for autonomy on Rutia IV. Kyril Finn leads them. They have been fighting for 70 years.

Antarean Brandy

beverage served in Classic Trek episode "Is There In Truth No Beauty?" It is blue, and served on special occasions.

Antarean Glow Water

in Classic Trek episode "The Trouble With Tribbles," Cyrano Jones has Antarean glow water to sell, as well as tribbles. It appears to be something like perfume, though it could be simply merchandise of a decorative nature.

ANTARES, U.S.S.

referred to in Classic Trek episode "Charlie X," it is a science vessel with a crew of 20. Captain Ramart is her commander, and she is destroyed by Charlie's mental powers after they rescue him and turn him over to the *Enterprise*.

Antares Class Freighter

freighters that carry cargo, mentioned in TNG episodes "Face of the Enemy" and "Ensign Ro."

Antede III

in TNG episode "Manhunt," this world's inhabitants are fish-like beings. They are afraid of space travel, and travel in a self-induced catatonia. When the *Enterprise* transports two of these beings to Pacifica, they turn out to be assassins.

ANTEDIAN DELEGATE

character played by Mick Fleetwood in TNG episode "Manhunt." He represents Antede III, but is an assassin in disguise.

ANTHONY, LARRY

actor who played Ensign Berkeley in "Dagger of the Mind." His credits include "The Man From UNCLE."

ANTHONY, RICHARD

actor who played Rider in "Spectre of the Gun."

Antica

mentioned in TNG episode "Lonely Among Us," its inhabitants are canine-like. The planet, located in the Beta Renner system, is at war with its neighbor, Selay.

Anticontamination Suit

seen in Classic Trek episode "The Naked Time," this suit is worn by Spock and Tormolen. It is red and pliant, like a plastic coverall.

Antigravity

something that defies gravity despite its weight and mass. This term often refers to devices that can be attached to a heavy object to move or lift it. Antigravity devices are used to carry Nomad in Classic Trek episode "The Changeling," and to bring Kollos aboard the *Enterprise* in "Is There In Truth No Beauty?" In the Classic Trek episode "The Cloud Minders," Stratos City uses antigravity elevation. Antigravity chambers are seen on board the *Enterprise* in the Classic Trek episodes "Space Seed" and "The Lights Of Zetar." Antigravity gurneys are used in the movies and on "The Next Generation" and "Deep Space 9" to move

patients to sickbay, as well as for antigravity handles which are attached to heavy cargo for ease of movement. These are sometimes referred to as 'antigravs.'

Antimatter

a dangerous and mysterious substance used along with matter for warp propulsion in all "Star Trek" series. In the animated episode "The Counter-Clock Incident," the *Enterprise* enters an antimatter universe.

ANTONIO, LOU

actor who played Lokai in the Classic Trek episode "Let That Be Your Last Battlefield." He was also in "The Snoop Sisters" ('73), "Dog and Cat" ('77), and "Makin' It" ('79). His films include "Hawaii" ('66) and "Partners in Crime" ('73). He is also a producer.

Antos IV

a planet mentioned in Classic Trek episode "Whom Gods Destroy." It was on this world that Garth learned the talent of cellular metamorphosis.

ANYA

character in TNG episode "The Dauphin" who is an allasomorph, a shapeshifter whose natural state is pure light. Anya is the guardian of future leader Salia and is from Daled IV's third moon. She appears as an older woman played by Paddi Edwards, as a teenage girl played by Madchen Amick, and as a beast played by Cindy Sorenson.

APELLA
character in Classic Trek episode "A Private Little War" played by Arthur Bernard. He is the headman of a village.

APGAR, MANUA
character from TNG episode "A Matter Of Perspective" played by Gina Hecht. The wife of Dr. Nel Apgar, she is a Tanugan who accuses Riker of trying to rape her.

APGAR, DR. NEL
Tanugan scientist and creator of a Krieger wave converter from TNG episode "A Matter Of Perspective." His wife is Manua. He destroys himself when he blows up the space station he lives on. Apgar is played by Mark Margolis.

Aphasia
the diagnosis of what seems to be effecting the people of DS9 in the episode "Babel." Aphasia victims suffer from a condition that leaves the thought processes unaffected but redirects all aural and visual stimuli. The victims in "Babel" begin speaking using nonsense words.

Apnex Sea
located on Romulus, it is mentioned by Jarok as where his home is located in TNG episode "The Defector."

APOLLO
character in Classic Trek episode "Who Mourns For Adonais?" played by Michael Forest. He is one of the mythical Greek gods, apparently really a highly advanced alien being, who wants the *Enterprise* crew to settle on Pollux IV and worship him. He dies by spreading himself upon the wind and disintegrating.

APPEL, ED
character on Classic Trek episode "Devil In The Dark" played by Brad Weston. He is a chief engineer on Janus VI.

APPLE, The
written by Max Ehrlich and Gene L. Coon, directed by Joseph Pevney, this second season Classic Trek episode aired 10/13/67. The landing party beams down to a seemingly idyllic planet only to find it filled with poisonous plants that throw darts, and inhabited by humanoid beings whose lives are controlled by an entity called Vaal. The beings never age, never reproduce and never die. Guest stars: John Winston, Keith Andes, Celeste Yarnall, Shari Nims, David Soul (of Starsky and Hutch fame,) Mal Friedman, Jerry Daniels, Jay Jones, Dick Dial.

APRIL, COMMODORE ROBERT
the first captain of the *Enterprise*. He appears in the animated "The Counter-Clock Incident," and has a wife, Sarah.

APRIL, DR. SARAH
the first medical officer of the *Enterprise*. She appears in the animated "The Counter-Clock Incident," and is married to Commodore Robert April.

APTER, HAROLD
scriptwriter of TNG episode "Data's Day."

Aquans
water-breathing beings on the planet Argo seen in the animated episode "The Ambergris Element." They have webbed feet and hands, green hair and dorsal fins.

Aquashuttle
a shuttlecraft aboard the *Enterprise* that can be piloted underwater. It is seen in the animated episode "The Ambergris Element."

AQUIEL
see entry for Uhnari, Lieutenant Aquiel.

AQUIEL
this sixth season TNG episode was written by Brannon Braga, Ronald D. Moore and Jeri Taylor, and directed by Cliff Bole. The Klingons have picked up Lt. Aquiel Uhnari in a shuttle she used to leave Subspace Relay Station 47. She left because she feared for her life when her co-worker, Rocha, tried to kill her and then killed himself on the station. She is suspected of murdering him. The only person who believes her story is Geordi, who has been reading the journals and letters she left behind. He has grown very fond of her. Guest stars: Renee Jones.

ARAN
character in TNG episode "When The Bough Breaks" who was supposed to be Alexandra's Aldean father.

Arboretum
a place on board the *Enterprise* where there is park-like scenery.

Arcanis
planet referred to in Classic Trek episode "Arena."

Arch
mentioned in TNG episode "Elementary, Dear Data," it is a computer-interface system within the holodeck that contains a fantasy scenario.

Archer IV
at the end of TNG episode "Yesterday's Enterprise," this is the *Enterprise*'s destination.

Archon, U.S.S.
a starship that had been missing for one hundred years before the *Enterprise* found out she had been pulled into the atmosphere of the planet Beta III in Classic Trek episode "The Return of the Archons."

Archons
what the survivors of the destroyed ship *U.S.S. Archon* were called by the inhabitants of Beta III in Classic episode "The Return of the Archons." It became a general term in reference to anyone who comes from outside the world to resist the hypnotic control of Landru. The *Enterprise* crew were, thus, Archons.

Archos
a civilian ship of the Federation mentioned as lost in TNG episode "Legacy."

Arcturian
an alien on the recreation deck in "Star Trek: The Motion Picture" played by an extra.

Arcturian fizz
in TNG episode "Menage A Troi," Lwaxana refers to this drink as having aphrodisiac qualities.

Arcturus
referred to in Classic episode "The Conscience of the King" as a culture from which the actors borrowed their props and costuming. They staged the play *MacBeth* as if it occurred in that culture.

ARDAN
character who is never seen in TNG episode "Too Short A Season." He is a dead Mordanite terrorist.

Ardana
a mining planet in Classic Trek episode "The Cloud Minders" over which Stratos City presides. The planet is the only known source of zienite.

ARDRA
the devil of Ventax II in TNG episode "Devil's Due." Myth says the people struck a bargain with Ardra to have a millennium of peace.

ARENA
written by Gene L. Coon and Frederick Brown, and directed by Joseph Pevney, this first season Classic Trek episode aired 1/19/67. The Enterprise is chasing a Gorn ship when they are stopped in space by all-powerful beings called Metrons who

are appalled at the violence of both ships. Kirk and the Gorn captain are then transported to the surface of a planet to battle to the death. Guest stars: Carole Shelyne, Jerry Ayres, Grant Woods, Tom Troupe, James Farley, Sean Kenney. Of note: This episode is, like the Theodore Sturgeon episode "Shore Leave," based on a science fiction short story. This story, "Arena" by Frederick Brown, was first published in *Astounding* in 1944. An "Outer Limits" episode called "Fun and Games" was also based on this story.

ARENBERG, LEE
actor who guest-starred in DS9 episode "The Nagus."

ARESCO, JOEY
actor who played Brull in TNG episode "The Vengeance Factor."

AREX, LT.
recurring character in the animated series. He is a navigator with three arms and three legs. The Edoan is orange-skinned with an oddly shaped (by human standards) head. James Doohan provided the voice for the character.

Argelius II
a planet visited by the *Enterprise* in Classic episode "Wolf In The Fold." It is a popular shore leave planet because the inhabitants are hedonists and live for pleasure. There is little crime on this world, and no jealousy.

Argo
a water planet visited by the *Enterprise* in the ani-

mated episode "The Ambergris Element." It has underwater cities inhabited by Aquans (see entry), a water-breathing alien species.

Argolis Cluster
a region of space the *Enterprise* charts in TNG episode "I, Borg." It is also mentioned in "True Q."

Argus River
referred to in Classic episode "Wolf In The Fold." It is a river on Rigel IV with carvings done by hill people that are famous throughout the galaxy.

Argus subspace telescope array
an automated installation that has been malfunctioning which the *Enterprise* visits in TNG episode "The Nth Degree."

Argus X
this planet is where Kirk meets the vampire cloud creature for the second time in Classic Trek episode "Obsession."

ARGYLE, BLAKE
an engineering officer on board the *Enterprise* in TNG episodes "Where No One Has Gone Before" and "Datalore." He is played by Biff Yeager.

ARIANA
a dying Tarellian refugee in TNG episode "Haven." She is played by Danitza Kingsley.

Ariannus
planet referred to in Classic Trek episode "Let That Be Your Last Battlefield"

which the *Enterprise* saves from a bacterial invasion by spraying decontaminants.

Ariel
a science ship containing a crew of six in the animated episode "The Eye of the Beholder."

ARIEL
in TNG episode "Angel One," she is the assistant to Beate in love with Captain Ramsey. She is played by Patricia MacPherson.

Aries, U.S.S.
Riker is offered command of this ship in TNG episode "The Icarus Factor."

Arkaria
planet where Riker and crew are briefly held in TNG episode "Starship Mine." According to Data, the Akaria is an egalitarian culture.

Arkarian horn
birds that sometimes darken the sky over Arkaria, mentioned in TNG episode "Starship Mine."

Arloph IX
referred to in TNG episode "The Neutral Zone."

ARMAGNAL, GARY
actor who played McNary in TNG episode "The Big Goodbye."

ARMEN, MARGARET
scriptwriter whose credits include "The Gamesters of Triskelion," "The Paradise Syndrome," "The Cloud Minders" (with David Gerrold and Oliver Crawford), "The Lorelei

Signal," and "The Ambergris Element." She's also written for "The Rifleman," "The Big Valley," and "Barnaby Jones."

ARMENIAN, DAWN
actress who played Miss Gladstone in TNG episode "The Child."

ARMOR, GENE
actor who played the Bajoran Bureaucrat in DS9 episode "Emissary."

ARMRITRAJ, VIJAY
actor who played the role of Starship Captain in "The Voyage Home." Born in India, Vijay won the David Cup in tennis. Acting credits include: "Octopussy" ('83), and the tv series "Fantasy Island."

ARMSTRONG, DAVE
actor who played Kartan in "Operation: Annihilate!" His other credits include "Sex And The Married Woman" ('77) and "The Man From UNCLE."

ARMSTRONG, VAUGHN
actor who played Korris in TNG episode "Heart of Glory."

ARMUS, BURTON
scriptwriter who wrote TNG episodes "The Outrageous Okona" and "A Matter of Honor." Also a producer.

ARMUS
creature that looked like a puddle of tar in TNG episode "Skin of Evil." The sadist killed Tasha Yar. Armus was played by Mart

McChesney, with the voice of Ran Gans.

Armus IX
referred to in TNG episode "Angel One" as the place where Riker wore feathers to honor the leaders.

ARNDT, JOHN
actor who played crewmen in "Miri," "Dagger of the Mind," "Balance of Terror" (crewman Fields), and "Space Seed."

Arneb
a star that can be seen from 'aucdet IX mentioned in the TNG episode "The Child."

ARNETT, CAMERON
actor in TNG episode "Disaster."

ARNOLD, KACEY INCE
scriptwriter who wrote TNG episode "Final Mission."

ARNOLD, STEVE
actor who played Zabo in Classic Trek episode "A Piece of the Action."

AROESTE, JEAN LISETTE
scriptwriter of Classic Trek episodes "Is There In Truth No Beauty?" and "All Our Yesterdays."

ARON, MICHAEL
actor who played Jack London in TNG episode "Time's Arrow."

ARON
character in TNG episode "The Dauphin" played by Peter Neptune. He is an *Enterprise* officer.

ARRANTS, ROD
actor who played Rex in TNG episode "Manhunt."

Arret
the planet where Kirk, Spock and McCoy discover the spheres containing the energy essences of Sargon, Thalessa and Henoch in Classic episode "Return To Tomorrow." Its atmosphere was ripped away half a million years before in a terrible war. In the antimatter universe of the animated "The Counter-Clock Incident," Arret is a planet where people age backward, and the sky darkens when the sun rises.

ARRIDOR, DR.
character from TNG episode "The Price" played by Dan Shor. He is a Ferengi scientist who is lost on the other side of an unstable wormhole.

ARSENAL OF FREEDOM, The
This first season TNG episode was written by Maurice Hurley, Bob Lewin, Richard Manning and Hnas Beimer, and directed by Les Landau. The *Enterprise* encounters the planet Minos whose people destroyed themselves in a terrible war, but whose weapons still exist. Guest stars: Vincent Schiavelli, Marco Rodriguez, Vyto Ruginis, Julia Nickson, George De La Pena.

Artemis, S.S.
in TNG episode "The Ensigns of Command," this is the ship that transported colonists to Tau Cygna V,

though its original destination was Septimis Minor. The ship's guidance system failed, and 15,253 Artemis ancestors have ended up on Tau Cygna V.

ARTHURS, BRUCE D.
scriptwriter who wrote TNG episode "Clues."

Artonian lasers
referred to in TNG episode "The Vengeance Factor," these are weapons found at a Gatherer camp.

ASHMORE, KELLY
actress who played Francine in TNG episode "We'll Always Have Paris."

ASIMOV, ISAAC
(1920-1992)
science consultant for Classic Trek film "Star Trek: The Motion Picture." Born in Russia, he immigrated to the USA at age four. He wrote over 400 books, both fiction and non-fiction books explaining science, religion and literature to the lay reader. Asimov is most famous for his Robot series and Foundation series, and won numerous awards for his work, including science fiction's Hugo and Nebula awards. His wife, Janet Asimov, is a doctor and, now, also a writer. He has a son and daughter. *Asimov's SF*, a magazine, was named after him. He never pretended the science of Star Trek was possible but offered valuable advice nonetheless.

Asmodeus
a demon referred to by Megan in the animated "The Magicks of Megas-Tu."

He claims he was once Asmodeus.

ASOTH
character in DS9 episode "Past Prologue" played by Bo Zenga.

Asphia
referred to in TNG episode "Angel One" as the planet where the *S.S. Odin* crash-landed.

ASSAEL, DAVID
scriptwriter who wrote TNG episode "The Icarus Factor."

ASSIGNMENT: EARTH
written by Art Wallace and Gene Roddenberry, directed by Marc Daniels, this final second season Classic Trek episode aired 3/29/68. This episode was a pilot for a new series that never got off the ground. Gary Seven is an operative from a highly advanced alien society which recruits humans and trains them as agents to interfere with potential planetary disasters before they happen. Kirk and Spock go back in time to observe Earth history and get in Seven's way. Guest stars: Robert Lansing, Terry Garr, Don Keefer, Morgan Jones, Lincoln Demyan. Of note: Barbara Babcock provides the voice for the cat Isis. Majel Barrett's voice is used for the incredible Beta 5 computer which Seven uses to help him thwart disaster.

ASSISTANT MANAGER, The
character in TNG episode "The Royale" who is the desk clerk of the Hotel Royale. He was played by Sam Anderson.

ASTAR, SHAY
actress who guest-starred in TNG episode "Imaginary Friend."

ASTER, JEREMY
character in TNG episode "The Bonding" played by Gabrial Damon. He is a 12-year-old boy whose mother was killed in a landing party mishap. This leaves him orphaned, but he does have an aunt and uncle on Earth.

ASTER, LIEUTENANT MARLA
an *Enterprise* archeologist from TNG episode "The Bonding" played by Susan Powell. She is the mother of Jeremy Aster who dies while on a landing party commanded by Worf. Her husband had died five years earlier of a Verustin infection. The energy beings called Koinonians recreate her image for her son, Jeremy, in order to get him to agree to accompany them to their planet where they will raise him. They do not succeed.

Astral Queen
the ship in Classic Trek episode "The Conscience of the King" that is supposed to transport the Karidian players to Benecia. The *Enterprise* transports them instead, and that ship is never seen.

Astral
Five Annex is a Federation cataloguing terminal referred to in TNG episode "Booby Trap."

Atalia VII
in TNG episode "The Chase," the *Enterprise* is supposed to attend a diplomatic conference there, but Picard has other plans.

Atavachron
device used in Classic episode "All Our Yesterdays" to 'prepare' a time-traveler's biochemistry to the time he wishes to visit on the planet Sarpeidon. Without it, he will die in a matter of hours.

ATIENZA, FRANK
actor who played the executioner in Classic Trek episode "The Omega Glory."

ATKINS, YEOMAN DORIS
character who appears in Classic episode "The Deadly Years." She is played by Carolyn Nelson.

Atlek
planet of the Coalition of Madina. It has a twin planet named Streleb. Both are located in the Omega Sagitta XII system. It is referred to in the TNG episode "The Outrageous Okona."

Atlek ship
a ship mentioned in TNG episode "The Outrageous Okona." The class 7 ship carries a crew of 26. Debin is its commander.

ATOZ, MR.
character on Classic episode "All Our Yesterdays" who is the Sarpeidon 'time-travel' librarian. Played by Ian Wolfe, he has made android replicants of himself to help tend the library.

ATWATER, BARRY
actor who played Surak in "The Savage Curtain." Atwater died in the '70s. He played the vampire in the movie "The Night Stalker" ('72). Other credits include "The Man From UNCLE," "Voyage To The Bottom Of The Sea," and "One Step Beyond."

AUBERJONOIS, RENE
actor who plays Odo on DS9. He was also in Classic Trek film "Star Trek VI: The Undiscovered Country." Born in 1940, he has done much stage work, including "Coco" with Audrey Hepburn, winning a Tony Award for that performance. His film debut was the movie "M*A*S*H." He's also starred in the movies "Pete 'N Tillie," "The Hindenberg," "King Kong" ('76), and "Police Academy 5" among others. He won an Emmy twice for his work in "The Legend of Sleepy Hollow." Rene also won an Emmy for "best supporting actor in a comedy" for his work on the tv series "Benson" in which he played regular Clayton Endicott III. He has also been seen on "L.A. Law," "Matlock," and "Civil Wars." He is the voice of the chef in Disney's "The Little Mermaid." In the Trek Classic film "The Undiscovered Country" he played the assassin, Colonel West. He has a bachelor of arts degree in drama from Carnegie-Mellon University.

AURELAN
see Kirk, Aurelan.

Aurelia
a planet referred to in the animated episode "Yesteryear" which has birdlike natives.

Aurora
the small stolen ship containing Dr. Sevrin and his followers in Classic episode "The Way To Eden." It is destroyed when its engines overload, just as the *Enterprise* beams its crew aboard.

Auto-destruct sequence
this is used throughout the series. Kirk uses it to destroy the *Enterprise* with a Klingon boarding party on board in the Classic Trek film "The Search For Spock." It is also used, and aborted, several times in "Star Trek" and "The Next Generation." In TNG episode "The Defector," Jarok uses it on his ship before he leaves so he will not leave behind top secret Romulan information.

Auxiliary Control
a part of the ship in the center of the saucer where, in a state of emergency, complete control of the ship can be transferred. In Classic Trek "The Immunity Syndrome," it is said to reside on deck 8. In TNG, it is referred to as a Battle Bridge.

Avadney IV
in TNG episode "Clues," this is the destination of the *Enterprise* after leaving Ngame Nebula.

AVARI, ERICK
actor in TNG episode "Unification, Part I."

Aveda III
referred to in TNG episode "The Arsenal of Freedom" as a colony world where Beverly Crusher lived for awhile with her grandmother as a child. A disaster on the planet threatened colonist's lives, and Beverly's grandmother saved many people with her knowledge of the Avedan plants.

Avian
a birdlike creature seen in the animated "Mudd's Passion."

Away Team
term used in "The Next Generation" for a landing party. This term is not used in Classic Trek, just as the term landing party is not used in TNG. However, the two terms seem interchangeable.

Axanar
referred to in Classic episode "Court Martial," it is a planet where there was a war. Kirk took part in the peace mission to Axanar and was awarded the Palm Leaf of the Axanar Peace Mission. The planet is also referred to by Garth in "Whom Gods Destroy."

AYELBORNE
character in Classic episode "Errand of Mercy" played by Jon Abbott. He is the chairman of the elders on Organia, and is actually an energy being, though he appears humanoid until the end of the episode.

AYRES, JERRY
actor who played O'Herlihy in "Arena" and Rizzo in "Obsession." His credits include "Message To My Daughter" ('73), "Attack On Terror," "The FBI Versus the Ku Klux Klan" ('75), and "Disaster On The Coastliner" ('79).

B'TARDAT
Kaelon administrator and scientist in TNG episode "Half A Life." He was played by Terence McNally.

BA'EL
half Romulan-half Klingon girl Worf meets at the Romulan camp in TNG episode "Birthright Part I and II."

BABCOCK, BARBARA
actress who appeared in many Classic Trek episodes. She was the voice of Trelane's mother in "The Squire of Gothos," Mea 3 in "A Taste of Armageddon," the voice of Isis the cat in "Assignment: Earth," and Philana in "Plato's Stepchildren." She won an Emmy for her role in "Hill Street Blues." She was also on "Dallas," and in the movies "Salem's Lot" ('79) and "Lords of Discipline" ('83).

Babel
planet mentioned in Classic Trek episode "Journey To Babel." It is the destination of the ambassadors on board the *Enterprise*. There they will attend the Babel Conference which will decide if Coridan will be admitted to the Federation.

BABEL
first season DS9 episode written by Michael McGreevey, Naren Shankar, Sally Caves and Ira Stephen Behr, and directed by Paul Lynch. Something is wrong with the food replicators on DS9. People are catching aphasia, a disease that affects the brain so speech becomes nonsense and they cannot communicate. Eventually, the condition attacks the nervous system, leaving the victims only 12 hours to live. Guest stars: Jack Kehler, Matthew Faison, Ann Gillespie, Geraldine Farrell, Bo Zenga, Kathleen Wirt, Lee Brooks, Richard Ryder, Frank Novak, Todd Feder.

BACHELIN, FRANZ
art director of original Classic Trek pilot "The Cage."

BADAR N'D'D
leader of the Antican party on TNG episode "Lonely Among Us."

BADER, DIETRICH
actor who played Tactical Crewman in TNG episode "The Emissary."

BADER, HILLARY
scriptwriter of TNG episodes "The Loss" and "Hero Worship."

BAILEY, DENNIS
scriptwriter of TNG episodes "Tin Man" and "First Contact."

BAILEY, LIEUTENANT DAVE
character in Classic Trek episode "The Corbomite Maneuver" played by Anthony Hall. He is the *Enterprise* navigator who stays with Balok as a human ambassador on a first contact mission to the First Federation.

Bajor
homeworld of the Barjorans. This world has recently been at war with the Cardassians, who tried to conquer Bajor with superior technology. The Bajorans have their world back now, but are still reeling from the effects of the war. Bajor is an Earth-like world not yet a member of the Federation, but well on its way. It is very close to a newly discovered wormhole used to travel to the Gamma Quadrant, a neighbor to the space station Deep Space Nine.

Bajoran Death Chant
a two-hour long ritual mentioned in TNG episode "The Next Phase."

Bajorans
native to the planet Bajor, they are humanoid with ridges on the bridge of the nose. They are a highly spiritual race, whose religion and culture involves mysterious orbs that show selected people scenes from the future. These orbs come from the wormhole itself. They mystify scientists. Nearly all Bajorans wear a decorative earring on their right ear that is a a cuff chained to a post or ring. This piece of jewelry seems to denote pride in their race, a kind of brotherhood. Ensign Ro of TNG is Bajoran, as is Major Kira Nerys of DS9.

BAKER
character played by Barbara Baldavin in Classic episode "Space Seed."

BAKEY, ED
actor who played the role of first fop in "All Our Yesterdays." He also appeared in "Dead and Buried" ('81), "Zapped!" ('82), and "The Philadelphia Experiment" ('84).

BAKKE, BRENDA
actress who played Rivan in TNG episode "Justice."

BAL, JEANNE
actress who played the older Nancy Crater in the Classic Trek episode "The Man Trap." Her credits include "Love and Marriage" (1959 60), "Bachelor Father" ('61), and "Mr. Novak" (1964-65).

BALANCE OF TERROR
written by Paul Schneider and directed by Vince McEveety, this first season Classic Trek episode aired 12/15/66. The Enterprise's first encounter with war-like Romulans shows how much like Vulcans they appear. Bigotry is one theme, with Spock its unfortunate victim. Guest stars: Mark Lenard (who later plays Sarek, Spock's Vulcan father), Paul Comi, Lawrence Montaigne (who later plays Stonn in "Amok Time"), John Warburton, Stephen Mines, Barbara Baldavin. Of note: The introduction of the famous Romulan cloaking device.

BALCER, RENE
scriptwriter of TNG episode "Power Play."

BALDAVIN, BARBARA
actress who played Angela Martine in the Classic Trek episodes "Balance of Terror" and "Shore Leave," Baker in "Space Seed," and the communications officer in "Turnabout

Intruder." Her credits include "Medical Center" and "The Bionic Woman."

BALLARD, LIEUTENANT
character in TNG episode "The Offspring" played by Judyann Elder. She is a teacher on the *Enterprise*.

Ballerina
an Enterprise crewwoman on TNG episode "Where No One Has Gone Before" who fantasizes a dance on the holodeck. She was played by Victoria Dillard.

BALOK
character from Classic Trek episode "The Corbomite Maneuver" played by Clint Howard. He is a small, almost child-like alien encountered by the *Enterprise*. He hides behind a monstrous mask when communicating with unknown ships. His flagship, the *Fesarius*, tests the *Enterprise* for hostile intentions.

Balthazar's Syndrome
a Klingon malady suffered by J'Dan in TNG episode "The Drumhead."

Bandi
people who live on Deneb IV, also known as Farpoint, in TNG episode "Encounter At Farpoint."

Bandi shopkeeper
played by David Erskine in TNG episode "Encounter At Farpoint."

BANKS, EMILY
actress who played Tonia Barrows on "Shore Leave." Credits include "The Tim Conway Show" and

"When Hell Was In Session" ('79).

BAR-DAVID, S
pen name for scriptwriter Shimon Wincelberg. He wrote the Classic Trek episodes "Dagger of the Mind" and "The Galileo Seven" (with Oliver Crawford).

BARASH
an alien boy abandoned on Alpha Onias III in TNG episode "Future Imperfect." He was also known as Jean-Luc and Ethan. He was played by Chris Demetral.

BARBARA
one of the android series in Classic episode "I, Mudd" played by twins Maureen and Colleen Thornton.

BARCLAY, LT. ENDICOTT REGINALD, THE THIRD
character in TNG episodes "Hollow Pursuits," "The Nth Degree," and "Realm of Fear." He is called Reg by his friends, and also bears the unflattering nickname "Broccoli." He is an expert engineer. Socially, however, he lacks many skills. He stutters around his peers, acts nervous, and fails to join in group activities. His favorite drink in Ten Forward is warm milk. A self-taught fencer, he is a man with a vivid imagination seen in his holodeck fantasies.

BARIS, NILZ
character in Classic Trek episode "The Trouble With Tribbles" played by William Schallert. He is in charge of agricultural

affairs on Space Station K-7 and Sherman's Planet. He is the one who sends the *Enterprise* a priority distress signal, though his station is not apparently under any threat.

BARLOW, JENNIFER
actress who played Ensign Gibson in TNG episode "The Dauphin."

BARNETT, GREGORY
stunt man who was Spock's double in the Classic Trek films "The Voyage Home" and "The Final Frontier."

BARNHART
crewman in Classic Trek episode "The Man Trap" who is killed by the salt vampire.

Barolians
mentioned in TNG episode "Unification," they are a race who conducted trade negotiations with the Romulans prior to Spock going to Romulus.

BARON, MICHAEL
scriptwriter of TNG episode "Code of Honor."

BARONA
in Classic Trek episode "Errand of Mercy," Kirk goes by the Organian name of Barona in hopes the Klingons won't recognize him as a Starfleet officer.

BARRETT, MAJEL
also known as M. (Majel) Leigh Hudec, the actress played Nurse Christine Chapel in the original series, and the voice of Christine and M'Ress and numerous other characters

in the animated series, as well as Number One in the Classic Trek pilot "The Cage." Majel reappeared as Chapel in the movies "Star Trek: The Motion Picture," and "The Voyage Home." Majel also plays Lwaxana Troi, Deanna Troi's mother, in The Next Generation and the voice of the computer in the Classic Trek movies, TNG, and Deep Space Nine. Born in Columbia, OH, she married Gene Roddenberry. They have a son together, Gene. The much accomplished actress and businesswoman has appeared in other Roddenberry productions and runs Lincoln Enterprises, which sells many types of merchandise associated with Star Trek. She was born Feb. 23.

BARRETT, STAN
actor who played the jailor in "All Our Yesterdays."

BARRETT, LIEUTENANT
she is an officer on *Enterprise* D in TNG episode "Yesterday's Enterprise."

BARRIER, MICHAEL
actor who played DeSalle in the Classic Trek episodes "The Squire of Gothos," "This Side of Paradise," and "Catspaw." He played a guard in "The City On The Edge Of Forever." He was also in "Voyage To The Bottom Of The Sea."

BARRON, DR.
in TNG episode "Who Watches The Watchers," he is the chief scientist of the Mintakan Anthropological Station played by James Greene.

BARROWS, YEOMAN TONIA
character in the Classic Trek episode "Shore Leave" who is Dr. McCoy's girlfriend. She is played by Emily Banks.

BARRY, CAROLYN
actress who plays the female engineer in the TNG episode "Home Soil."

BARRY, PATRICK
scripwriter of TNG episode "Angel One."

BARSTOW, COMMODORE
in Classic Trek episode "The Alternative Factor," Barstow orders the *Enterprise* to investigate what he thinks is a massive invasion from another universe. He is played by Richard Derr.

BARTHOLOMEW, COUNTESS REGINA
partner and love interest for Professor Moriarty in TNG episode "Ship In A Bottle."

Baryon particles
the *Enterprise* goes to Arkaria to be swept clear of baryon particles that build up from the ship's warp drive over time in TNG episode "Starship Mine."

Barzan II
the world whose inhabitants own the Barzan wormhole. This world is hostile to all life except the native inhabitants. It is seen in the TNG episode "The Price."

Barzan Wormhole
the only stable wormhole known to exist at this point, noted in TNG episode "The Price." It appears every 233 minutes and leads to the Gamma Quadrant. It is a worthless galactic phenomenon located by the world Barzan II.

BASCH, HARRY
actor who played Dr. Brown in "What Are Little Girls Made Of?" Credits: "Falcon Crest" (1982-84).

BASHIR, DR. JULIAN
the doctor of station Deep Space 9. A human male about 28 years old, he'd just graduated from the Starfleet Medical Academy before taking the DS9 assignment. He is enthusiastic about everything, a man who dreams of adventure. An expert in alien species medicine, Julian loves his work. His curiosity helps solve problems on DS9. It also gets him into trouble. He has a crush on Dax, who thinks he's cute but she's not interested in romance. Sisko is a good calming influence on him, and they get along, but Kira and O'Brien still don't completely trust him. He may be naive and a little arrogant, but his heart is in the right place. He sees everything as a challenge to surmount. The character has great potential, his puppy dog energy and slight immaturities countered by obvious genius, and overall good nature. When he's working on a medical problem, he's all business. Dark hair, dark eyes, and a

lean body add to his attraction. His British accent is icing on the cake.

Basotile
a priceless piece of art in TNG episode "The Most Toys."

BASS, BOBBY
actor who played a crewman in the Classic Trek episodes "Space Seed" and "This Side Of Paradise," and a Klingon guard in "Errand of Mercy." His credits include "Megaforce" ('82), "Blood Beach" ('81), and "Star 80" ('83).

Bass Player
member of the holodeck band in TNG episode "11001001" played by Abdul Salaam El Razzac.

Bat'tehl
a Klingon sword Worf uses to teach Alexander in TNG episode "Rightful Heir."

BATANIDES, ARTHUR
actor who played D'Amato in "That Which Survives." Credits include: "Cry Tough" ('59), "The Feminist and the Fuzz" ('71), "The Heist" ('73), "Lost In Space," "The Man From UNCLE," and "The Rifleman."

BATANIDES, ENSIGN MARTA
one of Picard's friends at the Academy he meets again courtesy of Q while reliving his Academy days in TNG episode "Tapestry."

Batareal
a Hahliian holiday spot Aquiel mentions to her sister, Sheana, in TNG episode "Aquiel."

BATES, RUSSELL
scriptwriter of the animated "How Sharper Than A Serpent's Tooth" (written with David Wise).

BATES, BROTHER JOHN
character in TNG episode "The Defector" who is in Data's Henry V holodeck simulations. He is played by S.A. Templeton.

BATES, DR. HANNAH
a chief physicist on Moab IV who leaves her society to join the Federation in TNG episode "The Masterpiece Society." She was played by Dey Young.

BATESON, CAPTAIN MORGAN
captain of the *U.S.S. Bozeman* which had been lost for 80 years in a time-space continuum in TNG episode "Cause and Effect." He is played by Kelsey Grammer.

Batris
a Telarian ship commandeered by Klingons and found by the *Enterprise* in TNG episode "Heart of Glory."

BATTLE, The
first season TNG episode written by Larry Forrester and Herbert Wright, and directed by Rob Bowman. Ferengi Commander DaiMon Bok gives Picard his lost ship, the *Stargazer*. On board is a mind control device which takes Picard back to the past on the ship. Guest stars: Frank Corsentino, Doug Warhit, Robert Towers.

Battle of Maxia
a first battle between the Federation and the Ferengi in TNG episode "The Battle." Picard's ship, the *Stargazer*, was destroyed.

Batur
one of Duras scheming sisters, a Klingon, who appears in the TNG episode "Redemption," and returns in DS9 episode "Past Prologue." Her sister is Lursa. She is played by Gwynyth Walsh.

BAUER, ROBERT
actor who played Kuivas in TNG episode "Heart of Glory."

BAXLEY, PAUL
stunt man who played Kirk's double in the Classic Trek episodes "What Are Little Girls Made Of?" and "Amok Time," the Black Knight in "Shore Leave," Ensign Freeman in "The Trouble With Tribbles" a patrol leader in "A Private Little War" a trooper in "Patterns of Force" and the security chief in "Assignment: Earth." His credits also include "The Man From U.N.C.L.E."

BAXTER, GEORGE
actor who played David in TNG episode "Unnatural Selection."

BAY, SUSAN
actress who played the admiral in DS9 episode "Past Prologue." She is Leonard Nimoy's wife.

BAYER, JOHN
actor who played the policeman in "The City On The Edge Of Forever."

Credits include "The Life and Legend of Wyatt Earp" (1955-56).

BAYLE, HAYNE
actor who played one of the Ten Forward crew in TNG episode "The Offspring."

BAYLOR, HAL
actor who played the guard in the Classic Trek episode "Elaan of Troyius."

BEACH
crewmember on the *Reliant* in the Classic Trek film "The Wrath of Khan" played by Paul Kent.

BEACHAM, STEPHANIE
actress who played Countess Regina Bartholomew in TNG episode "Ship In A Bottle."

BEAGLE, PETER S.
scriptwriter of TNG episode "Sarek."

Beagle, U.S.S.
ship destroyed in Classic episode "Bread and Circuses" after Captain Merik had his crew beam to Planet 892-IV. Six years later, the *Enterprise* encountered the debris, visited the world and discovered the few survivors.

BEAR, GREG
author who wrote Pocket Classic Trek novel *Corona.* He is a science fiction writer of repute who has won several awards for his novels.

BEATE
official of Angel One on TNG episode "Angel One"

played by Karen Montgomery.

BEAUMONT, GABRIELLE
director of the TNG episodes "The Booby Trap," "The High Ground," "Suddenly Human," "Disaster," "Imaginary Friend," and "Face of the Enemy."

BEAUREGARD
a plant in Sulu's botanical garden in Classic episode "The Man Trap." It is a pet that responds to humans by swaying and singing. Sulu calls it Gertrude; Rand calls it Beauregard.

BECK, NURSE
obstetrics specialist who comes aboard the *Enterprise* from Starbase 218 in TNG episode "Lessons."

BECKER, JAMES
actor who played Ensign Youngblood in many TNG episodes.

BECKER, ROBERT
director of TNG episodes "We'll Always Have Paris" and "The Outrageous Okona." He died in a tragic car accident on May 6, 1993.

BEECHER, BONNIE
actress who played Sylvia in the Classic Trek episode "Spectre of the Gun."

BEECROFT, GREGORY
actor who played Mickey D in TNG episode "The Royale."

BEGGS, HAGEN
actor who played Lt. Hanson in the Classic Trek episodes "The Menagerie"

and "Court Martial." Film credits: "I Love a Mystery" ('73), "Hey I'm Alive" ('75), "Star 80" ('83).

BEHAN, JOHNNY
character in Classic Trek episode "Spectre of the Gun" played by Bill Zuckert. He appears to be the sheriff of Cochise County but is actually a Melkot in disguise.

BEHAR, ELI
actor who played the therapist in the Classic Trek episode "Dagger of the Mind."

BEHR, IRA STEPHEN
scriptwriter of TNG episodes "Yesterday's Enterprise," "Captain's Holiday," and "Q Pid." He also wrote the story for DS9 episode "Babel" (with Sally Caves) and the teleplay for "The Nagus." He is also a producer.

BEIMLER, HANS
scriptwriter of TNG episodes "The Arsenal of Freedom," "Symbiosis," "The Schizoid Man," "The Emissary," "Shades of Grey," "Allegiance," "Who Watches The Watchers," and "Yesterday's Enterprise." He is also co-producer with Richard Manning.

BELANOFF, ADAM
scriptwriter of "The Masterpiece Society."

BELE
character in the Classic Trek episode "Let That Be Your Last Battlefield" played by Frank Gorshin.

He is the hunter of Lokai, whom he blames for the destruction of his civilization. The left side of his face is white, the right side black.

BELGREY, THOMAS
actor who played a crewman in TNG episode "Realm of Fear."

BELL, FELECIA M.
actress who guest-starred in DS9 episode "Emissary."

BELL, MICHAEL
actor who played Groppler Zorn in the TNG episode "Encounter At Farpoint."

BELL, DAN
character in TNG episode "The Big Goodbye" played by William Boyett. He was the police chief in 1941 San Francisco on the holodeck.

Bell Boy
character in TNG episode "The Royale." He is played by Leo Garcia. He died defending the honor of his love, Rita

BELLAH, JOHN
actor who played a crewman in the Classic Trek episodes "Charlie X" and "The Naked Time." Credits include: "The Man From U.N.C.L.E.," "The Amazing Howard Hughes" ('77), "A Few Days In Weasel Creek" ('81), "Ghost Dancing" ('83).

BELLI, CAESAR
actor who played Stevie in the Classic Trek episode "And The Children Shall Lead." His father, attorney Melvin Belli, appears as Gorgon in the same episode.

BELLI, MELVIN
actor who played Gorgon in the Classic Trek episode "And The Children Shall Lead." He is a famous attorney whose brief acting career included stints in "Wild In The Streets" ('68), "Gimme Shelter ('70), "The Lady of the House" ('78), and the game show "Whodunnit?" ('79). Born in Sonora, CA in 1907, Belli defended Jack Ruby, the man who shot Lee Harvey Oswald after Oswald was accused of assassinating President John F. Kennedy. He has also defended other notables including Jim and Tammy Bakker.

Beltane IX
mentioned in TNG episode "Coming of Age" as the place to which Jake Kurland will escape.

Belzoidian Flea
Q mentions this in TNG episode "Deja Q."

**BEM,
COMMANDER ARI BN**
character in animated episode "Bem." A native of Pandro, he can break his body into small, independent parts. James Doohan provides the voice of Bem.

BEM
written by David Gerrold, this animated episode aired 9/14/74. Commander Ari bn Bem is a guest of the *Enterprise* from the planet Pandro. After he beams down with a landing party to investigate Delta Theta III, the *Enterprise* crewmen learn he can split his body into several parts that operate independently of each other. The natives of the planet are supervised by a planet intelligence that demands the landing party leave and not interfere. They want to comply, but Bem runs away and they can't leave before they find him. Guest voices: Majel Barrett (M'Ress, Alien), James Doohan (Arex, Commander Ari bn Bem). Of note: David Gerrold admits to naming his alien Bem because the initials stand for *bug-eyed-monster*. This is just one of many injokes Trek episodes contain.

BENBECK, MARCUS
keeper of the customs and traditions of the Moab colony in TNG episode "The Masterpiece Society" played by Ron Canada.

BENDER, SLADE
thug who tried to kill Dixon Hill in TNG episode "Manhunt" played by Robert Costanzo.

Bendii Syndrome
disease afflicting Sarek in TNG episode "Sarek." The rare malady affects Vulcans over the age of 200 forcing the victim to project emotions instead of supressing them. There is no cure.

Benecia Colony
mentioned in Classic episode "The Conscience of the King," as the destination of the Karidian players after they leave Planet Q. It is also the planet where Janice Lester wants to maroon Kirk, whose essence is trapped in her body, in "Turnabout Intruder."

Benjisidrine
the heart medication Sarek secretly takes in "Journey To Babel."

BENKO, TOM
director of the TNG episodes "Transfigurations" and "Devil's Due."

BENNETT, FRAN
actress in TNG episode "Redemption, Part II."

BENNETT, HARVE
scriptwriter/producer on the Classic Trek films "The Wrath of Khan," "The Search For Spock," and "The Voyage Home." He also supplied the voice of the flight recorder in "The Search For Spock," and had a walk-on role as a starfleet chief of staff in "The Final Frontier." He won an Emmy as executive producer of "A Woman Called Golda" (which starred Leonard Nimoy), and produced tv including "The Six Million Dollar Man," "The Bionic Woman," "The Gemini Man," and "The Powers of Matthew Starr."

BENNETT, ENSIGN
Enterprise conn officer in TNG episode "Captain's Holiday."

**BENSMILLER,
KURT MICHAEL**
scriptwriter of the TNG episode "Time Squared" and DS9 episode "The Storyteller."

BENSON, BJORN
chief engineer of the terraforming project on Velara III in TNG episode "Home Soil" played by Gerard Prendergast.

BENTON, CRAIG
actor in TNG episode "Violations."

BENTON
lithium miner in Classic episode "Mudd's Women" played by Seamon Glass.

BENZALI, DANIEL
actor who played the surgeon who operates on Picard in TNG episode "Samaritan Snare."

BENZAN
the son of Kushell of Streleb in love with Yanar in TNG episode "The Outrageous Okona" played by Kieran Mulroney.

Benzar
home planet of the Benzites in TNG episode "A Matter of Honor." The world is a member of the Federation.

Benzite
Mordok in TNG episode "Coming of Age" is a Benzite. He has a breathing aparatus and grey skin and is larger than a human. Mordok is the first of his race to attend Starfleet Academy.

BERATIS
in Classic episode "Wolf In The Fold," this name is applied to the Jack The Ripper entity by Sybo.

BEREL
member of the medical staff at the hospital Riker is taken to in TNG episode "First Contact" played by George Hearn.

Berengaria VII
planet Spock mentions to Leila in Classic Trek episode "This Side of Paradise." He says he's seen dragons there.

BERGERE, LEE
actor who played Abraham Lincoln in the Classic Trek episode "The Savage Curtain." Credits include: "One Step Beyond," "The Man From UNCLE," "Hot l Baltimore," "Dynasty," "Evening In Byzantium" ('78).

BERGMAN, ALAN
actor who played Lal in the Classic Trek episode "The Empath." His credits include "Welcome Home Johnny Bristol" ('72) and "Cannon."

BERKELEY, ENSIGN
young transporter officer in Classic Trek episode "Dagger of the Mind" played by Larry Anthony.

Berlin, U.S.S.
starship patrolling the Neutral Zone in TNG episode "The Neutral Zone."

BERMAN, RICK
Executive producer of The Next Generation and creator and executive producer (with Michael Piller) of Deep Space 9. His other credits include work on "McGyver," "Cheers," and "Family Ties." He won an Emmy for his work on "The Big Blue Marble" (1977-82). He is scriptwriter of the TNG episodes "Brothers," "Ensign Ro," "A Matter of Time," "Unification Part I and II,"

and "Brothers." He also wrote, with Michael Piller, the DS9 episode "Emissary."

BERNARD, JOSEPH
actor who appeared as Tark in the Classic Trek episode "Wolf In The Fold." Credits include "The Immortal" ('69), "The Challenge" ('70), "The Winds of Kitty Hawk" ('78), "The Man Who Loved Women" ('83).

BERNARD, DR. HARRY
Enterprise doctor in TNG episode "When The Bough Breaks" who has a son named Harry. He is played by Dierk Torsek.

BERNARD, HARRY JR.
character played by Philip N. Waller
on TNG episode "When The Bough Breaks" whose father is an *Enterprise* doctor, Dr. Harry Bernard. He is kidnapped by the Aldeans.

BERNHEIM, ROBIN
scriptwriter of the TNG episode "The Hunted."

BERNSEN, CORBIN
actor who played Q2 in TNG episode "Deja Q."

BERRYMAN, MICHAEL
actor who played the starfleet display officer in the Classic Trek film "The Voyage Home" and Captain Rixx of the *U.S.S. Thomas Paine* in the TNG episode "Conspiracy." Credits: "Doc Savage Man of Bronze" ('75), "Deadly Blessing" ('81), "Invitation To Hell" ('84).

Bersallis III
world swept by firestorms every seven years. The *Enterprise* loses eight crewmembers in the rescue of these colonists in TNG episode "Lessons."

Berthold Rays
in Classic Trek episode "This Side of Paradise," these rays would be deadly to humans if it weren't for the protection of the spores on Omicron Ceti III. They are mentioned again in TNG episode "Deja Q" as being part of a Calamarain probe.

BESCH, BIBI
actress who played Dr. Carol Marcus in the Classic Trek film "The Wrath of Khan." She has numerous credits, including an appearance on "Northern Exposure" that led to her winning an Emmy in '92.

**BEST OF
BOTH WORLDS, The**
the first part was a third season TNG episode written by Michael Piller and directed by Cliff Bole; the second part a fourth season TNG episode written by Michael Piller and directed by Cliff Bole. A Borg vessel, the advance ship of a vast invading armada, is engaged by the *Enterprise*. The Borg kidnap Picard and turn him into their leader, a Borg named Locutus. The Borg continue to attack Starfleet, then head toward Earth. The only way to defeat them is to command them to go into a regenerative cycle and sleep. Picard is brought back aboard ship and his

Borg 'parts' surgically removed. Guest stars: Elizabeth Dennehy, George Murdock, Whoopi Goldberg, Todd Merrill, Colm Meaney (last two, second part only).

Beta Agni II
in TNG episode "The Most Toys," Kivas Fajo contaminates this planet's water supply with tricyanite to lure the *Enterprise* to him so he can kidnap Data. It is a Federation colony world.

Beta Antares IV
in Classic Trek episode "A Piece of the Action," Kirk says this planet is where he learned to play Fizzbin. He is, of course, making up this story.

Beta Aurigae
in Classic Trek episode "The Ultimate Computer," the binary system towards which the *Enterprise* heads to join the *Potemkin* and study gravitational effects.

Beta Canopus
in animated episode "The Pirates of Orion," the drug strobolin can be found on this planet.

Beta Cassius System
Haven from TNG episode "Haven" is in this system.

Beta Geminorum
mentioned in Classic episode "Who Mourns For Adonais?," it is in the system of the planet Pollux IV where Apollo lives.

Beta III in Star System 6-11
the planet where the *U.S.S. Archon* was lost in Classic episode "The Return of the Archons." This is where Landru rules.

Beta Kupsik
the *Enterprise*'s destination after they leave Starbase Montgomery in TNG episode "The Icarus Factor."

Beta Lyrae
a conglomerate of differently colored and sized stars considered one of the wonders of the universe. It is seen in the animated episode "The Slaver Weapon."

Beta Magellan System
Bynaus from TNG episode "11001001" is located here.

Beta Niobe
the star that is about to go nova and destroy all life on Sarpeidon in Classic episode "All Our Yesterdays." It is also encountered in the animated "The Counter-Clock Incident."

Beta Portalan System
in Classic Trek episode "Operation: Annihilate!" this is the location of the flying parasites' first victims, an ancient civilization that died of insanity many centuries before.

Beta Renner System
the worlds Antica and Selay from TNG episode "Lonely Among Us" are located in this system.

Beta Stromgren
in TNG episode "Tin Man," the probe Vega Nine returns from here with evidence the star will go supernova.

Beta V Computer
the computer Gary Seven keeps in his apartment in Classic episode "Assignment: Earth." The voice of the computer is provided by Majel Barrett.

Beta VI
the *Enterprise* I's destination before being detained by Trelane in Classic episode "The Squire of Gothos."

Beta XIIA
mentioned in Classic episode "Day of the Dove" where supposedly a hundred Federation citizens were murdered by Klingons. The story is not true.

Betazed
Troi and Lwaxana are natives of this world. (Troi is half-human.) Inhabitants are called Betazoids (see entry). The planet is a member of the Federation.

Betazoid Kitten
Deanna owned one as a child as mentioned in TNG episode "Pen Pals." Her mother did not get along with it.

Betazoids
natives of the planet Betazed. They look human. Deanna Troi and Lwaxana Troi are Betazoids, though Troi is half-human. They can read each other's thoughts and communicate telepathically but are limited to reading emotions of alien species. They cannot read Ferengi emotions. Betazoids usually develop their abilities in adoles-cence, but in TNG episode "Tin Man," Tam Elbrun was born telepathic and found the mental 'noise' too painful to endure. In the TNG episode "Manhunt" it is shown that one of their customs is to ring a chime during a meal to give thanks for their food. In TNG episode "The Child," it is revealed that a Betazoid gestation period is ten months. Betazoids are a matriarchal society, and believe men to be a commodity.

Beth Delta I
in TNG episode "Evolution," the character Stubbs tells Troi he will show her "New Manhattan on Beth Delta I as she has never seen it."

BETHUNE, IVY
actress who played Duana, Wesley's 'adopted mother' on Aldea in TNG episode "When The Bough Breaks."

Beyond Antares
the song Uhura sings in Classic episodes "The Conscience of the King" and "The Changeling."

BEYOND THE FARTHEST STAR
written by Samuel A. Peeples, this animated Classic Trek episode aired 12/22/73. The *Enterprise* is pulled by the gravity of a negative star mass to discover a giant ship that makes their ship look like a mere speck. On board the alien ship is a dead crew of an insectile race that destroyed themselves because they were invaded by a deadly lifeform. It is

still alive, and invades the *Enterprise*. Kirk pretends to destroy his ship to trick the alien into vacating the *Enterprise*. Guest voices: James Doohan (Kyle, engineer, Commander of Alien Starship, Alien).

Bezaride
planet of the Pallas 14 system mentioned in animated episode "One Of Our Planets Is Missing."

BHAVANI, PREMIER
planetary leader of Barzan II in TNG episode "The Price" played by Elizabeth Hoffman.

Bi-Dyttrium
powerful energy source sought by the Cardassians in DS9 episode "Past Prologue."

BICKELL, ANDREW
actor who played Wagnor in TNG episode "The Hunted."

BIG GOODBYE, The
first season TNG episode written by Tracy Torme and directed by Joseph L. Scanlan. On the *Enterprise* holodeck, Picard and crew visit 1940s San Francisco. A computer mishap leaves them stranded in a very real, very deadly scenario. Guest stars: Mike Genovese, Dick Mller, Carolyn Alport, Rhonda Aldrich, Eric Cord, Lawrence Tierney, Harvey Jason, William Boyett, David Selburg, Gary Armagnal. This episode won the Peabody Award.

BIKEL, THEORDORE
actor who guest-starred in TNG episode "Family."

Biko, U.S.S.
in TNG episode "A Fistful of Datas," the *Enterprise* is delayed on its way to meet the *Biko*.

Bilana III
location of the wave propulsion method test in TNG episode "New Ground."

BILAR
character from Classic episode "The Return Of The Archons" played by Ralph Maurer. He directs the *Enterprise* crew to a place to stay.

BILLINGS, EARL
actor in TNG episode "The Drumhead."

BILLY, MICHELE AMEEN
actress who played the Epsilon Lt. in the Classic Trek film "Star Trek: The Motion Picture." She was assistant to Harold Livingston at the time.

BINGHAM, MICHAEL J.
scriptwriter of the TNG episode "The Naked Now."

BINNEY, GEOFFREY
actor who played Compton in "Wink Of An Eye." Credits include: "The Appearances of Pretty Boy Floyd" ('74), "Once An Eagle" ('77), "Swan Song" ('80).

Biobeds
beds used in the medical ward in TNG episode "Contagion."

Biocomputer
a portable was used in Classic episode "Miri."

Biofilter
filter for harmful bacteria used in the transporter. It is referred to by Dr. Pulaski in TNG episode "Shades of Gray."

Biomolecular Specialist
a doctor who operates on Picard in TNG episode "Samaritan Snare" played by Tzi Ma.

Bioplast Sheeting
Data is composed of this element, as stated in TNG episode "The Most Toys."

Bird of Prey
Romulan ships in Classic Trek; both Romulan and Klingon ships in the Classic movies, The Next Generation and Deep Space 9.

Biridium Pellet
implant in Worf's neck inserted at the Carraya prison colony in TNG episode "Birthright Part II."

BIRK, RAYE
actor who played Wrenn in the TNG episode "Haven."

BIRKIN, DAVID TRISTAN
actor who guest-starred in TNG episode "Rascals."

BIRTHRIGHT, PART I AND II
sixth season TNG episode written by Brannon Braga (part I), and Rene Echevarria (part II), and directed by Winrich Kolbe (part I), and Dan Curry (part II). Worf visits Deep Space 9 and meets a Yridian named Shrek who tells him he can help Worf find his father, a prisoner in a Romulan-run camp holding refugees from the Khitomer massacre. Meanwhile, Data hallucinates when he is knocked unconscious, and the visiting Dr. Bashir tells him he experienced a dream. Worf finds the camp and discovers it is more of a village than a prison, and that Romulans and Klingons are living together in peace, even marrying and having families. Worf is appalled. He tries to convince the Klingons born in the camp but now young adults that they must embrace the Klingon way to be true to their heritage. Guest stars: Siddig El Fadil, James Cromwell, Alan Scarfe, Richard Herd, Christine Rose, Sterling Macer, Jr., Jennifer Gatti.

BISCHOFF, DAVID
scriptwriter of the TNG episodes "Tin Man" and "First Contact." He also wrote Pocket TNG novel *Grounded*.

BISHOP, ED
actor who was the voice of the Megan Prosecutor in the animated "The Magicks of Megas-Tu." Bishop is famous to sf fans for his role as Ed Straker in the British tv series "UFO."

BISSELL, WHIT
actor who played Lurry in "The Trouble With Tribbles." Born in 1919, he died in 1981. His credits include "The Time Tunnel," "Creature From The Black Lagoon" ('54), "Invasion of the Body

Snatchers" ('56), "The Time Machine" ('60), and "Soylent Green" ('73).

BIXBY, JEROME
scriptwriter who penned the Classic Trek episodes "Mirror, Mirror," "By Any Other Name" (with D.C.Fontana), "Day of the Dove," and "Requiem For Methuselah."

BLACK, JOHN D.F.
scriptwriter/producer who wrote "The Naked Time" and produced Star Trek's first season. He also wrote the TNG episode "The Naked Now," and early drafts of "Justice." He has won the Edgar award for "Thief," was nominated for an Emmy, wrote the original "Wonder Woman," and wrote and produced "A Shadow In The Streets" ('75) and "The Clone Master" ('78).

Black Cluster
an uncharted part of the galaxy mentioned in TNG episode "Hero Worship." The Black Cluster refelcts deflector shield power back at a ship when it tries to enter the area.

Black Knight
a synthetic character in Classic episode "Shore Leave" that attacks and kills McCoy.

BLACKBURN, BILL
stunt double who played The White Rabbit in the Classic Trek episode "Shore Leave," an extra in "A Taste of Armageddon," a guard in "The Alternative Factor," "Lt. Hadley in "A Piece of the Action," and a storm

trooper in "Patterns of Force."

Blackjack
a card game Data plays at the Royale in TNG episode "The Royale."

BLACKMAN, ROBERT
TNG and DS9 costume designer.

BLANTON, ARELL
actor who played Lt. Dickerson in "The Savage Curtain." Credits include "Pennies From Heaven" ('81). He also works on soft porn films.

BLISH, JAMES
author who wrote *Star Trek 1-12* (#12 was written with his wife J.A. Lawrence, who finished the book after he died in 1975), and *Spock Must Die!*, all published by Bantam.

BLOCH, ROBERT
scriptwriter who penned the Classic Trek episodes "What Are Little Girls Made Of?," "Catspaw," and "Wolf In The Fold." A horror writer of great repute, his episodes are darker than most Trek. Born in 1917, he is most famous for his script "Psycho" directed by Alfred Hitchcock. He also wrote "The Cabinet of Dr. Caligari" ('62) and "The House That Dripped Blood" ('71), as well as many short stories and novels.

BLOOM, JOHN
actor who played the behemoth alien in the Classic Trek film "The Undiscovered Country."

BLOOM, COMMANDER
a person Riker meets at the asylum in TNG episode "Frame of Mind." She claims to be the commander of the *Yorktown*, but her real name is Jaya.

Blue Parrot Cafe
in TNG episode "We'll Always Have Paris," this cafe is on Sarona VIII. It serves the famous Blue Parrot.

Bluejay 4
the code name of Captain Christopher's jet in Classic episode "Tomorrow Is Yesterday."

BLUM, KATHERINE
actress who played the Vulcan Child in the Classic Trek film "The Search For Spock." This ended up on the cutting room floor.

BOCHRA
Romulan Centurion who survives a crash on Galorndon Core in TNG episode "The Enemy" played by John Snyder.

Body, The
term used in Classic Trek episode "The Return Of The Archons." A person who has been 'absorbed' and controlled by Landru, the computer that runs the planet, is considered 'of the Body.'

BOEN, EARL
actor who played Nagilum in TNG episode "Where Silence Has Lease."

BOK
Ferengi commander on TNG episode "The Battle." His son was killed by Picard

nine years before. He is played by Frank Corsentino.

Bolan
blue-skinned, one of these people appear in DS9 episode "Emissary." He is the tactical officer on the *U.S.S. Saratoga* who drags Sisko to safety when the ship is attacked by the Borg. He is played by Stephen Davies.

BOLDER, CAL
actor who played Keel in "Friday's Child." His credits include "The Man From UNCLE."

BOLE, CLIFF
director of the TNG episodes "Lonely Among Us," "Hide and Q," "Conspiracy," "The Royale," "The Emissary," "The Ensigns of Command," "The Hunted," "A Matter of Perspective," "Hollow Pursuits," "The Best of Both Worlds Part 1 and 2," "Remember Me," "First Contact," "Q-Pid," "Redemption Part 1," "Silicon Avatar," "Unification Part II," "The Perfect Mate," "Realm of Fear," "Aquiel," "Starship Mine," and "Suspicions."

Bolians
natives of Bolius IX, humanoid with green skin and a ridge in the middle of the head (like Klingons). They appear in TNG episodes "Conspiracy" and "Allegiance."

BOMA, LIEUTENANT
astrophysicist in Classic episode "The Galileo Seven" played by Don

Marshall. He is one of the survivors of the *Galileo's* crash landing on Taurus II.

BONANNO, MARGARET WANDER
author of the Classic Trek novels *Probe*, *Strangers From the Sky*, and *Dwellers in the Crucible.*

BONAVENTURE, RUTH
one of the three women, the brunette, whom Harry Mudd is transporting to Rigel XII in Classic episode "Mudd's Women." She is played by Maggie Thrett.

Bonaventure
mentioned in animated episode "Time Trap" as the first ship to be fitted with the warp drive.

BOND, NANCY
scriptwriter of TNG episode "Silicon Avatar."

BOND, TIMOTHY
director of the TNG episodes "The Vengeance Factor" and "The Most Toys."

BONDING, The
third season TNG episode written by Ronald D. Moore, and directed by Winrich Kolbe. A young boy's mother is killed on an Away Team mission, but she returns to comfort him and try to get him to come away with her. She is really an alien who wants to raise the boy. Guest stars: Susan Powell, Gabriel Damon, Colm Meaney.

BONES
nickname Kirk uses to address his friend McCoy.

(See entry for McCoy, Dr. Leonard.)

Bonestell Recreation Facility
in TNG episode "Samaritan Snare," this facility is located at Starbase Earhart.

BONNE, SHIRLEY
actress who played Ruth in "Shore Leave." Credits: the tv series "My Sister Eileen" (1960-61).

BONNEY, GAIL
actress who played the second witch in "Catspaw." Her credits include "One Step Beyond," "The Priest Killer" ('71), "The Devil's Daughter" ('73), "Death Scream" ('75), and "Kingston The Power Play" ('76).

BONSALL, BRIAN
actor who played Alexander, Worf's son, in TNG episodes "New Ground," "Ethics," "Cost of Living," "Imaginary Friend," "A Fistful of Datas," and "Rascals." He also starred as Andrew in the last couple of seasons of the hit series "Family Ties."

BOOBY TRAP
third season TNG episode written by Michael Wagner, Ron Roman, Michael Piller, and Richard Danus, and directed by Gabrielle Beaumont. The *Enterprise* gets caught in a 1000-year-old booby trap left behind by a war, and discover a derelict Promelian ship also from that war. Geordi reconstructs an image of Dr. Leah Brahms, designer of the

Enterprise propulsion systems, on the holodeck to help escape the trap. Guest stars: Susan Gibney, Whoopi Goldberg, Albert Hall, Julie Warner, Colm Meaney.

Book of the People
term for a book of history and knowledge to be given to the people of Yonada when they arrive at their destination in Classic Trek episode "For The World Is Hollow And I Have Touched The Sky."

BOONE, WALKER
actor who played Leland T. Lynch in TNG episode "Skin of Evil."

BOOTH, JIMMIE
actor who played a Klingon in Classic Trek film "Star Trek: The Motion Picture."

BOOTHBY
groundskeeper of Starfleet Academy in TNG episode "The First Duty" played by Ray Walston.

BORATIS
character played by Michael Champion in TNG episode "Captain's Holiday." Apparently a Vorgon security agent from the 27th century, he is really a thief trying to steal the Tox-Uthat.

Boratis System
system of thirteen colonies, all new. In TNG episode "The Emissary," the *Enterprise* picks up Special Emissary K'Ehleyr from this system.

Boreth
a frozen Klingon world mentioned in TNG episode "Rightful Heir" where Kahless is supposed to reappear someday.

Borg
cybernetically enhanced beings that look human with the exception of lots of mechanical parts. They have a mission to destroy and/or absorb all life in the galaxy. They possess a hive mind and are the Federation's most ruthless enemy until Picard sends Hugh back to them with a virus in his programming. They are responsible for destroying Guinan's home system. They appear in several TNG episodes, first in "Q Who."

Borgia Plant
in Classic episode "The Man Trap," it is a poisonous plant found on planet M-113. It is thought to have killed Darnell.

Borgolis Nebula
destination of the *Enterprise* when they are called to Bersallis III in TNG episode "Lessons."

Boridium
in Classic episode "Wolf In The Fold," the knife used by the killer has a boridium blade.

Borkaas
what Bajorans call 'ghosts' in TNG episode "The Next Phase."

Bortas
a Klingon ship seen in TNG episode "The Defector" and later an

attack cruiser of the same name used by Gowron in "Reunion Part I."

BORYER, LUCY
actress who played Janeway in TNG "Man of the People."

Botany Bay, U.S.S.
ship enountered in Classic episode "Space Seed" that carries Khan's people in sleep stasis.

BOTSFORD, DIANA DRU
scriptwriter of TNG episode "Rascals."

BOTSFORD, WARD
scriptwriter of TNG episode "Rascals."

BOUCHET, BARBARA
actress who played Kelinda in "By Any Other Name." She was born in Germany and has been a model in commercials. Credits include: "Casino Royale" ('66), "Sweet Charity" ('69).

Bounty
name McCoy gives to the Klingon ship Kirk and crew have inherited in the Classic Trek film "The Voyage Home." He names the ship after the Bounty in *Mutiny on the Bounty*.

BOVA, VANESSA AND JESSICA
twin actresses who played Alexandra, a girl kidnapped from the *Enterprise* in the TNG episode "When The Bough Breaks."

BOWERS, ANTOINETTE
actress who played Sylvia in "Catspaw." Her redits include "The Man From UNCLE," "Perry Mason,"

and "Mission: Impossible," plus the films "The Scorpio Letters" ('67), "Death of Innocence" ('71), "First You Cry" ('78), "Blood Song" ('81), "The Thorn Birds" ('83), and "The Evil That Men Do" ('84).

BOWMAN, ROB
director of the TNG episodes "Where No One Has Gone Before," "The Battle," "Datalore," "Too Short A Season," "Heart Of Glory," "The Child," "Elementary, Dear Data," "A Matter of Honor," "The Dauphin," "Q Who," "Manhunt," "Shades of Gray," and "Brothers."

Box, Talking
in TNG episode "Haven," this device is a box that has a face and speaks. It speaks with the voice of Armin Shimerman.

BOY
12-year-old Ansata separatist in TNG episode "The High Ground" played by Christopher Pettiet.

BOYCE, DR. PHILLIP
ship's doctor in Classic pilot "The Cage" played by John Hoyt. He is a surgeon as well as an amateur psychologist/philosopher.

BOYER, KATY
actress who played a Citizen of Bynus, a Bynar, in TNG episode "11001001."

BOYETT, WILLIAM
actor who played police chief Dan Bell in TNG episode "The Big Goodbye," and played a police man in "Time's Arrow Part II."

Bozeman, U.S.S.
commanded by Captain Morgan Bateson, this ship was lost 80 years before in a time/space continuum in TNG episode "Cause and Effect."

BRACK, MR.
the man who bought the planet Holbert 917G. This name is an alias for Flint in Classic episode "Requiem For Methuselah."

BRACTOR, DaiMON
leader of the Ferengi ship *Krik'ta* in TNG episode "Peak Performance" played by Armin Shimerman.

Bradbury, U.S.S.
in TNG episode "Menage A Troi," Wesley is supposed to board this ship for a trip to Starfleet Academy. He misses his ride.

BRADEN, KIM
actress who guest-starred in TNG episode "The Loss."

BRADLEY, PAUL
actor who played Ensign Freeman in "The Trouble With Tribbles."

BRADLEY, ARTHUR GLINTON
unseen husband of Jessica Bradley in TNG episode "The Big Goodbye."

BRADLEY, JESSICA
murder victim in the Dixon Hill holo projection in TNG episode "The Big Goodbye" played by Carolyn Allport.

BRAGA, BRANNON
scriptwriter for TNG episodes "Identity Crisis," "Power Play," "The Game,"

" Schisms," "Realm of Fear," "A Fistful of Datas," "Aquiel," "Cause and Effect," "Imaginary Friend," "Birthright, Part I," "Reunion," "Frame of Mind," and "Timescape."

BRAHMS, JOHANNES
one of Flint's past identities from Classic episode "Requiem For Methuselah."

BRAHMS, DR. LEAH
character in TNG episode "Booby Trap" who is a propulsion engineer and a graduate of the Daystrom Institute Theoretical Propulsion Group. She is Geordi's personal hero. He programs her image in a holo-fantasy to help solve the ship's problems. She is played by Susan Gibney.

BRALVER, ROBERT
stunt man who played Grant in the Classic Trek episode "Friday's Child" and who appeared in the Classic Trek film "Star Trek: The Motion Picture." He also served as stunt driver of the car in "Knight Rider," and appeared in "The Bionic Woman" and "The Man From UNCLE."

BRAMLEY, WILLIAM
actor who played the policeman in the Classic Trek episode "Bread and Circuses." His credits include the movies "Jaws 3-D" ('83) and "The Wild Life" ('84) as well as the tv series "The Girl From UNCLE," "Iron Horse," "Petrocelli," and "Barnaby Jones."

BRANAGH, KENNETH
mentioned in TNG episode "The Defector," he is an actor/director Data wants to study.

BRANCH, COMMANDER
Epsilon station commander in the Classic Trek film "Star Trek: The Motion Picture."

BRAND, ADMIRAL
the superintendent of Starfleet Academy in TNG episode "The First Duty" played by Jacqueline Brookes. A Vulcan, Captain Satelk, is her assistant.

BRANDT, VICTOR
actor who played Watson in the Classic Trek episode "Elaan of Troyius" and Tongo Rad in "The Way To Eden." Credits: "Nobody's Perfect" ('80), "Strange Homecoming" ('74), "The Deadly Triangle" ('77), "Zuma Beach" ('78), "Wacko" ('83).

BRANNEN, RALPH
actor who played a crewman in the Classic Trek film "Star Trek: The Motion Picture."

Braslota System
the location of the Starfleet battle simulation between the *U.S.S. Hathaway* and the *Enterprise* shown in TNG episode "Peak Performance." It is located in the Oneamisu sector. Its worlds include Kei, Yuri, and Totoro.

Brattain, U.S.S.
science ship of Starfleet found by the *Enterprise* with all but one of its crew dead in TNG episode "Night Terrors."

Bre'el IV
world threatened by a falling asteroid in TNG episode "Deja Q." Q intervenes and saves the world.

BREAD AND CIRCUSES
written by Gene Roddenberry, Gene L. Coon, and John Kneubuhl, directed by Ralph Senensky, this second season Classic Trek episode aired 3/15/68. The wrecked ship *S.S. Beagle* is found orbiting planet 892-IV. The world below exhibits 20th century technology, but ancient Roman culture, complete with gladiatorial fights to the death. Claudius Marcus, the proconsul of the Empire, controls who is left alive of the *Beagle's* crew, and attempts to gain control of the *Enterprise*. Guest stars: William Smithers, Logan Ramsey, Ian Wolfe, Rhodes Reason, Lois Jewell. Of note: Introduction of Hodgkin's Law of Parallel Planets, which conveniently explains why many aliens speak English but not why they have Earth gods and customs.

Brechtian Cluster
where the *Enterprise* meets for the second time with the crystalline entity in TNG episode "Silicon Avatar."

Breen
a race with attack ships that use disruptors and cloaking devices encountered in TNG episode "The Loss" and mentioned in "Hollow Worship."

Brekka
this planet, the fourth world of the Delos system, holds felicium, a cure for a plague on Ornara in TNG episode "Symbiosis."

BRENNER, EVE
actress who guest-starred in TNG episode "Violations."

BRENNER, FAYE
script supervisor for "The Undiscovered Country."

BRENT, LIEUTENANT
minor character on the bridge in Classic Trek episode "The Naked Time" played by Frank da Vinci.

BRETON, BROOKE
associate producer of the Classic Trek film "The Voyage Home."

BREVELLE, ENSIGN
a member of LaForge's Away Team to Tarchannen III absorbed by the group of indiginous humanoid lifeforms in TNG episode "Identity Crisis." He was played by Paul Tompkins.

BRIAM, AMBASSADOR
envoy from Krios to Valt Minor played by Tim O'Connor in TNG episode "The Perfect Mate."

BRIAN, DAVID
actor who played John Gill in "Patterns of Force." Born in 1914, his credits include "Mr. District Attorney" (1954- 55), "The Immortal" ('70), "Million Dollar Mermaid" ('52), and "How The West Was Won" ('62).

BRIANON, KAREEN
ward of Dr. Ira Graves in TNG episode "The Schizoid Man" played by Barbara Alyn Woods. He is in love with her.

BRIGGS, BOB
head of the Cetacean Institute in the Classic Trek film "The Voyage Home" played by Scott DeVenney.

BRILL, CHARLIE
actor who played Arne Darvin in the Classic Trek episode "The Trouble With Tribbles." He also appeared on "Rowan and Martin's Laugh In" and "Supertrain," and in the films "Young Love, First Love" ('79) and "Your Place Or Mine" ('83).

Brincas V
in TNG episode "The Loss," Geordi remembers skindiving on this world.

Bringloid
a colony in the Ficus Sector in TNG episode "Up The Long Ladder." Bringloid means 'dream' in Gaelic. The inhabitants are Irish humans who left Earth to develop their own world independently in 2123.

BRISLANE, MIKE
actor who played the Saratoga science officer in "The Voyage Home."

BROCCO, PETER
actor who played Claymare in "Errand of Mercy." Credits include films "Alian Smith and Jones" ('71), "Raid On Entebbe" ('77), "Jeckyl and Hyde: Together Again"

('82), "Twilight Zone: The Movie" ('83) and tv credits gpt "Chase," "Voyage to the Bottom of the Sea," and "The Man From UNCLE."

BROCKSMITH, ROY
actor who played Sirna Kolrami in TNG episode "Peak Performance."

BRODY, LARRY
scriptwriter of the animated episode the Classic Trek episode "The Magicks of Megas-Tu." He has also written scripts for "Cannon" and "Barnaby Jones," and several tv movies.

BRONKEN, TRENKA
mentioned in TNG episode "The Ensigns of Command," he is a concert violinist whose style Data emulates.

BRONSON, FRED
scriptwriter of the TNG episodes "Menage A Troi" and "The Game."

BROOKES, ADMIRAL
mentioned in TNG episode "Suspicions" as the senior officer Beverly will have to report to for a formal inquiry after Dr. Reyga, the Ferengi scientist, is murdered.

BROOKS, AVERY
actor who plays Commander Benjamin Sisko in Deep Space 9. Born and raised in Indiana, Brooks graduated from Oberlin College and performed on the stage. His tv credits include being a regular on "Spencer For Hire" as the character Hawk, and starring in the short

lived series spin-off "A Man Called Hawk." He plays jazz, and often teaches. He is a tenured professor at Rutgers University, where he has taught for 20 years. He is married and currently lives in Los Angeles with his wife, a daughter, and two sons.

BROOKS, LEE
actor who played the aphasia victim in DS9 episode "Babel."

BROOKS, JACQUELINE
actress in TNG episode "The First Duty."

BROOKS, JAMES E.
scriptwriter who wrote the story for TNG episode "Rightful Heir."

BROOKS, JOEL
actor who guest-starred in DS9 episode "Move Along Home."

BROOKS, ROLLAND M.
art director of Classic Star Trek's first season.

BROOKS, STEPHEN
actor who played Garrovick in "Obsession." His other tv credits include "The Nurses," "The FBI," and "The Interns."

BROPHY, BRIAN
actor who played Commander Bruce Maddox in TNG episode "The Measure of a Man."

BROTHERS
fourth season TNG episode written by Rick Berman, and directed by Rob Bowman. Data meets his creator, his father, Dr. Soong, played by Brent

Spiner. Soong wants to give Data feelings, but gives the special chip to Lore instead, who becomes crazed, assaults Soong and runs away. Data is rescued just as his father dies. Guest stars: Cory Danziger, Adam Ryen, James Lashly, Colm Meaney.

Browder IV
a world being terraformed in TNG episode "Allegiance," the *Enterprise* is en route to rendezvous with the *U.S.S. Hood.*

BROWN, CAITLIN
actress who guest-starred in DS9 episode "The Passenger."

BROWN, FREDRIC
writer whose original story, "Arena," published in *Astounding Science Fiction Stories* in 1944 was the foundation for the Classic trek episode "Arena." The original story was republished in *Starlog* #4.

BROWN, GEORGIA
actress who starred in TNG episode "Family."

BROWN, MARCIA
actress who played Alice in the Classic trek episode "Shore Leave."

BROWN, MARK ROBERT
actor who played Don in the Classic trek episode "And The Children Shall Lead."

BROWN, ROBERT
actor who played Lazarus in the Classic trek episode "The Alternative Factor." He also starred in "Here

Come The Brides" and "Primus."

BROWN, ROGER AARON
actor who played the Epsilon tech in the Classic trek film "Star Trek: The Motion Picture." His film credits include "McNaughton's Daughter" ('76), "Death on the Freeway" ('79), "Don't Cry, It's Only Thunder" ('82) and "Sins of the Past" ('84).

BROWN, RON
actor who played Drummer in the holodeck band in TNG episode "11001001."

BROWN, WREN T.
actor who played the transport pilot in TNG episode "Manhunt."

BROWN, DR.
Dr. Korby's android assistant in Classic episode "What Are Little Girls Made Of?" played by Harry Basch.

BROWNE, KATHIE
actress who played Deela in "Wink Of An Eye. Tv credits include "Slattery's People" and "Hondo," with film credit for "Berlin Affair" ('70). She is married to actor Darren McGavin, best known as Kolshak of "The Night Stalker."

BRUCK, KARL
actor who played King Duncan in "The Conscience of the King." Born in 1906, he died in 1987. His film credits include "Escape of the Birdmen" ('71) and "Escape From the Planet of the Apes" ('71.) He is a survivor

of the holocaust, and was a regular on "The Young And The Restless."

BRULL
the leader of the Gatherers on Gamma Hromi II in TNG episode "The Vengeance Factor" played by Joey Aresco.

Brute, The
character in the prison who fights Kirk in the Classic Trek film "The Undiscovered Country" played by Tom Morga. Apparently his genitals are where his knees should be.

BRY, ELLEN
actress who guest-starred in TNG episode "The Quality of Life."

BRYANT, URSALINE
actress who played Captain Tryla Scott of the USS Renegade in the TNG episode "Conspiracy."

BRYCE, RANDI
biologist in animated episode "The Eye Of The Beholder," with voice played by Majel Barrett. She is a.

BUCKLAND, MARC
actor who played Katik Shaw in TNG episode "The High Ground."

BUDRON, ADMIRAL
mentioned in TNG episode "Frame of Mind" as the person who denied Riker was a member of Starfleet.

Buffers
information processors worn by the Bynars around their waists in TNG episode "11001001."

Bulgalian Sludge Rat
what Rondon calls Wesley when he meets him in TNG episode "Coming of Age."

BUNDY, BROOKE
actress who plays Sarah MacDougal, chief of engineering in TNG episode "The Naked Now."

Buoy, Melkotian
the *Enterprise* encounters this buoy in Classic episode "The Spectre of the Gun." It supposedly speaks telepathically and in the native language of each listener. James Doohan supplied the voice.

BURDETTE, MARLYS
actress who played Krako's Gun Moll in the Classic Trek episode "A Piece of the Action."

BURKE, ENSIGN
tactical officer on the *Enterprise* who takes Worf's place when Worf goes to the *Hathaway* in TNG episode "Peak Performance." He was played by Glenn Morshower.

BURKE, JOHN
mentioned in Classic episode "The Trouble With Tribbles" as the person who mapped Sherman's Planet.

BURNS, ELKANAH J.
actor who played Temarek in TNG episode "The Vengeance Factor."

BURNS, JUDY
scriptwriter for "The Tholian Web" (with Chet Richards). She's also written for "Mission: Impossible," "Toma" and uncounted others.

BURNS, TIM
actor who played Russ in "The Doomsday Machine." Film credits include: "Gargoyles" ('72), "Monkey Grip" ('83).

BURNSIDE, JOHN
actor who was an extra in "A Taste of Armageddon."

BURTON, LeVAR
actor who plays Geordi LaForge on The Next Generation. Born Feb. 16, 1957 in Landsthul, West Germany, he played Kunta Kinte in the epic "Roots." Other film credits include "Looking For Mr. Goodbar," "The Hunter," and "The Supernaturals" (which also starred Nichelle Nichols). He hosts "Reading Rainbow," a PBS show for children. His tv movies include "Dummy," "One In A Million: The Ron LeFlore Story," "Grambling's White Tiger," "The Guyana Tragedy: The Story of Jim Jones," "Battered," "Billy: Portrait of a Street Kid," and the mini-series "Liberty." He was a Star Trek fan long before landing the role, and entered a Catholic seminary at age 13, his goal: to become a priest. His interest in philosophy led him to read Lao Tzu, Kierkegaard, and Neitzche by the time he was fifteen. After he left the seminary, he won a scholarship to USC, where he was when at age 19 he

landed the grand role in "Roots." He got an Emmy nomination for his portrayal of Kinte. Burton lives in Los Angeles with his German Shepherd Mozart. His character is named after a real Star Trek fan who died of muscular dystrophy in 1975. Burton also directed TNG episode "Second Chances."

Buruk
a Klingon Bird of Prey commanded by Gowron in TNG episode "Reunion."

BUTLER, MEGAN
actress who starred as a lieutenant in DS9 episode "Emissary."

BUTLER, NATHAN
psuedonym of scriptwriter and sf writer Jerry Sohl who wrote the Classic Trek episode "This Side of Paradise."

BUTLER, ROBERT
director of the Classic Trek episodes "The Cage" and "The Menagerie, Part II." His directing credits include Disney's "The Computer Wore Tennis Shoes" ('69) and "Now You See Him, Now You Don't" ('71). He won an Emmy in 1973 for Director of the Year, and another for his work on "Hill Street Blues." He is co-creator of "Remington Steele."

BUTRICK, MERRITT
actor who played David Marcus, Kirk's son, in the Classic Trek films "The Wrath of Khan" and "The Search For Spock." He played T'Jon in The Next Generation episode

"Symbiosis." Before he died of AIDs in 1990, he starred in many tv series, including "Beauty and the Beast," and as a regular on the series "Square Pegs" where he played Johnny Slash. His film credits include "Zapped!," "When Your Lover Leaves," and "Shy People."

BY ANY OTHER NAME
written by D.C. Fontana and Jerome Bixby, directed by Marc Daniels, this second season Classic Trek episode aired 2/23/68. Aliens from the galaxy Andromeda, as a prelude to invasion, hijack the Enterprise for the 300 year journey back to their home. They reduce everyone but the command crew to compressed, mineral-like hexagonal boxes. The command crew must find a way to take back control of the ship. Guest stars: Warren Stevens, Barbara Bouchet, Steward Moss, Robert Fortier, Carol Byrd, Leslie Dalton, Julie Cobb.

BYERS, RALPH
actor who played a crewman in "Star Trek: The Motion Picture." Film credits: "Blind Ambition" ('79), "The Cradle Will Fall" ('83.)

Bynars, The
characters in TNG episode "11001001" who are linked by an organic computer and work in pairs. The small beings are named 11, 00, 10, and 01. They steal the *Enterprise* from Starbase 74. They are played by Katy Boyer, Alexandra Johnson, Iva Lane, and Kelly Ann McNally.

Bynaus
home world of the Bynars from TNG episode "11001001." They are a race who exist as part of an organic computer.

BYRAM, AMICK
actor who guest-starred in TNG episode "Identity Crisis."

BYRAM, CASSANDRA
actress who played the communications officer in DS9 episode "Emissary."

BYRD, CARL
actor who played Lt. Shea in the Classic Trek episode "By Any Other Name."

CABOT, ENSIGN
Enterprise junior officer who wants a transfer in TNG episode "Lessons."

CADIENTE, DAVE
played a Klingon in "The Search For Spock."

Cairo, U.S.S.
Excelsior Class ship from TNG episode "Chain of Command" commanded by Captain Edward Jellicoe.

Caitian
feline people covered with fur, bearing tails. M'Ress from the animated series is a Caitian.

Calamarain
Q torments these people, a race comprised of ionized gas, in TNG episode "Deja Q."

CALDER, THOMAS
scriptwriter of the TNG episode "The Emissary."

Caldonians
beings committed to pure research in TNG episode "The Price."

CALENTI, VINCE
actor who played a security guard in the Classic Trek episode "The Alternative Factor."

CALL, ANTHONY
actor who played Lt. Dave Bailey in the Classic Trek episode "The Corbomite Maneuver."

CAMERON, LAURA
actress who played Bajoran Woman in DS9 episode "Q Less."

CAMPBELL, WILLIAM
actor who played Captain Koloth in Classic Trek episode "The Trouble With Tribbles," and Trelane in the episode "The Squire of Gothos." Campbell was born in 1926 and has many tv credits, including "Gunsmoke," and the Gene Roddenberry produced movie "Pretty Maids All In A Row."

CAMPBELL, WILLIAM O.
actor who played Captain Thaddiun Okona in TNG episode "The Outrageous Okona."

CAMPIO
third minister of the conference of judges on Kostolain who is going to marry Lwaxana Troi until they discover incompatibilities in TNG episode "Cost of Living." Campio is played by Tony Jay.

Camus II
planet in Classic Trek episode "Turnabout Intruder" where Janice Lester and her team of scientists explored the ruins of a dead civilization and discovered the device that switched her essence with Kirk's. In TNG episode "Legacy," the *Enterprise* bypasses this world.

CANADA, RON
actor in TNG episode "Masterpiece Society."

Canar
a Hahliian device used to augment a telepathic link with others. It is seen in TNG episode "Aquiel."

CANON, PETER
actor who played the gestapo lieutenant in the Classic Trek episode "Patterns of Force." TV credits include: "The Wackiest Ship In The Army."

Canopus
in Classic Trek episode "Where No Man Has Gone Before," Gary Mitchell quotes from a poem called "Nightingale Woman" which was written by Phineas Tarbolde who was from Canopus.

Canopus III
place where Kirk saw a beast that resembled the fire-breathing iguana of Lactra VII mentioned in animated episode "Eye of the Beholder."

CANSINO, RICHARD
actor who played Dr. Garin in TNG episode "Deja Q."

Cantaba Street
where Morla lives in Classic Trek episode "Wolf In The Fold."

Capella IV
small world with red seas valued for its deposits of topaline, a substance used in life support systems on planetoid colonies in Classic episode "Friday's Child." The Federation and the Klingons compete for the allegiance of the planet. This planet is also mentioned in the animated episode "Counter-Clock Incident" as the location of one of the most beautiful flowers in the galaxy.

Capellan Power Cat
fiercest beast in the galaxy, mentioned in the animated episode "How Sharper Than A Serpent's Tooth." The untamable animal is like a bobcat with red fur and gold eyes with brown spines down its back. It possesses a white, glowing aura of electricity and can throw jolts at its victims.

Capellan Salute
shown in Classic episode "Friday's Child," it consists of forming the right hand into a fist, holding it against the center of the chest, then extending it outward with the palm up.

Capellans
tall human-like warriors seen in Classic episode "Friday's Child." They believe only the strong should survive and hold lit-tle value for medicine. They enjoy combat and interpret any show of force as a challenge to battle.

CAPRA, FRANK (III)
assistant director of the Classic film "The Voyage Home." He is the grandson of director Frank Capra. He also worked on the film "Zapped!"

CAPTAIN'S HOLIDAY
third season TNG episode written by Ira Stephen Behr, and directed by Chip Chalmers. Picard takes a holiday on Risa, which turns out to be anything but restful. He first meets Vash in this episode. Together they search for the Tox-Uthat, which the Ferengi and two Vorgons from the 27th century are also after. Guest stars: Jennifer Hetrick, Max Grodenchik, Karen Landry, Michael Champion, Deirdre Imershein.

Captain's Woman
see entry for Moreau, Marlena.

CAPTIVE PURSUIT
first season DS9 episode written by Jill Sherman Donner and Michael Piller, and directed by Corey Allen. An reptilian alien from the Gamma Quadrant visits DS9 with a damaged spacecraft. O'Brien befriends him only to learn that Tosk is bred to be prey in a great chase to the death, and is being pursued. Guest stars: Gerrit Graham, Scott MacDonald, Kelly Curtis.

CARABATSOS, STEPHEN W.
writer and producer who scripted the Classic Trek episodes "Court Martial" and "Operation: Annihilate!" He was a producer during Classic Trek's first season.

CARAPLEDES, UNA
character mentioned as having been killed in an accident by Starfleet in TNG episode "Conspiracy."

Carbon Cycle Life Form
the creature on Excalbia in Classic episode "The Savage Curtain" is one.

Cardassians
members of a hostile race whose leaders love to conquer, they are involved in a bitter war with Bajor. Ridges seem to attach their necks to their shoulders and make them look awkward. Except for their somewhat ridged foreheads, they are otherwise humanoid in appearance with hair on top of their heads. They appear often on DS9 as the resident villains. In TNG episode "Chain of Command," their leader shows a sadistic side when they torture and attempt to brainwash the captured Picard. Occasional episodes show that not all Cardassians are inherently evil, although they live under a barbaric regime.

CARETAKER, The
character on Classic episode "Shore Leave" who oversees the recreational facilities on the planet. He is played by Oliver McGowan. He dies in the animated episode "Once Upon A Planet."

CAREY, DIANE
author of TNG novel *Ghost Ship*, Classic Trek novels *Best Destiny, Final Frontier, Dreadnought!, Battlestations!,* and *The Great Starship Race.*

CARHART, TIMOTHY
actor in TNG episode "Redemption Part II."

CARLISLE, LIEUTENANT
security officer in Classic Trek pilot "The Cage" played by Arnold Lessing.

CARLYLE, RICHARD
played Karl Jaeger in the Classic Trek episode "The Squire of Gothos." TV credits include: "One Step Beyond" and "Cannon."

CARMEL, ROGER C.
layed Harcourt Fenton Mudd in "Mudd's Women," "I, Mudd," and the voice of Mudd in the the animated episode "Mudd's Passion." His tv credits include being a regular on "The Mother's In-Law" and "Fitz and Bones," as well as guest-starring in such shows as "I, Spy," "The Man From UNCLE," "The Alfred Hitchcock Show," and "Voyage To The Bottom of the Sea." He is famous as the voice of Senor Naugles (for a Mexican fast food restaurant chain) and Smokey The Bear. He died in 1986 of an apparent drug overdose. Before his death he made several convention appearances.

CARMICHAEL, MRS.
landlady in 19th century San Francisco who keeps demanding the rent from Picard in TNG episode "Time's Arrow Part II." She is played by Pamela Kosh.

Carnel
world where Picard and Tasha first met mentioned in TNG episode "Legacy."

Carolina, U.S.S.
vessel mentioned in Classic episode "Friday's Child" as the supposed origin of a second distress signal that draws Scotty away from the planet where the landing party remains. He does not heed this signal when he decides the Klingons are tricking him.

CARR, PAUL
played Lee Kelso in "Where No Man Has Gone Before." His tv credits include "The Rifleman," "Voyage To The Bottom Of The Sea," "The Green Hornet," "The Six Million Dollar Man," "Buck Rogers in the 23rd Century," and "Highway To Heaven."

Carraya IV
location of the Romulan prison camp that Worf invades in TNG episode "Birthright."

Carrel
viewing area in the library on Sarpeidon in Classic episode "All Our Yesterdays."

CARREN, DAVID BENNETT
scriptwriter of the TNG episode "Future Imperfect."

CARRIGAN-FAUCI, JEANNE
scriptwriter of DS9 episode "Move Along Home."

CARROLL, LARRY J.
scriptwriter of the TNG episode "Future Imperfect."

CARSON, DAVID
director of TNG episodes "The Enemy," "Yesterday's Enterprise," "Redemption Part II," and "The Next Phase." He also directed DS9 episodes "The Emissary" and "Move Along Home." His other directing credits include "Northern Exposure," "Alien Nation," "Homefront," "Doogie Howser, M.D.," and "L.A. Law." He moved his family from England to the U.S. only a few years ago.

CARSON, FRED
played First Denevan in the Classic Trek episode "Operation: Annihilate!"

CARTER, CARMEN
author of TNG novels *The Children of Hamlin, Doomsday World, The Devil's Heart, Dreams of the Raven.*

CARTER, DR.
doctor of the *Exeter* who died from the disease the landing party brought back from Omega IV on Classic episode "The Omega Glory." Played by Ed McCready.

CARTWRIGHT, ADMIRAL
member of Starfleet Command played by Brock Peters in "The Voyage Home" and "The Undiscovered Country."
Cartwright is one of the traitors involved in the conspiracy to assassinate the Klingons.

CARUSO, ANTHONY
played Bela Oxmyx in Classic Trek episode "A Piece of the Action." Born in 1915, his career includes singing as well as acting. He is well known for his portrayal of gangsters in various tv shows.

CARVER, STEPHEN JAMES
actor in DS9 episode "A Man Alone."

CARVER
security guard who beams down to Taurus II with the landing party in the animated episode "The Lorelei Signal."

CARY-HIROYUKI
played Mandarin Bailiff in TNG "Encounter At Farpoint."

CASCONE, NICHOLAS
played Ensign Davies in TNG episode "Pen Pals."

CASSEL, SEYMOUR
played Hester Dealt in TNG episode "The Child."

CASSIDY, TED
played Ruk in the Classic Trek episode "What Are Little Girls Made Of?" He also provided the voice of Balok in "The Corbomite Maneuver" and the voice of the Gorn in "Arena." Born in 1932, he is best known for his portrayal of Lurch in the tv series "The Addams Family." He died in 1979.

CASTILLO, LIEUTENANT RICHARD
helmsman and later senior officer of *Enterprise* C in TNG episode "Yesterday's Enterprise." He is in love with Tasha. He is played by Christopher McDonald.

CATCHING, BILL
stunt double for Spock in the Classic Trek episode "This Side of Paradise," as well as stunt double for Lazarus in "The Alternative Factor." He also appears in "Operation: Annihilate!"

CATRON, JERRY
played Second Denevan in the Classic Trek episode "Operation: Annihilate!" and Montgomery in "The Doomsday Machine." His career includes playing henchmen and monsters on various tv shows of the Sixties.

CATSPAW
written by famous horror writer Robert Bloch, directed by Joseph Pevney, this second season Classic Trek episode aired 10/27/67. The Enterprise investigates a ghostly, haunted planet where alien creatures have the power to generate illusions. Guest stars: Michael Barrier, Antoinette Bower, Theo Marcuse, Jimmy Jones. Of note: This was obviously planned as a 'Halloween' episode, and not one of the best.

CATTRALL, KIM
played Valeris in the Classic Trek film "The Undiscovered Country." Her film debut was "Mannequin," and she has recently appeared in many

threatrical and tv movies, including the surreal, virtual reality mini-series "Wild Palms," and "Big Trouble In Little China."

Catullan Ambassador
mentioned in Classic episode "The Way To Eden" as being the father of Tongo Rad, one of the group of 'space hippies' the *Enterprise* brings aboard.

CAUSE AND EFFECT
fifth season TNG episode written by Brannon Braga, and directed by Jonathan Frakes. The *Enterprise* is caught in a time loop and keeps repeating the same day over and over and over and over. Guest stars: Kelsey Grammer, Michelle Forbes.

CAVENS, AL
played Second Fop in the Classic Trek episode "All Our Yesterdays."

CAVES, SALLY
scriptwriter of the TNG episode "Hollow Pursuits."

CAVETT, JON
played a guard in the Classic Trek episode "Devil In The Dark."

Celebium
the type of radiation Janice Lester was exposed to on Camus II in Classic episode "Turnabout Intruder." She deliberately exposed the rest of her team to get the *Enterprise* to rescue them. Her team died.

Celestial Temple
term the Bajorans use for their rough equivalent of heaven. They believe the

Orbs come from the Celestial Temple.

Cellular Casting
what the creatures on the recreational planet in Classic episode "Shore Leave" are made of.

Centauri VII
mentioned in Classic episode "Requiem For Methuselah" as the home planet of Taranallus, a lithographer. Flint collects his work. Spock sees one titled "The Creation" displayed on a wall in Flint's living room.

Centurion
older Romulan man who appears to be second in rank, 'centurion,' to the commander in Classic episode "Balance of Terror" played by John Warburton. He dies when the debris from an attack falls on him.

Cepheus
an Arachna sun with one planet orbiting it mentioned in animated episode "The Terratin Incident."

Cerberan Youth Drug
drug invented by Admiral Jameson to reverse the aging process in TNG episode "Too Short A Season."

Cerberus
location of the school McCoy's daughter attended mentioned in animated episode "The Survivor."

Cerberus II
world on which Admiral Jameson developed a rejuvenation process in TNG

episode "Too Short A Season."

Cestus III
world of the Federation colony attacked by the Gorns in Classic episode "Arena."

Ceti Alpha V
planet where Khan and his people are exiled by Kirk in Classic episode "Space Seed." Chekov mistakes this planet for Ceti Alpha VI (which was unknowingly destroyed) in "The Wrath of Khan," and, with Captain Terrell, runs into the survivors of Khan's party.

Ceti Alpha VI
world that blew up and effected the orbit of Ceti Alpha V, making it nearly unlivable. Chekov thinks he's on Ceti Alpha VI in "The Wrath of Khan."

Ceti Eels
slug-like creatures indiginous to Ceti Alpha V that destroyed many of Khan's people. Their young enter a person's body through the ear and wrap themselves around the cerebral cortex. As they feed and grow, the person experiences pain and insanity, then death.

Cha'Dich
term for a Klingon attorney. Kurn is Worf's Cha'Dich in TNG episode "Sins of the Father."

CHADWICK, ROBERT
played Romulan Scope Operator in Classic Trek episode "Balance of Terror."

CHAIN OF COMMAND, PART I AND II
sixth season TNG episode written by Ronald D. Moore (part I) and Frank Abetemarco (part I and II) and directed by Robert Scheerer (part I) and Les Landau (part II). Picard, Crusher, and Worf go on a secret mission to learn if the Cardassians have a hidden base on Celtris III, but they walk into a trap. Worf and Crusher escape, but Picard is captured by the Cardassians, one of whom, Gul Madred, tortures him mercilessly for his own sadistic pleasure. Guest stars: Ronny Cox, David Warner.

Chalice of Rixx
a clay pot growing mold which belongs to Lwaxana in TNG episode "Menage A Troi."

CHALMERS, CHIP
director of TNG episodes "Captain's Holiday," "The Loss," "The Wounded," and "Ethics." He is also assistant director of various episodes.

Chalna
homeworld of the Chalnoth people, a race of warriors, including Esoqq. Picard visited while captain of the *Stargazer* in TNG episode "Allegiance."

Chalnoth
anarchists, warrior inhabitants of the world Chalna. Esoqq in TNG episode "Allegiance" is a Chalnoth, and, in their language, his name means 'fighter'.

Chamber of the Ages

in Classic episode "The Devil In The Dark," the Horta refers to her 'nest' of silicon eggs as the Chamber of the Ages and the Altar of Tomorrow.

Chameleon Rose

flower presented by Wyatt to Deanna in TNG episode "Haven." This flower changes color according to the mood of the person holding it.

CHAMPION, MICHAEL

played Boratis in TNG "Captain's Holiday."

CHANDLER, ESTEE

played Mirren Oliana in TNG episode "Coming of Age."

CHANDRA, CAPTAIN

member of Kirk's trial board when Kirk is tried for the murder of Ben Finney in Classic episode "Court Martial." He is played by Reginald Lalsingh.

Chandra

Child that talks in riddles telling pieces how to get past obstacles during game Quark plays with the Waddi in DS9 episode "Move Along Home." She is played by Clara Bryant.

Chandra V

planet mentioned in TNG episode "Tin Man." Tam Elbrun is the only Federation delegate assigned there.

Chandrans

peaceful inhabitants of Chandra V encountered in TNG episode "Tin Man."

For them, saying 'hello' can involve a three-day ritual.

CHANG, LIEUTENANT

tactical officer in TNG episode "Coming Of Age" who is Wesley's proctor for his Academy exam. He was played by Robert Ito.

CHANG

Klingon warrior in the Classic Trek film "The Undiscovered Country" played by Chirstopher Plummer. He frames Kirk for the murder of Gorkon and attacks the *Enterprise* at Khittomer.

CHANGELING, The

written by John Meredyth Lucas, directed by Marc Daniels, this second season Classic Trek episode aired 9/29/67. Nomad is a probe that merged with another machine, Tan Ru, altering its programming from seeking out life to destroying it. It believes Kirk is its creator because Kirk's name resembles that of its maker, and so does not immediately destroy the Enterprise. Guest stars: Blaisdell Makee, Barbara Gates, Arnold Lessing, Vic Perrin (voice of Nomad) Of note: The plot of the Classic film "Star Trek: The Motion Picture" derives much from this episode.

Changeling

term used in Classic episode "The Changeling" referring to a fairy tale in which a human child is replaced by a child of faerie. The machine Nomad is called a 'changeling' because it is not the same as when Earth

sent it off to explore life in the year 2002. It merged with a machine called Tan Ru and became a murdering machine. This term is also used to describe Odo in DS9 episode "Vortex." Crodon calls him a changeling since he's met the race in the Gamma Quadrant and they are shapeshifters. He is lying, retelling a myth, but Odo could still be related to changelings. It is a mystery he has been trying to solve all his life.

Channel E

the channel Nilz Baris uses to contact the *Enterprise* in Classic episode "The Trouble With Tribbles."

CHANNING, DR.

dilitium theorist Wesley studies mentioned in TNG episode "Lonely Among Us.".

Chant

in Classic episode "And The Children Shall Lead," the five kids chant: "Hail, hail, fire and snow,/call the angel we will go/far away for to see/friendly angel come to me." They stand in a circle with their hands placed in the center, one on top of the other. After they finish the chant, Gorgon appears to tell them what to do.

CHAO, ROSALIND

actress who played Keiko in TNG episodes "Data's Day," "The Wounded," "Night Terrors," "In Theory," "Disaster," "Violations," and "Power Play." She is also a regular on DS9. Her character is

married to Mile O'Brien; they have a small daughter.

CHAPEL, NURSE (AND DOCTOR) CHRISTINE

recurring character on Classic Trek played by Majel Barrett. She is the head nurse on the *Enterprise*, and by "Star Trek: The Motion Picture" has become a doctor. She has a secret, unrequited crush on Spock. Her fiancee, Dr. Roger Korby, died on Exo III in Classic episode "What Are Little Girls Made Of?," the first episode to present Chapel. After that incident, she becomes McCoy's head nurse. Although recurring, she remains a minor character. Little else is known of her.

CHAPMAN, LANEI

actress who played Rager in TNG "Galaxy's Child," "Night Terrors," and "Relics."

Charleston, U.S.S.

this ship was to rendezvous with the *Enterprise* in TNG episode "The Neutral Zone."

CHARLIE X

first season, Classic Trek, episode aired 9/15/66 penned by D.C. Fontana and Gene Roddenberry. Larry Dobkin directs a story involving an orphan, Charlie Evans, marooned on an alien planet and raised by psychokinetic energy beings who teach him their powers. Guest stars: Robert Walker, Jr. Of note: In this episode, Uhura sings a song to/about Spock, Janice Rand gets

smacked on the behind, and Spock first plays his Vulcan harp (or lyre, or lytherette).

CHARNO, SARA
scriptwriter of TNG episodes "The Wounded," "New Ground," and "Ethics" (with Stuart Charno).

CHARNO, STUART
scriptwriter of TNG episodes "The Wounded" (with Cy Chermak), "New Ground," and "Ethics" (with Sara Charno).

Charnoks' Comedy Cabaret
club simulated by Data on the holodeck in TNG episode "The Outrageous Okona."

Charybdis
lost NASA exploratory ship launched July 23, 2037 from America. Mentioned in the TNG episode "The Royale."

CHASE, The
sixth season TNG episode written by Joe Menosky and Ronald D. Moore, directed by Jonathan Frakes. An old archeology professor of Picard's, Galen, comes aboard the *Enterprise* with knowledge of a rare discovery on a microscopic level. He dies when his shuttle is attacked by Yridians in an attempt to steal his information, which is of galactic proportion. It is a message from a long dead race who seeded many worlds, hoping that by the time the offspring of their seedings had the technology to unravel the mes-

sage, they would be living in a world of peace and fellowship. Guest stars: Norman Lloyd, Linda Thorson, John Cothran, Jr., Maurice Roeves, Salome Jens.

CHATTAWAY, JAY
composer of music in TNG "Tin Man."

Chaya VII
place Leah Brahms visited mentioned in TNG episode "Booby Trap."

Chech'tluth
Klingon drink seen in TNG episode "Up The Long Ladder."

CHEKOV, ENSIGN PAVEL
major character in Classic Trek played by Walter Koenig. He appears in second season beginning with the episode "Who Mourns For Adonais?" A Russian, the *Enterprise* navigator. is supposedly only 22 when first seen. He is very proud of his Russian heritage, and often jokes that Russians invented almost everything good in Earth history. Little is known of his family. He is apparently single, and becomes close friends with Sulu. They take leave together in "The Final Frontier," only to get lost hiking through a forest on Earth. They are beamed back to the ship by Uhura. Chekov achieves the rank of 'commander' by the time of the Star Trek movies, and is the first officer of the ship *Reliant* under the command of Captain Terrell in "The Wrath of Khan." In "The

Motion Picture" he is the *Enterprise* weapons officer. In the later films, he is restationed on the *Enterprise*. In "Mirror, Mirror," Chekov is an assassin.

CHEKOV, PIOTR
mentioned in Classic episode "Day Of The Dove," he is supposedly Chekov's brother who was killed by Klingons in a raid on an outpost. This is not a true memory as Chekov never had a brother according to Sulu.

CHENEY, ENSIGN
in TNG episode "Lessons," she plays in a chamber music trio with Data and Lt. Commander Nella Daren.

CHERMAK, CY
scriptwriter of TNG episode "The Wounded" (with Sara and Stuart Charno).

Cheron, Battle of
a battle in which the Federation humiliated the Romulans mentioned in TNG episode "The Defector."

Cheron
homeworld of Lokai and Bele in Classic episode "Let That Be Your Last Battlefield" which was completely destroyed by race wars.

CHESS, JOE
camera operator on DS9.

Chess, 3-D
Kirk and Spock's favorite pastime is a three-dimensional form of chess. They are good opponents for

each other as Kirk often wins utilizing intuition rather than formal logic, easily fooling Spock. Kirk uses a chess move code to communicate to the *Enterprise* from Elba II in the Classic Trek episode "Whom Gods Destroy."

Chicago Mobs of the Twenties
title of the book left behind on Iotia by the *Horizon* that directed their whole culture in Classic episode "A Piece Of The Action."

Chief Officer, Commission of Political Traitors
Bele's official title in Classic episode "Let That Be Your Last Battlefield."

CHILBERG, JOHN E.
art director of the Classic Trek film "The Search For Spock."

CHILDRESS, BEN
character played by Gene Dynarski in Classic episode "Mudd's Women" who is a lithium miner on Rigel XII. He marries Eve McHuron.

Chime, Betazoid
chime customarily used during a Betazoid meal as a means for giving thanks seen in the TNG episode "Haven."

Chiya VII
mentioned in TNG episode "Booby Trap" as a site for many intergalactic caucuses.

CHOMSKY, MARVIN
director of Classic Trek episodes "And The

Children Shall Lead," "Day of the Dove," and "All Our Yesterdays." Born in 1929, he directed "Assault On The Wayne" ('70— starring Leonard Nimoy), "Holocaust" ('78), "Attica," and "Inside The Third Reich" ('81), winning an Emmy each time.

CHORGON
leader of the Gatherers in TNG episode "The Vengeance Factor" played by Stephen Lee.

Chorus
a group of people —a woman, a scholar, a warrior —who are a team that communicates for Riva, a famous mediator in TNG episode "Loud As A Whisper." The chorus translates his emotions but are later killed in an accident leaving Riva uncommunicative.

CHRISTINA
O'Brien's pet tarantula which he found on Titus IV and mentioned in TNG episode "Realm of Fear."

CHRISTOPHER, CAPTAIN JOHN
20th century Air Force pilot beamed aboard the *Enterprise* in Classic Trek episode "Tomorrow Is Yesterday" played by Roger Perry. The action threatens to change history because Christopher's future son, Shaun Geoffrey, is destined to man an Earth-Saturn probe significant in the exploration of space. The *Enterprise* must return him to Earth without effecting history. At the time, Christopher has a wife and

two children, both daughters, as he tells Spock he has no son.

CHRISTOPHER, COLONEL SHAUN GEOFFREY
future son of Captain John Christopher who will head the Earth-Saturn probe, a significant moment in space exploration history mentioned in Classic Trek episode "Tomorrow Is Yesterday."

CHRISTOPHER, DR.
subspace theoretician whose wife, Dr. T'Pan, and he criticize Dr. Reyga's theories in TNG episode "Suspicions."

Chrysalians
peaceful race encountered in TNG episode "The Price."

CHUFT, CAPTAIN
leader of the Kzin in animated episode "The Slaver Weapon."

Chula, Valley of
mentioned as being on the planet Romulus in TNG episode "The Defector."

CIGNONI, DIANA
actress who plays Dabo Girl in DS9.

Circausian Plague Cat
pet Geordi had when he was eight mentioned in TNG episode "Violations."

Circonea
world having a dispute with the Rekkags mentioned in TNG episode "Man of the People."

CITY ON THE EDGE OF FOREVER, The
first season Classic Trek scripted by award-winning author Harlan Ellison directed by Joseph Pevney aired 4/6/67. McCoy, delirious from an accident, beams down to the mysterious planet the *Enterprise* is investigating. The landing party discovers The Guardian of Forever portal, and McCoy jumps through to a different time. Somehow his actions change the future and the *Enterprise* no longer orbits. Kirk and Spock follow to save the future they all know. Guest stars: David L. Ross, Hal Boylor, Joan Collins, John Harmon, John Winston. Of note: The original, uncut version of Ellison's script is published in *Six Science Fiction Plays*, edited by Roger Elwood. Ellison never approved of Gene Roddenberry's changes to his script, and never hid that his Star Trek experience was an unhappy one. The episode won the Hugo Award for Best Dramatic Presentation in 1967.

CLAIBORNE, BILLY
member of the Clanton gang Chekov is supposed to be in Classic episode "Spectre of the Gun."

CLANCY, ENSIGN
assistant engineer on the *Enterprise* who later became the ops officer in TNG episodes "Elementary, Dear Data" and "The Emissary." She is played by Anne Elizabeth Ramsey.

CLANTON, BILLY
the member of the Clanton gang Scotty is supposed to be in Classic episode "Spectre of the Gun."

CLANTON, IKE
leader of the Clanton gang Kirk is supposed to be in Classic episode "Spectre of the Gun."

CLAPP, GORDON
actor in DS9 episode "Vortex."

CLARK, BOB
actor who played the Gorn in the Classic Trek episode "Arena." He also was a stunt man in "Return of the Archons," an extra in "Mirror, Mirror," and a native in "The Apple." His other tv credits include "Bonanza" and "Gunsmoke."

CLARK, JOSH
actor who played bridge position in TNG episode "Justice."

CLARK, DOCTOR HOWARD
head of the Federation science team on Ventax II in TNG episode "Devil's Due" played by Paul Lambert.

Class 1 Probe
mentioned in TNG episodes "Time Squared," "Yesterday's Enterprise," "The Defector," and "Pen Pals." They are used to get information at a distance.

Class 2 Probe
launched from the *Enterprise* in TNG episode "The Most Toys" to deliver hytritium to the water

source contaminated by tricyanate.

Class 3 Probe
machine with a neutrino beacon sent to the Galorndon Core in TNG episode "The Enemy."

Class 8 Probe
can travel at warp 9 and is seen in TNG episode "The Emissary."

Class J Cargo Ship
referred to in Classic episode "Mudd's Women" as the size of Harry Mudd's ship.

Class J Starship
older vessels used for trainees mentioned in Classic episode "The Menagerie."

Class M Planet
Earthlike world suitable for human survival also known on TNG as a class M atmosphere.

CLAUDIUS MARCUS
see entry for Marcus, Claudius.

CLAYMARE
Organian elder in Classic episode "Errand Of Mercy" played by Peter Brocco.

CLEARY, LIEUTENANT
crew member of the *Enterprise* played by Michael Roygas in the Classic Trek film "The Motion Picture."

CLEMONS, L.Q. 'SONNY'
cryonically frozen human from TNG episode "The Neutral Zone" played by Leon Rippy. He died of drug abuse and was brought back to life in the 24th century.

Cleponji
thousand years old Promellian battlecruiser commanded by Galek Sar found by the *Enterprise* in TNG episode "Booby Trap." It was trapped in the Menthar booby trap.

Cliffs of Heaven
place an officer of the *Enterprise* jumps off in a holodeck recreation, straining her shoulder in TNG episode "Conundrum."

Cloaking Device
invisibility shield used by Romulans first encountered in Classic episode "Balance of Terror." Kirk and Spock later steal the technology in a complex undercover plot in "The Enterprise Incident."

Cloth, Mintakan
ornament given as a gift to Picard by Nuria and Haki in TNG episode "Who Watches The Watchers." Seen again in "Sarek."

Cloud City
see entry for Stratos.

Cloud Creature
several cloud-like creatures are encountered in the series. Kirk encounters the vampire cloud in the Classic Trek episode "Obsession." In TNG episode "Lonely Among Us" the *Enterprise* and several of its crew are taken over by another cloud creature.

CLOUD MINDERS, The
written by Margaret Armen, David Gerrold and Oliver Crawford, this third season Classic Trek episode aired 2/28/69. The *Enterprise* pays a visit to Ardana, a world with a vast cloud city. The ship needs to shuttle the zeenite from Ardana's mines to a nearby world where it is the only known cure for a plague. Kirk and Spock become embroiled in a struggle between the cloud city dwellers and the miners on the planet below, and the ship and millions of people awaiting the shipment are threatened. Guest stars: Jeff Corey, Diana Ewing, Charlene Polite, Fred Williamson, Ed Long.

CLOUD WILLIAM
a Yang, one of the group fighting the Kohms, played by Roy Jenson in Classic Trek episode "The Omega Glory."

CLOW, CHUCK
stunt man in the Classic Trek episode "Friday's Child."

CLOWES, CAROLYN
author of Classic Trek novel *The Pandora Principle.*

CLUES
fourth season TNG episode written by Bruce D. Arthurs and Joe Menosky, directed by Les Landau. The crew discovers that 24 hours of their lives has been lost, and they investigate. Data interferes with the investigation, even lying to Picard. Guest stars: Whoopi Goldberg, Rhonda Aldrich, Pamela Winslow, Colm Meaney, Thomas Knickerbocker.

Coalition of Madina
twin planets Atlek and Streleb mentioned in TNG episode "The Outrageous Okona."

Coalsack
term for a dark spot in the galaxy used in Classic episode "Let That Be Your Last Battlefield." Cheron is located near a coalsack.

COBB, JULIE
actress who played Yeoman Leslie Thompson in the Classic Trek episode "By Any Other Name." She held regular roles in the tv series "A Year At The Top," "The DA," and "Charles In Charge." Tv movies include: "The Death Squad" ('74), "Salem's Lot" ('79), "Brave New World" ('80).

COBURN, DAVID
actor in TNG episode "The Nth Degree."

COCHRANE, ZEFREM
inventer of the warp drive in Classic episode "Metamorphosis" played by Glenn Corbett. He has been marooned on an asteroid with the 'companion,' a cloud creature that keeps him young and healthy and immortal. When Kirk, Spock, and McCoy encounter him, he is over 200 years old, and has been alone for a long time. The 'companion' brought the shuttlecraft to the asteroid so Cochrane could have human company.

Cochrane Deceleration Maneuver
battle maneuver mentioned by Spock in Classic episode "Whom Gods Destroy." In TNG episode "Menage A Troi," Riker refers to a Cochrane distortion.

Coco-no-no
drink Geordi offers Christy in TNG episode "Booby Trap."

Code 1
warning used when war or invasion will occur. It appears in the Classic episodes "The Alternative Factor" and "Errand of Mercy."

Code 2
code the Romulanas break in Classic episode "The Deadly Years." A forgetful, aging Kirk mistakenly orders this code used to send messages.

Code 3
code the Romulans do not break in Classic episode "The Deadly Years."

Code 47
emergency transmission for captain's eyes only mentioned in TNG episode "Conspiracy."

Code 710
term used by the planet Eminiar VII which means under no circumstances to approach their world in Classic episode "A Taste of Armageddon."

CODE OF HONOR
first season TNG episode written by Kathryn Powers and Michael Baron, direct-
ed by Russ Mayberry. Yar is kidnapped by the leader, Lutan, on a planet named Ligon II. She is forced to fight a death duel. Guest stars: Jessie Lawrence Ferguson, Karole Selmon, James Louis Watkins, Michael Rider.

Code One, Alpha Zero
code for a Federation starship in distress in TNG episode "Relics."

COE, GEORGE
actor in TNG episode "First Contact."

COFFEY, GORDON
actor who played a Romulan soldier in the Classic Trek episode "The Enterprise Incident."

COGAN, RHODIE
actress who played First Witch in Classic Trek episode "Catspaw."

COGLEY, SAMUEL T.
Kirk's lawyer in Classic episode "Court Martial" played by Elisha Cook, Jr. He loves books and is a brilliant defender. When Kirk is acquitted of killing Finney, Cogley defends Finney against charges brought against him for trying to frame Kirk.

COGSWELL, THEODORE R.
author of the Classic Trek novel *Spock Messiah!* (with Charles A. Spano, Jr.)

COLE, MEGAN
actress in TNG episode "The Outcast."

COLEMAN, DR. ARTHUR
character in Classic Trek episode "Turnabout Intruder" played by Harry Landers. He was in love with Janice Lester, and helped her try to take over Kirk's body and the *Enterprise.* He also helped her murder a scientific team by exposing them to celebium radiation.

COLICOS, JOHN
actor who played Kor, the Klingon commander in the Classic Trek episode "Errand of Mercy." He also was a regular in the science fiction tv series "Battlestar Galactica." He was born in Canada in 1928.

COLLA, RICHARD
director of TNG episode "The Last Outpost."

Colleena
young woman Picard makes a date with in TNG episode "Tapestry." She later slaps him in front of his friends because he made a simultaneous date with Penny.

COLLINS, CHRISTOPHER
actor who plays Grebnedlog in TNG episode "Samaritan Snare," and Captain Kargan in "A Matter of Honor." He is also in the DS9 episode "The Passenger."

COLLINS, JOAN
actress who played Edith Keeler in the Classic Trek episode "The City on the Edge of Forever." Born in London in 1933, her credits are numerous. She is most famous for her role as a villianous woman on the tv
series "Dynasty." Her sister Jackie Collins is a best-selling author.

COLLINS, SHELDON
actor who played the young boy in the Classic Trek episode "A Piece of the Action."

COLLINS, STEPHEN
actor who played Commander Will Decker in Classic Trek film "Star Trek: The Motion Picture." The character is the son of Matt Decker ("The Doomsday Machine"). The actor was born in 1947 in Iowa and appeared on Broadway and guest-starred in many tv shows including "The Waltons" and "Charlie's Angels." His tv series include "Tales of the Gold Monkey." One of his best performances is opposite Whoopie Goldberg in the film "Jumpin' Jack Flash."

COLLIS, JACK T.
production designer of the Classic Trek film "The Voyage Home." Other credits include: "The Four Seasons" ('81), "Paternity" ('81), "Tex" ('82), "Night Shift" ('82), "Nation Lampoon's Vacation" ('83), "Splash" ('84).

COLLISON, FRANK
actor in TNG "Ensign Ro."

Colony V
the *Enterprise's* destination for Charlie in Classic episode "Charlie X." Apparently Charlie has relatives there.

COLT, YEOMAN J.M.
young woman with a crush on Captain Pike in Classic pilot "The Cage" ("The Menagerie") played by Laurel Goodwin.

Coltair IV
planet that experiences the time distortion mentioned in TNG episode "We'll Always Have Paris."

Columbia, U.S.S.
ship in Classic pilot "The Cage" from which Vina, horribly crippled, was the only survivor.

Columbus
shuttlecraft on board the *Enterprise* first seen in Classic episode "The Galileo Seven."

COMBS, DAVID Q.
actor who played a mediator in TNG episode "Justice."

COMI, PAUL
actor who played the centurion in the Classic Trek episode "Balance of Terror." His tv credits include "Voyage to the Bottom of the Sea" and "Barnaby Jones." Films include "Warlock" ('59), "Pork Chop Hill" ('59), "Cry Rape!" ('73).

Comic
character played by Joe Piscopo on Data's holodeck recreation in TNG episode "The Outrageous Okona."

COMING OF AGE
first season TNG episode written by Sandy Fries and directed by Michael Vejar. Wesley takes the Starfleet Academy entrance exam on Relva VII while an investigation is undertaken to test Picard's loyalties to Starfleet. Guest stars: Estee Chandler, Daniel Riordan, Brendan McKane, Wyatt Knight, Ward Costello, Robert Schekkan, Robert Ito, John Putch, Stephan Gregory, Tasia Valenza.

Command Level
reference to the level of DS9 that holds the ops center.

Common Cold, The
by the time of Star Trek, the cure for the common cold has been found. This is mentioned in TNG episode "Angel One."

Communicator
device like a futuristic walkie-talkie or cellular phone. In Classic Trek, it is a square box with a grid that flips up. In "The Motion Picture" it is a wrist bracelet. On TNG and DS9 it is the insignia pin on the Starfleet uniforms.

Companion, The
misty cloud being in Classic episode "Metamorphosis" who takes care of 'the man', Zefrem Cochrane, maintaining his health and youth for 150 years and communicating by surrounding him with its energy. It exists on the asteroid remnant of the destroyed planet Gamma Canaris N. It the shuttlecraft to the asteroid against its will to provide human companionship for the lonely Cochrane. Voice is provided by Majel Barrett.

Complete Klingon Culture Index
book Wesley reads to find out about the Klingon custom the Age of Ascension in TNG episode "The Icarus Factor."

COMPTON, RICHARD
actor/director who played Washburn in Classic Trek episode "The Doomsday Machine" and the technical officer in "The Enterprise Incident." He also directed TNG episode "Haven."

COMPTON, CREWMAN
character played by Geoffrey Binney in Classic episode "Wink of an Eye." He is accelerated to the level of the Scalosians only to die of a minor injury that causes his cellular structure to age and decompose.

Comptronics
computer technology invented by Dr. Richard Daystrom in Classic episode "The Ultimate Computer."

Computer
the *Enterprise* computer is a vast voice command system that helps run the ship. The voice is provided by Majel Barrett. Other computers run the society in Classic episode "The Return of the Archons," the Bynars in TNG episode "11001001," and the Borg on TNG. In Classic Trek "For The World Is Hollow And I Have Touched The Sky," Yonada is run by a computer. In "A Taste of Armageddon," Eminiar and Vendikar conduct war by computers. There are portable computers, desk computers, diagnostic computers, library computers, and many others mentioned throughout all three series and movies.

Con
command of the bridge; short for "consoles."

Condition Green
code Kirk uses in Classic episode "Bread and Circuses" that means the landing party is in danger but the *Enterprise* must not interfere.

CONLEY, LAWRENCE V.
scriptwriter of TNG episode "Silicon Avatar."

CONOR, AARON
Troi's lover and leader of the Moab IV colony in TNG episode "The Masterpiece Society" played by John Snyder.

CONRAD, BART
played Captain Krasnowsky in the Classic Trek episode "Court Martial." His TV credits include "Perry Mason."

CONSCIENCE OF THE KING, The
first season Classic Trek episode written by Barry Trivers and directed by Gerd Oswald aired 12/8/66. A troupe of actors come aboard the Enterprise and Kirk thinks the star is really the infamous Kodos The Executioner of Tarsus IV who killed thousands of people to prevent all from dying of starvation. Kirk was on Tarsus as a child when this happened, and

he and Lt. Kevin Riley are two of only three survivors still alive. Guest stars: Arnold Moss, Barbara Anderson, Bruce Hyde, Eddie Paskey, William Sargent.

Of note: The return of Kevin Thomas Riley delighted fans, "Hamlet" by Shakespeare is performed for the crew, and Uhura sings "Beyond Antares" (words written by Gene L. Coon) to Riley.

CONSPIRACY
first season TNG episode written by Robert Sabaroff and Tracy Torme, and directed by Cliff Bole. Picard is warned there is a conspiracy to undermine Starfleet by top officials by his old friend Walker Keel. Walker's ship is then destroyed, leading Picard on a journey during which he discovers an invasion via parasites into the bodies of some very powerful Starfleet officials. Guest stars: Michael Berryman, Ursaline Bryant, Henry Darrow, Robert Schenkkan, Jonathan Farwell.

Constantinople
Federation transport ship in distress in TNG episode "The Schizoid Man."

Constellation, U.S.S.
starship attacked by the doomsday device in Classic episode "The Doomsday Machine." All hands are lost after Captain Decker beams them down to a nearby world, supposedly to save them, only to watch in horror as the machine eats the world. The ship is damaged, used

in conjunction with the *Enterprise* to destroy the deadly war device, and, ultimately, destroyed.

Constellation Class Starship
the *U.S.S. Stargazer* commanded by Picard was one of this class of starship with four warp nacelles.

Constitution Class Starship
the first *Enterprise* from Classic Trek is of this class of starship.

CONTAGION
second season TNG episode written by Steve Gerber and Beth Woods, and directed by Rob Bowman. A computer virus that is transmitted to the *Yamato* destroys it, and the *Enterprise* becomes infected. Meanwhile, a Romulan ship is in orbit about Iconia, where the virus seems to originate. Guest stars: Thalmus Rasulala, Carlyn Seymour, Dana Sparks, Folkert Schmidt, Colm Meaney.

Control Coils
integral parts of Ornaran frieghters mentioned in TNG episode "Symbiosis."

Controller, The
in Classic episode "Spock's Brain" the Eymorgs refer to Spock's brain as the Controller.

CONUNDRUM
fifth season TNG episode written by Paul Schiffer, Barry M. Schkolnick and Joe Menosky, and directed by Les Landau. The Lysians wipe the minds of the

Enterprise crew who awaken to find themselves in the middle of a war. Nobody recognizes the new bridge crewman who has always experienced the memory loss. Guest stars: Erich Anderson, Kieran MacDuff, Michelle Forbes, Liz Vassey, Erick Weiss.

CONWAY, JAMES L.
director of TNG episodes "Justice," "The Neutral Zone," and "Frame of Mind."

CONWAY, KEVIN
played the cloned Kahless in TNG episode "Rightful Heir."

COOK, ELISHA JR.
played Samuel T. Cogley, attorney at law in the Classic Trek episode "Court Martial." Born in San Francisco in 1906, his film credits include "The Maltese Falcon," "The Big Sleep," "Shane," "Rosemary's Baby," "Carny." TV credits: "The Bionic Woman," and "The Man From UNCLE" among others.

COOMBS, GARY
stunt man in Classic Trek episodes "The Galileo Seven," "Arena," "Errand of Mercy," "Space Seed," "The Alternative Factor," and "Operation: Annihilate!"

COON, GENE L.
writer/producer of Classic Trek who also wrote under the name Lee Cronin. He wrote "Arena," "Space Seed," "A Taste of Armageddon," "Devil In The Dark," "Errand of Mercy," "The Apple,"

"Metamorphosis," "A Piece of the Action," "Bread and Circuses," "Spock's Brain," "Spectre of the Gun," "Wink of an Eye," and "Let That Be Your Last Battlefield." He also worked with Gene Roddenberry on the movie "The Questor Tapes," and died in 1974.

COOPER, CHARLES
played K'mpec on TNG episode "Sins of the Fathers," and acted in "Reunion."

COOPER, SONNI
author of the Classic Trek novel *Black Fire*.

COPAGE, JOHN
played Elliot in Classic Trek episode "The Doomsday Machine."

Copernicus
shuttlecraft on the *Enterprise* first referred to in animated episode "The Slaver Weapon."

Cor Caroli V
world cured of a phyrox plague in TNG episode "Allegiance."

Coradrenalin
medication for treating frostbite and exposure McCoy needs in Classic episode "All Our Yesterdays."

CORBETT, GLENN
played Zefrem Cochrane in Classic Trek episode "Metamorphosis." Born in 1934, his many credits include "Midway," "Route 66," "The Road West," and "Dallas."

Corbomite
imaginary substance Kirk fantasizes to delay the people of the First Federation from attacking the *Enterprise* in Classic episode "The Corbomite Maneuver." Kirk says it is a substance that is contained in the ship's hull that will will blow up when the ship is destroyed and reflect the energy back on the attacker.

CORBOMITE MANEUVER, The
written by Jerry Sohl and directed by Joe Sargent, this Classic Trek first season episode aired 11/10/66. The Enterprise encounters a space buoy that blocks them and then threatens to destroy them. The word 'corbomite' refers to a nonexistent substance Kirk makes up to 'bluff' aliens into a less hostile approach. Guest stars: Anthony Call, Clint Howard (Ron Howard's younger brother.)

CORD, ERIK
played a thug in TNG episode "The Big Goodbye."

Cordrazine
miracle drug that can save a deathly ill person or kill them, depending upon the dosage and problem. McCoy accidentally injects himself with cordrazine in Classic episode "The City On The Edge of Forever," goes insane, and leaps through the Guardian of Forever into Earth's past, changing all of history.

COREY, JEFF
played Plasus in Classic Trek episode "The Cloud

Minders." Born in 1914, he also taught acting. His films include "The Man Who Wouldn't Die," "Seconds," and "Beneath The Planet Of The Apes."

Coridan
system of worlds that wishes admission to the Federation. In Classic episode "Journey to Babel," the Babel Conference is being held to decide this issue. Orion mining pirates have, in the past, raided the Coridan system because its worlds are rich in minerals.

Corinth IV
location of a starbase mentioned in Classic episode "Metamorphosis."

Cornelian system
destination of the *Enterprise* when it is trapped in a void in TNG episode "Where Silence Has Lease."

CORRELL, CHARLES
director of photography of "The Search For Spock." Other credits include "Cheech and Chong's Nice Dreams" and "The Joy of Sex."

Correllium Fever
disease on Nahmi IV in TNG episode "Hollow Pursuits."

CORREY, LEE
author of the Classic Trek novel *The Abode of Life*.

CORRIGAN
old friend of Kirk's who turns his back on him when Kirk walks into the bar on the starbase in

Classic episode "Court Martial."

CORSENTINO, FRANK
played Bok in TNG episode "The Battle," and DaiMon Tog, Ferengi captain of the *Krayton* in TNG episode "Menage A Troi."

Cortropine
stimulant McCoy uses to keep the crew alive in animated episode "The Lorelei Signal."

Corvallens
mercenary race that Troi senses will betray the Romulans in TNG episode "Face of the Enemy."

CORY, DONALD
character played by Key Luke in Classic Trek episode "Whom Gods Destroy" who runs the penal colony on Elba II.

COST OF LIVING
fifth season TNG episode written by Peter Allan Fields, and directed by Winrich Kolbe. Parasites are eating the *Enterprise*. Meanwhile, Lwaxana takes a lonely Alexander under her wing and entertains him on the holodeck. Guest stars: Majel Barrett, Brian Bonsall, Tony Jay, Carel Struycken, Patrick Cronin, Albie Setznick, David Oliver, Tracy D'Arcy, George Edie, Christopher Halste.

COSTANZO, ROBERT
played Slade Bender in TNG "Manhunt."

COSTELLO, WARD
played Admiral Gregory Quinn in TNG episode

"Coming of Age," and "Conspiracy."

COSTER, NICOLAS
played Admiral Anthony Haftel in TNG episode "The Offspring." He has numerous acting credits, including recurring roles on "The Facts of Life" and in movies such as "Little Darlings." (In 1993, he showed up on "As The World Turns.")

COTHRAN, JOHN, JR.
played Klingong Nu'Daq in TNG episode "The Chase."

COTTRELL, MICKEY
actor in TNG episode "The Perfect Mate."

COUCH, CHUCK
stunt man in Classic Trek episode "Space Seed."

COUCH, WILLIAM
stunt man in "Star Trek: The Motion Picture." Has also worked on the films "Dead and Buried" and "Brainstorm."

Council of Elders
the head leaders of Organia from Classic episode "Errand of Mercy."

Council of Nobles
the ruling class of Elas from Classic episode "Elaan of Troyius."

COUNTER-CLOCK INCIDENT, The
written by John Culver, this animated Classic Trek episode aired 10/12/74. The first captain of the *Enterprise*, Commodore Robert April and his wife, Sara April, are being transported by the ship to Babel. En route, they encounter a

ship heading straight for a nova, Beta Niobe. They lock onto the ship trying to save it but are pulled into the nova and an antimatter universe where the sky is white, the stars are black and time flows backwards. There they encounter a race of beings on the planet Arret. The crew rapidly ages backwards until they are toddlers and cannot run the ship. April and his wife must save the day, since they were older to begin with and are now young adults who can still remember how to run the ship.

COURAGE, ALEXANDER
composer who scored the original series theme. He also wrote much of the music for the episodes. Born in 1919, his credits include "Voyage To The Bottom Of The Sea" and "Lost In Space," and the musicals "Porgy and Bess," "Doctor Doolittle," and "Fiddler on the Roof." Gene Roddenberry wrote the words to the Star Trek theme as the poem "Star Trek."

COURT-MARTIAL
first season Classic Trek episode written by Don M. Mankiewicz and Stephen W. Carabatsos, and directed by Marc Daniels aired 2/2/67. Kirk stands accused of the death of a crewman. He will lose everything unless he can prove he did not make the error, but the video records, (as we have learned almost 30 years later in the '90s,) are very damning. Guest stars: Percy Rodriguez, Elisha Cook, Jr.,

Joan Marshall, Richard Webb, Alice Rawlings, Hagen Beggs.
Of note: Kirk kisses his old flame on the bridge of the Enterprise, showing he has no grudge against her even though she was the prosecutor in the trial.

COURTNEY, CHUCK
played Davod in the Classic Trek episode "Patterns of Force."

COUSINS, BRIAN
actor in TNG "The Next Phase."

COX, RICHARD
played Kyril Finn in TNG "The High Ground."

COX, RONNY
guest-star in TNG episode "Chain of Command."

COX, NIKKI
played Sarjenka in TNG "Pen Pals." She has done movies and TV commercials.

CRAIG, YVONNE
played Marta in Classic Trek episode "Whom Gods Destroy." Born in 1941, her numerous credits include Batgirl in the "Batman" series.

CRANDELL, MELISSA
author of Classic Trek novel *Shell Game.*

CRATER, NANCY
McCoy's old girlfriend who apparently reappears in Classic episode "The Man Trap." Actually it is a creature that has taken her shape from McCoy and Professor Crater's minds to fool the *Enterprise* crew.

The real Nancy actually died at the hands of the creature. She called McCoy by the nickname 'Plum'.

CRATER, PROFESSOR ROBERT
archeologist on planet M-113 played by Alfred Ryder in Classic episode "The Man Trap" who is protecting a creature that killed his wife.

CRAWFORD, JOHN
played Commissioner Ferris in Classic Trek episode "The Galileo Seven." Born in 1926, his credits include "Satan's Satellites" (with Leonard Nimoy), "Voyage To The Bottom Of The Sea," and a semi-regular stint on "The Waltons."

CRAWFORD, OLIVER
scriptwriter who penned Classic Trek episodes "The Galileo Seven," "Let That Be Your Last Battlefield," and "The Cloud Minders." He also wrote scripts for TV shows including "Voyage To The Bottom Of The Sea," "The Rifleman," "The Bionic Woman," and "Perry Mason."

Crazy Horse, U.S.S.
attack ship in TNG episode "Descent."

CREAGHAN, DENNIS
actor in TNG episode "Family."

Credit
monetary unit of the Federation in all three series, though gold-pressed latnum seems to be favored on DS9.

Crimson Force Field
term Riker makes up in TNG episode "Samaritan Snare" to describe the exhaust of the hydrogen collectors he pretends is a force field.

Crisalians
race of beings negotiating on the bidding for the Barzan wormhole in TNG episode "The Price."

CRISPIN, A.C.
author of Classic Trek novels *Yesterday's Son*, *Time For Yesterday*, and TNG novel *The Eyes of the Beholders.*

CRIST, PAULA
played a crewmember in "Star Trek: The Motion Picture." She has also done stunt and extra work in such films as "Logan's Run."

CROCKETT, DICK
stunt director who played Kirk's double in Classic Trek episode "Where No Man Has Gone Before," and an Andorian in "The Gamesters of Triskelion." He was also a Klingon in "The Trouble With Tribbles."

CRODON
character played by Cliff DeYoung who kills one of the Miradorn twins in self-defense in DS9 episode "Vortex" and is then jailed and tried for murder.

CROMWELL, JAMES
played Prime Minister Nayrock in TNG episode "The Hunted," and Yaglom Shrek in "Birthright Part I."

CROMWELL

launch director at McKinley Rocket Base played by Don Keeferin in Classic episode "Assignment: Earth."

CRONIN, LEE

scriptwriter credited for Classic episodes "Spock's Brain," "Spectre of the Gun," "Wink of an Eye," and "Let That Be Your Last Battlefield." Pen name for Gene L. Coon.

CRONIN, PATRICK

actor in TNG episode "Cost of Living."

Cronitron Field

Data tracks this throughout the *Enterprise* to help determine Ro and Geordi are still alive in TNG episode "The Next Phase."

CROSBY, DENISE

played Tasha Yar in TNG's first season, then returned in "Yesterday's Enterprise," and as Yar's daughter Sela in "Redemption," "The Mind's Eye," and "Unification." Film credits include "48 Hours," "Miracle Mile," and "The Eliminators." She also has numerous television credits. She is the granddaughter of Bing Crosby, and has also been a model, which she did not enjoy, and worked on the stage.

CROSIS

Borg captured in TNG episode "Descent."

CRUCIS, JUD

scriptwriter who wrote the story for Classic Trek episode "A Private Little War."

Crucis System

located near Romulan space, it is mentioned in TNG episode "Disaster."

CRUSHER, DR. BEVERLY C.

regular character in "The Next Generation" played by Gates McFadden. She is the *Enterprise* head doctor. Her husband, Jack Crusher, died under Picard's first command, when he was on an away team from the *Stargazer*. Her son, Wesley, is a genius who becomes an ensign on the *Enterprise* even before he leaves to attend Starfleet Academy. She left the *Enterprise* for one year with no explanation and was replaced by Dr. Pulaski, then returned in the third season. She and Picard are very good friends, even though she once blamed him for the death of her husband. They have breakfast together every morning, and though they seem to be attracted to one another, they rarely act on that attraction. Beverly lived on Aveda III when she was a child.

CRUSHER, WESLEY

regular character in the first 83 episode of "The Next Generation" played by Wil Wheaton. He is a child genius who helps solve many problems and is made acting ensign and then full ensign. He left the *Enterprise* to attend Starfleet Academy where he ran into trouble when involved in a cover-up of the death of a classmate. He returns to visit the *Enterprise* every once in

awhile. In the TNG episode "Hide and Q," he becomes an adult played by actor William A. Wallace.

CRUSHER, LIEUTENANT COMMANDER JACK R.

first officer of the *Stargazer* and husband of Dr. Beverly Crusher who died under Picard's command. He is the father of Wesley Crusher.

Cryonetrium

gaseous substance flooded into the injector pathway conduits to lower their temperature in TNG episode "Hollow Pursuits."

Cryptobiolin

one of the elements used to create perfect soldiers in TNG episode "The Hunted."

Crystalline Entity

destructive entity that feeds off energy emanations of life forms encountered in TNG episode "Datalore." It destroyed many planets in its path until it was killed in TNG episode "Silicon Avatar."

Cueller System

system in which the *Enterprise* investigates the destruction of a Cardassian station in TNG episode "The Wounded."

CULBREATH, MYRNA

author (with Sondra Marshak) of the Classic Trek novels *The Price of the Phoenix*, *The Fate of the Phoenix*, *Triangle*, *The Prometheus Design*, and editor of *Star Trek The New Voyage* and Star Trek The New Voyages 2. She also

wrote (with Sondra, and William Shatner) *Shatner Where No Man*, a biography of the actor long out of print. It will never see print again because William Shatner, not liking how it turned out, bought all the rights to it.

CULEA, MELINDA

actress in TNG episode "The Outcast."

CULLUM, J.D.

actor in TNG "Redemption."

CULVER, JOHN

scriptwriter who penned the animated "The Counter-Clock Incident."

CUMMINGS, BOB

played Klingon Gunner in "The Search For Spock."

CUPO, PATRICK

played Bajoran Man in DS9 episode "A Man Alone."

CURRY, DAN

visual effects supervisor on various TNG episodes, as well as director of TNG episode "Birthright, Part II."

CURTIS, KELLY

actress in DS9 episode "Captive Pursuit."

CURTIS, ROBIN

played Saavik (after Kirstie Alley did not return) in "The Search For Spock" and "The Voyage Home." She also appeared in a seventh season TNG episode as a Vulcan disguised as a Romulan.

CURZON

the best friend and mentor of Benjamin Sisko whose

body Dax occupied before becoming Jadzia Dax. Curzon's memories continue to be a part of Jadzia Dax. Curzon lived a long life, and died an old man. He is seen in DS9 episode "Emissary," played by Frank Owen Smith. See entries for Trills and Dax.

CUSHMAN, MARC
scriptwriter of TNG episode "Sarek."

Custodian, The
supercomputer built by progenitors on Aldea in TNG episode "When The Bough Breaks."

Cygnet XIV
all-female world where the *Enterprise* had its computer system overhauled. The computer was given a personality that caused it to fall in love with Kirk in Classic episode "Tomorrow Is Yesterday."

Cygnia Minor
mentioned in Classic episode "The Conscience of the King" as a world which is regularly threatened by famine.

Cylodin
poison self-inflicted by the Starnes expedition under the influence of the Gorgon in Classic episode "And The Children Shall Lead." Only the children survive.

Cytherians
Barclay inadvertantly becomes the Cytherians emissary when they temporarily make him the most intelligent human in the universe in TNG episode "The Nth Degree." The curious humanoid Cytherians meant no harm.

D'ABO, OLIVIA
guest starred in TNG "True Q." Best known for her recurring role as Karen in "The Wonder Years," D'Abo has also starred in several films, including "Beyond The Stars."

D'AMATO, ENSIGN
is put on report by Worf in TNG episode "Sarek."

D'AMATO, LIEUTENANT
Enterprise geologist, played by Arthur Batanides, killed by Losira in Classic episode "That Which Survives."

D'ARCY, TRACY
actress in TNG "Cost of Living."

D'SORA, ENSIGN JENNA
Enterprise engineering officer who plays the flute and is courted by Data in TNG episode "In Theory." Data finds he cannot give Jenna, played by Michele Scarabelli, what she needs and the relationship ends.

D'Voris
a Romulan ship under command of Admiral Mendak in TNG episode "Data's Day."

D Y 100
a class of ship from the late 1990's. The sleeper ship *Botany Bay* from Classic episode "Space Seed" is of this class.

D Y 500
a class of ship from the 21st century mentioned in Classic episode "Space Seed."

DA VINCI, FRANK
played Lt. Brett in Classic Trek "The Naked Time" and a crewmember in "The Lights of Zetar."

Dabo
a gambling game played in Quark's bar on *Deep Space 9.*

Dachlyds
a culture of stubborn people for whom Picard mediated a trade dispute mentioned in TNG episode "Captain's Holiday."

DAGGER OF THE MIND
first season Classic Trek episode written by Shimon Wincelberg (who also writes under the name S. Bar David) which aired 11/3/66. Directed by Vince McEveety, the story involves an asylum, or penal colony on Tantalus V where criminals and the mentally ill receive treatment. A new device, the neural neutralizer, which empties the brain of all thought and memory and allows the victim to be open to new suggestions, gives the head doctor Tristan Adams full control over his patients as well as his staff. Guest stars: James Gregory, Morgan Woodward (who later plays Captain Tracy in "Omega Glory"), Marianna Hill, and Suzanne Wasson. Of note: This is the first time we see the famous Vulcan mind meld performed, an ability attrib-

uted as much to Leonard Nimoy as to the show's writers.

Dahk'ta
Klingon dagger Worf sees rusting in a drawer at the Carraya prison camp in TNG episode "Birthright."

DAILY, CAPTAIN JON
captain of the *Astral Queen,* ship originally designated to transport the Karidian players to Benecia in Classic episode "Conscience of the King."

Daled IV
homeworld of Salia, the shapechanger from TNG episode "The Dauphin."

DALTON, LESLIE
played Drea in Classic Trek "By Any Other Name."

DALY, JAMES
played Flint in Classic Trek "Requiem For Methuselah." Also famous for his regular role in the TV series "Medical Center."

DALY, JANE
played Varria in TNG "The Most Toys."

DAMIAN, LEO
played Warrior/Adonis in TNG "Loud As A Whisper."

DAMON, GABRIEL
played Jeremy Aster in TNG "The Bonding."

DANAR, GUL
commander of the Cardassian warship in DS9 "Past Prologue."

DANAR, ROGA
a perfect soldier and an Angosian veteran of the

Tarsian War who yearns for his freedom. Played by Jeff McCarthy in TNG "The Hunted."

DANESE, CONNIE
played Toya in TNG "When The Bough Breaks.

DANG, TIMOTHY
played main bridge security in TNG "Encounter At Farpoint."

DANIELS, JERRY
played Marple in Classic Trek "The Apple."

DANIELS, MARC
directed Classic Trek episodes "The Man Trap," "The Naked Time," "The Menagerie," "Court Martial," "Space Seed," "Who Mourns For Adonais," "The Changeling," "Mirror, Mirror," "The Doomsday Machine," "I, Mudd," "A Private Little War," "By Any Other Name," "Assignment: Earth," "Spock's Brain," and Roddenberry's pilot "Planet Earth." He also wrote the script for the animated "One Of Our Planets Is Missing" and has directed numerous other TV shows.

DANO, KAL
scientist from the 27th century who invented the Tox Uthat and hid it on Risa in TNG episode "Captain's Holiday." He later died in the 22nd century.

DANTE, MICHAEL
played Maab in "Friday's Child." Often cast in Native American roles because of his dark looks, his films

include "Kid Galahad," "Willard," "Shining Star" and "Winterhawk." He is also a writer.

Danula II
the planet on which Cadet Picard won a marathon as mentioned in TNG episode "The Best of Both Worlds."

DANUS, RICHARD
wrote TNG episodes "Deja Q" and "Booby Trap" and became the show's executive story editor during its third season.

DANZINGER, CORY
appears in TNG episode "Brothers."

DARA
Dr. Timicin's daughter, played by Michelle Forbes, who wants him to accept his honorable, but early death as is the Kaelon custom in TNG episode "Half A Life." Forbes also played Ensign Ro. See entry.

Darabin V
planet where Lt. Uhnari was posted prior to her job on the Subspace Relay Station 47 in TNG episode "Aquiel."

Daran V
in danger of being hit by the spaceship world Yonada if its course is allowed to continue in Classic episode "For The World Is Hollow And I Have Touched The Sky."

DARAS
member of the Ekosian underground, played by Valora Noland, who poses as a hero of the Fatherland

in Classic episode "Patterns of Force."

DARBY, KIM
played Miri in Classic Trek episode "Miri." Born in 1948, some of her other credits include "True Grit" (with John Wayne) and "The People" (with William Shatner.)

DAREN, LT. COMMANDER NELLA
head of Stellar Cartography, and a pianist, on the *Enterpise*, she and Captain Picard have a brief liaison but part, still very much in love, when they realize a shipboard romance is impossible without jeopardizing their professional concerns. She asks for a transfer, and they agree to see each other during shore leaves and continue a long distance friendship.

Daren herbal tea #3
drink Lt. Commander Nella Daren programs into the food replicators in TNG episode "Lessons." Picard doesn't like the tea.

DARIS, JAMES
played a savage in Classic Trek "Spock's Brain."

Dark Matter
exists in the Mar Obscura Nebula and can cause depressurization on board starships as their hulls phase in and out of existence. Mentioned in TNG episode "In Theory."

DARMOK
fifth season TNG episode written by Philip Lazebnik and Joe Menosky, and

directed by Winrich Kolbe. A ship manned by a species which calls themselves the Children of Tama is met by the *Enterprise*, but communication is nearly impossible because the Tamans speak in metaphors alluding to their own history and myth, which the *Enterprise* and its universal translator know nothing about, but must learn. Guest stars: Paul Winfield, Richard Allen, Colm Meaney, and Ashley Judd.

Darnay's disease
illness afflicting Graves in TNG episode "The Schizoid Man."

DARNELL
crewman, played by Michael Zaslow, killed by the salt vampire in Classic episode "The Man Trap" and found with a piece of borgia plant in his mouth.

DARO, GLEN
a member of the Cardassian delegation, played by Time Winters, that comes aboard the *Enterprise* in TNG episode "The Wounded."

DARROW, HENRY
played Admiral Savar in TNG episode "Conspiracy."

DARSON, CAPTAIN
commander of the ship *Adelphi* who died in the Ghorusda disaster in TNG episode "Tin Man."

DARVIN, ARNE
a Klingon, played by Charlie Brill, disguised as an assistant to Nilz Baris on Space Station K 7 in Classic

episode "The Trouble With Tribbles."

DATA, LT. COMMANDER

android operations officer of the *Enterprise* played by Brent Spiner, in "The Next Generation." Created by Dr. Noonian Soong on Omicron Theta IV, he was first found by the ship *U.S.S. Tripoli* and later attended Starfleet Academy. When a Turing Test declared him sentient, he was awarded several different posts on Starfleet vessels before coming aboard the Enterprise. Data and his twin, Lore, were designed in their father Soong's image. Data and Lore, who was created first, have very pale skin, yellow eyes, and are physically human in every way, except for off switches on their backs. Data's fondest wish is to know what it is like to be mentally and emotionally human. He comes close many times to attaining feeling, but each attempt results in disaster. His hobbies include music, acting, writing poetry, his cat Spot, painting, stand-up comedy, solving mysteries (his favorite sleuth is Sherlock Holmes) and playing poker. He says he cannot speak in contractions, yet he does so easily when imitating a human, or acting out a role. An accomplished engineer, often assisting Geordi with mechanical problems, Data is also an expert on many subjects, and can pilot the *Enterprise* out of tough situations with ease. Although designed to be completely rational, he is one of the

most compassionate crewmembers on the *Enterprise*. He even breaks the Prime Directive in TNG episode "Pen Pals," going against command orders to save a little girl calling for help from a doomed world. (For more, see entry on Androids.)

DATA'S DAY

fourth season TNG episode written by Harold Apter and Ronald D. Moore, and directed by Robert Wiemer. The camera follows Data on the start of a typical day which ends up highly unusual. First, Data is to give Keiko away in the O'Brien's wedding, until Keiko calls the wedding off. Then a Vulcan ambassador beams aboard on a mission of utmost secrecy. Guest stars: Rosalind Chao, Sierra Pecheur, Alan Scarfe, Colm Meaney, V'Sal, and April Grace.

DATALORE

first season TNG episode written by Bob Lewin, Maurice Hurley and Gene Roddenberry, and directed by Rob Bowman, in which Data discovers he has a twin brother, named Lore. (Both characters are played by Brent Spiner.) Created before Data, Lore does have emotions but no conscience, a combination which makes him selfish and deadly. Guest star: Biff Yeager.

DATHON, CAPTAIN

Tamarian ship captain, played by Paul Winfield in TNG episode "Darmok," who is killed on the world of El-Adrel.

DAUGHERTY, HERSCHEL

director of Classic Trek episodes "Operation: Annihilate!" "The Savage Curtain" and numerous other TV shows.

DAUPHIN, THE

second season TNG episode written by Scott Rubenstein and Leonard Mlodinow, and directed by Rob Bowman. Salia, future ruler of Daled IV, comes aboard the *Enterprise* for transport and falls for Wesley, who doesn't know she is a shapechanger. Guest stars: Paddi Edwards, Jamie Hubbard, Madchen Amick, Cindy Sorenson, Jennifer Barlow, and Peter Neptune.

DAVID, PETER

wrote the Classic Trek novel *The Rift*, TNG novels *Imzadi, Vendetta, Strike Zone, Doomsday World, Q-In Law, A Rock and a Hard Place*, and the DS9 novel *The Seige*. Also wrote a number of TNG comic book stories.

DAVID, DEBORAH DEAN

wrote script for TNG episode "We'll Always Have Paris."

DAVID

child, played by George Baxter, Pulaski beams aboard the shuttlecraft in TNG episode "Unnatural Selection."

DAVIES, STEPHEN

plays tactical officer in DS9.

DAVIES, ENSIGN

played by Nicholas Cascone, assists Wesley in

solving the Secundi Drema system problem in TNG episode "Pen Pals."

DAVILA, CARMEN

an official on Melona IV, played by Susan Diol, who is attracted to Riker and is killed by the Chrystalline Entity in TNG episode "Silicon Avatar."

DAVIS, DANIEL

played Professor James Moriarty in TNG shows "Elementary, Dear Data" and "Ship In A Bottle."

DAVIS, JOE W.

played the young Spock in the film "The Search For Spock."

DAVIS, TEDDY

played a transporter technician in TNG "Sins of the Fathers."

DAVIS, WALT

played a therapist in Classic Trek "Dagger of the Mind," a Romulan crewman in "Balance of Terror," and a Klingon soldier in "Errand of Mercy." Other credits include "Alias Smith and Jones" and "The Bionic Woman."

DAVOD

a Zeon, played by Chuck Courtney, on Classic episode "Patterns of Force."

DAWSON, BOB

special effects supervisor in films "The Wrath of Khan" and "The Search For Spock."

DAX, JADZIA

a regularly featured character on DS9 made up of two different species. Dax is a member of the symbiotic species known as the Trill. Jadzia, a 28-year-old female humanoid with a series of intricate, freckle-like markings from her temples down to her shoulders, is the host body. As a symbiote, Dax resembles a large worm, and Jadzia is his seventh host, meaning he has lived seven lifetimes and is over 300 years old. Jadzia shares his many lives' memories once they are physically fused and become one being. Dax is a brilliant scientist. Jadzia is also brilliant, with several doctorates and degrees in exobiology, zoology, astrophysics, and exoarcheology, studying all her life in order to be chosen as a host, which is the greatest honor a Trill can give.

DAX

in this first season DS9 episode, written by D.C. Fontana and Peter Allen Fields, Dax is accused of a murder he allegedly committed while occupying his former host, Curzon. Should Jadzia stand trial for crimes committed when she was essentially another person? Guest stars: Gregory Itzin, Anne Haney, Richard Lineback, and Fionnula.

DAY OF THE DOVE, THE

written by Jerome Bixby and directed by Marvin Chomsky, this third season Classic Trek episode aired 11/1/68. An entity which feeds off violent thoughts and actions causes the *Enterprise* crew and a Klingon crew to misunderstand each other and fight.

No one, however, dies in these skirmishes. When deadly blows instantly heal, both crews realize an alien influence is at work. Guest stars: Michael Ansara, Susan Johnson, David L. Rose, and Mark Tobin.

DAYSTROM, DR. RICHARD

computer science genius, played by William Marshall, and winner of the Nobel Prize and the Z Magnees Prize, he creates the M 5 computer which takes over the *Enterprise* and kills the crew of the *Excalibur*. At the end of Classic episode "The Ultimate Computer," he suffers a mental breakdown.

Daystrom Annex

located on Galor IV, part of the Daystrom Institute (see entry.)

Daystrom Institute

major Federation/Starfleet research facility named after Dr. Daystrom from Classic episode "The Ultimate Computer."

Daystrom Institute Theoretical Propulsion Group

school from where Dr. Brahms graduated and mentioned in TNG episode "Booby Trap."

DAYTON, CHARLES

played a crewmember in TNG "Where No One Has Gone Before."

DE LA PENA, GEORGE

played Solis in TNG "The Arsenal of Freedom."

DE VRIES, JON

played Wilson Granger in TNG "Up The Long Ladder."

DEADLY YEARS, THE

written by David P. Harmon, directed by Joseph Pevney, this second season Classic Trek episode aired 12/8/67. *Enterprise* crewmembers visit Gamma Hydra IV and are infected by a disease which prematurely ages them. Kirk loses command when he begins to act senile. Guest stars: Charles Drake, Sarah Marshall, Beverly Washburn, Felix Locher, Laura Wood, and Carolyn Nelson. Of note: The Next Generation episode "Unnatural Selection" involves a similar plotline.

DEADRICK, VINCE

played Matthews in Classic "What Are Little Girls Made Of?" a Romulan crewman in "Balance of Terror," a native in "The Apple," as well as stunt work for McCoy in "Mirror, Mirror," and stunts in "Shore Leave," and "The Doomsday Machine." Film credits include "Romancing the Stone."

DEADWOOD, SOUTH DAKOTA

location of Alexander and Worf's holodeck simulation of the wild west in TNG episode "A Fistful of Datas."

DEALT, HESTER

Lieutenant Commander and medical trustee of the Federation Medical Collection Station, played

by Seymour Cassel, in TNG episode "The Child."

DEAN, LIEUTENANT

character, played by Dan Kern, in TNG episode "We'll Always Have Paris" with whom Picard fenced.

DEBIN

leader of the planet Atlek, played by Douglas Rowe, in TNG episode "The Outrageous Okona."

DECIUS

Romulan officer, played by Lawrence Montaigne, in Classic episode "Balance of Terror."

Decius

a Romulan warship which transports Ambassador Tomalak, Picard and Troi to the *Enterprise* in TNG episode "Future Imperfect."

DECKER, COMMODORE MATTHEW

captain of the *Constellation*, played by William Windom, and sole survivor of the destructive device in Classic episode "The Doomsday Machine" who later dies trying to destroy the device. He is the father of Will Decker who appears in "The Motion Picture."

DECKER, COMMANDER WILLARD

captain of the *Enterprise*, played by Stephen Collins, from whom Kirk takes control during an emergency in "The Motion Picture." The son of Commodore Matt Decker, Willard is in love with the Deltan navigator Ilia, and ends up dissipating into a higher being

at the end of the movie. Supposedly TNG character Riker is patterned after Willard, as TNG's Deanna is patterned after Ilia.

DEELA

queen of the Scalosians who falls in love with Kirk. Deela, played by Kathie Brown, and her people live in an accelerated time frame in Classic episode "Wink of an Eye."

Deep Space Four

space station mentioned in TNG episode "The Chase," where Professor Galen wanted to start his micropaleontology search.

Deep Space Nine

space station located in the Bajor sector which aided the Bajoran government in repairs after their system was pillaged by the Cardassians. Worf visits DS9 in TNG episode "Birthright." DS9, located near the only connecting wormhole through which travel to the distant, virtually unexplored Gamma Quadrant is possible, became the setting for the series of the same name and is commanded by Benjamin Sisko.

DEFECTOR, THE

third season TNG episode written by Ronald D. Moore, and directed by Robert Scheerer. A Romulan defector claims the Romulans are about to wage war, but Picard does not trust him. Guest stars: James Sloyan, Andreas Katsulas, John Hancock, and S.A. Templeman.

Defiant, U.S.S.

starship lost in interphase between universes in Classic episode "The Tholian Web." Kirk is a member of the landing party on the ship when he disappears and is presumed dead.

Deflectors

force shield which protects starships from attack.

DeHAAS, TIM

scriptwriter of TNG episode "Identity Crisis."

DEHNER, DR. ELIZABETH

ship's psychiatrist, who, along with Gary Mitchell, develops heightened telepathic powers when the *Enterprise* hits the barrier rim at the edge of the galaxy. Played by Sally Kellerman, she dies defending Kirk against Mitchell.

DEIGHAN, DREW

scriptwriter of TNG episodes "Sins of the Father" and "Reunion."

DEJA Q

third season TNG episode written by Richard Danus and directed by Les Landau. Q, deprived of his powers, visits a populated world threatened by an asteroid as punishment by his own people and learns what it's like to be human. Guest stars: John deLancie, Whoopi Goldberg, Richard Cansino, Betty Muramoto, and Corbin Bernsen.

Dekyon field

field used by Data to transmit a message to his alternate self in TNG episode "Cause and Effect."

DEL ARCO, JONATHAN

guest starred as Hugh in TNG "I, Borg."

DeLANCIE, JOHN

plays Q in TNG episodes"Encounter At Farpoint," "Hide and Q," "Q Who," "Deja Q," "QPid," "True Q," "Tapestry" and the DS9 episode "Q Less." He also appears in the Peter Weir movie "Fearless" with Jeff Bridges.

DELANO, LEE

played Kalo in Classic Trek "A Piece of the Action." Film credits include "Blood Sport," "In The Glitter Palace" and "Splash!"

DeLaure Belt

mentioned in TNG episode "The Ensigns of Command" as an area, located in the Tau Cygna V region, of hyperonic radiation.

Delos IV

location of Dr. Crusher's medical residency under Dr. Dalen Quince as mentioned in the TNG episode "Remember Me."

Delos System

location of the planets Brekka and Ornara as mentioned in the TNG episode "Symbiosis." Also the site of a sun which had an unstable magnetic field for a short period.

Delphi Ardu

outpost world of the Tkon Empire, which became extinct thousands of years before, in TNG episode "The Last Outpost."

Delta 05

science station, bordering the destroyed Neutral Zone, mentioned in the TNG episode "The Neutral Zone."

Delta Quadrant

part of the galaxy 200 lights years away from the Alpha Quadrant, where the shuttle and Ferengi craft come out on the other side of the wormhole in the TNG episode "The Price."

Delta Rana System

location of the planet Rana IV mentioned in the TNG episode "The Survivors."

Delta rays

injured Captain Pike while on a cadet training vessel, as mentioned in the Classic episode "The Menagerie."

Delta Theta

class M world visited in animated episode "Bem."

Delta Triangle Region

region of the galaxy where many starships have disappeared in the animated episode "Time Trap."

Delta Vega

desolate world and site of an automated lithium-cracking station in Classic episode "Where No Man Has Gone Before." Kirk hopes to strand Gary Mitchell on Vega, where the ore freighters call only once every twenty years. Instead both Mitchell and Elizabeth Dehner die there.

Deltans

a hairless race from Delta IV, of which Ilia is a member, which projects

pheromones, causing male sexual arousal. First introduced in "The Motion Picture," They are also empaths, and when mated, bond mentally as well as physically. A bonded Deltan pair working with Dr. Marcus on Regula are killed by Khan in "The Wrath of Khan."

Deltived Asteroid Belt
Q2 mentions he misplaced this galactic anomaly in the TNG episode "Deja Q."

DELUGO, WINSTON
played Timothy in Classic Trek "Court Martial."

DEMENT, CAROL DANIELS
played Zora in Classic Trek "The Savage Curtain."

DEMETRAL, CHRIS
actor in the TNG episode "Future Imperfect."

DEMOS
head of security police on planet Dramia in animated episode "Albatross."

DEMPSEY, MARK
played the Air Force captain in Classic Trek "Tomorrow Is Yesterday."

DEMYAN, LINCOLN
played St. Lipton in Classic Trek "Assignment: Earth."

Denasian
Iconian language of Deneus III mentioned in the TNG episode "Contagion."

DENBERG, SUSAN
played Maggie Kovas in Classic Trek "Mudd's Women." Film credits include "The Wackiest Ship In The Army."

Deneb II
a Jack The Ripper entity, named Kesla, struck this world in Classic episode "Wolf In The Fold."

Deneb IV
planet inhabited by the Bandi and site of the Farpoint Station from the TNG episode "Encounter at Farpoint." Deneb IV, also referred to as "Farpoint" after the space station, is mentioned in the Classic episode "Where No Man Has Gone Before" as the place where Kirk once shared a wild shore leave with Gary Mitchell.

Deneb V
planet where Harry Mudd sold the rights to a Vulcan fuel synthesizer he did not own; an act for which he was subsequently sentenced to death in the Classic episode "I, Mudd."

Denebian Alps
programmed into the holodeck by Wesley in TNG episode "Angel One" so he and a friend can go skiing.

Denebian slime devil
Korax's unflattering description of Kirk in the Classic episode "The Trouble With Tribbles."

Deneva
considered one of the most beautiful colony planets in the Federation and home to Kirk's brother Sam and his family before a parasitic invasion in the Classic episode "Operation: Annihilate!"

DENGEL, JAKE
played the Ferengi Mordoc in the TNG episode "The Last Outpost."

DENIS, WILLIAM
played Ki Mendrossen in the TNG episode "Sarek."

Denius III
world in the TNG episode "Contagion" where Captain Varley of the *Yamato* discovered evidence which led him to the ruined Iconian homeworld.

Denkiri Arm
located in the Gamma Quadrant, the final home of the Barzan probe featured in the TNG episode "The Price."

Denkirs
unit of measurement used by the Fajo in the TNG episode "The Most Toys."

DENNEHY, ELIZABETH
played Lt. Commander Shelby in the TNG episode "The Best of Both Worlds."

DENNIS, CHARLES
played Sunad in the TNG episode "Transfigurations."

Denorios Belt
area of heavy neutrino activity mentioned in DS9 episode "Emissary," where most of the Bajoran Orbs were found.

DENVER, MARYESTHER
played Third Witch in the Classic Trek "Catspaw."

Denver
ship which hits a mine in the TNG episode "Ethics." The *Enterprise* saves most of the people on board.

DePAUL, LIEUTENANT
an *Enterprise* navigator in Classic episodes "Arena" and "A Taste of Armageddon."

Deridium
valuable element necessary to the survival of a dying race in the DS9 episode "The Passenger."

DERR, RICHARD
played Commodore Barlow in Classic Trek episode "The Alternative Factor," and Admiral Fitzgerald in "The Mark of Gideon." Other TV credits include "Perry Mason," "Barnaby Jones" and "Cannon."

DeSALLE, LIEUTENANT VINCENT
a relief navigator, played by Michael Barrier, in Classic episodes "The Squire of Gothos" and "This Side of Paradise," and later promoted to assistant chief of engineering in "Catspaw."

DESCENT, PART I
sixth season TNG episode written by Ronald D. Moore and Jeri Taylor. A new breed of Borg, led by Data's twin Lore, ambush a Federation outpost on Ohniaka III. A stranded *Enterprise* landing party bands together with an underground Borg resistance group of which Hugh is a part and attempt to stop Lore. Guest stars: Jim Norton, Stephen Hawking.

DeSEVE, ENSIGN STEFAN

defected to the Romulan empire 20 years before working with Spock in the Romulan underground in the Classic episode "Face of the Enemy."

DeSOTO, CAPTAIN JEREMIAH

commander of the *U.S.S. Hood*, and Riker's former commanding officer, mentioned in the TNG episode "Encounter At Farpoint."

Detrian System

the *Enterprise* goes to this system to watch the birth of a new star in the TNG episode "Ship In A Bottle."

Deuterium Gas

element leaked from a reactor on the planet Battress in the TNG episode "Heart of Glory."

DEVENNY, SCOTT

played Klingon Chancellor Azetbur in "The Undiscovered Country."

DEVEREAUX, TERRY

scriptwriter of the TNG episode "Manhunt."

Devidia II

Data's head is found in a cave on this world, located in the Marrab sector, in the TNG episode "Time's Arrow." Also mentioned in "Timescape."

DEVIL IN THE DARK, THE

written by Gene L. Coon and directed by Joseph Pevney, this first season Classic Trek episode aired 3/9/67. Miners, working in a resource-rich planet, are being killed by a

mysterious beast. The *Enterprise* investigates and discovers the miners are inadvertently destroying the creature's eggs. The creature is later determined to be intelligent and refers to herself as a Horta. Guest stars: Ken Lynch, Barry Russo, Brad Weston, John Cavett, Janos Prohaska, Biff Elliot, and Dick Dial. Of note: While filming this episode, William Shatner learned of his father's death but insisted filming continue.

DEVIL'S DUE

fourth season TNG episode written by Philip Lazebnik and William Douglas Lansford and directed by Tom Benko. The Ventaxians made a deal with a type of metaphysical devil named Ardra for 1,000 years of peace and prosperity. Now the 1,000 years are up and the being is thought to have returned to collect. Picard, however, doesn't believe Ardra is what the Ventaxians think it is. Guest stars: Marta Dubois, Paul Lambert, Marcelo Tubert, William Glover, Thad Lamey, and Tom Magee.

Devisor

Klingon Battle cruiser featured in animated episode "More Trouble, More Tribbles."

Devna

an Orion woman marooned on the planet Elysia in animated episode "Time Trap."

Devo

Ferengi ship encountered in TNG episode "The Last Outpost."

DEVOR

member of a team trying to steal trilithium from the

Enterprise in TNG episode "Starship Mine."

DEVOS, ALEXANA

police director on the planet Rutia, played by Kerrie Keane, in TNG episode "The High Ground."

Dewan

Iconian language mentioned in TNG episode "Contagion."

DEWEESE, GENE

authored Classic Trek novels *Renegade*, *Chain of Attack*, *The Final Nexus*, and the TNG novel *The Peacekeepers*.

DeYOUNG, CLIFF

played Crodon in DS9 episode "Vortex."

Dikironium

elemental ingredient in planet Tycho IV's vampire cloud in Classic episode "Obsession."

Diagnostic Panel

panels located above sickbay beds.

Diagnostic Scanner

hand-held scanner used to diagnose a patient.

DIAL, DICK

stuntman who played Sam in Classic Trek "Devil In the Dark," Kaplan in "The Apple" and Kirk's double in "Arena." Also appears in "Friday's Child" and "The Immunity Syndrome." Other TV credits include several shows of the 1960's, including "The Man From U.N.C.L.E."

Diburnium Osmium Alloy

alloy used to build the Kalandan outpost in Classic episode "That Which Survives."

DICKERSON, LIEUTENANT

Enterprise security officer, played by Arell Blanton, in Classic episode "Savage Curtain."

DICKSON, LANCE

scriptwriter of TNG episode "The Outrageous Okona."

Dicosilium

element delivered to Dr. Apgar by the *Enterprise* in TNG episode "A Matter of Perspective."

DIEGHAN, LIAM

philosopher mentioned in TNG episode "Up The Long Ladder" who preached getting 'back to nature' and founded the 22nd century neo-transcendentalists.

Dierdre, S.S.

subject of a fake distress call made by the Klingons asking for emergency assistance in Classic episode "Friday's Child."

DIERKOP, CHARLES

played Morla in Classic Trek "Wolf In The Fold." Also appeared regularly on "Police Woman," and has numerous other TV credits.

DiFALCO, CHIEF

relief navigator of the *Enterprise*, played by Marcy Lafferty (William Shatner's wife) in "The Motion Picture."

Dilinea IV
planetary home to scientists who designed a transporter modification to eliminate transporter psychosis, mentioned in TNG episode "Realm of Fear."

Dilithium
rare crystal which powers Starfleet starships' warp drive.

DILLARD, J.M.
authored Classic Trek novels *Mindshadow, Bloodthirst, Demons, The Final Frontier, The Undiscovered Country, The Lost Years,* and the DS9 book *Emissary.*

DILLARD, VICTORIA
played ballerina in TNG episode "Where No One Has Gone Before."

Dimensional Shifter
device used by the Ansata to transport anywhere on the planet Rutia in TNG episode "The High Ground." The device's major side effects involve DNA breakdown and accelerated cellular aging.

Dimorus
mentioned in Classic episode "Where No Man Has Gone Before," as a world visited by Kirk and Gary Mitchell where the inhabitants attacked them and Mitchell shielded Kirk from a poison dart, saving his life.

Dinonicus VII
planet where the *Enterprise* schedules a rendezvous with the *Bilko* in TNG episode "A Fistful of Datas."

Diomidian scarlet moss
substance Dr. Crusher is growing in her lab when she notices a time difference in its growth patterns in TNG episode "Clues."

DION, SUSAN
actress in TNG "Silicon Avatar."

DIOYD
young-looking Platonian with black hair, played by Derek Patridge, in Classic episode "Plato's Stepchildren."

DIRGO, CAPTAIN
shuttle pilot, played by Nick Tate, who dies after his shuttle crashes on a nearby moon while taking Picard and Wesley to Pentarus V in TNG espisode "Final Mission."

DISASTER
fifth season TNG episode written by Ron Jarvis, Philip A. Scorza and Ronald D. Moore, directed by Gabrielle Beaumont. After the ship is nearly wrecked hitting a cosmic string fragment, Picard finds himself trapped in the turbolift with three panicking *Enterprise* school kids and Keiko goes into labor while trapped in Ten Forward. Guest stars: Rosalind Chao, Colm Meaney, Michelle Forbes, Erika Florews, John Christian Graas, Max Supera, Cameron Arnett, and Jana Marie Hupp.

Disruptor
weapon carried on Klingon ships. They also use hand-held versions. The Eminian weapons in Classic episode "A Taste of

Armageddon" are also referred to as disruptors.

Disruptors
name the Stratos dwellers use for terrorist Troglytes in Classic episode "The Cloud Minders."

DITMARS, IVAN
music composer in Classic Trek episode "Requiem For Methuselah."

DIVOK
young Klingon who has a vision of Kahless in TNG episode "Rightful Heir."

DOBKIN, LARRY
director of the Classic Trek episode "Charlie X." Also an actor and writer, he guest starred in TNG episode "The Mind's Eye." TV credits include "Streets of San Francisco" and "The Rifleman."

DOE, JOHN
transforming Zalkonian played by Mark LaMura in TNG episode "Transfigurations."

DOHLMAN
ruler and warlord of Elas. Elaan in Classic episode "Elaan of Troyius" is also a dohlman.

DOKACHIN, KLIN
a Zakdorn administrator, played by Graham Jarvis, of the Zed 15 surplus depot at Qualor II in TNG episode "Unification."

DOLAK, GUL
a Cardassian, played by Frank Collison, in on a conspiracy with Admiral Kennelly in TNG episode "Ensign Ro."

DOLINSKY, MEYER
scriptwriter of the Classic Trek "Plato's Stepchildren."

Domjot
a game like pool played by Academy cadets in TNG episode "Tapestry."

DOMINGUEZ, COMMANDER JOSE
a friend of Kirk's mentioned in Classic episode "The Man Trap" as the commander of a starbase on Corinth IV.

DON
one of the little boys in "And The Children Shall Lead." See entry for Linden, Don.

Don Juan
Yeoman Tonia Barrows runs into a version of the famous romancer, played by James Grusaf, on the recreational planet in Classic episode "Shore Leave."

DONAHUE, ELINOR
played Commissioner Nancy Hedford in Classic Trek "Metamorphosis." A regularly featured character on TV series "Father Knows Best," she also guest starred in many other series and TV movies.

DONALD, JULI
played Tayna in TNG "A Matter of Perspective."

Donatu V
disputed territory, mentioned in Classic episode "The Trouble With Tribbles," over which a battle was fought with the Klingons.

DONNER, JACK
played Subcommander Tal in Classic Trek "The Enterprise Incident."

DONNER, JILL SHERMAN
scriptwriter for DS9 episode "Captive Pursuit."

DOOHAN, JAMES
played Lt. Commander (later promoted to Commander and Captain) Montgomery Scott, the engineer of the Classic Trek *Enterprise*. Voice-over credits for aliens include father's voice in "The Squire of Gothos," Sargon, the Melkot buoy, M 5 in "The Ultimate Computer," and Lt. Arex in the animated series. Born in Vancouver, Canada, he started his career doing voices on the radio. His TV credits include "Bonanza," "Hazel," "The Virginian," "Blue Light," "Daniel Boone," "The FBI," "The Gallant Men," "Gunsmoke," "The Man From U.N.C.L.E.," "Outer Limits," "Peyton Place," "Shenandoah," "Then Came Bronson," "The Twilight Zone," "Voyage To The Bottom Of The Sea," "The Fugitive," "Iron Horse," "Ben Casey" and "Bewitched." He also appeared in the Saturday morning series "Space Academy" (with "And The Children Shall Lead" actors Brian Tochi and Pamelyn Ferdin,) and had a recurring role in "Jason of Star Command." Doohan appeared in the Roddenberry-produced movie "Pretty Maids All In A Row," and is an accomplished carpenter and wood carver. He has also appeared in all six Trek movies, as well as the TNG episode "Relics" reprising his role of Scotty. He has four children from his first marriage. His second wife, Anita Yagel, was a Paramount secretary he met on the lot. He recently wrote his memoirs, to be published by Pocket Books, which were untitled when this encyclopedia went to press. In the late 1980's, he suffered a heart attack but has completely recovered.

DOOMSDAY MACHINE, The
written by noted science fiction author and critic Norman Spinrad and directed by Marc Daniels, this second season Classic Trek episode aired 10/20/67. A device which devours planets for fuel is discovered after the *Enterprise* encounters the *U.S.S. Constellation* empty and adrift, with only the captain, Matthew Decker, left on board. Guest stars: William Windom, Elizabeth Rogers, John Copage and Richard Compton. Of note: Captain Decker, who dies in this episode, is the father of Will Decker who later shows up in "Star Trek: The Motion Picture" (and 'dies.') This episode was nominated for a Hugo Award for Best Dramatic Presentation of 1967.

Doomsday Machine
planet and starship killing device referred to as a doomsday machine by Spock in the Classic episode of the same name.

Doraf I
mentioned as a world scheduled for terraforming in TNG episode "Unification."

DORAN
character played by Lynnda Fergusson which appeared in DS9 episode "Emissary."

Dorian
ship Ambassador Olcar leaves to come aboard the *Enterprise* in TNG episode "Man of the People."

DORN, MICHAEL
an avid Star Trek fan, Dorn was very excited to land the role of the Klingon Worf on *The Next Generation* series. Prior to TNG, he was a regular on the series "Chips," a background extra (a writer in the newsroom) on the last two years of "The Mary Tyler Moore Show" and appeared in "Days of Our Lives" and "Capitol." His film credits include "Demon Seed," "Rocky" and "The Jagged Edge." Born in Liling, Texas, Dorn grew up in Pasadena, California and performed in a rock band during high school and college. He also played a Klingon public defender in the Classic episode "The Undiscovered Country" (he does his best to defend McCoy and Kirk who are being tried for murder,) and has done voice-overs for the TV series "Dinosaurs." Still interested in rock music, he does occasional studio work as a bass player and writes music in his spare time.

DORNISCH, WILLIAM P.
film editor on "The Wrath of Khan."

Doublejack
form of solitaire Eve is playing with round cards in Classic episode "Mudd's Women."

DOUGLAS, PAMELA
scriptwriter of TNG episode "Night Terrors."

DOUGLAS, PHYLLIS
played Yeoman Mears in Classic Trek "The Galileo Seven," and Girl in "The Way To Eden."

DOUGLASS, CHARLES
played Haskell in TNG "Where Silence Has Lease."

Douwd
immortal who can take on any form and is thousands of years old when the *Enterprise* encounters it in the form of Kevin Uxbridge in TNG episode "The Survivors."

DOWNEY, DEBORAH
played Girl in Classic Trek "The Way To Eden."

DOWNEY, GARY
played a Tellerite in Classic Trek "Whom Gods Destroy," and did stunt work as Kirk's double in "Catspaw."

Draconians
natives of Sigma Draconis who steal Spock's brain in the Classic episode of the same name. Women run the society and control the men, who are reduced to savages, with a pain-inducing device.

DRAKE, CHARLES

played Commodore George Stocker in Classic Trek "The Deadly Years."

DRAKE, LAURA

played the Klingon Vekma in TNG "A Matter of Honor."

Drake, U.S.S.

captained by Paul Rice, this ship was destroyed by a weapon called Echo Papa 607 in TNG episode "The Arsenal of Freedom."

Draken IV

home of a Starfleet base near the Kaleb sector in TNG episode "Face of the Enemy."

DREA

a Kelvin, played by Leslie Dalton, in Classic episode "By Any Other Name."

Dream of the Fire, The

title of a book, written by the Klingon Karatok, Worf gives Data in TNG episode "The Measure of a Man."

Drella

the Jack the Ripper entity, which feeds off fear, is compared to a Drella, an entity which lives off love, in the Classic episode "Wolf In The Fold."

DRESDEN, JOHN

played a security officer in "Star Trek: The Motion Picture." Other TV credits include "Barnaby Jones."

Drill Thralls

slaves on the planet Triskelion in Classic episode "The Gamesters of Triskelion."

DROMM, ANDREA

played Yeoman Smith in Classic Trek "Where No Man Has Gone Before."

DROXINE

Diana Ewing plays the spoiled aristocratic daughter of Plasus, high advisor to the city of Stratos, who becomes fascinated with Spock in Classic episode "The Cloud Minders."

Drubidium Calamus

a plant Keiko brings back with her from Marlonia in TNG episode "Rascals."

DRUMHEAD, The

fourth season TNG episode written by Jeri Taylor and directed by Jonathan Frakes. Admiral Satie comes aboard the *Enterprise* to investigate a Klingon exchange student charged with treason. Satie is so paranoid, however, that she sees conspiracy everywhere, to the point of putting Picard on trial as well as an innocent Vulcan ensign who hid the fact he is part Romulan to avoid prejudice. Guest stars: Jean Simmons, Bruce French, Spencer Garrett, Earl Billings, Henry Woronicz and Ann Shea.

DRUSILLA

slave, played by Lois Jewell, given to Kirk for the night in Classic episode "Bread and Circuses."

Dryworm

creature mentioned in Classic episode "Who Mourns For Adonais?" which, if it grows to its largest size, can control

energy outside its body like Apollo does.

DUANA

Wesley's adopted mother, played by Ivy Bethune, in TNG episode "When The Bough Breaks."

DUANE, DIANE

author of the Classic Trek novels *The Wounded Sky*, *The Romulan Way*, *My Enemy, My Ally*, *Doctor's Orders*, *Spock's World*, and the TNG novel *Dark Mirror*. Also wrote the script for TNG episode "Where No One Has Gone Before."

DUBOIS, MARTA

actress in TNG "Devil's Due."

DUFFY

an engineer, played by Charley Lang, in Geordi's crew in TNG episode "Hollow Pursuits."

DUKAT, GUL

a Cardassian leader who became the administrator of Bajor when the Cardassians conquered the planet.

DUMONT, ENSIGN SUZANNE

a girl with whom Wesley has a date in TNG episode "Sarek."

DUNCAN, LEE

played Evans in Classic Trek "Elaan of Troyius."

DUNCAN

played by Karl Bruck, character who plays King Duncan from *MacBeth* in Classic episode "The Conscience of the King."

DUNN, MICHAEL

played Alexander in Classic Trek "Plato's Stepchildren." He was most well known for his recurring role as Dr. Lovelace in the TV series "Wild, Wild West."

Dunsel, Captain

term used to refer to Kirk, meaning someone who is useless, in Classic episode "The Ultimate Computer."

Duotronics

computer technology, mentioned in Classic episode "The Ultimate Computer," Daystrom used to develop the M 5 computer and the Starfleet computer system.

DURAND, JUDI

plays the computer voice on DS9.

Duranium

element used in the bulkheads of the *Enterprise* as mentioned in TNG episode "A Matter of Perspective." Also used as an alloy in shuttlecrafts as mentioned in Classic episode "Metamorphosis."

DURAS

son of Worf's father's greatest enemy in TNG episode "Sins of the Father." Although he sits on the Klingon High Council, it is actually his father who was the traitor on Khitomer, not Worf's father.

DURBIN, JOHN

played Bada N'D'D' in TNG episode "Lonely Among Us."

Durenia IV
destination of the *Enterprise* when Dr. Crusher disappears into Wesley's warp field in TNG episode "Remember Me."

DURKIN, CHANCELLOR AVILL
leader of Malcoria III, played by George Coe, who thinks his world is not ready for Federation or outside contact in TNG episode "First Contact."

DURNHAM, BRETT
played the security chief in Classic Trek "The Menagerie."

DUROCK, DICK
played an Elasian guard in Classic Trek "Elaan of Troyius."

DURYEA, PETER
played Jose Tyler in Classic Trek "The Menagerie."

DUSAY, MARJ
played Kara in Classic Trek "Spock's Brain." Dusay has appeared in several TV shows, including "Facts of Life," and does stage work.

DUUR
Capellan warrior, played by Kirk Raymone, who is killed by Klingon Kras in Classic Trek episode "Friday's Child."

DVORKIN, DANIEL
authored the TNG novel *The Captain's Honor* (with David Dvorkin.)

DVORKIN, DAVID
wrote the Classic Trek novels *The Trellisane Confrontation, Timetrap,* and the TNG novel *The*

Captain's Honor (with Daniel Dvorkin.)

DYLAPLANE
governor of Pacifica, mentioned in TNG episode "Conspiracy."

Dylovene
drug McCoy uses on Sulu who was bitten by a poisonous retlaw in animated episode "The Infinite Vulcan."

DYNARSKI, GENE
played Ben Childress in Classic Trek "Mudd's Women," Krodak in "The Mark of Gideon," and base commander Orfil Quinteros in TNG episode "11001001." Other TV credits include "Voyage To The Bottom Of The Sea" and "Iron Horse." Film credits include Spielberg's "Duel," "The Sound of Anger," "Double Indemnity" and "Sins of the Past."

Dyson Sphere
structure built around a G type star named after the 20th century American engineer and theorist who first came up with the idea of building one in TNG episode "Relics."

Dytalix Mining Corporation
company which mines the world Dytalix B mentioned in TNG episode "Conspiracy."

Dytalix B
the fifth of six planets located in the Mira system, it is mined by the Dytalix Mining Corporation and the site of a Starfleet con-

spiracy in TNG episode "Conspiracy."

Earl Grey
Picard's favorite brand of tea.

EARP, MORGAN
character, played by Rex Holman, known historically as "the man who kills on sight" and who 'kills' Chekov in Classic episode "Spectre of the Gun."

EARP, VIRGIL
character in Classic episode "Spectre of the Gun" played by Charles Maxwell. Historically, he was the town marshall of Tombstone, but not in this episode.

EARP, WYATT
marshall of Tombstone, played by Ron Soble, who is knocked down by Kirk at the O.K. Corral in Classic episode "Spectre of the Gun."

Earth
a class M planet.

Earth Saturn Probe
a pivotal mission in space exploration to be manned by Captain John Christopher's son, Shaun Christopher, as mentioned in Classic episode "Tomorrow Is Yesterday."

Earther
Klingons use this term to refer to Terrans, also called Earthlings, in Classic episode "The Trouble With Tribbles."

EASTON, ROBERT
played the Klingon judge in "The Undiscovered Country."

ECHEVARRIA, RENE
scriptwriter of TNG episodes "The Offspring," "Transfigurations," "The Mind's Eye," "The Perfect Mate," "True Q," "I, Borg," "Face of the Enemy," "Ship In A Bottle," "Birthright Part II" and "Second Chances."

Echo Papa 607
weapon designed by the Minos which a salesman tries to sell to Picard in TNG episode "The Arsenal of Freedom."

ECKLAR, JULIA
science fiction writer nominated for several writing awards and author of Classic Trek novel *The Kobayashi Maru.*

ED
Tombstone barkeep, played by Charles Seel, in Classic episode "Spectre of the Gun."

EDE, GEORGE
appeared in TNG "Cost of Living."

Edelman Neurological Institute
school from which Dr. Toby Russel graduated in TNG episode "Ethics."

Eden
mythical planet sought by a gang from Classic episode "The Way To Eden." Spock thinks he finds its location in Romulan space, only to discover that the beautiful world's plant life is acid-

based and poisonous to nonindigenous life.

Edo
 inhabitants of the planet Rubicam III encountered by the *Enterprise* in TNG episode "Justice." The Edo are guided by a superior energy force.

Edoans
 species featured in the animated episodes with three arms and three legs, and orange skin. Lt. Arex, a navigator for the *Enterprise*, is an Edoan.

EDOURD
 the maitre'd, played by Jean Paul Vignon, of the Parisian cafe re-created with the holodeck in TNG episode "We'll Always Have Paris."

EDWARDS, PADDI
 played Anya in TNG "The Dauphin."

EDWARDS, TONY
 played the helicopter pilot in "The Voyage Home." His also appeared in "Starman."

EDWELL, CAPTAIN
 mentioned in TNG episode "Starship Mine" as an amazing officer, born on Gaspar VII, to whom Picard is compared by Hutchison.

Eel birds
 in Classic episode "Amok Time," Spock refers to the giant Eel birds of Regulus V when trying to explain to Kirk the nature of pon farr. The Eel birds must return every eleven years to mate in the caverns in which they were hatched, or die trying.

EFROS, MEL
 coproducer of "The Final Frontier."

Egg, The
 a probe invented by Dr. Paul Stubbs to examine the Kavis Alpha system in TNG episode "Evolution."

EHRLICH, MAX
 scriptwriter of Classic Trek "The Apple." His other writing credits include "Voyage To The Bottom Of The Sea."

Eichner Radiation
 radiation emitted by subspace phase inverters. The creature Ian in TNG episode "The Child" is a source of this kind of radiation.

Eight Eleven, East 68th Street, Apartment 12B
 Gary Seven's New York address in Classic episode "Assignment: Earth."

EISENERG, ARON
 plays the recurring character of the young Ferengi, Nog, in DS9. He appears in the pilot, "Emissary," as well as several other episodes.

EISENMANN, IKE
 played Peter Preston in "The Wrath of Khan." He also appeared in the Disney movies "Escape To Witch Mountain" and "Return To Witch Mountain," and in the science fiction TV series "Fantastic Journey."

EITNER, DON
 played the navigator in Classic Trek "Charlie X," and Kirk's double in "The

Enemy Within." Also appeared in "Lost In Space."

EKLUND, GORDON
 author of Classic Trek novels *The Starless World*, and *Devil World*.

EKOR
 a Scalosian, played by Eric Holland, in Classic episode "Wink of an Eye."

Ekos
 planet in the M43 Alpha sector at war with its peace-loving neighbor, Zeon, in Classic episode "Patterns of Force."

EL FADIL, SIDDIG
 stars as Dr. Julian Bashir in DS9. He also appeared in TNG episode "Birthright, Part I." El Fadil was born in the Sudan, but grew up in London, England. He began to study acting out of a desire to become a director and has acted in, and directed, several stage plays . His British television debut was as a Palestinian in the six-part miniseries "Big Battalions." He later landed the small role of King Faisel in the British production of "A Dangerous Man: Lawrence After Arabia." The role did not attract much attention, but by luck Rick Berman, co-executive producer of DS9 saw it and considered the then 24-year-old El Fadil for the role of Commander Sisko. Berman, however, thought El Fadil was older than he actually was because he was aged with make up for the King Faisel role. Although the producers wanted an older actor to play Commander

Sisko, they were impressed enough with the now 26-year-old El Fadil to give him the role of the 27-year-old doctor. He currently resides in West Hollywood.

EL RAZZAC, ABDUL SALAAM
 played the bass player in TNG "11001001."

El Adrel IV
 in TNG episode "Darmok," Picard and Dathon beam down to this world to try gain an understanding of their peoples.

El Baz
 Enterprise shuttle pod five, named after NASA geologist Farouk El Baz, in which Picard is found unconscious in TNG episode "Time Squared." The shuttle pod also appears in "Transfigurations."

ELAAN
 the name of the Dohlman of Elas, played by Fance Nuyen, sent to marry the ruler of Troyius so their worlds can at last have peace in Classic episode "Elaan of Troyius." She does not want to marry him, but must fulfill her duty. Elasian women's tears are supposed to have a biochemical affect on men. It is said that once a man touches an Elasian woman's tears, he falls in love with her and can refuse her nothing.

ELAAN OF TROYIUS
 written and directed by John Meredyth Lucas, this third season Classic Trek episode aired 12/20/68. The *Enterprise* must transport

the spoiled princess Elaan, the Dohlman of Elas, to Troyius for her marriage to the Troyian leader, insuring peace between the two historically hostile people. Elaan has a substance in her tears that can make a man fall in love with her, and uses her 'weapon' on Kirk when he becomes impatient with her while teaching her manners. A Klingon ship also gives the *Enterprise* trouble. Guest stars: France Nuyen, Jay Robinson, Tony Young, Victor Brandt, K.L. Smith and Lee Duncan.

Elas
world located in the Tellan system and ruled by the Dohlman Elaan and a Council of Nobles, who decide Elaan should marry the ruler of Troyius in the interests of peace, in Classic episode "Elaan of Troyius."

Elba II
planet with a poisonous atmosphere and site of an insane asylum which an inmate, Garth of Izar, takes over in Classic episode "Whom Gods Destroy." The asylum is contained within a large dome and covered by a force field to protect it from the planet's air.

ELBRUN, TAM
a Betazoid telepath, played by Harry Groener, who is a specialist in first contact. Born with telepathy (most Betazoids develop it in adolescence) he is highly sensitive and is hospitalized for stress related to his abilities in the TNG episode "Tin Man."

ELDER, JUDYANN
played Lt. Ballard in TNG "The Offspring."

Elected One
Beate is the Elected One, or the head of state of Angel One in the TNG episode of the same name.

Electromagnetic Synthomomometer
tool used by Soong to construct Data and Lore in TNG episode "Datalore."

ELEEN
pregnant Capellan wife, played by Julie Newmar, of the ruler the Teer Akaar in Classic episode "Friday's Child."

ELEMENTARY, DEAR DATA
second season TNG episode written by Brian Alan Lane and directed by Rob Bowman. When Data, Pulaski and Geordi reenact a Sherlock Holmes mystery in the holodeck, one of the characters, Moriarty, takes on a consciousness and will of his own and takes over the *Enterprise* using the holodeck computer. Guest stars: Daniel Davis, Alan Shearman, Biff Manard, Diz White, Anne Ramsay and Richard Merson.

ELIAS, LOUIS
played the first technician in Classic Trek "And The Children Shall Lead."

ELIG, DR. DEKON
thought to be the creator of a virus which causes a form of aphasia in DS9 episode "Babel." When he cannot be found, it is his assistant, Surmak Ren, who finds the cure for the virus and admits that Elig did create it.

ELINE
Kamin's wife, played by Margot Rose, in TNG episode "The Inner Light." Picard is Kamin in another reality and has two children with Eline, Meribor and Batai.

ELLENSTEIN, DAVID
played a doctor in "The Voyage Home."

ELLENSTEIN, ROBERT
played the Federation Council President in "The Voyage Home," and the character Stephen Miller in TNG "Haven." His other acting credits include "The Man From U.N.C.L.E.," "One Step Beyond" and "Bonanza."

ELLIOTT, BIFF
played Schmitter in Classic Trek "Devil In The Dark." His credits include "Voyage To The Bottom Of The Sea," "Planet of the Apes" and "Cannon."

ELLIOTT, KAY
played Stella Mudd in Classic Trek "I, Mudd." Other credits include "The Man From U.N.C.L.E."

ELLIS, MR.
mentioned but never seen as the first officer of the *Antares*, in Classic episode "Charlie X."

ELLISON, HARLAN
scriptwriter of Classic Trek "The City on the Edge of Forever." Famous in science fiction circles and winner of several Hugo and Nebula awards, Ellison also wrote under the pen name Cordwainer Bird. He has written many film scripts, including "A Boy and His Dog," TV teleplays, novels and short stories. TV script credits includes "The Voyage To The Bottom Of The Sea," "The Starlost," "The Man From U.N.C.L.E.," "The Outer Limits" and "Twilight Zone." Also a noted reviewer and critic, Ellison is a popular speaker at science fiction conventions and has done some quite elegant car commercials. His relationship with Hollywood has been rocky, however. Several of Ellison's story ideas have been stolen in the past but he has successfully sued for compensation. He is married to Susan Ellison and lives in the Los Angeles area.

Elway Theorem
theorem which helps the *Enterprise* crew understand how the Ansata rebels are transporting themselves from location to location in TNG episode "The High Ground."

Elysia
located in the Delta Triangle region where many ships are reported lost, the *Enterprise* visits this planet in the animated episode "Time Trap."

Em/3/Green
green skinned character in the animated episode "Jihad" whose voice was played by David Gerrold.

Emila II

destination of the *Enterprise* at the end of TNG episode "A Matter of Perspective."

Eminiar VII

planet ruled by Anan 7 and located in star cluster NGC 321 which has warred for 500 years with its neighbor, Vendikar. The struggle is carried on via computer when the *Enterprise* visits the two planets in Classic episode "A Taste of Armageddon."

EMISSARY, The

second season TNG episode written by Thomas H. Calder, Richard Manning, Hans Beimer and directed by Cliff Bole. K'Ehleyr, a half human, half Klingon emissary and Worf's past lover, comes aboard ship to meet with a group of Klingons stuck in suspended animation for 100 years who are still set on attacking and conquering the Federation. Guest stars: Suzie Plakson, Lance, Georgann Johnson, Colm Meaney, Anne Elizabeth Ramsay and Dietrich Bader.

EMISSARY

first season DS9 episode written by Michael Piller, Rick Berman, and directed by David Carson. Sisko comes aboard DS9 as its new commander and meets his crew for the first time. Additionally, he must deal with memories of losing his wife in the Borg attack at Wolf 359, and with the fact that he is the emissary for whom the Bajorans are waiting. The wormhole is also discov-

ered. Guest stars: Patrick Stewart, Camille Saviola, Felecia M. Bell, Marc Alaimo, Joel Swetow, Aron Eisenerg, Stephne Davies, Max Grodenchik, Steve Rankin, Lily Mariye, Cassandra Byram, John Noah Hertzler, April Grace, Kevin McDermott, Parker Whitman, William Powell Blair, Frank Owen Smith, Lynnda Fergusson, Megan Butler, Stephen Power, Thomas Hobson, Donald Hotton, Gene Armor and Diana Cignoni.

Emmis I

a Federation colony under Borg attack in TNG episode "Descent."

EMPATH, The

written by Joyce Muskat and directed by John Erman, this third season Classic Trek episode aired 12/6/68. When the *Enterprise* arrives to evacuate researchers from the planet Minara II, they are unable to find them. Landing party members then begin to vanish, one by one, reawakening in an underground chamber where creatures called Vians torture them, and they meet Gem, a mute empath. Guest stars: Kathryn Hays, Willard Sage, Alan Bergmann, David Roberts and Jason Wingreen.

Empathic Metamorph

Kamala is an empathic metamorph with the ability to bond with only one person and become their perfect mate in TNG episode "The Perfect Mate."

Empaths

being with a talent for reading or feeling another's emotions. Gem, from Classic episode "The Empath," is an example, but who additionally can heal physical wounds on another by touching them and taking the wound onto herself. Deanna Troi of TNG is an empath, who can sense feelings in others with the exception of Ferengis but who is a full telepath with her own species, Betazoid. (See entry on Betazoids.) Ilia, the Deltan, from "The Motion Picture" also has empathic powers to some extent. (See entry on Deltans.)

ENBERG, ALEXANDER

played a reporter in TNG "Time's Arrow Part II."

ENCOUNTER AT FARPOINT

first season TNG episode written by Dorothy Fontana and Gene Roddenberry. Directed by Corey Allen, it is shown in two parts and involves the *Enterprise's* maiden voyage to Deneb IV, or Farpoint. They encounter Q for the first time while trying to solve the mystery of the Bandi, builders of Farpoint. Guest stars include: John DeLancie, Michael Bell, DeForest Kelley, Colm Meaney, Cary Hiroyuki, Timothy Dang, David Erskine, Evelyn Guerrero, Chuck Hicks and Jimmy Ortega. Of note: McCoy from Classic Trek appears, though his name is never spoken. This show was made in both a two part TV and movie format

although the episodes made for TV are cut down and some scenes heavily edited. The unedited versions are available from Paramount on video or laser disc.

ENDAR, CAPTAIN

a Talarian, played by Sherman Howar, who adopts a human son in TNG episode "Suddenly Human."

Endeavor, U.S.S.

ship used as a blockade in the Klingon civil war mentioned in TNG episode "Reunion." In "The Game," the *Endeavor's* crew is one of the first to become addicted to the Ktaran game.

Endicor System

destination of the *Enterprise* before it is picked up by the time vortex and almost destroyed in TNG episode "Time Squared."

Endroki

another game mentioned in TNG episode "Tapestry" in reference to billiards.

ENEG

played by Robert Horgan, a member of the underground on Ekos on Classic episode "Patterns of Force."

ENEMY, The

third season TNG episode written by David Kemper and Michael Piller and directed by David Carson. Geordi is stranded on the Galorndan Core with a Romulan crash victim and the two must learn to trust each other in order to sur-

vive. Guest stars: John Snyder, Andreas Katsulas, STever Rankin and Colm Meaney.

ENEMY WITHIN, The

first season Classic Trek episode written by science fiction author Richard Matheson and directed by Leo Penn which aired 10/6/66. A transporter malfunction divides Kirk into twins, one evil, one good. Guest stars: Jim Goodwin (who also shows up as Farrell in "Mudd's Women," "Miri," and others,) Edward Madden and Garland Thompson. An alien unicorn dog, played by DeForest Kelley's dog, appears as well. Fans find the plot flawed because it never occurs to the characters to send a shuttle to the planet below to rescue the freezing men, but the shuttlecraft had not yet been conceived by Trek writers. Of note: This is the first time Spock uses his Vulcan neck pinch, invented by William Shatner and Leonard Nimoy in their spare time.

Energy Barrier

potent energy field which surrounds the entire galaxy at its rim and destroys most ships that attempt to cross it. It is first discovered in Classic episode (and second pilot) "Where No Man Has Gone Before," and again in "By Any Other Name" and "Is There In Truth No Beauty?"

ENGLELBERG, LESLIE
appeared in DS9 "Vortex."

Ennan VI

in TNG episode "Time Squared," Pulaski says the ale she brings to dinner comes from Ennan VI.

ENSIGN, MICHAEL

played Krola in TNG "First Contact."

ENSIGN RO

fifth season TNG episode written by Rick Berman and Michael Piller, and directed by Les Landau. Ro Laren, a Bajoran who was court martialed for disobeying her commanding officer's orders and causing deaths, has served her prison sentence and is assigned aboard the *Enterprise*. She must figure out the mysterious destruction of a colony near Cardassian territory. Guest stars: Michelle Forbes, Cliff Potts, Whoopi Goldberg, Ken Thorley, Jeffrey Hayenga, Frank Collison, Scott Marlowe and Harley Venton.

ENSIGNS OF COMMAND, The

third season TNG episode written by Melinda M. Snodgrass and directed by Cliff Bole. Human settlers on Tau Cygna V are in violation of a treaty with the Sheliak, and must be evacuated before the Sheliak come to destroy them. Guest stars: Eileen Seeley, Grainger Hines, Mark L. Taylor, Richard Allen, Mart McChesney and Colm Meaney.

Enterprise, U.S.S.

a Constitution Class starship first commanded by Robert April. Its various commanders include Christopher Pike, James Kirk, Will Decker, Spock and Jean Luc Picard (though Picard's ship is referred to in TNG as a Galaxy Class ship.) It was destroyed in "The Search For Spock" but rebuilt by the end of "The Voyage Home." It has gone through many stages of revision. The *Enterprise* of "The Next Generation" looks very different from the original version in "The Cage." In Classic Trek it housed 432 crewmembers. In TNG it holds over one thousand, many of them crewmembers' families. A legendary ship in Starfleet history, it is one of the only starships to come back from its first five year mission relatively intact. Her call numbers are NCC 1701. Other versions are identified with additional letters, such as NCC 1701C, an Ambassador class ship, captained by Rachel Garrett, from an alternate timeline that was supposedly destroyed in Picard's ship's timeline 22 years ago, in TNG's "Yesterday's Enterprise." NCC 1701D is the streamlined, modernized starship Picard commands in TNG. This fifth starship *Enterprise* is said to have been manufactured at the Utopia Planetia shipyards on Mars.

Enterprise, I.S.S.

pirate starship from a mirror universe captained by James Kirk and owned run by the Empire in Classic episode "Mirror, Mirror."

ENTERPRISE INCIDENT, The

written by D.C. Fontana and directed by John Meredyth Lucas, this third season Classic Trek episode aired 9/27/68. Kirk and Spock get secret orders to infiltrate the Romulan Neutral Zone, allow themselves to be captured, and sneak aboard the Romulan vessel to steal the infamous cloaking device. Guest stars: Joanne Linville, Jack Donner and Richard Compton. Of note: In this episode Spock's ability to lie is tested and he admits to having another, unpronounceable name.

ENWRIGHT, COMMODORE

unseen character who orders the *Enterprise* to test the M 5 computer in Classic episode "The Ultimate Computer."

Epidermal Mold

material Soong used to construct Data and Lore in TNG episode "Datalore."

Episilon Canaris III

planet on the verge of war and destination of peacekeeper Commissioner Nancy Hedford in Classic episode "Metamorphosis" before the shuttlecraft is diverted to an asteroid housing Zefrem Cochrane and the Companion.

EPPERSON, VAN

played Bajoran Clerk in DS9 "Q Less," and the morgue attendant in "Time's Arrow Part II."

Epsilon Indi

system in which the planet Triacus is located, home of the Gorgon which caused the scientific team to kill themselves in Classic episode "And The Children Shall Lead." The *Enterprise* rescues the children from Triacus, unaware they are bringing the Gorgon on board with them. The planet Andor is also located in the system as stated in TNG episode "The Child."

Epsilon IX Sector

the *Enterprise*'s destination in TNG episode "Samaritan Snare."

Epsilon Monitoring Station

station which monitored the progress of the ship *Vejur*'s attack on the Klingon ships and reported back to Starfleet in "The Motion Picture." It was eventually destroyed by the Vejur.

Epsilon Mynos System

planet where Aldea from TNG episode "When The Bough Breaks" is located.

EPSTEIN, PROFESSOR TERENCE

mentioned in TNG episode "11001001" as Dr. Crusher's favorite instructor who teaches at Starbase 74.

Eraclitus

character, played by Ted Scott, who played psychokinetic chess with Alexander from Classic episode "Plato's Stepchildren."

ERB, STEPHANIE

played Liva in TNG "Man Of The People."

ERKO

played by Patrick Cronin, aid and master of protocol to Campio in TNG episode "Cost of Living."

ERMAN, JOHN

director of Classic Trek "The Empath," and many other movies and TV series.

ERRAND OF MERCY

written by Gene L. Coon and directed by John Newland, this first season Classic Trek episode aired 3/23/67. Kirk and Spock beam down to Organia to get permission from the inhabitants to build a Federation base on the planet. Tensions erupt, however, when the Klingons decide they want to build there as well. Guest stars: David Hillary Hughes, Jon Abbott, John Colicos, Peter Brocco, Victor Lundin, George Sawaya and Walt Davis. Of note: This episode results in the famous Organian Peace Treaty and introduces the Klingon mind sifter. First appearance, as well, of Kirk and Spock in tights.

Ersalrope Wars

the planet Ersalrope was destroyed in these wars by weapons made by the Minos in TNG episode "The Arsenal of Freedom."

ERSKINE, DAVID

played a Bandi Shopkeeper in TNG "Encounter at Farpoint."

Erstwhile, S.S.

a class 9 cargo freighter captained by Thaddiun Okona in TNG episode "The Outrageous Okona."

ERWIN, BILL

played Dr. Dalen Quaice in TNG "Remember Me."

ERWIN, LEE

scriptwriter of Classic Trek "Whom Gods Destroy."

ERWIN, LIBBY

played a technician in Classic Trek "The Lights of Zetar."

ESOQQ

Chalnoth warrior, played by Reiner Schone, in TNG episode "Allegiance" who is kidnapped along with Picard, Tholl and Haro.

ESPINOZA, RICHARD

second assistant director on "The Wrath of Khan." His other film credits include "Vice Squad," and "Yellowbeard."

Essex, U.S.S.

ship lost 200 years ago in TNG episode "Power Play." The *Enterprise* finds it apparently haunted by its dead crew, but they are not ghosts, simply the Ux Mal prisoners trying to escape and take over the *Enterprise*.

ESTRAGON, PROFESSOR SAMUEL

legendary archeologist mentioned in TNG episode "Captain's Holiday," who searched for the Tox Uthat and tracked it to Risa, but died before he could find it. Vash was his assistant.

ETHAN

another name the boy Barash calls himself in TNG episode "Future Imperfect." (See entry for Barash.)

ETHICS

fifth season TNG episode written by Stuart and Sara Charno and Ronald D. Moore, and directed by Chip Chalmers. Worf has an accident that severs his spinal cord and could leave him permanently paralyzed. A new doctor, however, has been experimenting with a procedure that could help him. Meanwhile Worf considers a ritualistic suicide. Guest stars: Caroline Kava, Brian Bonsall and Patti Yasutake.

Eugenics Wars

occurred in Earth's late 20th century (the 1990's) and resulted in the last World War on Earth. The "supermen" who were genetically created and bred for the war took over Earth for awhile, until they were chased out of power. Khan, of Classic episode "Space Seed" and who reappears in "The Wrath of Khan," is a "superman" left over from the Eugenics Wars.

Evadne IV

destination of the *Enterprise* when they meet the "forgettable" Paxans in TNG episode "Clues."

EVANS, RICHARD

played Isak in Classic Trek "The Patterns of Force" and a regular of "Peyton Place."

EVANS, CHARLIE

orphan with undisciplined and deadly mind powers, marooned on Thasus after a colony ship crashed on the planet. He attempts to take over the *Enterprise* in Classic episode "Charlie X."

EVANS

crewman, played by Lee Duncan, in Classic episode "Elaan of Troyius."

EVERS, JASON

played Rael in Classic Trek "Wink of an Eye." Born in 1922, Evers numerous TV credits include guest spots on "Gunsmoke" and "Fantastic Journey."

EVOLUTION

third season TNG episode written by Michael Piller and Michael Wagner and directed by Winrich Kolbe. Wesley accidentally lets loose some nanites he has been experimenting with, which infest the ship and cause many malfunctions. Guest stars: Ken Jenkins, Whoopi Goldberg, Mary McCusker, Randall Patrick, Scott Grimes and Amy O'Neill.

EWING, DIANA

played Droxine in Classic Trek "The Cloud Minders."

Excalbia

world where the rock creature, Yarnek, of Classic episode "The Savage Curtain" brings Kirk and crew to fight with heroic and evil figures of the past. A patch of Earth-like territory is created to protect the humans from the planet's poisonous atmosphere.

Excalibur, U.S.S.

commanded by Captain Harris, this starship is attacked by the M 5 computer in Classic episode "The Ultimate Computer" and the entire crew is killed. Another version of this ship is commanded by Riker in TNG episode "Redemption."

Excelsior, U.S.S.

this is a fat bellied version of a starship seen in "The Search For Spock," and captained by Stiles. Later, in "The Undiscovered Country," Sulu is captain of the *Excelsior*. His yeoman is a young man who closely resembles Christian Slater (see entry for Slater.) Another officer aboard the ship is Commander Rand.

Exeter, U.S.S.

ship, commanded by Captain Ronald Tracey, the *Enterprise* finds adrift about the planet Omega IV in Classic episode "The Omega Glory."

Exo III

cold, frozen world where Dr. Korby and his androids are found living in underground caves in Classic episode "What Are Little Girls Made Of?"

EYE OF THE BEHOLDER, The

written by David P. Harmon, this animated Classic Trek episode aired 1/5/74. Giant intelligent slug beings of the planet Lactra put Kirk, Spock and McCoy into a zoo. The telepathic Lactrans don't understand that humans are intelligent because the

officers cannot communicate on their level. Spock finally communicates with them using his rudimentary Vulcan telepathy on a Lactran child. Guest voices: James Doohan (Lt. Arex, Lt. Commander Tom Markel,) and Majel Barrett (Randi Bryce.)

Eymorgs

name the mentally childlike females of Sigma Draconis call themselves. The men, called Morgs by the women, refer to the women as "the Givers of Pain and Delight" in Classic episode "Spock's Brain."

Fabrina

the sun of the Fabrini system which once had eight planets before it went nova. The people of Yonada are the survivers as mentioned in Classic episode "For The World Is Hollow And I Have Touched The Sky."

Fabrini

the people of Fabrina who now live on the spaceship world Yonada in Classic episode "For The World Is Hollow And I Have Touched The Sky." The Fabrini records contain a cure for xenopolycythemia, the disease from which McCoy is dying when he meets Natira.

FACE OF THE ENEMY

sixth season TNG episode written by Naren Shankar and Rene Echevarria, and directed by Gabrielle Beaumont. Troi awakens to find herself on board a Romulan vessel, disguised as a Romulan. She has been

kidnapped by N'Vek who wants her to impersonate Rakal of the Tal Shiar of Imperial Romulan Intelligence to help him get three members of the Romulan underground, held in stasis in the ship's cargo bay, to Federation space. Guest stars: Carolyn Seymour and Scott MacDonald.

FAGA, GARY

played the airlock technician who gets neck pinched by Spock in "Star Trek: The Motion Picture." He also played one of the prison guards watching McCoy in "The Search For Spock."

Fairmont Hotel

mentioned by Dixon Hill's secretary in TNG episode "The Big Goodbye."

FAISON, MATTHEW

guest starred in DS9 "Babel."

FAJO, FATHER

a wealthy thief and Kivas Fajo's father, mentioned in TNG episode "The Most Toys."

FAJO, KIVAS

Zibalian trader from TNG episode "The Most Toys." A collector of rare objects, played by Saul Rubinek, who steals Data for his collection.

FALLOW

leader of the Waddi who is in charge of the game Quark plays in which the pieces are really Sisko, Kira, Julian and Dax in DS9 episode "Move Along Home."

Famen
an *Enterprise* shuttlecraft in TNG episode "Chain of Command."

FAMILY
fourth season TNG episode written by Ronald D. Moore from a premise by Susanne Lambdin and Bryan Stewart, and directed by Les Landau. Still recovering from his experience as a Borg, Picard takes a leave on Earth and visits his family in Labarre, France. Worf also sees his parents, and Wesley sees a message from his long dead father. Guest stars: Jeremy Kemp, Samantha Eggar, Theodore Bikel, Georgia Brown, Whoopi Goldberg, Colm Meaney, Dennis Creaghan, David Tristan Birken and Doug Wert.

FANCY, RICHARD
appeared in TNG "The First Duty."

FAREK, DR.
a Ferengi doctor on the ship *Krayton* in TNG episode "Menage A Troi."

FARLEY, JAMES
played Lt. Lang in Classic Trek "Arena."

FARLEY, MORGAN
played Hacom in Classic Trek "Return of the Archons," and Marak Scholar in "The Omega Glory." Film credits include "A Killing Affair," "Orphan Train" and "Charlie and the Great Balloon Race."

Farpoint
complex built and inhabited by the Bandi, but discov-

ered to be a life form all its own in TNG episode "Encounter At Farpoint."

FARR, KIMBERLY
played Lango in TNG "Symbiosis."

Farragut, U.S.S.
commanded by Captain Garrovick, the ship Kirk first served on as a lieutenant during his first deep space assignment, when the ship ran into the vampire cloud that killed Garrovick. Kirk meets up with the cloud creature again, eleven years later in Classic episode "Obsession."

FARRALON, DR.
the director of the mining facility at Tyrus VIIA in TNG episode "The Quality of Life."

FARRELL, BRIONI
played Tula in Classic Trek "Return of the Archons." Her movie credits include "Keefer" and "My Tutor." She also guest starred on the TV shows "The Man From U.N.C.L.E." and "The Bionic Woman."

FARRELL, GERALDINE
guest starred in DS9 "Babel."

FARRELL, TERRY
stars as Jadzia Dax on DS9. Born in Cedar Rapids, Iowa, Farrell signed on with the Elite modeling agency at 16 and has appeared on the covers of *Mademoiselle* and *Vogue*. Her first TV role was the short lived series "Paper Dolls" (with Jonathan Frakes.) She also appeared in an episode of the reincarnated "The Twilight Zone,"

and guest starred on "The Cosby Show," "Family Ties" and "Quantum Leap." Films include "Back To School" (with Rodney Dangerfield,) "Beverly Hills Madam," (with Faye Dunaway,) "The Deliberate Stranger" (as a victim of Ted Bundy played by Mark Harmon,) and "Hellraiser III: Hell On Earth" (in which she was spotted by TNG producers Rick Berman and Michael Piller.) She was a Star Trek fan when she was a little girl, and even owned a tribble. Other coincidences: She knew Michael Dorn prior to getting the role, and she and Marina Sirtis have a mutual friend. She lives in Los Angeles with her dog, Freckles.

FARRELL, LIEUTENANT JOHN
ship's navigator, played by Jim Goodwin, in Classic episodes "The Enemy Within," "Miri" and "Mudd's Women." as the ship's navigator.

FARRELL
Kirk's personal guard, played by Pete Kellert, in mirror universe in Classic episode "Mirror, Mirror."

Farspace Starbase Earhart
location of the Bonestell Recreation Facility and mentioned in TNG episode "Samaritan Snare" as the only frontier outpost before the Klingons joined the Federation.

FARWELL, JONATHAN
played Captain Walker Keel in TNG "Conspiracy."

Fearless, U.S.S.
Excelsior Class starship seen in TNG episode "Where No One Has Gone Before."

FEDER, TODD
played Federation Man in DS9 "Babel."

Federation
the United Federation of Planets, founded in 2161 as mentioned in TNG episode "The Outcast."

Federation Undersecretary for Agricultural Affairs
Nilz Baris' title in Classic episode "The Trouble With Tribbles."

Feinburger
medical scanner used by McCoy and named after Irving Feinburg, a famous 20th century technician.

Fek'lhr
Klingon demon in TNG episode "Devil's Due."

Felicium
narcotic, mentioned in TNG episode "Symbiosis," which cured the Breckans and the Ornarans of a deadly plague 200 years before.

Feline Supplement 127
food Data gives his cat which shows up in the replicators on several decks in TNG episode "A Fistful of Datas."

FELLINI, COLONEL
man, played by Ed Peck, who captures Kirk at the Omaha Air Force Base on 1960s Earth in Classic episode "Tomorrow Is Yesterday."

Felodesine chip
orange wafer that contains poison in TNG episode "The Defector."

FELTON, ENSIGN
Enterprise con officer, played by Sheila Franklin, who appears in several TNG episodes.

FENTO
Mintakan wise man, played by John McLiam, in TNG episode "Who Watches The Watchers."

FERDIN, PAMELYN
played Mary Janowski in Classic Trek "And The Children Shall Lead." As a child, she was a familiar face in television shows of the 1960's and 70's. Her credits include Disney movies as well as a regular character on the Saturday morning TV series "Space Academy."

Ferengi
small, bald and large-eared species, driven by greed and immature relative to their technology, which was stolen. The women are considered inferior, are not educated and never wear clothing. Ferengi are hostile to the Federation, though more like irritating, dangerous children than threatening enemies. Quark of DS9 is a Ferengi, and though motivated by greed, he seems to show some integrity in certain situations as the series progresses, giving his character more depth. Their ears are their most sensitive spot. They refer to their "lobes" as one of their most errogenous zones when sexually aroused. They also rate another Ferengi's courage or masculinity by the size of their "lobes." Betazoids can read most alien beings' emotions, but cannot read Ferengis'.

FERGUSON, BRAD
wrote Classic Trek novels *Crisis on Centaurus, A Flag Full of Stars.*

FERGUSON, JESSIE LAWRENCE
played Lutan in TNG "Code of Honor.'

FERGUSSON, LYNNDA
played Doran in DS9 "Emissary."

Fermi
an *Enterprise* shuttle seen in TNG episode "True Q" and later destroyed in "Rascals."

FERRER, MIGUEL
played first officer of the *Excelsior* in "The Search For Spock." He has guest starred on "Miami Vice," "Magnum P.I.," and many other TV series. His film credits include "Deep Star Six" and "Robocop." He was a regular in the acclaimed TV series "Twin Peaks" and returned to play the same role in the Twin Peaks movie "Fire Walk With Me." He is the son of Jose Ferrer. He is also the drummer in a rock band whose lead singer is Bill Mumy (from "Lost In Space.")

FERRIS, HIGH COMMISSIONER
Federation official on his way to Makus III, played by John Crawford, who wants Kirk to abandon his search for the *Galileo* in Classic episode "The Galileo Seven."

Fesarius
name of Balok's First Federation flagship in Classic episode "The Corbomite Maneuver."

Festival
celebrated by the people of Beta III, also called Zero Hour, during which they go wild for twelve hours and riot in the streets as seen in Classic episode "Return of the Archons."

Feynman
shuttlepod seen in TNG episode "The Nth Degree."

FGC 13
cluster scanned by the *Enterprise* in TNG episode "Schisms."

FGC 47
nebula studied by the *Enterprise* in TNG episode "The Icarus Factor."

Ficus Sector
mentioned in TNG epiode "Up The Long Ladder" as as system with severe sunflares and the location of two Earth colonies, although there is no record of them. The inhabitants of Planet Five, a class M world in the system, have no modern technology.

FIEDLER, JOHN
played Hengist in Classic Trek "Wolf In The Fold." His numerous film credits include "True Grit," "Double Indemnity," "Woman of the Year" and "The Cannonball Run." He was a regular on "The Bob Newhart Show," and has appeared in "Kolchak, The Night Stalker" and "Buffalo Bill." He continues to guest star in various TV series.

FIEDLING, JERRY
music composer of Classic Trek episodes "The Trouble With Tribbles" and "Spectre of the Gun." His other scores include "The Bionic Woman," and "Hogans's Heroes," as well as the movies "The Wild Bunch," "The Enforcer" and "The Gauntlet."

FIELDS, JIMMY
played a guard in Classic Trek "The Cloud Minders."

FIELDS, PETER ALLEN
scriptwriter and story editor of TNG "Half A Life," "Silicon Avatar," "The Inner Light" and "Cost of Living." He also wrote DS9 episode "Dax" with D.C. Fontana. He is now coproducer of DS9, which he enjoys more than writing for TNG. He likes the fact that the characters don't all get along and believes Gene Roddenberry made TNG too perfect. He was quoted in *Starlog* as saying, "For me as a writer, as someone who likes character conflict, this show is very exciting."

Finagle's Folly
a green drink McCoy tells Kirk he makes well in Classic episode "The Ultimate Computer."

Finagle's Law
"Any port chosen for leave or liberty should not be one's own home port," Kirk

quotes in Classic episode "Amok Time."

FINAL MISSION
fourth season TNG episode written by Kacey Arnold Ince and Jeri Taylor, and directed by Corey Allen. Wesley is leaving the ship to enter Starfleet Academy, but before he leaves he accompanies Picard in a shuttle to Pentarus V. The shuttle crashes, however, and Wesley must use all his knowledge to save Picard from death. Guest stars: Nick Tate, Kim Hamilton and Mary Kohnert.

FINELLI, DARIO
scriptwriter of the animated episode "Albatross."

FINN, KYRIL
an artist and leader of the Ansata terrorists, using dimensional shift devices to attack their enemy, the Rutians, he kidnaps Dr. Crusher in TNG episode "The High Ground." Played by Richard Cox, he dies in the episode.

FINNEGAN
practical joker, played by Bruce Mars, who plagued Kirk at the Academy and with whom Kirk meets again on a recreational planet in Classic episode "Shore Leave."

FINNERMAN, GERALD PERRY (JERRY)
director of Classic Trek photography, he also worked on "Planet of the Apes," "Moonlighting" and others.

FINNEY, JAMIE
daughter of Kirk's good friend Ben Finney and Kirk's namesake, played by Alice Rawlings. She thinks Kirk killed her father in Classic episode "Court Martial."

FINNEY, LIEUTENANT COMMANDER BENJAMIN
Enterprise records officer who frames Kirk for his own murder as revenge for Kirk's reporting him for negligence on duty. Finney, played by Richard Webb, turns out to be alive and later suffers a nervous breakdown in Classic episode "Court Martial."

Finoplak
a salve that dissolves Data's uniform in TNG episode "The Most Toys."

FIONNULA
appears in DS9 as "Dax."

First Citizen
title of Merik (or Mericus), Lord of the Games and Chief Magistrate of the Condemned on Planet 892 IV in Classic episode "Bread And Circuses."

FIRST CONTACT
fourth season TNG episode written by Marc Scott Zicree, Dennis Russell Bailey, David Bischoff, Joe Menosky, Michael Piller and Ronald D. Moore and directed by Cliff Bole. Riker is injured while on a first contact mission on Malkor and taken to a local hospital where the inhabitants discover he is an alien. Meanwhile, Picard and Troi reveal themselves to top officials, who aren't sure

their world is ready for outside contact, with the exception of one scientist who has dreamed for years of making first contact. Guest stars: Georte Coe, Carolyn Seymour, Michael Ensign, George Hearn, Steven Anderson, Sachi Parker and Bebe Neuwirth.

FIRST DUTY, The
fifth season TNG episode written by Ronald D. Moore and Naren Shankar, and directed by Paul Lynch. Wesley's nova squadron is responsible for the death of one of their own when they participate in a forbidden flying formation. Fearing punishment or possible expulsion from Starfleet Academy, they attempt to cover their tracks but their lies get more exaggerated. Guest stars: Wil Wheaton, Ray Walston, Jacqueline Brookes, Robert Duncan McNeill, Ed Lauter, Richard Fancy, Walker Brandt, Shannon Fill and Richard Rothenberg.

First Electorine
title of the administrator on the planet Haven in the TNG episode of the same name.

First Federation
Balok in Classic episode "Court Martial" is from the First Federation.

First Security Guard
played by Colm Meaney in TNG episode "Lonely Among Us."

FISHER, TECHNICIAN
geologist, played by Edward Madden, and a member of the landing party on Alfa 177 who falls and hurts himself in Classic episode "The Enemy Within." He is beamed up before Kirk, but the ore on his uniform causes the transporter to malfunction.

FISTFUL OF DATAS, A
sixth season TNG episode written by Robert Hewitt Wolfe and Brannon Braga and directed by Patrick Stewart. During a lay over at a starbase, Worf goes to the holodeck with Alexander to play out a western with his son but things go wrong when the computer locks the program and pits Data against them in a deadly game of kidnapping and murder. Guest star: Brian Bonsall.

FITTS, RICK
guest starred in TNG "Violations."

FITZGERALD, ADMIRAL
admiral, played by Richard Derr, Spock calls for help when he runs into trouble searching for the missing Kirk in Classic episode "Mark of Gideon."

FITZPATRICK, ADMIRAL
admiral, played by Ed Reimer, who orders Kirk to protect the quadro triticale on Space Station K 7 in Classic episode "The Trouble With Tribbles."

FIX, PAUL
played Dr. Mark Piper in Classic Trek "Where No Man Has Gone Before."

Born in 1901, his many credits include the movie "Night of the Lepus" with DeForest Kelley. A regular character in the TV series "The Rifleman," Fix died in 1983.

Fizzbin

a game Kirk creates to distract the guards in Classic episode "A Piece of the Action." It has very odd rules such as: Each player gets six cards except the player on the dealer's right who gets seven. The second card is turned up except on Tuesdays (though Kirk turns all the cards up as he deals.) Two Jacks is a half fizzbin and three is a sralk and disqualifies the player. The player then needs a King of duece, except at night when he needs a Queen or four. It is excellent if another Jack is dealt, unless the next card is a six, in which case the player must forfeit a card to the dealer unless it's a black six in which case the player gets another card. The object of the game is to get a royal fizzbin, but the odds are astronomical of that happening. The last card dealt is called a kronk. Kirk doesn't get to finish explaining the rest.

FLAHERTY, COMMANDER

the *Ares* first officer who speaks 40 languages as mentioned in TNG episode "The Icarus Factor."

FLANAGAN, KELLIE

played the little blond girl in Classic Trek "Miri."

FLAVIUS, MAXIMUS

worshipper of the "Son," played by Rhodes Reason, who is killed defending Kirk in the arena in Classic episode "Bread and Circuses."

FLECK, JOHN

played Commander Taibak in TNG "The Mind's Eye."

FLEETWOOD, MICK

lead singer of the famous musical group "Fleetwood Mac" who played the Andedian Delegate in TNG "Manhunt."

FLETCHER, ROBERT

costume designer for "Star Trek: The Motion Picture," "The Wrath of Khan," "The Search For Spock" and "The Voyage Home." His other costume credits include "Caveman" and "The Last Starfighter."

Flex Coordinating Sensor

device Wesley studies in preparation for his Academy exams in TNG episode "Coming of Age."

FLIEGEL, RICHARD

scriptwriter of TNG "Imaginary Friend."

FLINT

immortal human who is six thousand years old when found by the crew in Classic episode "Requiem For Methuselah." Born Akharin, he realized he was immortal when he was struck through the heart in battle and didn't die. He claims to have actually been Leonardo da Vinci and Johannes Brahms and

to have known Alexander the Great and Galileo. He created Reena as his perfect wife. He also uses the name Mr. Brack. (See entry for Brack, Mr.)

FLOOD, ELOISE

author of TNG novel *Chains of Command.*

FLORES, MARISSA

played by Erika Flores, the child winner of the primary school science fair aboard the *Enterprise* who is given the temporary title of Ensign by Picard because of her proven leadership skills in TNG episode "Disaster."

Flux Capacitor

term borrowed as a joke from "Buckeroo Banzai" and mentioned as a system on the *Enterprise* in TNG episode "Hollow Pursuits."

FLYNN, MICHAEL J.

played Zayner in TNG "The Hunted."

FOLEY, LIEUTENANT

found evidence that the three people the *Enterprise* is looking for were kidnapped in TNG episode "Menage A Troi."

Folsom Point

Spock thinks the weapons used by the creatures in Classic episode "The Galileo Seven" are Folsum points, reminiscent of the old Folsum culture found on Earth in New Mexico.

FONTANA, D.C. (DOROTHY)

scriptwriter of Classic Trek episodes, "Charlie X," "Tomorrow Is Yesterday,"

"This Side of Paradise," "Journey To Babel," "Friday's Child," "By Any Other Name," "The Ultimate Computer," "The Enterprise Incident" and the animated episode "Yesteryear." Her other writing credits include the TV series "Logan's Run," "Fantastic Journey," "Buck Rogers" and "Dallas." She has written the novelization of the movie "The Questor Tapes" (scripted by Gene Roddenberry and Gene L. Coon,) and the Classic Trek novel *Vulcan's Glory.* She also co-wrote the TNG pilot "Encounter At Farpoint," and episodes "Heart of Glory" and "Too Short A Season." Her most recent addition to the Trek trilogy is the script for DS9 episode "Dax" (with TNG writer Peter Allen Fields.)

Food Synthesizers

the machines, later called replicators in TNG and DS9, that make and deliver food in Classic Trek.

Foolie

in Miri's world, a game or trick played on someone in Classic episode "Miri."

FOR THE WORLD IS HOLLOW AND I HAVE TOUCHED THE SKY

written by Rick Vollaerts and directed by Tony Leader, this third season Classic Trek episode aired 11/8/68. Yonada, a completely enclosed spaceship world, is on a collision course which must be corrected without violating the Prime Directive. McCoy, suffering from a rare, incurable disease, decides he wants to stay on the world and marry its leader, Natira. A cure for his disease is found in the vast Fabrini library on this spaceship world and its course is corrected. Guest stars: Kate Woodville, Byron Morrow and Jon Lormer.

FORBES, MICHELLE
played Dara in TNG "Half a Life." She also played Ensign Ro in "Ensign Ro," "Disaster," "Power Play," "Cause and Effect" and "The Next Phase." The role of Kira Nerys in DS9 was originally created for her, but was altered when she announced she could not be in the series.

Force Field
an invisible barrier used in the brig and in certain spots on DS9 for sealing off an area.

FORCHION, RAYMOND
played Ben Prieto in TNG "Skin of Evil."

FORD, JOHN M.
author of Classic Trek novels *The Final Reflection* and *How Much For Just The Planet?*

FOREST, MICHAEL
played Apollo in Classic Trek "Who Mourns For Adonais?" His TV credits include "Gunsmoke," "Branded" and "The Rifleman."

FORESTER, LARRY
scriptwriter of TNG "The Battle."

Formazine
McCoy, who says it is a vitamin supplement, gives

Hanar this drug which makes him edgy, in Classic episode "By Any Other Name."

FORREST, BRAD
played an ensign in Classic Trek "That Which Survives."

FORTIER, ROBERT
played Tomar in Classic Trek "By Any Other Name."

FOSTER, ALAN DEAN
scriptwriter on "Star Trek: The Motion Picture." He is also the author of numerous science fiction books, as well as novelizations of movies such as "Aliens," "The Last Starfighter" and "Clash of the Titans." He also wrote all the Log Books, which novelize the animated Trek series' scripts.

FOSTER, STACIE
played Bartel in TNG "Relics."

FOSTER
a trainee on board the *Enterprise*, played by Phil Morris (son of Greg Morris) in "The Search For Spock." Both father and son starred in "Mission: Impossible" and the new "Mission: Impossible" respectively.

FOX, AMBASSADOR ROBERT
ambassador to Eminiar VII, played by Gene Lyons, who wants to help the planet make peace with Vendikar in Classic episode "A Taste Of Armageddon."

FRAKES, JONATHAN
stars as William Riker, also called Number One, on The Next Generation. His other acting credits include "Falcon Crest," "Paper Dolls," "Bare Essence," and a regular appearance on the soap opera "The Doctors." A stage actor both on and off Broadway, he also appeared in the TV movie "The Nutcracker," and in the miniseries "Dream West" and "North and South." Born in Pennsylvania, he attended Penn State and Harvard to study psychology. He currently lives in Los Angeles and is married to actress Genie Francis (Laura of Luke and Laura fame on "General Hospital," and a regular on "Days of Our Lives.") He has also directed the TNG episodes "The Offspring," "The Drumhead," "Reunion," "Cause and Effect," "The Quality of Life" and "The Chase."

FRAME OF MIND
sixth season TNG episode written by Brannon Braga and directed by Jim Conway. Riker keeps phasing out from reality and finding himself in a mental institution where he is told his entire life is a mental hallucination and he is very ill. Guest stars: Andrew Prine, Gary Werntz, David Selburg and Susanna Thompson.

FRANCINE
Gabrielle's friend, played by Kelly Ashmore, in TNG episode "We'll Always Have Paris."

FRANCIS, AL
director of photography for many third season Classic Trek episodes.

FRANCIS, JOHN H.
played science crewman in TNG "Sarek."

FRANKENSTEIN
a doctor Guinan once knew and with whom she compares Wesley in TNG episode "Evolution."

FRANKHAM, DAVID
played Lawrence Marvick in Classic Trek "Is There In Truth No Beauty?" He has also appeared in the films "The Return of the Fly," "Winter Kill," "Eleanor, First Lady Of The World" and "Wrong Is Right."

FRANKLIN, SHEILA
guest starred in TNG "A Matter of Time," "The Masterpiece Society" and "Imaginary Friend."

FRANKLIN, MATT
unseen officer, who dies from a pattern degradation when teleported with Scotty to the transport ship *Jenolan*, in TNG episode "Relics."

FRANKLIN
an *Enterprise* security guard killed when Borg beam aboard the bridge in TNG episode "Descent"

FREDERICKS
officer on *Enterprise* C in TNG episode "Yesterday's Enterprise."

FREEMAN, ENSIGN
Enterprise officer, played by Paul Bradley, given a Tribble by Uhura in Classic

episode "The Trouble With Tribbles."

FRENCH, BRUCE
played Sabin in TNG "The Drumhead."

FREWER, MATT
guest starred as Professor Berlinghoff Rasmussen in TNG "A Matter of Time." A well known comedian and actor, he starred in the series "Max Headroom" and other TV shows and has also made many film appearances.

FRIDAY'S CHILD
written by D.C. Fontana and directed by Joseph Pevney, this second season Classic Trek episode aired 12/1/67. The Federation and the Klingons are vying for control of Capella IV. The Enterprise crew is forced to retreat to the hills when their ship doesn't answer and fight for their lives. Guest stars: Julie Newmar, Tige Andrews, Michael Dante, Cal Bolder and Ben Gage. Of note: In an unusual move, this episode was obviously shot in real, California country (probably the back lot), not on a sound stage using fake plants and painted skies.

FRIED, GERALD
music composer for the Classic Trek episodes "Shore Leave," "Amok Time," "The Apple," "Catspaw," "Journey To Babel," "Friday's Child," "Wolf In The Fold" and "The Paradise Syndrome." He also worked on "The Man From U.N.C.L.E.," "The Cabinet of Dr. Caligari,"

"Soylent Green" and "Roots."

FRIEDMAN, MAL
played Hendorff in Classic Trek "The Apple."

FRIEDMAN, MICHAEL JAN
wrote TNG novels *A Call To Darkness*, *Doomsday World*, *Fortune's Light*, *Reunion*, *Relics*, and the Classic novel *Faces of Fire*.

FRIES, SANDY
scriptwriter of TNG "Coming of Age."

FROMAN, DAVID
played Captain K'Nera on TNG "Heart Of Glory."

Fusing Pitons
used by Worf, Crusher and Picard in TNG episode "Chain of Command" to climb to the secret Cardassian base on Seltris III.

Fusion Bombs
kind of bomb supposedly used in the war between Eminiar VII and Vendikar, but are really imaginary bombs in a war being fought by a computer in Classic episode "A Taste of Armageddon."

FUTURE IMPERFECT
fourth season TNG episode written by J. Larry Carroll and David Bennett Carren, and directed by Les Landau. Riker wakes up to find himself captain of the Enterprise sixteen years in the future and is told he had a virus which wiped out all his memories for the last sixteen years. Guest stars: Andreas Katsulas,

Chris Demetral, Carolyn McCormick, April Grace, Patti Yasutake, Todd Merrill and George O. Hanlon, Jr.

GABRIELLE
played by Isabel Lorca, reminds Picard of Jenice Manheim in the Paris holoimage in TNG episode "We'll Always Have Paris."

GAETANO
an *Enterprise* radiation technician, played by Peter Marko, who is the second member of the shuttlecraft to be killed on Taurus II in Classic episode "The Galileo Seven."

Gagarin IV
location of the Darwin Genetic Research Station mentioned in TNG episode "Unnatural Selection."

GAGE, BEN
played Akaar in Classic Trek "Friday's Child." He was a guest star in many TV shows of the 1960's, including "Iron Horse."

Gakh
"serpent worms," a Klingon delicacy, served up in TNG episode "A Matter of Honor."

Gal Ga'thong
area on Romulus where firefalls occur, mentioned in TNG episode "The Defector."

Galactic Cultural Exchange Project
organization mentioned as sponsoring the Karidian players in Classic episode "The Conscience of the King."

Galaxy Class
the Federation's most powerful class of ship. The *Enterprise* is of this class.

GALAXY'S CHILD
fourth season TNG episode written by Maurice Hurley and Thomas Kartozian, and directed by Winrich Kolbe. Dr. Leah Brahms comes aboard the ship but is not what Geordi expected. Meanwhile an alien lifeform, believing the *Enterprise* to be its mother, attaches itself to the ship and drains its power. Guest stars: Susan Gibney, Whoopi Goldberg, Jana Marie Hupp, April Grace and Lanei Chapman.

GALEN, PROFESSOR RICHARD
a famed archeologist and one of Picard's past teachers who tries to get the captain to accompany him on a micropaleontology quest. He is later killed in TNG episode "The Chase."

Galen IV
the Talarians attacked this Federation colony ten years before, where Jeremiah Rossa, whose Talarian father is Endar, was raised by Talarians. Galan IV is mentioned in TNG episode "Suddenly Human."

Galileo, NCC 1701/7
an *Enterprise* shuttlecraft which breaks up in orbit over Taurus II in Classic episode "The Galileo Seven." It is later replaced and seen again in "Metamorphosis." Supposedly the real life sized model of the shuttle

sits in a fan's garage in Los Angeles.

GALILEO SEVEN, The
written by Oliver Crawford and S. Bar David and directed by Robert Gist, this first season Classic Trek episode aired 1/5/67. Spock's first command mission, of a shuttle called Galileo, crash lands on Taurus II where large creatures threaten the crew and kill two members. Guest stars: Don Marchall, Peter Marko, Reese Vaughn, Grant Woods, Phyllis Douglas and John Crawford. Of note: The shuttlecraft is destroyed in this episode, but is later replaced and used in "Metamorphosis."

GALLEGOS, JOSHUA
played a security officer in "Star Trek: The Motion Picture." Other film credits include "Survival of Diana" and "The Mystic Warrior."

Gallian, The
title of a magazine seen on Planet 892 IV in Classic episode "Bread and Circuses."

GALLIULIN, IRINI
played by Mary Linda Rapelye, member of a gang of "space hippies" from Classic episode "The Way To Eden." She and Chekov met previously at the Academy and appear to share a strong attraction for each other.

GALLOWAY, LIEUTENANT
Enterprise security officer, played by David L. Ross, in Classic episodes "Miri," "A Taste Of Armageddon" and

"The Omega Glory" in which he is killed by Captain Tracey.

Galor IV
location of an annex of the Daystrom institute and a Starfleet research center. Also the birthplace of Haftel from TNG episode "The Offspring."

Galorndon Core
referred to in "The Defector," and the site of a Romulan scout vessel crash landing in TNG episode "The Enemy."

GALT
master thrall, played by Joseph Ruskin, in Classic episode "The Gamesters of Triskelion."

Galvan V
world where, according to Data in TNG episode "Data's Day," a marriage is successful only if children are produced within one year.

GALWAY, LIEUTENANT ARLENE
member of the landing party and chief biologist on the *Enterprise, played by Beverly Washburn*, in Classic episode "The Deadly Years" who contracts the deadly Gamma Hydra IV radiation which ages her prematurely and kills her of old age before a cure is found in Classic episode "The Deadly Years."

GAME, The
fifth season TNG episode written by Susan Sackett, Fred Bronson and Brannon Braga, and directed by Corey Allen. Riker brings a

game from Risa aboard the *Enterprise* and soon everyone is addicted to it and neglecting their duties. Guest stars: Wil Wheaton, Ashley Judd, Colm Meaney, Katherine Moffat and Diane M. Hurley.

Gamelan V
in TNG episode "Final Mission," is subjected to deadly radiation from an abandoned garbage scow. Gamelan's leader is Songi.

GAMESTERS OF TRISKELION, The
written by Margaret Armen and directed by Gene Nelson, this second season Classic Trek episode aired 1/5/68. Kirk, Uhura and Chekov are kidnapped and transported to Triskelion as slaves to entertain three powerful mind beings called "The Providers." Guest stars: Joseph Ruskin, Angelique Pettyjohn, Steve Sandor, Mickey Morton, Victoria George, Jane Ross and Dick Crockett.

Gamma 400 System
mentioned as the location of Starbase 12 in Classic episode "Space Seed."

Gamma 7A Solar System
system wiped out by the giant space amoeba in Classic episode "The Immunity Syndrome."

Gamma Arigulon
site of radiation anomalies the Enterprise is studying in TNG episode "Reunion."

Gamma Canaris N
small planetoid much like Earth, inhabited by Zefrem Cochrane, to which the shuttle is steered by the Companion in Classic episode "Metamorphosis."

Gamma Erandi Nebula
area where the *Enterprise* is incommunicado when Riker, Deanna and Lwaxana are kidnapped in TNG episode "Menage A Troi."

Gamma Field
force which kills the nanites in TNG episode "Evolution."

Gamma Hromi II
location of the Gatherer encampment in TNG episode "The Vengeance Factor."

Gamma Hydra IV
a class M world, close to the neutral zone and within the jurisdiction of Starbase 10, where a deadly radiation from a comet's tail killed the colonists by causing them to age rapidly in Classic episode "The Deadly Years."

Gamma II
world to which Kirk, Uhura and Chekov are beaming when they are snatched by the Providers' long-range transport beam and brought to Triskelion to become thralls in Classic episode "The Gamesters of Triskelion."

Gamma Quadrant
a virtually unexplored section of the galaxy only accessible since the discovery of the wormhole near

Bajor and Deep Space 9, located in the Alpha Quadrant. The Barzan wormhole leads there, as well, but is an unstable wormhole.

Gamma Sequence
evasive maneuver used by the *Enterprise* in TNG episode "Yesterday's Enterprise."

Gamma Tauri IV
planet from which the Ferengi stole a K 9 converter, mentioned in TNG episode "The Last Outpost."

Gamma Trianguli VI
visited by the Enterprise crew in Classic episode "The Apple," a very warm, jungle-like planet where the inhabitants are ruled by a machine called Vaal.

Gamma Vertis IV
Gem's planet in Classic episode "The Empath" where the inhabitants are mutes with the empathic healing powers to survive great catastrophes.

Gamma VII Sector
where the *U.S.S. Lantree* was patrolling in TNG episode "Unnatural Selection."

Gandhi, U.S.S.
ship on which the second Riker, created by a transporter field distortion and still a lieutenant, accepts a position in TNG episode "Second Chances."

Ganges
runabout used on Deep Space 9.

GANINO, TRENT CHRISTOPHER
scriptwriter who penned TNG "Yesterday's Enterprise."

GANS, RON
the voice of Armus in TNG "Skin of Evil."

Ganymede
Jupiter moon where Scotty claims he got his "green" drink in Classic episode "By Any Other Name."

Garadius IV
destination of the *Enterprise* after it answers a Romulan ships' distress call in TNG episode "The Next Phase."

Garaman Sector
destination of the *Enterprise* in TNG episode "Rightful Heir" when Worf tries to have a vision of the Klingon "god" Kahless.

GARCIE, LEO
played the bellboy in TNG "The Royale."

Gardeners of Eden
a terraforming project on Velara mentioned in TNG episode "Home Soil."

GARIN, DR.
leader, played by Richard Cansino, of Bre'el's research team in TNG episode "Deja Q."

GARION, BUDDY
played Krako's gangster in Classic Trek "A Piece of the Action." His other credits include "The Death Squad" ('74).

GARISON, C.P.O.
Enterprise officer, played by Adam Roarke, under the command of Captain Pike in Classic episode "The Menagerie."

GARNER, SHAY
played a scientist in TNG "A Matter of Time."

Garo VII System
location of Pandro, Commander Ari Bem's home world from animated episode "Bem."

Garon II
planet mentioned in TNG episode "Ensign Ro" where, as a member of an away team, Ensign Ro disobeyed orders causing eight people to die; an act for which she went to prison.

GARR, TERRI
played Roberta Lincoln in Classic Trek "Assignment: Earth." Garr has guest starred on many TV series including "The Ken Berry Wow Show," "The Burns and Schrieber Comedy Hour," "The Girl With Something Extra" and "The Sonny and Cher Comedy Hour." Her most famous film credits are "Young Frankenstein," "The Black Stallion," "Tootsie" and "Mr. Mom." She is a favorite guest of David Letterman, appearing regularly on his talk show, and recently appeared on "Murphy Brown."

GARRETSON, KATY E.
second assistant director on "The Undiscovered Country."

GARRETT, JOHN
played a lieutenant in TNG "Loud As A Whisper."

GARRETT, SPENCER
played Simon Tarses in TNG "The Drumhead."

GARRETT, CAPTAIN RACHEL
captain, played by Tricia O'Neil, of the *Enterprise* C who was killed in a Klingon attack in TNG episode "Yesterday's Enterprise."

GARROVICK, CAPTAIN
captain of the *Farragut*, and the commander during Kirk's first deep space assignment who died when the vampire cloud creature attacked his ship.

GARROVICK, ENSIGN
an *Enterprise* security officer, played by Stephen Brooks, and the son of Captain Garrovick (Kirk's first deep space commander) who blames himself for the deaths of the men killed by the vampire cloud creature when it attacks the *Enterprise*.

GARTH OF IZAR
a brilliant starship commander and tactician, played by Steve Inhat, who is an Academy hero. He suffers from a mental breakdown and is sent to the asylum on Elba II which he takes over and where he tortures Kirk and Spock and the aslyum's governor, Cory in Classic episode "Whom Gods Destroy." He has learned cellular metamorphosis from an alien race, which further complicates matters. When finally

cured, he has no memory of his aberrant behavior.

Garum
a Romulan condiment served with roasted sparrows on Planet 892 IV in Classic episode "Bread and Circuses."

GATES, BARBARA
played the astrochemist in Classic Trek "The Changeling." Her other credits include "The Young Country" ('70.)

Gatherers
nomadic raiders, led by Chorgon, who left Acamar III because of blood feuds in TNG episode "The Vengeance Factor."

GATTI, JENNIFER
guest starred in TNG episode "Birthright."

Gault
farm world where Worf was raised by human parents along with a human step brother after he was found at the Khitomar Outpost as mentioned in TNG episode "Heart of Glory."

GAUTREAUX, DAVID
played Commander Branch in "Star Trek: The Motion Picture." He was originally hired to play Xon in the new Star Trek TV series before Nimoy agreed to return as Spock and the first movie was made.

GAV
a Tellerite, played by John Wheeler, who opposes Coridan's entry to the Federation in Classic

episode "Journey To Babel" and is later murdered by an Orion.

GEARY, RICHARD
played an andorian in Classic Trek "Whom Gods Destroy." His other credits include "The Man From U.N.C.L.E.," and "Perry Mason."

GEDEON, CONROY
played the agent at the bar in "The Search For Spock."

GEER, ELLEN
played Dr. Kila Marr in TNG "Silicon Avatar."

GEHRING, TED
played a police officer in Classic Trek "Assignment: Earth." His credits include "The Intruders," "The Rockford Files," "Captains and the Kings," "The Legend of the Lone Ranger," "The Night The Bridge Fell Down," "Little House On The Prairie," "Alice" and "Dallas." He was a regular on the TV series "The Family Holvak."

GEM
an empath named by Dr. McCoy, played by Kathryn Hays, who has a special ability by which she can heal severe wounds in another with a touch of her hand. The Minarans, who can save only one planet as their sun goes nova, choose to save Gem's world, Gamma Vertis IV in the Minara system, in the Classic episode "The Empath."

Gemarians
people for whom Picard mediated a dispute, men-

tioned in TNG episode "Captain's Holiday." Their neighbors are the Dachlyds.

Gemaris V
mentioned in TNG episode "Captain's Holiday" as a world where Picard mediated a dispute.

GENDEL, MORGAN
scriptwriter of TNG "The Inner Light," "Starship Mine" and of DS9 "The Passenger."

General Order Number One
another term for the Prime Directive. (See entry for Prime Directive.)

General Order Number Seven
order, quoted in Classic episode "The Menagerie," which allows no vessel under any circumstances to approach Talos IV.

General Order Number Six
supposedly a ship's self-destruct sequence automatically activated 24 hours after the entire crew has died as mentioned in animated episode "The Albatross."

General Order Number Twenty Four
directs an entire world to be destroyed if the galaxy is threatened. Kirk gives this order to Scotty in Classic episode "A Taste Of Armageddon."

Genesis
a device, developed by the science team headed by Dr. Carol Marcus on Regula I in "The Wrath of Khan,"

which creates a living world from a lifeless planet.

Genesis Planet
an unstable world created when Khan activated the Genesis wave in an attempt to destroy the *Enterprise*. Because David Marcus had put proto-matter into the device, against Dr. Carol Marcus' wishes, the world aged too quickly and was breaking up even as the *Enterprise* and the *Grissom* arrived on it in "The Search For Spock."

Genetronic Replicator
an experimental device that creates a new spinal column for Worf in TNG episode "Ethics."

GENGHIS KHAN
considered the most ruthless of military geniuses, played by Nathan Jung, he is encountered in Classic episode "The Savage Curtain," but is really an image taken from Kirk's mind.

GENOVESE, MIKE
played the desk sergeant in TNG "The Big Goodbye."

GENTILE, ROBERT
played the Romulan technician in Classic Trek "The Enterprise Incident."

GEORGE, VICTORIA
played Ensign Jana Haines in Classic Trek "The Gamesters of Triskelion."

GEORGE
name of the male humpback whale the *Enterprise* transports to the 23rd century in "The Voyage Home."

GERBER, STEVE
scriptwriter of TNG "Contagion."

GERROLD, DAVID
scriptwriter for Classic Trek "I, Mudd," "The Trouble With Tribbles," "The Cloud Minders," and the animated "More Tribbles, More Troubles" and "BEM." He also scripted the TNG episode "Encounter At Farpoint" and helped create the show and its characters. He provided the voice of two characters in the animated series Korax in "More Tribbles, More Troubles," and M 3 Green in "Jihad" and has written scripts for other TV series including "Logan's Run" and the new "The Twilight Zone." He is the author of the books *The Trouble With Tribbles*, *The World of Star Trek*, the Classic Trek novel *The Galactic Whirlpool* and the TNG novel *Encounter At Farpoint*. A noted science fiction writer outside the Trek genre as well, he has many short stories and novels to his credit, including his most recent, War Against the Chtorr series. He lives with his son in the Los Angeles area.

Gettysburg, U.S.S.
ship once commanded by Admiral Mark Jameson mentioned in TNG episode "Too Short A Season."

Ghaimon
exotic language Flaherty speaks in TNG episode "The Icarus Factor."

Ghorusda
Tam Elbrun's destination in TNG episode "Tin Man" where an apparently very alien, very complex culture lives.

Ghorusda Disaster
a first contact situation in which 47 people were killed, including the captain of the *Adelphi* and two friends of Riker's, as mentioned in TNG episode "Tin Man."

GI'RAL
a Klingon female, captured at Khitomer, whose daughter, Ba'el, is half Klingon, half Romulan. Her husband is the Romulan commander of the Carraya System colony in TNG episode "Birthright Part I and II."

GIBNEY, SUSAN
played Dr. Leah Brahms in TNG "Booby Trap" and "Galaxy's Child."

GIBSON, ENSIGN
Enterprise officer, played by Jennifer Dauphin, in TNG episode "The Dauphin."

Gideon
a world where over population, due to a lack of disease and the long life span of the people, has become such a problem that the government is willing to infect their own biosphere with a deadly disease to control it. Kirk is kidnapped and held on the planet in Classic episode "Mark of Gideon."

GIERASCH, STEFAN
played Dr. Hal Moseley in TNG "A Matter of Time."

GILDEN, MEL
author of TNG novel *Boogeymen*, and Classic Trek novel *The Starship Trap*.

Giles Belt
mentioned in TNG episode "The Most Toys."

GILL, JOHN
a historian and Kirk's former teacher, played by David Brian, who went to Ekos as a cultural observer but ended up violating the Prime Directive when he tried to help bring the people together. His attempts resulted in the creation of a Nazi-type regime he could not control in Classic episode "Patterns of Force."

GILLESPIE, ANN
played Hildebrandt in TNG "Pen Pals" and also appeared in DS9 "Babel."

GILLESPIE, ENSIGN
an *Enterprise* officer, played by Duke Moosekian, in TNG episode "Night Terrors."

GILMAN, SAM
played Doc Holliday in Classic Trek "Spectre of the Gun." He was a regular in the TV series "Shane," and also guest starred on many shows of the 1960's including "The Rifleman."

GILNOR
a dead terrorist mentioned in TNG episode "Too Short A Season."

GIMPEL, SHARON
played the creature, a the salt vampire, in Classic Trek "The Man Trap."

Gin'tak
a Klingon warrior spear seen in TNG episode "Birthright Part I and II."

GIOTTO, LT. COMMANDER
head of the Janus VI security in Classic episode "The Devil In The Dark," played by Barry Russo.

Gisborne, Sir Guy of
adversary Picard is forced to duel in the Robin Hood scenario Q creates in TNG episode "Q Pid."

GIST, ROBERT
director of Classic Trek episode "The Galileo Seven."

Givers of Pain and Delight
name the Morgs give the Eymorgs in Classic episode "Spock's Brain." (See entry for Eymorgs.)

GLADSTONE, MISS
nursery attendant, played by Dawn Armenian, on board the *Enterprise* in TNG episode "The Child."

GLASS, SEAMON
played Benton in Classic Trek "Mudd's Women." TV credits include "Buck Rogers in the 25th Century," and the films "The Other Side of Hell," "She's Dressed To Kill," "Gideon's Trumpet" and "Partners."

Glavyn
a Ligonian weapon which looks like a bird worn over the hand, in TNG episode "Code of Honor."

GLEASON, CAPTAIN
captain of the *U.S.S. Zhukov*, Barclay's old ship, who gives Barclay a very high performance rating as mentioned in TNG episode "Hollow Pursuits."

GLEE, MONA
scriptwriter of the original story TNG story "The Neutral Zone."

Glob fly
a Klingon fly with an unpleasant buzzing sound mentioned in TNG episode "The Outrageous Okona."

Globe Illustrated Shakespeare, The
title of book shown to Q by Picard who keeps it in his ready room in TNG episode "Hide and Q."

Glommer
the tribbles only natural enemy, seen in animated episode "More Tribbles, More Troubles."

GLOVER, EDNA
played one of the Vulcan masters in "Star Trek: The Motion Picture."

GLOVER, KIRSTIN
camera operator for "The Undiscovered Country."

GLOVER, WILLIAM
played Marley in TNG "Devil's Due."

Goddard, U.S.S.
ship with which the *Enterprise* is to rendezvous in TNG episode "The Vengeance Factor."

Gol
area on Vulcan, seen in "The Motion Picture,"

where a temple exists for the acolytes of Kolinahr. The students learn to purge all emotion from their minds and live like monks or hermits.

GOLAS, THADDEUS
played Controller in "The Voyage Home."

Gold-pressed latnum
currency used on DS9 by gamblers. Quark deals in gold-pressed latnum which is made in the form of heavy bars.

GOLDBERG, WHOOPI
stars semi-regularly as Guinan on TNG. She started her career as a highly successful comedienne, then went on to win an Oscar nomination for her role in "The Color Purple." She also starred in the movies "Jumpin' Jack Flash," "Burglar," "Fatal Beauty," "Clara's Heart," "Ghost," (for which she won an Oscar for best supporting actress,) "The Long Walk Home," "Soapdish," "Sister Act" and "Saraphina." She starred in the TV series "Bagdad Cafe" with Jean Stapleton, and won an Emmy for her guest role on "Moonlighting." A former talk show host as well, she is one of the stars of Comic Relief (along with Billy Crystal and Robin Williams,) an annual telethon which raises money for the homeless. A Star Trek fan as a child, (her hero was Nichelle Nichols,) the role of Guinan was created specifically for her after producers found out

she really wanted to be a part of the series.

GOLDEN, MURRAY
director of Classic Trek "Requiem For Methuselah." He also directed an episode of "The Rifleman" and "The Wackiest Ship In The Army."

GOLDIN, STEPHEN
author of Classic Trek novel *Trek To Madworld*.

GOLDSMITH, JERRY
composer who wrote the theme and score for "Star Trek: The Motion Picture." The same theme is now used in "The Next Generation." Born in Los Angeles in 1930, he composed scores for such TV series as "Climax!," "Playhouse 90" and "Gunsmoke." He also wrote the famous theme from "The Man From U.N.C.L.E.," as well as the movies "Planet of the Apes," "Papillon," "The Omen," (for which he won an Oscar,) and "The Secret of NIMH."

GOLDSTONE, JAMES
director of Classic Trek episodes "Where No Man Has Gone Before," and "What Are Little Girls Made Of?" Born in 1931, his directing credits include "Iron Horse" (which he created with Stephen Kandel,) "They Only Kill Their Masters," "The Day The World Ended," "Earth Star Voyager" "Voyage to the Bottom of the Sea" and "Kent State" for which he won an Emmy.

GOMEZ, MIKE
played DaiMon Taar in TNG "The Last Outpost."

GOMEZ, ENSIGN SONYA
recent Academy graduate, played by Lycia Naff, who was handpicked by Geordi from Rayna VI. She appears in TNG episodes "Q Who" and "Samaritan Snare."

GOODHARTZ, SHARI
scriptwriter of TNG episodes "The Most Toys," "Night Terrors" and "Violations."

GOODWIN, JIM
played Lt. John Farrell in Classic Trek episodes "The Enemy Within," "Mudd's Women" and "Miri." His character was played by a different actor during the show's second season. His TV and film credits include "Perry Mason" and "Ten Seconds To Hell" ('59).

GOODWIN, LAUREL
played Yeoman Colt in Classic Trek pilot "The Cage" and appears in "The Menagerie."

GORDON, BARRY
appeared in DS9 "The Nagus."

GORDON, JAY
boy, played by John Christian Graas, who wins the primary school science fair on the *Enterprise* in TNG episode "Disaster."

GORGON
an alien entity, played by the famous attorney Melvin Belli, which thrives on negative energy. It attempts to take control of the *Enterprise*, and ulti-

mately the galaxy, using five children whose parents it killed. The last inhabitant of an ancient race from the planet Triacus, he ends up being destroyed by the childrens' positive thoughts of love, happiness and grief over the memories of their parents.

Gorkon, U.S.S.
ship commanded by Vice Admiral Alina Nechayev during an attack on the Borg in TNG episode "Descent Part I."

GORKON
the Klingon chancellor, played by John Warner, who wants peace in "The Undiscovered Country." He is assassinated by his own general, Chang, and Kirk is framed for the murder.

Gorla
a colony that exists in the mirror universe in Classic episode "Mirror, Mirror."

Gorn
an alien species resembling a gigantic lizard, which appears in Classic episode "Arena," played by both Garry Coombs and Bobby Clark. It has green skin, speaks with a hissing sound and is bred for fighting. Gorns are also encountered in the animated episode "Time Trap."

GORO
father, played by Richard Hale, of Miramanee in Classic episode "The Paradise Syndrome."

GORSHEVEN
leader of Tau Cygna V, played by Grainger Hines (whose name does not appear in the credits) in TNG episode "The Ensigns of Command."

GORSHIN, FRANK
played Bele in Classic Trek "Let That Be Your Last Battlefield." Gorshin guest starred in many TV series, including "Batman."

GOSS, DaiMON
Ferengi leader, played by Scott Thomson, in TNG episode "The Price."

Gossamer Mice
transparent mice McCoy keeps in his lab in animated episode "The Terratin Incident."

GOSSETT, HERB
miner, played by Jon Kowal, on Rigel XII in Classic episode "Mudd's Women" who ends up marrying one of them.

GOTELL, WALTER
played Kurt Mandl in TNG "Homesoil."

Gothos
Trelane's moveable planet, located in space where no sun or stars exist, which follows the Enterprise and where he keeps Kirk and crew after kidnapping them in Classic episode "The Squire of Gothos."

GOUW, CYNTHIA
played Caitlin Dar in "The Final Frontier."

GOWANS, JOHN D.
played transporter assistant in "Star Trek: The Motion Picture."

GOWRON
Klingon warrior, played by Robert o'Reilly, who sits on the Klingon High Council. The character is regularly featured in "The Next Generation."

GRAAS, JOHN CHRISTIAN
played Jay Gordon in TNG "Disaster."

GRACE, APRIL
a Hubbell in "Future Imperfect," and a transporter technician in TNG "Reunion," "Data's Day," "Galaxy's Child" and "The Perfect Mate." She also played the transporter chief in DS9 "Emissary."

GRACIE
the pregnant, female whale the Enterprise transports to the 23rd century in "The Voyage Home."

GRAF, L.A.
author of Classic Trek novels Ice Trap and Death Count.

GRAF, KATHRYN
played Bajoran woman in DS9 "A Man Alone."

GRAFFEO, CHARLES M.
set decorator for "The Wrath of Khan."

GRAHAM, GERRIT
appeared in DS9 "Captive Pursuit."

GRAK TAY
composer Data reprogrammed himself to sound

like in TNG episode "Sarek."

GRAMMER, KELSEY
played Captain Bateson in TNG "Cause and Effect." Most famous for his portrayal of Frasier Crane in the sitcom "Cheers" and its spin-off show "Frasier."

GRANGER
Granger clones made from a combined archetype of Wilson Granger, Prime Minister of Maripose, and Victor Granger, Minister of Health, played by Jon de Vries, in TNG episode "Up The Long Ladder."

GRANT
security guard, played by Robert Bralver, and member of the landing party to Capella IV who is killed when he sees the Klingon Kras and automatically reaches for his weapon in Classic episode "Friday's Child."

GRAVES, DAVID MICHAEL
played one of the Edo Children in TNG "Justice."

GRAVES, DR. IRA
cyberneticist and Dr. Noonian Soong's teacher, played by W. Morgan Sheppard, living on Graves' World with his assistant in TNG episode "The Schizoid Man."

Graves' World
home and research center of Dr. Ira Graves and Kareen Brianon in TNG episode "The Schizoid Man."

Gravitic mine
the *Denver* hits a gravitic mine leftover from the Federation-Cardassian war in TNG episode "Ethics." T

GRAX, REITTAN
a Betazoid conference director and Deanna's father's friend, played by Rudolph Willrich, who tells Picard that Deanna, Lwaxana and Riker have been kidnapped in TNG episode "Menage A Troi."

GRAY, PAMELA
scriptwriter of TNG "Violations."

GRAY, MIKE
scriptwriter of TNG episodes "Unnatural Selection" and "Violations." Also a producer.

GRAYSON, AMANDA
Spock's human mother, married to Sarek. (See entry for Amanda.)

GREBNEDLOG
captain, played by Christopher Collins, of the Pakled ship *Mondor*, who takes Geordi hostage in TNG episode "Samaritan Snare."

GREEN, GILBERT
played the SS Major on Classic Trek "Patterns of Force." His film appearances include the pilot for the TV series "Starsky and Hutch."

GREEN, CREWMAN
character, played by Bruce Watson, killed by the salt vampire on planet M 113 in Classic episode "The Man Trap." The creature then assumes Green's appearance to gain access to the *Enterprise*.

GREEN, COLONEL
supposedly a ruthless military man responsible for a genocidal war on Earth in the 21st century. His image, taken from Kirk's mind and played by Phillip Pines, is encountered in Classic episode "The Savage Curtain."

GREENBERGER, ROBERT
co-author of TNG novel *Doomsday World* and sole writer of Classic novel *The Disinherited*.

GREENE, VANESSA
scriptwriter of TNG "The Loss."

GREENE, JAMES
played Dr. Barron in TNG "Who Watches The Watchers."

GREGORY, STEPHEN
played Jake Kurland in TNG "Coming of Age."

GREGORY, JAMES
played Dr. Tristan Adams in Classic Trek "Dagger of the Mind." Born in 1911, his credits include "The Naked City," "The Sons of Katie Elder" and "Beneath The Planet of the Apes." An actor with extensive stage experience, he also appeared regularly on "The Paul Lynde Show," "Barney Miller" and "Detective School."

Grenthamen Water Hopper
a type of vessel mentioned in TNG episode "Peak Performance."

GRIMES, SCOTT
played Eric (in scenes later cut) in TNG "Evolution."

Grissom, S.S.
science ship, commanded by Captain Esteban, destroyed by Kruge in "The Search For Spock." Another *Grissom* is mentioned in TNG episode "The Most Toys" as sought by the *Enterprise* for help obtaining hytritium, but is unable to aid the *Enterprise* although it is the closest ship in the quadrant.

GRIST, ROBERT
director of Classic Trek episode "The Galileo Seven."

Grizellas
beings named as arbitors by Picard in the Treaty of Armens because of their long hibernation period which gives the *Enterprise* time to rescue people in TNG episode "The Ensigns of Command."

GRODENCHIK, MAX
played Sovak in TNG "Captain's Holiday," and Par Lenor in "The Perfect Mate." He also played the Ferengi Pit Boss in DS9 "Emissary" and appeared in DS9 "A Man Alone," "The Nagus" and "Vortex."

GROENER, HARRY
played Tam Elbrun in TNG "Tin Man."

GROMEK, ADMIRAL
starfleet Admiral, played by Georgann Johnson, in TNG episode "The Emissary."

Grubs
a favorite food of the Ferengi who eat them live in DS9 episode "The Nagus."

GRUDT, MONA
Graham in TNG "Identity Crisis."

Grum'ba
a Narsicaan word that means "guts" or courage in TNG episode "Tapestry."

Grup
name the children on Miri's planet use for adults in Classic episode "Miri."

GRUZAF, JAMES
played Don Juan in Classic Trek "Shore Leave."

GSK 783, Subspace Frequency 3
Aurelan Kirk uses this private communication wave to call the *Enterprise* for help from Deneva in Classic episode "Operation: Annihilate!"

Guardian of Forever
a gateway to the past on a ruined, windblown world seen in Classic episode "The City On The Edge Of Forever" and in the animated "Yesteryear."

Guernica system
destination of the *Enterprise* when Dr. Leah Brahms comes aboard in TNG episode "Galaxy's Child."

GUERRA, CASTULO
played Seth Mendoza in TNG "The Price."

GUERRERO, EVELYN
played an ensign in TNG "Encounter At Farpoint."

GUERZ, KARL
scriptwriter of TNG "Homesoil."

GUEST, NICHOLAS
played a cadet in "The Wrath of Khan." A stage actor as well, he has appeared in the movies "Trading Places" and "Cloak and Dagger."

GUINAN
recurring character, played by Whoopi Goldberg, in "The Next Generation." A member of a mysterious race that doesn't seem to age, Guinan is over 1000 years old. She has had many children and husbands but her family was wiped out by the Borg. She knew Q prior to his visits to the ship, but something unknown about their relationship is the reason she is currently aboard the *Enterprise* as head of the bar in Ten Forward. She and Picard share a very strong bond, they have a trust and an understanding that surpasses normal friendship and hints, in some episodes, at possible intimacy. In TNG episode "Booby Trap," she says she's attracted to bald men. She is the only one who can challenge Picard's orders, question them, even get him to change his mind. Data believes her perception goes beyond linear time, which is why she knew the timeline was altered in "Yesterday's Enterprise."

Gul
Cardassian command title, roughly the equivalent of "captain."

GUNNING, CHARLES
played Miners in TNG "The Perfect Mate."

GUNTON, BOB
played Captain Ben Maxwell in TNG "The Wounded."

GUSTAFSON, FLEET ADMIRAL
officer with whom Picard is to meet after a magnetic wave survey of the Parvenium sector in TNG episode "The Inner Light."

Haakona
Romulan ship onto which Picard steps when he goes through the Iconian teleporter in TNG episode "Contagion."

HACOM
rabid elderly Landru follower, played by Morgan Farley, in Classic episode "The Return of the Archons."

HADEN, ADMIRAL
commander, played by John Hancock, of the Starfleet station on Lya III in TNG episode "The Defector."

HADLEY, LIEUTENANT
Enterprise officer, played by William Blackburn, who takes over Spock's station in Classic episode "A Piece of the Action."

HAFTEL, ADMIRAL ANTHONY
officer, played by Nicholas Coster, who serves at research facility on Galor IV and wants to take Lal away from Data in TNG episode "The Offspring."

HAGAN, COUNSELOR ANDRUS
the catatonic Betazoid, played by John Vickery, who speaks to Deanna in dreams in TNG episode "Night Terrors."

HAGERTY, MICHAEL G.
played Larg in TNG "Redemption Part II."

HAGLER, LIEUTENANT
Enterprise officer whose blood is turned into liquid polymer in TNG episode "Schisms."

HAGON
played by James Louis Watkins, holds the title of Primary and First One To Yareena in TNG episode "Night Terrors."

Hahliia
world inhabited by partially telepathic aliens of which Lieutenant Aqueil Uhnari is one in TNG episode "Aquiel."

HAHN, ADMIRAL
mentioned in TNG episode "Menage A Troi."

HAIG, SID
played First Lawgiver in Classic Trek "Return of the Archons." His other credits include "Who Is the Black Dahlia?," "The Return of the World's Greatest Detective," "Evening In Byzantium," "Death On The Freeway," "Chu Chu And The Philly Flash" and "Galaxy of Terror."

HAIGHT, WANDA M.
scriptwriter of TNG "A Matter of Honor."

HAINES, ENSIGN JANA
Enterprise navigator, played by Victoria George, in Classic episode "The Gamesters of Triskelion."

HAJAR, CADET SECOND CLASS
member, played by Walter Brandt, of Wesley's Nova Squadron in TNG episode "The First Duty."

HAKI
a Mintakan child who gives Picard a piece of cloth as a gift in TNG episode "Who Watches The Watchers."

HALDEMAN, JOE
science fiction writer and author of Classic Trek novels *Planet of Judgment* and *World Without End*.

HALDEMAN, JACK C. II
author of Classic Trek novel *Perry's Planet*.

HALE, DOUG
played computer voice in "Star Trek: The Motion Picture." He appeared in the film "Charleston," and plays voices in "Terror At Alcatraz," and "Mothers Against Drunk Drivers."

HALE, RICHARD
played Goro in Classic Trek "The Paradise Syndrome." Born in 1893, his credits include "Julius Caesar" and "Ben Hur." He guest starred (as mostly Indian characters) in "Cheyenne" and "Iron Horse." He died in 1981.

HALF A LIFE
fourth season TNG episode written by Peter Allan Fields and Ted Roberts, and

directed by Les Landau. A Kaelon scientist has dedicated his entire life to experimenting with a process for reenergizing a dying star because his own world's sun is dying. Lwazana Troi meets him just as he is about to turn 60, an age when he must, according to his culture, submit himself to death. In love with him, she tries to persuade him to leave his homeworld and continue his experiments. Guest stars: Majel Barrett, David Ogden Stiers, Michelle Forbes, Terence McNally, Colm Meaney and Carel Struycken. Of note: When Lwaxana walks away from the mirror the boom microphone can be observed.

HALI
a Mintakan, played by James McIntyre, in TNG episode "Who Watches The Watchers."

Hali
a hellish place, mentioned in TNG episode "Heart of Glory."

Halkans
a peaceful people with whom the *Enterprise* is trying to negotiate dilithium mining rights when Kirk, Scott, McCoy and Uhura are transported to the another universe in Classic episode "Mirror, Mirror."

HALL, KEVIN PETER
played Leyor in TNG "The Price."

HALL, LOIS
played Mary Warren in TNG "Who Watches The Watchers."

Hall of Audiences
place where people come to see Landru in Classic episode "The Return of the Archons."

HALLOWAY, CAPTAIN THOMAS
commander of the *Enterprise* in an alternate future in TNG episode "Tapestry."

HALPERIN, MICHAEL
scriptwriter of TNG episode "Lonely Among Us."

HALSTE, CHRISTOPHER
played First Learner in TNG "Cost of Living."

HAMBLY, BARBARA
author of Classic Trek novels *Ishmael* and *Ghost Walker.*

HAMILTON, LAURELL K.
wrote TNG novel *Nightshade,* and has authored a fantasy novel and a three book vampire series.

HAMILTON, KIM
played Chairman Sonji in TNG "Final Mission."

HAMLET, PRINCE
role a Karidian actor, played by Marc Adams, assumes in Classic episode "The Conscience of the King."

HAMNER, ROBERT
scriptwriter of Classic Trek "A Taste of Armageddon" and episodes of "The Man

From U.N.C.L.E." and "Voyage To The Bottom Of The Sea." He also wrote "You Lie so Deep My Love," "Dallas Cowboys Cheerleaders" and "The Million Dollar Face." He is also a producer.

HANAR
Kelvin invader, played by Stewart Moss, to whom McCoy gives formazine in Classic episode "By Any Other Name."

HANCOCK, JOHN
played Admiral Haden in TNG episodes "The Defector" and "The Wounded."

HANEY, ANNE
appeared in DS9 "Dax."

HANLON, GEORGE O.
played the transporter chief in TNG "Future Imperfect."

Hanolin asteroid belt
location near Vulcan where a Ferengi shuttle crashes in TNG episode "Unification."

HANSEN, LIEUTENANT
an *Enterprise* helmsman, played by Hagan Beggs, in Classic episodes "Court Martial" and "The Menagerie."

HANSON, ADMIRAL J.P.
a Starfleet tactical officer, played by George Murdock, in TNG episode "The Best of Both Worlds."

HANSON, COMMANDER
commander, played by Garry Walberg, of Outpost IV which is destroyed by

the Romulans in Classic episode "Balance of Terror."

HANSON'S PLANET
mentioned in Classic episode "The Galileo Seven" as another world inhabited by furry creatures like those on Taurus II.

HARDER, RICHARD
played Joe in "The Voyage Home."

HARDIN, JERRY
played Radue on TNG "When The Bough Breaks," and Samuel Clemens in "Time's Arrow Part I and II."

HARITATH
played by Mark L. Taylor, character who supports Data and Ard'rian as they try to evacuate Tau Cygna V in TNG episode, "The Ensigns of Command."

Harkona
Romulan vessel commanded by Subcommander Taras in TNG episode "Contagion."

HARMON, DAVID P.
scriptwriter of Classic Trek episodes "The Deadly Years," "A Piece of the Action," and the animated "The Eye Of The Beholder." His TV scripts include "Honeymoon With A Stranger," "Killer By Night," "Rescue From Gilligan's Island" and "The Harlem Globetrotters On Gilligan's Island."

HARMON, JOHN
played Rodent in Classic Trek "The City On The Edge Of Forever," and Tepo in "A Piece Of The Action."

Other credits include a semi-regular part on "The Rifleman."

HARO, MITENA
a Bolian cadet and spy, played by Joycelyn O'Brien, kidnapped with Thool, Esoqq and Picard in TNG episode "Allegiance."

Harod IV
world from which the *Enterprise* rescues several miners in TNG episode "The Perfect Mate."

HAROLD, LIEUTENANT
survivor, played by Tom Troups, of the Gorn attack on Cestus III in Classic episode "Arena."

HARPER, JAMES
appeared in DS9 "The Passenger."

HARPER, ROBERT
played Lathal in TNG "The Host."

HARPER, ENSIGN
engineer, played by Sean Morgan, who is killed by the M 5 computer when he tries to shut it down in Classic episode "The Ultimate Computer."

Harrakis V
planet where the *Enterprise* finishes its work early in TNG episode "Clues."

HARRIS, JOSHUA
played Timothy in TNG "Hero Worship."

HARRIS, LEON
art director on "Star Trek: The Motion Picture" who also worked on the movie "The Devil and Max Devlin."

HARRIS, CAPTAIN
unseen captain of the *Excalibur* who is killed with his crew by the M 5 computer in Classic episode "The Ultimate Computer."

HARRISON, GRACIE
played Clare Raymond in TNG "The Neutral Zone."

HARRISON, DR.
tagger, played by John Bellah, who paints "Sinner Repent" and "Love Mankind" on the bulkheads of the *Enterprise* in Classic episode "The Naked Time".

HARRISON, TECHNICIAN
character on the bridge when Khan takes over in Classic episode "Space Seed."

HARRISON, WILLIAM B.
the last of Captain Merik's men to die in the arena during gladiatorial combat in Classic episode "Bread and Circuses".

HART, HARVEY
director of Classic Trek episode "Mudd's Women." A producer of several low budget movies, most of his work as a director is limited to television.

HARTLEY, MARIETTE
played Zarabeth in Classic Trek "All Our Yesterdays." Born in 1940, Hartley made guest appearances in many TV series of the 1960's, including "The Twilight Zone," and was a regular on "Peyton Place," "The Hero" and "Goodnight Beantown" (co-starring with Bill Bixby and Tracey

Gold.) She also starred in Roddenberry's "Genesis II," and won an Emmy for her guest star performance in "The Incredible Hulk" (again with Bill Bixby.)

HASKELL
an *Enterprise* crewman, played by Charles Douglass, killed in TNG episode "Where Silence Has Lease."

HASKINS, DR. THEODORE
one of the survivors, played by Jon Lormer, on Talos IV in Classic episode "The Menagerie" and "The Cage" and also has a role in "For The World Is Hollow And I Have Touched The Sky."

HATAE, HANA
played Molly in DS9 "A Man Alone."

Hathaway, U.S.S.
80-year-old derelict ship over which Riker is given command with 40 officers in order to participate in a simulated battle, in TNG episode "Peak Performance."

Havana
ship with which *Enterprise* has orders to rendezvous in TNG episode "Lessons,"

Haven
paradise world located in the Beta Cassius system and governed by First Electorine Valeda Innis in TNG episode "Haven."

HAVEN
Troi's mother, Lwaxana, is introduced in this first season TNG episode written by Tracy Torme and Lian

Okun and directed by Richard Compton. Wyatt Miller, to whom Troi has been promised in a Betazoid arranged marriage, also comes aboard, but he constantly sees images of another young woman who he believes is his true love. Guest stars: Danzita Kingsley, Carel Struycken, Anna Katarina, Raye Birk, Michael Rider, Majel Barrett, Rob Knepper, Nan Martin and Robert Ellenstein.

HAWKE, SIMON
author of TNG novel *The Romulan Prize.*

HAWKING, STEPHEN
famous quantum phycisist who made a cameo appearance in TNG episode "Descent."

Hawking
Enterprise shuttle, named after quantum physicist Stephen Hawking (who makes an appearance in TNG's seventh season) in TNG episode "The Host."

HAWKINS, AMBASSADOR
the leader of the diplomatic party on Mordan IV in TNG episode "Too Short A Season."

Hayashi system
location from which the *Enterprise* is called in TNG episode "Tin Man."

HAYENGA, JEFFREY
played Orta in TNG "Ensign Ro."

HAYNE
leader of the faction, played by Don Mirrault, on

Turkana IV in TNG episode "Legacy."

HAYNES, LLOYD
played Communications Officer Lt. Alden in Classic Trek "Where No Man Has Gone Before." Most famous for his starring role in the TV series "Room 222," his other credits include "Assault On The Wayne" (with Leonard Nimoy,) "Look What's Happened To Rosemary's Baby" and "Born To Be Sold." He died in 1986.

HAYMER, JOHNNY
played the constable in Classic Trek "All Our Yesterdays." His credits include feature roles on "M*A*S*H" and "Madame's Place." Film work includes "Mongo's Back In Town," "Ring of Passion" and "The Best Place To Be."

HAYS, KATHRYN
actress who played Gem in Classic Trek "The Empath." Her credits include a regular role on "The Road West" and guest roles on "The Man From U.N.C.L.E." and "Circle of Fear." She has appeared regularly as Kim on the soap opera "As The World Turns" for over 20 years.

Heading Out To Eden
song Adam sings in Classic episode "The Way To Eden."

HEARN, GEORGE
played Berel in TNG "First Contact."

HEART OF GLORY
first season TNG episode written by Maurice Hurley,

Herbert Wright, D.C. Fontana and directed by Rob Bowman. Klingons board the *Enterprise* and try to turn Worf against his fellow crewmembers in an attempt to capture the ship. Guest stars: Vaughn Armstrong, Robert Bauer, Brad Zerbst, Dennis Madalone and Charles H. Hyman.

HECHT, GINA
played Manua in TNG "A Matter of Perspective."

HEDFORD, NANCY
commissioner, played by Elinor Donahue, on her way to negotiate peace on Epsilon Canaris III when her shuttle is is taken off course by the Companion in Classic episode "Metamorphosis."

HEDRICK, CHIEF
transporter officer, played by Dennis Madalone, in TNG episode "Identity Crisis."

HEINEMANN, ARTHUR
scriptwriter of Classic Trek episodes "Wink of an Eye," "The Way To Eden" and "The Savage Curtain." He has also written scripts for the TV series "Cannon."

Hektah
Klingon ship commanded by Kurn, Worf's brother in TNG episode "Redemption."

HELD, CHRISTOPHER
played Lindstrom in Classic Trek "Return of the Archons."

Helglenian Shift
method used by Ligon transporters in TNG episode "Code of Honor."

HELLER, CHIP
played a warrior in TNG "Loud As A Whisper."

HENDORF
security guard, played by Mal Friedman, who is killed by thorns shot from a beautiful flower in Classic episode "The Apple."

HENGIST
administrator, played by John Fiedler, on Argelius II and a native of Rigel who is eventually discovered to be the murdering entity in Classic episode "Wolf In The Fold."

HENNESSY
Dr. Pulaski's patient in TNG episode "The Dauphin."

HENNINGS, SAM
played Ramsey in TNG "Angel One."

HENOCH
energy being which takes over Spock's body and decides it does not want to give it up in Classic episode "Return To Tomorrow."

HENRIQUES, DARRYL
played The Portal in TNG "The Last Outpost" and Nanclus in "The Undiscovered Country."

**HENRY,
ADMIRAL THOMAS**
officer, played by Earl Billings, who closes down Sadie's witch hunt in TNG episode "The Drumhead."

HENSEL, KAREN
played Admiral Brackett in TNG "Unification Part I."

HENSHAW, CHRISTY
character, played by Julie Warner, Geordi tries and fails to romance in TNG episodes "Transfigurations" and "Booby Trap."

HENTELOFF, ALEX
played Nichols in "The Voyage Home." His other credits include regular roles on TV series "Pistols 'n Petticoats," "The Young Rebels," "Needles And Pins" and "The Betty White Comedy Show." He also appeared in films "Partners In Crime," "The Invisible Man ('75)," "The Bastard," "Victims," "The Red" and Light Sting."

Herbarium
name of the arboretum on the *Enterprise* in Classic Trek "Is There In Truth No Beauty?"

HERBERT, ENSIGN
a transporter officer, played by Lance Spellerberg, in TNG episodes "We'll Always Have Paris" and "The Icarus Factor."

Hercos III
the Devinoni Ral's adopted world in TNG episode "The Price."

HERD, RICHARD
guest starred in TNG episode "Birthright." He is a popular character actor who has appeared on many TV series and movies.

HERMAN
series of androids, played by twin actors Tom and Ted LeGarde, created by Harry Mudd in Classic episode "I, Mudd."

Hermes, U.S.S.
starfleet ship participating in the Klingon blockade in Classic episode "Redemption."

HERO WORSHIP
fifth season TNG episode written by Hilary J. Bader and Joe Menosky and directed by Patrick Stewart. A young survivor of a terrible starship accident blames himself and tries to block his emotions by emulating Data in an attempt to become a robot himself. Guest stars: Joshua Harris and Steven Einspahr.

HERRON, ROBERT
played Pike's stunt double in Classic Trek pilot "The Cage" and Kahless in "The Savage Curtain."

HERTZLER, JOHN NOAH
played Vulcan Captain in DS9 "Emissary."

Het'ba
Klingon suicide ceremony Worf considers performing when he suffers paralysis in TNG episode "Ethics."

HETRICK, JENNIFER
played Vash in TNG "Captain's Holiday," "Q Pid" and DS9 "Q Less."

Hey Out There
gang song in Classic episode "The Way To Eden."

Hibishan Civilization
built elaborate tombs plundered by the Cardassians in TNG episode "Chain of Command."

HICKMAN, LIEUTENANT PAUL
officer, played by Amick Byram, on the *U.S.S. Victory* who steals a shuttlecraft in TNG episode "Identity Crisis."

HICKS, CATHERINE
played Gillian Taylor in "The Voyage Home." TV credits include regular roles in the series "Ryan's Hope" and "The Bad News Bears." She also won an Emmy for her portrayal of Marilyn Monroe in "Marilyn: The Untold Appearances." Film credits include "The Razor's Edge" and "Peggy Sue Got Married."

HICKS, CHUCK
played Military Officer in TNG "Encounter At Farpoint."

HIDE AND Q
first season TNG episode written by C.J. Holland and Gene Roddenberry and directed by Cliff Bole. Q gives Riker Q powers, but Riker turns down Q's offer to make him a Q permanently. Guest stars: John deLancie, Elaine Nalee and William A. Wallace.

HIGH GROUND, The
third season TNG episode written by Melinda Snodgrass and directed by Gabrielle Beaumont. Dr.

Crusher is kidnapped by terrorists on Rutia IV who need a doctor to help them combat a DNA breakdown caused by the use of their strange teleport device, the Invertor, which leads to death if overused. Finn, her kidnapper, also uses Crusher in an attempt to lure the *Enterprise* into the planet's conflict. Guest stars: Kerrie Keane, Richard Cox, Marc Buckland, Fred G. Smith and Christopher Pettiet.

Highway 949
road leading to McKinley Rocket Base and on which agents 201 and 347 died in a car crash in Classic episode "Tomorrow Is Yesterday."

HILDEBRANDT
member, played by Ann H. Gillespie, of the Selcundi Drema team who is married to Alans in TNG episode "Pen Pals."

HILL, MARIANNA
played Dr. Helen Noel on Classic Trek "Dagger of the Mind." Other TV credits include "Perry Mason" and the movies "Death At Love House," "Relentless," "Blood Beach" and "Invisible Strangler."

HILL, DIXON
role Picard assumes during his holodeck mystery recreations in TNG episode "Manhunt."

HILLYER, SHARON
played one of the "girls" in Classic Trek "A Piece Of The Action." She appeared regularly in the third sea-

son of "The Man From U.N.C.L.E."

HINES, GRAINGER
played Gosheven in TNG "The Ensigns of Command."

HOBSON, THOMAS
played young Jake in DS9 "Emissary."

HOBSON, LT. COMMANDER CHRISTOPHER
first officer, played by Timothy Carhart, of the *U.S.S. Sutherland* who gives Data a hard time in TNG episode "Redemption."

HOCK, ALLISON
scriptwriter of TNG "Rascals."

HOCKRIDGE, JOHN
first assistant director on "The Search For Spock."

Hodgkins' Law of Parallel Planet Development
theory, mentioned in Classic episode "Bread and Circuses," on why so many humanoid beings and cultures resembling Earth exist throughout the galaxy.

HODIN
Odona's father, played by David Hurst, who risks his daughter's life to solve the planet Gideon's population problem in Classic episode "Mark of Gideon".

HOFFMAN, ELIZABETH
played Bhavani in TNG "The Price."

Holberg 917G
ryetalin-rich planet, located in the Omega system, visited by the *Enterprise* in search of a cure for the Rigellian fever sweeping the ship and where they meet Flint and Reena in Classic episode "Requiem For Methuselah."

HOLLAND, C.J.
scriptwriter who penned TNG "Hide and Q."

HOLLAND, ERIK
played Ekor on Classic Trek "Wink of an Eye." TV credits include "The Man From U.N.C.L.E." and "Voyage To The Bottom Of The Sea." Film credits include" "Friendly Persuasion," "The French Atlantic Affair," "Little House: Look Back To Yesterday" and "Table For Five."

HOLLANDER, ELI
young gun hostile to Worf in TNG episode "A Fistful of Datas."

HOLLIDAY, DOC
Melkotian alien, played by Dam Gilman, in Classic episode "Spectre of the Gun."

HOLLIS
Enterprise security officer in TNG episode "Descent."

HOLLOW PURSUITS
third season TNG episode written by Sally Caves and directed by Cliff Bole. Engineer Reginald Barclay, addicted to the holodeck because of his shyness and inability to socialize with others, is needed to help solve the ship's problems.

Guest stars: Dwight Schultz, Whoopi Goldberg, Charley Lang and Colm Meaney.

HOLLOWAY, ROGER
played Mr. Lemli on Classic Trek "Turnabout Intruder."

HOLMAN, REX
played Morgan Earp in Classic Trek "Spectre of the Gun" and J'Onn in "The Final Frontier." His other film credits include "The Bounty Man," "The Legend of the Golden Gun" and "The Wild Women of Chastity Gulch."

HOLMES, SHERLOCK
role Data assumes in holodeck mystery recreations in TNG episode "Elementary, Dear Data."

Holodeck
recreation facility that creates crewmembers' fantasies in virtual reality.

Holodiction
addiction to the holodeck, to the point where reality is shunned. Barclay falls victim to holodiction in TNG episode "Hollow Pursuits."

Holosuites
sex fantasy programs run by Quark on Deep Space 9.

HOME SOIL
first season TNG episode written by Robert Sabaroff, Karl Guerz and Ralph Sanchez and directed by Corey Allen. A rare life form, called a "microbrain," living in the soil of Velara III, attempts to save itself from a Federation terraforming project by killing the scientists

involved. Guest stars: Walter Gotell, Elizabeth Lindsey, Gerard Pendergast, Mario Roccuzzo and Carolyn Barry.

HOMEIER, SKIP
played Melakon in Classic Trek "Patterns of Force" and Dr. Sevrin in "The Way To Eden." Born in 1930 as George Vincent Homeier, he made regular appearances on radio and in TV, including starring roles in "Dan Raven" and "The Interns." His film credits include "The Gunfighter," "Commanche Station" and "The Greatest."

HOMN, MR.
Lwaxana Troi's mute aide, played by Carel Struycken, first seen in TNG episode "The Big Goodbye."

Hood, U.S.S.
ship, commanded by Captain DeSoto, on which Riker served as first officer before transferring to the *Enterprise*, as mentioned in TNG episode "Encounter At Farpoint." The ship, encountered in several future episodes, is also involved in war games with the M 5 computer in Classic episode "The Ultimate Computer."

Hook Spiders, Talarian
insects with half meter long legs which supposedly infested Zera IV, as mentioned by O'Brien in TNG episode "Realm of Fear."

HOOKS, ROBERT
played Commander Morrow in "The Search For Spock." Born in 1937, his credits include "Hurry Sundown," "Airport '77"

and a starring role in the 1960's series "NYPD."

HORAN, JAMES
guest starred in TNG episode "Suspicions."

Horatio, U.S.S.
ship, commanded by Captain Walker Keel, destroyed in TNG episode "Conspiracy."

Horga'hn
symbol of sexuality on Risa, a stone statue of which Riker asks Picard to bring him from the captain's trip to the planet in TNG episode "Captain's Holiday."

HORGAN, PATRICK
played Eneg in Classic Trek "Patterns of Force." TV credits include the miniseries "George Washington" and a starring role in the series "Casablanca."

Horizon, U.S.S.
ship which made first contact with Iotia and left behind the book *Chicago Mods of the Twenties*, altering the culture, in Classic episode "A Piece Of The Action."

Hornbuck
Mintakan animal native mentioned in TNG episode "Who Watches The Watchers."

HORNER, JAMES
composed themes for "The Wrath of Khan" and "The Search For Spock." His other film scores include "Battle Beyond the Stars" (his first,) "Aliens" and "Brainstorm."

Hornet, U.S.S.
starship working with the Klingon blockade in TNG episode "Redemption."

Horta
intelligent rock creature whose nest the miners inadvertantly disturb in Classic episode "Devil in the Dark."

HORVAT, MICHEL
scriptwriter of TNG "The Host."

HOST, The
fourth season TNG episode written by Michel Horvat and directed by Marvin V. Rush. Dr. Crusher falls in love with a Trill, a being hosting a symbiotic life form. When the body is injured beyond repair, another body is ordered for him but the host turns out to be female, a turn of events Crusher cannot come to terms with. Guest stars: Franc Luz, Barbara Tarbuck, William Newman, Nicole Orth-Pallavicini, Robert Harper and Patti Yasutake.

HOTTON, DONALD
played Monk #1 in DS9 "Emissary."

Hoverball
a sport Picard is not particularly fond of in TNG episode "Captain's Holiday."

HOW SHARPER THAN A SERPENT'S TOOTH
written by Russell Bates and David Wise, this animated Classic Trek episode aired 10/5/74. The *Enterprise* encounters a ship which looks like a Kulkukan from Mayan or Aztec legend. The entity ship, angry at being forgotten by humans, gives the crew a puzzle to solve. Kirk, McCoy, Scott and Ensign Dawson Walking Bear are then transported to a city where they end up saving the entity's life. James Doohan guest stars as Arex the Kulkukan.

HOWARD, CLINT
played Balok in Classic Trek "The Corbomite Maneuver." Brother of actor/producer/director Ron Howard, he had regular starring roles in the TV series "The Bailey's of Balboa," "Gentle Ben" and "The Cowboys." His films include "Evilspeak," "Night Shift," "Splash!" and "Backdraft."

HOWARD, LESLIE C.
played a yeoman in "Star Trek: The Motion Picture."

HOWARD, SHERMAN
played Endar in TNG "Suddenly Human."

HOWARD, SUSAN
played Mara in Classic Trek "Day of the Dove." Other credits include "Quarantined," "Indict and Convict" (with William Shatner,) "Superdome" and "The Power Within." She also appeared regularly in "Petrocelli" and "Dallas."

HOWARD, VINCE
played "Uhura's Crewman" in Classic Trek "The Man Trap." He was featured regularly on the TV series "Mr. Novak" and appeared in the films "Vanished," "Love Is Not Enough" and "The Red Light Sting."

HOWDEN, MIKE
played Lt. Rowe in Classic Trek "I, Mudd," and a Romulan guard in "The Enterprise Incident."

HOY, ENSIGN
character in TNG episode "Who Watches The Watchers."

HOYT, CLEGG
played Transporter Chief Pitcairn in Classic Trek pilot "The Cage." His other TV credits include "The Man From U.N.C.L.E." and "The Rifleman."

HOYT, JOHN
played Dr. Philip Boyce in Classic Trek pilot "The Cage." Born in 1905, his film credits include "When Worlds Collide," "Duel At Diablo" and "Flesh Gordon." A regular on the TV series "Tom, Dick and Mey," and "Gimme A Break," he appeared in "The Man From U.N.C.L.E.," "Planet of the Apes" and "Voyage To The Bottom Of The Sea."

Hromi Cluster
location of the Gatherer camp in TNG episode "The Vengeance Factor."

HUBBARD, JAMIE
played Salia in TNG "The Dauphin."

HUBBELL, J.P.
played an ensign in TNG "Man of the People."

HUBBLELL, CHIEF
transporter tech, played by April Grace, in TNG episodes "Reunion," "Future Imperfect," "Galaxy's Child" and "The Perfect Mate."

HUDEC, M. LEIGH
see Barrett, Majel.

HUGH
Borg captured by the *Enterprise,* given individuality, and then sent back to the other Borgs with a virus in his system. Played by Jonathan del Arco, he appeared in TNG episode "I, Borg" and "Descent."

HUGHES, WENDY
guest starred as Nella Daren in TNG episode "Lessons."

HUGHES, DAVID HILLARY
played Trefayne in Classic Trek "Errand of Mercy."

HUMBOLT, CHIEF
chief of the computer section, played by George Sawaya, on Starbase Eleven in Classic episode "The Menagerie."

HUMMEL, SAYRA
played the engine room technician in "Star Trek: The Motion Picture."

HUNDLEY, CRAIG
played Peter Kirk in Classic Trek "Operation: Annihilate!" and Tommy Starnes in "And The Children Shall Lead."

HUNGERFORD, MICHAEL
played Roughneck in TNG "Time's Arrow, Part I."

HUNT, MARSHA
played Anne Jameson on TNG "Too Short A Season."

Hunt, The
official contest of an alien race from the Gamma Quadrant which hunts prey bred solely for the game. The *Enterprise* encounters a hunted creature, named Tosk, who is to be pursued until he dies in DS9 episode "Captive Pursuit."

HUNTER, JEFFREY
played Captain Christopher Pike in Classic Trek pilot "The Cage." Born in New Orleans in 1925, his credits include "Red Skies of Montana," "King of Kings," "The Longest Day" and a regular role in the series "Temple Houston." He died in 1969 from a brain injury while filming in Spain.

HUNTER, The
third season TNG episode written by Robin Bernheim and directed by Cliff Bole. Genetically superior soldiers, created by the government during a civil war on Angosia, are being held in prison during peace time. One of the soldiers, Roga Danar, escapes and asks the *Enterprise* for help but the ship refuses, leaving the society to resolve its own problems. Guest stars: Jeff McCarthy, James Cromwell, J. Michael Flynn, Andrew Bicknell and Colm Meaney.

HUPP, JANA MARIE
played Ensign Pavlik in TNG "Galaxy's Child" and Ensign Monroe in "Disaster."

Hurkos III
world to which Ral relocated at age 19 as mentioned in TNG episode "The Price."

HURLEY, CRAIG
played Peeples in TNG "Night Terrors."

HURLEY, DIANE M.
played "woman" in TNG "The Game."

HURLEY, MAURICE
scriptwriter of TNG "Datalore," "11001001," "Heart of Glory," "The Arsenal of Freedom," "The Neutral Zone," "The Child," "Time Squared," "Q Who," "Shades of Gray," "Galaxy's Child" and "Power Play."

Huron, S.S.
a dilithium cargo freighter commanded by Captain O'Shea in animated episode "The Pirates of Orion."

HURST, DAVID
played Hodin in Classic Trek "The Mark of Gideon."

Husnock
a race of 50 billion people mentally destroyed by Kevin Uxbridge after they kill his wife in TNG episode "The Survivors."

Husnock Vessel
a gigantic spectre ship five times the size of the *Enterprise* and fully armed in TNG episode "The Survivors."

HUTCHISON, COMMANDER CALVIN "HUTCH"
incredibly boring Starfleet officer assigned to Arkaria who hosts a party, which Picard orders the entire crew to attend, in TNG episode "Starship Mine." The commander is killed by theives attempting to steal the *Enterprise*'s trilithium at the end of the episode.

HUTZEL, GARY
responsible for visual effects in DS9.

HYDE, BRUCE
played Lt. Kevin Thomas Riley in Classic Trek "The Naked Time" and "The Conscious of the King."

Hydrogen Collectors
red areas located on the front of the warp nacelles which project hydrogen, referred to in TNG episode "Samaritan Snare."

HYMAN, CHARLES
played Konmil in TNG "Heart of Glory."

Hyperacceleration
time realm inhabited by the Scalosians who cannot be seen or heard, except for a faint buzzing sound, in Classic episode "Wink of an Eye."

Hyperonic Radiation
level of toxicity which interferes with phasers, sensors and transporters and is deadly to humans. The colonists of Tau Cygna adapted to the radiation after it killed a third of them as mentioned in TNG episode "The Ensigns of Command."

Hypo
a syringe without a needle, also called hypospray in TNG, used in Sick Bay.

Hyronalin
drug that cures the disease which causes rapid aging in Classic episode "The Deadly Years."

Hytritium
substance the *Enterprise* uses to cleanse the water supply, contaminated with tricyanate, on Beta Agni II in TNG episode "The Most Toys."

I, BORG
fifth season TNG episode written by Rene Echevarria and directed by Bob Lederman. A young and impressionable survivor from a crashed Borg ship is brought aboard the *Enterprise*, befriended by Geordi (who names him Hugh,) and is taught about independence. Guest stars: Jonathan del Arco and Whoopi Goldberg.

I, MUDD
written by Stephen Kandel and David Gerrold and directed by Marc Daniels, this second season Classic Trek episode aired 11/3/67. The plot, centered on the return of Harry Mudd, makes for a very humorous script involving a world of androids. Guest stars: Roger C. Carmel, Kay Elliot, Richard Tatro, Rhea and Alyce Andrece, Tom and Ted LeGarde, Maureen and Collen Thornton, Tamara and Starr Wilson, Mike Howden and Michael Zaslow.

I'Chaya
the name of Spock's sehlat in the animated episode "Yesteryear." The sehlat is also referred to, but not by name, in "Journey To Babel." (see entry for Sehlat.)

IAN
alien entity Deanna Troi gives birth to, born as a glowing white pulse of energy which takes the form of a human boy so it can experience humanoid life in TNG episode "The Child." He ages rapidly and dies when he learns he is emitting deadly Eichner radiation. Zachary Benjamin plays the younger Ian and R.J. Williams when he is older.

IBODAN
Bajoran murderer and black marketeer who is murdered, and Oko accused of the crime, in DS9 episode "A Man Alone."

ICARUS FACTOR, The
second season TNG episode written by David Assael and Robert L. McCullough, and directed by Robert Iscove. Riker's father, Kyle, comes aboard to tell his son that Will Riker has been promoted to command the starship *Ares*. Guest stars: Mitchell Ryan, Colm Meaney and Lance Spellerberg.

Icarus IV
comet through which the Romulan ship purposely passes to throw the *Enterprise* off its track in Classic episode "Balance of Terror."

Icobar
an Iconian language mentioned in TNG episode "Contagion."

Iconia
lost civilization's home-world located in the Neutral Zone in TNG episode "Contagion."

Icor IX
location of a symposium on Rogue Star Clusters mentioned in TNG episode "Captain's Holiday."

IDENTITY CRISIS
fourth season TNG episode written by Tim DeHaas and Brannon Braga and directed by Winrich Kolbe. Five years before, Geordi and a friend visited a planet on which all the colonists have since disappeared; and they may be experiencing the same phenomenon. Guest stars: Maryann Plunkett, Patti Yasutake, Amick Byram, Mona Grudt, Dennis Madalone and Paul Tompkins.

IDIC
Vulcan philosophy, meaning Infinite Diversity in Infinite Combinations, symbolized by a circle with a triangle sticking through it. Spock wears the symbol on a necklace in Classic episode "Is There In Truth No Beauty?" Gene Roddenberry created the theory, and its symbol, so he could sell the necklaces through the mail and make more money.

Idini Star Cluster
location through which the *Enterprise* passes in

TNG episode "Too Short A Season."

Igo
star system to which the *Enterprise* is sent to find the *Yosemite* in TNG episode "Realm of Fear."

ILIA
Deltan navigator and Will Decker's old flame, played by Persis Khambatta, who comes aboard the *Enterprise* in the film "Star Trek: The Motion Picture." She is attacked by the Vejur probe. The Vejur later sends a probe in her image to the *Enterprise* in order to learn about the humans on board.

Ilium 629
isotope in dilithium mentioned in TNG episode "Pen Pals."

Illicon
mentioned in TNG episode "We'll Always Have Paris" as a world which feels the time distortion.

Ilyra IV
a charming world where Mudd sold Starfleet Academy, mentioned in animated episode "Mudd's Passion."

IMAGINARY FRIEND
fifth season TNG episode written by Ronald Wilderson, Jean Matthias, Richard Fliegel, Edithe Swenson and Brannon Braga, and directed by Gabrielle Beaumont. The imaginary friend of an an *Enterprise* officer's daughter actually forms into a real being with super powers

and deliberately causes dangerous accidents on the ship. Guest stars: Noley Thornton, Shay Astar, Brian Bonsall, Jeff Allin, Patti Yasutake and Sheila Franklin.

IMAN
famous model who played Martia in "The Undiscovered Country." Her film work includes a Michael Jackson video and the movie "L.A. Story" with Steve Martin. She is married to the actor/rock star David Bowie.

IMERSHEIN, DIERDRE
played Joval in TNG "Captain's Holiday."

IMMUNITY SYNDROME, The
written by Robert Sabaroff and directed by Joseph Pevney, this second season Classic Trek episode aired 1/19/68. The *Enterprise* enters a dark rift in space and finds itself being pulled toward an amoeba-like creature that is miles long. They must find a way out or die. No guest stars. Of note: The *U.S.S. Intrepid*, a ship commanded by an all Vulcan crew, is lost with all hands, a loss Spock telepathically feels.

Imodene system
system mentioned as the place Geordi's father studied invertebrates in TNG episode "The Icarus Factor."

Impulse power
secondary, very slow propulsion used by the *Enterprise* when moving away from space docks or

planets, and when the warp drive is out.

Imzadi
Betazoid term meaning a "beloved" person mentioned in TNG episode "Shades of Gray." Troi refers to Riker with this endearment on occasion.

IN THEORY
fourth season TNG episode written by Ronald D. Moore and Joe Menosky and directed by Patrick Stewart. Data becomes involved romantically with a young ensign who just broke up with her lover. Latrer, as the *Enterprise* moves into a nebula cloud, things start going wrong, as if a poltergeist is on board. Guest stars: Michele Scarabelli, Rosalind Chao, Whoopi Goldberg, Pamela Winslow and Colm Meaney. Of note: During filming of this episode, a crewmember renamed a shuttlepod *Pontiac* to play a joke on Patrick Stewart.

INAD
Ullian historian, played by Eve Brennar, whose son, Jev, is a mind rapist in TNG episode "Violations."

Indri VIII
world destroyed by Klingon Captain Nu'Daq to stop anyone from finding the key to Professor Galen's micropaleontology mystery in TNG episode "The Chase."

Industrial Light and Magic
company responsible for the special effects in

"Encounter At Farpoint," but which continued to get credit throughout the TNG series because stock footage from the two hour episode is used universally.

INFINITE VULCAN, The
written by Walter Koenig, this animated Classic Trek episode aired 10/20/73. On the planet Phylos the crew encounters plant-like beings and a giant human, Dr. Stavos Keniclius, whom the beings refer to as Master or Savior. Keniclius kidnaps Spock and clones him in his laboratory into a giant immortal Vulcan. Guest voices: James Doohan (Dr. Keniclius 5, Agmar, Lt. Arex) and Nichelle Nichols as the computer.

INGALLS, DON
scriptwriter of Classic Trek "The Alternative Factor." He also wrote the scripts for the films "A Matter of Wife and Death," "Flood," "The Initiation of Sarah" and "Captain America."

INGLEDEW, ROSALIND
played Yanar in TNG "The Outrageous Okona."

Ingraham B
world invaded by parasites which destroy the inhabiting civilization in Classic episode "Operation: Annihilate!" two years before the invasion on Deneva.

INHAT, STEVE
played Captain Garth in Classic Trek "Whom Gods Destroy." Born in Czecheslovakia in 1934, his credits include "The Chase" and "Fuzz" as well as several

appearances in westerns such as "Iron Horse." He died in 1972.

INNER LIGHT, The
fifth season TNG episode written by Morgan Gendel and Peter Allan Fields and directed by Peter Lauritson. A strange, alien probe knocks Picard unconscious and installs in his conciousness memories as a native Katan, a now dead world. While unconcious, Picard lives an entire life on Katan as a man named Kaman, who marries, fathers two children, and dies an old man. When he wakes up, he is told he has been out for only minutes. Guest stars: Margot Rose, Richard Riehle, Scott Jaeck, Jennifer Nash, Daniel Stewart (Patrick Stewart's son) and Patti Yasutake. Of note: This episode won the Hugo award in 1993 for best science fiction dramatic presentation.

INNIS, VALEDA
the First Electorine of Haven played by Anna Katarina in TNG episode "Haven."

Inoprovaline
drug given to John by Dr. Crusher in TNG episode "Transfigurations."

INSOMOK, ADMIRAL
the officer Wesley is to report to when he arrives at the Starfleet Academy in TNG episode "Final Mission."

Inspector General's Officer
branch of Starfleet which insures Starfleet's integrity

mentioned in TNG episode "Coming of Age."

Instrument of Obedience
implant placed by the Oracle in the temple of the people of Yonada to control them from asking too many questions about the nature of their world, contained within an asteroid, in Classic episode "For The World Is Hollow And I Have Touched The Sky." The Oracle monitors the implants and can administer a severe dose of pain to questioners or even institute death.

Interceptor
type of airplane piloted by Captain John Christopher in Classic episode "Tomorrow Is Yesterday."

Interium
element used on Vulcan ships mentioned in TNG episode "Unification."

Intermix chamber
part of the ship's engines mentioned in Classic episode "The Naked Time."

Interphase
rip in the fabric of space through which the *Defiant* disappears and reappears at certain intervals which can be charted through space-time waves in Classic episode "The Tholian Web."

Intrepid, U.S.S.
ship docked at the Starbase for repairs in Classic episode "Court Martial." Mentioned as first on the site of the Khitomer disaster in TNG episode "Sins of

the Fathers," it is later destroyed by the giant amoeba in "The Immunity Syndrome."

Invidium
packing substance used by the Mikulaks which causes the technical systems of the *Enterprise* to malfunction in TNG episode "Hollow Pursuits."

Ion Propulsion
Eymorg's ship uses this propulsion system in Classic episode "Spock's Brain."

Ion Storm
caused Kirk, Scotty, McCoy and Uhura to be sent to an alternate universe in Classic episode "Mirror, Mirror." An ion storm also occurred in "Court Martial" and was supposedly responsible for Ben Finney's death.

Iotia
the planet where the intelligent, humanoid inhabitants' culture was based upon the book *Chicago Mobs of the Twenties*, left behind by the *Horizon* in Classic episode "A Piece of the Action."

Iraatan V
where Kivas Fajo claims he was educated in TNG episode "The Most Toys."

IRELAND, JILL
played Leila Kalomi in Classic Trek "This Side of Paradise." Born in London in 1936, she died after a long battle with cancer in 1991. Her credits include several roles in husband Charles Bronson's films,

including "Hell Drivers, "Breakheart Pass" and "Love and Bullets." A regular character on "Shane," she guest starred several times in "The Man From U.N.C.L.E." with her first husband David McCallum.

Iresine Syndrome
disease *Enterprise* crew members who have been mind raped by Jev are thought to be suffering from in TNG episode "Violations."

Irillium
substance which, when mixed with ryetalyn, renders ryetalyn useless in Classic episode "Requiem For Methuselah." (See entry for ryetalyn.)

Irish Unification of 2024
referred to by Data in TNG episode "The High Ground."

IS THERE IN TRUTH NO BEAUTY?
written by Jean Lissette Aroeste and directed by Ralph Senensky, this third season Classic Trek episode aired 10/18/68. The *Enterprise* transports the Medusan ambassador Kollos and his blind assistant back to his home planet. The assistant must be blind to work with Kollos, who is kept in a box, because it is said anyone who looks at the Medusan will go insane. In order to protect the ambassador from attempted murder, Spock inadvertantly sees him. Guest stars: Diana

Muldaur and David Frankham. Of note: In this episode, the Vulcan philosophical symbol, IDIC, makes its first appearance. Roddenberry wrote the symbol into the script because he wanted to sell the newly invented medallion through his company, Lincoln Enterprises.

ISAK
Zeon native, played by Richard Evans, whose brother is named Abrom in Classic episode "Patterns of Force."

ISCOVE, ROBERT
director of TNG "The Icarus Factor."

ISHIKAWA, KEIKO
see entry for O'Brien, Keiko.

ISIS
name of Gary Seven's sleek black cat, with which he seems to have some kind of mental telepathy, in Classic episode "Assignment: Earth." At the end of the episode, Roberta Lincoln sees the cat change into a woman for a few seconds, but what the cat's natural image actually is remains a mystery.

Isis III
destination of the *Enterprise* in TNG episode "Too Short A Season."

Isolinear chips
computer storage used by *Enterprise* in TNG episode "The Drumhead."

ITO, ROBERT
played Tactical Officer Chang in TNG "Coming of Age."

ITZKOWITZ, HOWARD
played the cargo deck ensign in "Star Trek: The Motion Picture." His credits include a regular role in the variety show "Marie" and the movie "Amateur Night At The Dixie Bar And Grill."

Iverson's Disease
disease for which Admiral Mark Jameson takes Cerberan youth drugs, which eventually kill him, in TNG episode "Too Short A Season."

Izar
home of Garth of Izar in Classic episode "Whom Gods Destroy."

J'DDAN
Romulan spy, played by Henry Woronicz, who masquarades as a Klingon exchange exobiologist during a visit to the *Enterprise* in TNG episode "The Drumhead."

J'naii
androgenous race which does not allow itself to act as a single gender in TNG episode "The Outcast."

J'ONN
man on Nimbus III, played by Rex Holman, who joins Sybok in his search for ShaKaRee in the film "The Final Frontier."

J25 system
location Q sends the *Enterprise* in TNG episode "Q Who" where they first encounter the Borg.

JA'ROD

Duras' father in TNG episode "Sins of the Fathers."

Jack The Ripper

an entity which feeds off fear and possesses people on various worlds, making them commit serial murders. It is called Redjac, Kesla and Beratis on the worlds it has visited. It inhabits the body of Hengist on Argelius II in Classic episode "Wolf In The Fold."

JACKSON, SHERRY

played Andrea in Classic Trek "What Are Little Girls Made Of?" Her credits include a regular role as one of the children in "The Danny Thomas Show," and appearances in "Lost In Space" and "Gunsmoke." Her films include "Wild Woman," "The Girl On The Late, Late Show," "Returning Home" and"Casino."

JACKSON

member, played by Jimmy Jones, of the landing party on Pyris VII who is killed and beamed back to the ship as a warning for others to stay away in Classic episode "Catspaw."

JACOBS, JAKE

scriptwriter for TNG "Sarek."

JACOBSEN, JILL

played Vanessa in TNG "The Royale."

JAEGER, LIEUTENANT KARL

member, played by Richard Carlyle, of the landing party on Gothos in

Classic episode "The Squire of Gothos."

JAGLOM SHREK

character in TNG episode "Birthright" who takes Worf to Carraya in search of his father.

JAHIL, CAPTAIN

captain of an alien ship in DS9 episode "Babel."

JAHN

Miri's paranoid and conniving friend, played by Michael J. Pollard, the oldest boy in Classic episode "Miri."

Jakmanite

element which can break down glass mentioned in TNG episode "Hollow Pursuits."

Jamaharohn

reference to sex on Risa in TNG episode "Captain's Holiday."

JAMAL, YEOMAN ZAHRA

member, played Maurisha Taliferro, of the landing party on Deneva in Classic episode "Operation: Annihilate!"

JAMES, ANTHONY

played Thei in TNG "The Neutral Zone."

JAMES, LOREN

stunt man for Norman in Classic Trek "I, Mudd."

JAMES, RICHARD D.

production designer of TNG.

JAMESON, ANNE

wife, played by Marsha Hunt, of Admiral Mark

Jameson in TNG episode "Too Short A Season."

JAMESON, MARK

a Starfleet Admiral, played by Clayton Rohner, who dies of a Cerberan rejuvenation drug overdose in TNG episode "Too Short A Season."

Janaran Falls

Betazoid location where Riker and Troi last met before Riker was stationed on the *Potemkin* in TNG episode "Second Chances."

JANOWSKY, MARY

young girl, played by Pamelyn Ferdin, whose parents commit suicide because of the Gorgon's influence in Classic episode "And The Children Shall Lead."

JANSSEN, FAMKE

played Kamala in TNG "The Perfect Mate."

Janus VI

mineral treasure house which had been mined by the Federation for fifty years before encountering the Horta in Classic episode "Devil In The Dark."

Jarada

mentioned by Riker in TNG episode "Samaritan Snare" and described as a new Federation ally with insectoid people obsessed by protocol In "The Big Goodbye."

JARIS

prefect of Argelius II whose wife Sybo is murdered by the entity inhabiting Hengist in Classic episode "Wolf In The Fold."

JAROK, ADMIRAL ALIDAR

officer, played by James Sloyan, who poses as Sublieutenant Setal in order to defect to the Federation but eventually commits suicide in TNG episode "The Defector."

Jaros II

location of the Starfleet prison facility where Ensign Ro was confined in TNG episode "Ensign Ro."

JARVIS, GRAHAM

played Klin Dokachin in TNG "Unification Part I."

JARVIS, RON

scriptwriter for TNG "Disaster."

JASAL, GUL

Cardassian character, played by Joel Swetow, in DS9 episode "Emissary."

JASON, HARVEY

played Felix Leech in TNG "The Big Goodbye."

Jat'yln

Klingon word meaning "taking the living by the dead" mentioned in TNG episode "Power Play."

JAY, TONY

played Campio in TNG "Cost of Living."

JAYA

asylum inmate who claims to be Commander Bloom of the *Yosemite* in TNG episode "Frame of Mind."

JEDDA

researcher on Regula I, played by John Vargas, who is killed in "The Wrath of Khan."

Jeffries Tube
tunnel-like area on the *Enterprise* through which crewmembers access various delicate parts of the ship for repair.

JELLICOE, CAPTAIN EDWARD
takes command of the *Enterprise* when Picard is captured by the Cardassians in TNG episode "Chain of Command." He immediately decorates the ready room with his young son's artwork depicting elephants and does not get along well with Riker.

JEMISON, MAE
guest-starred in TNG episode "Second Chances."

JENKINS, KEN
played Paul Stubbs in TNG "Evolution."

JENNINGS, JOSEPH R.
production designer on "The Wrath of Khan." He has also done work on the movies "Yellowbeard" and "Johnny Dangerously."

JENNINGS, JUNERO
played an engine room technician in "Star Trek: The Motion Picture." She has had other small roles, including an appearance in "Stone."

Jenok
Klingon necklace given to a girl who has come of age in TNG episode "Birthright."

Jenolan
transport ship which has been missing for 75 years and is found by the *Enterprise* crashed into the Dyson sphere in TNG

episode "Relics." Montgomery Scott, preserved in a transporter pattern, is found on the ship.

JENS, SALOME
actress who guest starred in TNG episode "The Chase."

JENSEN, KEITH L.
stunt man in "Star Trek: The Motion Picture."

JENSON, LEN
scriptwriter of the animated episode "Once Upon A Planet."

JENSON, ROY
played Cloud William in Classic Trek "The Omega Glory." His film credits include "Ride Lonesome," "Powerkeg," "Hit Lady," "Nightside," "Honkytonk Man" and "Last of the Great Survivors." He has also appeared on the TV shows "The Man From U.N.C.L.E." and "Voyage To The Bottom Of The Sea."

JETER, K.W.
author of DS9 novel *Bloodletter*.

JEV
character from Ullian, played by Ben Lemon, who mind rapes some of the *Enterprise* crew in TNG episode "Violations."

Jewel of Thesia
the prized possession of the planet Streleb (in the Coalition of Medina) thought to have been stolen by Captain Okona in TNG episode "The Outrageous Okona." It was actually taken by Benzan,

the son of Streleb leader Kushell, for a wedding gift.

JEWELL, AUSTEN
unit production manager for "Star Trek: The Motion Picture." He has also worked on the 1950's films "Gunfight At Dodge City" and "Cast A Long Shadow."

JEWELL, LOIS
played Drusilla in Classic Trek "Bread and Circuses."

JIHAD
written by Stephen Kandel, this animated Classic Trek episode aired 1/13/74. Kirk and Spock, along with other members of alien ships, are chosen for a secret mission to find the Soul of Skorr and stop the break out of a holy war. Guest voice: David Gerrold (Em/3/Green.)

JIL ORRA
young daughter of Picard's Cardassian tormentor, Bul Madred, in TNG episode "Chain of Command."

JILESTRA, SABIN
Admiral Satie's Betazoid aide, played by Bruce French, in TNG episode "Chain of Command."

JO'BRIL, DR.
Takaran scientist who fakes his own death but comes back to life while on a shuttle with Crusher who kills him in TNG episode "Suspicions."

JOAQUIM
Khan's right hand man, played by Judson Scott (whose name does not appear in the credits,) in the film "The Wrath of Khan."

JOAQUIN
Khan's right hand man, played by Mark Tobin, in Classic episode "Space Seed."

JOCHIM, ANTHONY
played a survivor in the Classic Trek pilot "The Cage." He has appeared in "The Big Fisherman" ('59) and "One Step Beyond."

JOHNSON, ALEXANDRA
played One Zero in TNG "11001001."

JOHNSON, GEORGANN
played Admiral Gromek in TNG "The Emissary."

JOHNSON, GEORGE CLAYTON
scriptwriter of Classic Trek "The Man Trap" and often a featured speaker at Star Trek conventions. A science fiction writer and the author of the movie and book "Logan's Run," he also wrote for "The Twilight Zone" among other TV shows.

JOHNSON, JOAN
played a guard in Classic Trek "Space Seed."

JOHNSON, JULIE
stunt woman who doubled for Yeoman Landon in Classic Trek "The Apple."

JOHNSON, KATIE JANE
played the "child Martia" who led Kirk and McCoy through small tunnels and out of prison in "The Undiscovered Country."

JOHNSON, ELAINE
old woman, played by Laura Wood, who is dying

in Classic episode "The Deadly Years."

JOHNSON, LIEUTENANT
man, played by David L. Ross, wounded in battle who heals quickly and rejoins the fray in Classic episode "Day of the Dove."

JOHNSON, ROBERT
old man, played by Felix Locher, in Classic episode "The Deadly Years" who is really 29 years old.

Joining
Betazoid marriage ceremony performed in the nude mentioned in TNG episode "Haven."

JOL, ETANA
leader of the Ktarans who gives an addictive game to Riker in TNG episode "The Game."

JONES, JAY
played Ensign Mallory in Classic Trek "The Apple" and Mirt in "A Piece Of The Action." He was also a stunt man in several episodes, including as a double for Scotty in "Who Mourns For Adonais." His other credits include "Man On The Outside" and "The Man From U.N.C.L.E."

JONES, JIMMY
played Jackson in Classic Trek "Catspaw."

JONES, JUDITH
played one of the Edo children in TNG "Justice."

JONES, MORGAN
played Colonel Nesvig in Classic Trek "Assignment: Earth." He also starred in the TV series "Blue Angels"

in 1960. His film credits include "Doctors' Private Lives," "Advice To The Lovelorn" and "The Red Light Sting."

JONES, RENEE
played Lt. Aquiel Uhnari in TNG episode "Aquiel."

JONES, RON
composer of incidental music for dozens of TNG episodes.

JONES, DR. MIRANDA
blind, telepathic aide, played by Diana Muldaur, to Kollos. Her jealousy, pride and bitterness about her handicap threatens the lives of others in Classic episode "Is There In Truth No Beauty?"

JONES, CYRANO
con man, played by Stanley Adams, who will sell anything to anyone. He is responsible for the tribble infestation on board the *Enterprise* and on Space Station K 7 in Classic episode "Is There In Truth No Beauty?" Adams was also a Trek scriptwriter. (See entry for Adams, Stanley.)

JORDAN, ENSIGN
android, played by Michael Zaslow, controlled by Harry Mudd, who takes over the *Enterprise* in Classic episode "I, Mudd."

JOSEPHS, LIEUTENANT
officer, played by James X. Mitchell, who finds Ambassador Gav's body in Classic episode "Journey To Babel."

Jouret IV
site of a colony completely wiped out by the Borg in TNG episode "The Best of Both Worlds."

JOURNEY TO BABEL
written by D.C. Fontana and directed by Joseph Pevney, this second season Classic Trek episode aired 11/17/67. Spock's parents, Amanda and Ambassador Sarek, who is dying from a heart condition, board the *Enterprise* which is shuttling ambassadors and their families to the important Babel Conference. Meanwhile someone is killing the ambassadors. Guest stars: Mark Lenard, Jane Wyatt, William O'Connell, Reggie Nalder and John Wheeler. Of note: Spock's childhood pet, a large furry beast with six inch fangs called a Sehlat, is mentioned in this episode.

JOVAL
flirtatious character, played by Dierdre Imershein, who tells Picard how to display the Horga'hn on Risa in TNG episode "Captain's Holiday."

Jovis
Kivas Fajo's ship in TNG episode "The Most Toys."

JUDD, ASHLEY
played Robin Lefler in TNG "Darmok" and "The Game." She is Naomi's younger daughter and Wynona's sister, of the former country superstar team The Judds.

JudgeAdvocate General's Corps
Starfleet legal affairs branch mentioned in TNG episode "The Measure of a Man."

JULIAN, HEIDI
production coordinator of DS9.

JUNG, NATHAN
played Genghis Khan in Classic Trek "The Savage Curtain."

Jupiter Eight
car seen in a magazine in Classic episode "Bread and Circuses."

JUSTICE
first season TNG episode written by Worley Thorne and Ralph Willis and directed by James L. Conway. The inhabitants of Rubicam III welcome the crew openly but their "god," orbiting overhead, does not want the *Enterprise* interfering with her children. Guest stars: Josh Clark, David Q. Combs, Richard Lavin, Judith Jones, Eric Matthew, Brad Zerbst and David Michael Graves.

JUSTMAN, ROBERT
associate producer of Classic Trek's first two seasons and supervising producer on "Star Trek: The Next Generation." He also worked on the show "Stoney Burke" and produced "Then Came Bronson" as well as the pilot for the series "The Man From Atlantis" (with Herb Solow) and "Planet Earth" (with Gene Roddenberry.)

Justman
Enterprise shuttlecraft upon which Dr. Reyga's experimental metaphasic shielding is tested. The shuttle is piloted into the star Vaytan in TNG episode "Suspicions."

K'EHLEYR
half Klingon, half human woman, played by Suzie Plakson, who had an affair with Worf six years prior to appearing as an emissary for the T'Ong situation in TNG episode "The Emissary."

K'MPEC
leader of the Klingon Council, played by Charles Cooper, in TNG episode "Sins of the Fathers."

K'NERA, CAPTAIN
commander, played by David Froman, of the Klingon vessel in TNG episode "Heart of Glory."

K'Tarans
race which attempts to take over Starfleet by using an addictive game to control the officers in TNG episode "The Game."

K'TEMOC
Klingon leader of the T'Ong, played by Lance LeGault, who had been in cryonic sleep for 75 years in TNG episode "The Emissary."

K'VADA, CAPTAIN
Klingon captain who takes Picard and Data to the Romulan homeworld in TNG episode "Unification."

K'vort Class Battlecruisers
class of ship named after Klingon birds of prey in TNG episode "Yesterday's Enterprise."

K 7, Space Station
located near Sherman's planet, the site of the battle of Donatu V mentioned in Classic episode "The Trouble With Tribbles."

Kabatris
world where Riker wore fancy robes to impress its leaders mentioned in TNG episode "Angel One."

Kaelon II
planet threatened by its dying star, where the inhabitants believe in involuntary suicide at age 60, performed in a ceremony called the Resolution. Dr. Timicin, a Kaelon scientist who is about to turn 60, developed a theory to relight his homeworld's star but his people insist he must fulfill the death ritual in TNG episode "Half A Life."

Kaferian apples
Mitchell creates Kaferian apple trees on Delta Vega with his newfound talents in Classic episode "Where No Man Has Gone Before."

KAGEN, JANET
noted science fiction author of Classic Trek novel *Uhura's Song* and winner of the Hugo award for science fiction.

KAHLESS
famous ancient Klingon, known as "The Unforgettable," responsible for bringing Klingon culture together into a warrior society. Klingon myth says he will reappear one day to lead Klingons into a new, gteater era. He appears in Classic episode "The Savage Curtain," played by Robert Herron, and in TNG episode "Rightful Heir" in which he is a clone of himself.

KAHLEST
Worf's nurse, played by Thelma Lee, and only survivor from the massacre at the Khitomer Outpost. She appears again after a long silence to help Worf in the TNG episode "Sins of the Fathers."

KAHN, JAMES
scriptwriter of TNG "The Masterpiece Society."

Kahs-wan
Vulcan test of manhood taken by all seven year old boys, during which they must journey alone into the desert and learn how to survive for ten days, mentioned in the animated episode "Yesteryear."

KAI
Bajoran term for an elder or revered member of society in DS9.

KAIL, JAMES
make up artist on "The Search For Spock."

Kalandans
dead civilization which succumbed to an unknown disease leaving behind only an outpost and the computer-generated vision of Losira in Classic episode "That Which Survives."

Kaldra IV
world to which the *Enterprise* is delivering a Ullian delegation of telepathic historians in TNG episode "Violations."

Kaleb Sector
location for a rendezvous between the Romulan warbird *Khazara* and a Corvallen ship in TNG episode "Face of the Enemy."

KALI
female Klingon in animated episode "Time Trap."

Kalifee
a Vulcan term meaning "challenge" used in Classic episode "Amok Time."

KALIN TROSE
see entry for Trose, Kalin.

Kallisko
ship whose crew is killed by the Crystalline Entity in TNG episode "Silicon Avatar."

KALO
one of Oxmyx's gunmen, played by Lee Delano, in Classic episode "A Piece of the Action."

KALOMI, LEILA
colony botanist, played by Jill Ireland, on Omicron Ceti III and Spock's friend six years before he has a "spore induced" love affair with her in Classic episode "This Side of Paradise."

KAMAL, JON

played the Vulcan Sonak in "Star Trek: The Motion Picture."

KAMAL, STANLEY

played Kosinski in TNG "Where No One Has Gone Before."

KAMALA

empathic metamorph from Krios, played by Famke Janssen, promised to be Chancellor Alrik of Valt's wife but who accidentally bonds with Picard. She carries out her duty, however, and marries the Chancellor although he can no longer be her perfect mate in TNG episode "The Perfect Mate."

KAMIN

Picard's name on Kataan where, according to a memory installed in his subconcious, he plays the flute and has a son, Batai, a daughter, Maribor, and a wife, Eline in TNG episode "The Inner Light."

KANDEL, STEPHEN

scriptwriter of Classic Trek "Mudd's Women," "I, Mudd," and the animated episodes "Mudd's Passion" and "The Jihad." A co-creator of the series "Iron Horse," he also wrote for "Green Hornet" and "Wonder Woman" and was producer of the series "McGiver."

KANG

captain of a Klingon ship, played by Michael Ansara, in Classic episode "Day of the Dove."

Kanutu

one of a tribe of Neural hill people who have knowledge of herbs and roots which can cure sickness in Classic episode "A Private Little War."

KAPEC, REENA

Flint's android ward, played by Louise Sorel, who dies from emotional overload when she is forced to choose between her newfound love for Kirk and her loyal love for Flint in Classic episode "Requiem For Methuselah."

KAPLAN, SOL

composer for Classic Trek episodes "The Enemy Within," "The Doomsday Machine," "The Deadly Years," "Obsession," "The Immunity Syndrome" and "The Ultimate Computer." He has also written scores for such movies as "Tales of Manhattan" and "The Spy Who Came In From The Cold."

KAPLAN

security guard, played by Dick Dial, killed by a lightning bolt in Classic episode "The Apple."

KARA

cafe dancer, played by Tania Lemani, on Argelius II in Classic episode "Wolf In The Fold." In "Spock's Brain," a woman named Kara, played by Marj Dusay, is the Eymorg who steals Spock's brain. Her planet is Sigma Draconis VI.

KARAPLEEDEEZ, ONNA

Starfleet officer who was a victim of a Starfleet conspiracy in TNG episode "Conspiracy."

KARAS, GREG

played the intern in "The Voyage Home."

KARATOK

author of *The Dream of Fire*, a book given to Data in TNG episode "The Measure of a Man."

KAREEL

name of the female body, played by Nicole Orth-Pallaviicini, which hosts the Trill Ambassador Odan who was Dr. Crusher's lover while hosted in a male body in TNG episode "The Host."

KARELKIE

Enterprise security officer on the away team to Ohniaka in TNG episode "Descent."

Karema III

world mentioned as a mining possibility in TNG episode "The Quality of Life."

KAREN, ANNA

played "woman" in Classic Trek "All Our Yesterdays."

KARF

gunman, played by Buddy Garion, for Krako in Classic episode "A Piece of the Action."

KARGAN, CAPTAIN

commander, played by Christopher Collins, of the Klingon ship *Pagh* in TNG episode "A Matter of Honor."

KARIDIAN, ANTON

actor, played by Arnold Moss, who heads the Karidian players, and whom Kirk thinks is really Kodos the Executioner responsible for the execution of half the population of Tarsus IV during a famine. Karidian is later killed by his own daughter, Lenore, in Classic episode "The Conscience of the King." (See entry for Kodos.)

KARIDIAN, LENORE

nineteen year old member, played by Barbara Anderson, of the Karidian company of players and daughter of Anton Karidian. She went insane as a child when she secretly found out her father was responsible for a mass genocide. She accidentally phasers him to death in Classic episode "The Conscience of the King."

Karidian Players

travelling troupe of actors, sponsored by the Galactic Cultural Exchange Program, who have been performing together for nine years in Classic episode "The Conscience of the King."

Karl 4

Karla 5's son from animated episode "The Counter Clock Incident" who is from Arret where time runs backwards.

KARLA 5

character from Arret who ages backwards in the animated episode "The Counter Clock Incident."

KARNAS

governor of Mordan IV, played by Michael Pataki, who kidnaps a group of Starfleet people as revenge against Admiral Jameson in TNG episode "Too Short A Season."

Karst Topography

planet filled with sinkholes, underground caverns and rivers which confuse the *Enterprise* sensors in TNG episode "Who Watches the Watchers."

Kartag

Klingon ship in TNG episode "Heart of Glory."

KARTAN

Denevan native, played by Fred Carson, in Classic episode "Operation: Annihilate!"

KARTOZIAN, THOMAS

scriptwriter of TNG "Galaxy's Child."

Kataan

world where Picard lives an entire life in virtual reality while inside a probe in TNG episode "The Inner Light." His experience makes him the foremost authority on the dead civilization.

KATARINA, ANNA

played Valeda Innis in TNG "Haven."

KATIE

one of the children, played by Jandi Swanson, kidnapped by the Aldeans in TNG episode "When The Bough Breaks."

Katra

Vulcan term for the soul which they can supposedly transfer to another person at death as seen in "The Search For Spock."

KATSULAS, ANDREAS

played Commander Tomalak in TNG "The Enemy" and "Future Imperfect."

KAVA, CAROLINE

played Dr. Toby Russell in TNG "Ethics."

Kavis Alpha IV

site of the new nanite colony in TNG episode "Evolution."

Kavis Alpha Sector

location to which the *Enterprise* travels to study a stellar explosion that happens once every 196 years in TNG episode "Evolution."

KAYRON

Ferengi, played by Tracey Walter, under command of DaiMon Tarr in TNG episode "The Last Outpost."

KAZ

Klingon officer, second in command to Kor in animated episode "Time Trap."

KAZAGO

Ferengi first officer, played by Doug Warhit, under command of DaiMon Bok in TNG episode "The Battle."

Kazanga

genius as big as Einstein or the Vulcan Sikar, mentioned in Classic episode "The Ultimate Computer."

Kazis Binary System

location where an Earth capsule is found mentioned in TNG episode "The Neutral Zone."

KEEFER, DON

played Cromwell in Classic Trek "Assigment: Earth." Other credits include "Angel," "The Guns of Will Sonnett" and "Iron Horse." His films include "The Bait," "The Immigrants," "Marathon," "The Five Of Me" and "Creepshow."

KEEL, ANNE AND MELISSA

sisters of Walker Keel who never appear but are mentioned in TNG episode "Conspiracy."

KEEL, CAPTAIN WALKER

officer, played by Jonathan Farwell, who warns Picard of a Starfleet conspiracy in TNG episode "Conspiracy." He served with Picard and Jack Crusher aboard the *Stargazer* and introduced Beverly to Jack.

KEEL

Capellan, played by Cal Bolder, who kills the Klingon Kras in Classic episode "Friday's Child."

KEELER, EDITH

socialworker, played by Joan Collins, on Earth during the 1920's with whom Kirk falls in love in Classic episode "The City On The Edge Of Forever." McCoy changes history when he saves her life but her eventual death when she is hit by a truck restores history as we know it.

Keeper

Talosian zoo keeper, played by Meg Wyllie, in Classic episodes "The Menagerie" and "The Cage." Malachi Throne plays the zoo keeper's voice.

KEEVE, FALOR

Bajoran member of the underground in TNG episode "Ensign Ro."

KEHLER, JACK

appeared in DS9 "Babel."

KEHOE, PATRICK

first assistant director on "The Voyage Home." He was also assistant director on "Poltergeist," "Things Are Tough All Over," "Bad Boys," "Twilight Zone: The Movie" and "The Philadelphia Experiment."

KEIKO O'BRIEN

see entry for O'Brien, Keiko.

KELINDA

Kelvin female, played by Barbara Bouchet, and Rojan's apparent love interest whom Kirk tries to distract by seducing her in Classic episode "By Any Other Name."

KELL, AMBASSADOR

Klingon official in league with the Romulans who brainwashes LaForge into attempting the assassination of Governor Vagh in TNG episode "The Mind's Eye."

KELLER, DORE

played a crewman in TNG "The Child."

KELLERMAN, SALLY

played Dr. Elizabeth Dehner on Classic Trek "Where No Man Has Gone Before." Born in 1938, her other film credits include "M*A*S*H," "Reform School Girl," "Lost Horizon," "Serial," and others. She studied under actor Jeff Corey, who played Plasus in "The Cloud Minders."

KELLETT, PETE

played Kirk's henchman in Classic Trek "Mirror, Mirror." He had a recurring role on "Branded" and "The Man From U.N.C.L.E."

KELLEY, DEFOREST

starred as Dr. Leonard (Bones) McCoy in the Classic and animated series and all six Trek movies. He also appeared as the old doctor in TNG "Encounter At Farpoint." Born in Atlanta, Georgia in 1920, the son of a Baptist minister, he moved to California at age seventeen after graduating from high school. He did radio work before signing on with Paramount in the 1940's, after which he worked as a stage and TV actor in both New York and Los Angeles. His TV credits include "Schlitz Theatre," "Playhouse 90," "Gunsmoke," "You Are There," "Navy Log," "Science Fiction Theatre," "Zane Grey Theatre," "Rawhide" and "Bonanza." He appeared in the films "Fear In The Night," "Canon City," "Gunfight At Comanche Creek," "Illegal," "Marriage on the Rocks," "The Men," "Variety Girl," "View From Pompey's Head," "Waco," "Duke of Chicago," "House of Bamboo," "Tension At Table Rock," "Gunfight At the O.K. Corral," "Raintree Country," "The Law and Jake Wade," "Black Spurs," "Town Tamer," "Warlock," "Gunfight," "Johnny Reno," "Apache Uprising" and "Where Love Has Gone." Roddenberry originally wanted Kelley for the role of Mr. Spock, but Kelley refused, taking the small role of a lieutenant instead in the series, his first. He did two other (non Trek) pilots for Roddenberry before the producer decided to give him the role of the doctor (after a series of other doctor characters did not work out.) A fortune teller once told Kelley during the 1940's that his greatest success would not occur until after he reached 40, and she was right. However, Kelley, who likes to be called "De," had a difficult time playing second fiddle to William Shatner and Leonard Nimoy. Kelley claims a Star Trek producer once wrote an episode which did not include him and the writer later apologized, explaining that Kelley's exclusion was an oversight. His favorite episode is "The Deadly Years," because of the challenge involved playing an aging McCoy. It is a well known Classic Trek tradition that McCoy gets the best, and often the last, lines in each episode.

KELLEY, IRENE

played Sirah in Classic Trek "The Omega Glory."

KELLICK, ROBIN

stand-in in the movie "The Search For Spock."

KELLY, CHIEF ENGINEER

officer of the *Yosemite* killed while trying to take cover in a transporter stream in TNG episode "Realm of Fear."

KELLY

security guard killed by the Horta in Classic episode "Devil in the Dark."

KELOWITZ, LIEUTENANT LEE

security guard, played by Grant Woods, who searches for the shuttle on the wrong world in Classic episode "The Galileo Seven". Kelowitz also appears in "Arena" and "This Side of Paradise."

KELSEY

leader who dies, along with her team, while trying to steal trilithium from the *Enterprise* in TNG episode "Starship Mine." Devor, Kiros, Neil and Pompet are other members of the team.

KELSO, CHIEF

Enterprise transporter tech in TNG episode "The Quality of Life."

KELSO, LIEUTENANT LEE

helmsman, played by Paul Carr, who is strangled by Gary Mitchell with a cord in Classic episode "Where No Man Has Gone Before."

Kelvans

multi-tendrilled creatures from Kelva, a planet ruled by the Kelvan empire in the Andromeda galaxy, who disguise themselves as humans and try to take over the *Enterprise* in Classic episode "By Any Other Name." They want to conquer the Milky Way because their own Andromeda Galaxy will not be able to support life in the future.

KELVEN, MAX

played Maximus in Classic Trek "Bread and Circuses."

KEMP, JEREMY

played Robert Picard in TNG "Family."

KEMPER, DAVID

scriptwriter of TNG "Peak Performance" and "The Enemy."

KENICLIUS, DR. STAVOS

scientist, whose voice is played by James Doohan, responsible for the Eugenics Wars when people were cloned into super humans. He traveled to the planet Phylos where he cloned himself several times before the *Enterprise* encounters him in the animated episode "The Infinite Vulcan."

KENNELLY, ADMIRAL

Starfleet officer, played by Cliff Potts, who conspires with the Cardassian Gul Dolak to kill the Bajoran rebel leader Orta in TNG episode "Ensign Ro."

KENNER, COMMANDER

mentioned in Classic episode "Mirror, Mirror," as a man who plans to temporarily take Marlena, the captain's woman, after she moves out of Kirk's cabin.

KENNEY, SEAN
played the injured Captain Pike in Classic Trek "The Menagerie Parts I and II," and Lt. DePaul in the episodes "Arena" and "A Taste of Armageddon."

KENT, PAUL
played Beach in "The Wrath of Khan." Other film credits include "The Astronaut," "Pray For The Wildcats" (with William Shatner,) "The Night They Took Miss Beautiful" and "If Things Were Different." He also appeared on the TV series "The Man From U.N.C.L.E.," "Alias Smith and Jones" and "Griff."

KENTOR
played by Richard Allen, a supporter of Data in TNG episode "The Ensigns of Command."

KENWITH, HERB
director of the Classic Trek "The Lights of Zetar."

KEPPLER, WERNER
make up artist on "The Wrath of Khan."

KEPROS, NICHOLAS
played Movar in TNG "Redemption Part I and II."

KERN, DAN
played Lt. Dean in TNG "We'll Always Have Paris."

Kesla
one of several names used to refer to the Jack the Ripper entity in Classic episode "Wolf In The Fold."

Kevas
a dealer in kevas and trillium, which are never defined, mentioned in Classic episode "Errand of Mercy."

KHAMBATTA, PERSIS
starred as Ilia in "Star Trek: The Motion Picture." Born in Bombay, India in 1950, she first worked as a model and was crowned Miss India at age 16. Her film credits include "The Wilby Conspiracy," "Conduct Unbecoming," "Nighthawks" and "Megaforce." She has also guest starred on the TV series "Hunter," "McGiver" and "The New Mike Hammer."

KHAN, GHENGIS
character, played by Nathan Jung, who appears to fight Kirk, Spock, Lincoln and Surak in Classic episode "The Savage Curtain."

KHAN
see entry for Singh, Khan Noonian.

Khazara
name of the Romulan ship on which Troi awakens in TNG episode "Face of the Enemy."

Khitomer
mentioned as the site of Worf's father's death during a Romulan attack called the Khitomer Massacre in TNG episode "Sins of the Fathers." It is also the location of a peace conference between the Federation and the Klingons, during which an attempt to assassinate the Federation president is thwarted by Kirk in "The Undiscovered Country."

Khoth'va
Klingon term meaning "ritual hunt" mentioned in TNG episode "Birthright."

KIM, DR. LUISA
assistant director, played by Elizabeth Lindsey, of the Gardeners of Eden on Velara III in TNG episode "Home Soil."

KING DUNCAN
a member of the Karidian players, played by Karl Bruck, in Classic episode "The Conscience of the King."

KINGSBRIDGE, JOHN
scriptwriter of Classic Trek "Return To Tomorrow."

KINGSLEY, DANITZA
played Ariana in TNG "Haven."

KINGSLEY, DR. SARA
chief researcher, played by Patricia Smith, at the Darwin Genetic Research Station in TNG episode "Unnatural Selection."

KINO, LLOYD
played Wu in Classic Trek "The Omega Glory." His credits include "Seizure: The Appearance of Kathy Morris," (with Leonard Nimoy,) "Hammett" and "Forced Vengeance." Other TV appearances include "The Man From U.N.C.L.E." and "Voyage To The Bottom Of The Sea."

KIR
Scalosian extra in Classic episode "Wink of an Eye."

KIRA, MAJOR
see entry for Nerys, Major Kira.

KIRK, AURELAN
played by Joan Swift, wife of George Samuel "Sam" Kirk, James Kirk's brother, both of whom die when infected by the stinger of the parasites in Classic episode "Operation: Annihilate!" Her son, Peter, survives.

KIRK, GEORGE SAMUEL
James Kirk's older brother, a research biologist, who dies, with his wife Aurelan, in Classic episode "Operation: Annihilate!" All that is known about him is that Kirk calls him "Sam" and he had (according to *The Making of Star Trek*) three sons. One son, Peter, survives the parasite attack and is rescued from Deneva but the other two are never mentioned. Sam's only appearance is as a corpse and the actor who played him is not credited.

KIRK, JAMES TIBERIUS
captain of the *Enterprise* in Classic Trek and the six films. He is promoted to Admiral by the "The Motion Picture" but in "The Voyage Home" he is reduced back to captain as punishment for going against orders to rescue Spock from Genesis. The youngest captain in Starfleet when he took command of the *Enterprise* at age 34, his heroes include Abraham Lincoln and Garth of Izar. He seems well versed in literature, sometimes quoting famous poetry, and he loves books, antiques, Earth history and sports. He is very ambitious, a natural leader with a great imagination and a

tendency to use it to get what he wants. Kirk does not want to grow old gracefully and resents age although in the films it does not seem to hamper his ability to command. His best friends are Spock and McCoy. He had a son with Carol Marcus, David, who was killed by Kruge in "The Search For Spock." Kirk's only other child died unborn when the child's mother, Miramanee, was killed in Classic episode "The Paradise Syndrome." However Kirk could have other, unknown children since he has had several affairs with women in the past. Kirk is excited by challenge; even while on vacation he will find risky things to do (such as free climbing in Yosemite in "The Final Frontier.") He is excellent in hand to hand combat, has a quick mind and a great sense of humor, qualities which have made him a great Starfleet hero and a legend across the galaxy.

KIRK, PETER
son-in-law of James Kirk and son of Sam Kirk, he is the only Kirk, played by Craig Hundley (who also played Tommy Starnes in "And the Children Shall Lead") mentioned as a survivor of the parasite attack on Deneva in Classic episode "Operation: Annihilate!"

Kirok
name Miramanee calls Kirk when she can't remember his entire name in Classic episode "The Paradise Syndrome."

Kironide
substance which is found in Platonion food which affects the pituitary gland, allowing the Platonians to experience psychokinesis in Classic episode "Plato's Stepchildren."

KIROS
member of a team trying to steal trilithium from the *Enterprise* in TNG episode "Starship Mine."

Kithara
musical instrument given to Spock as a gift by the Platonians in Classic episode "Plato's Stepchildren."

KIVEL, BARRY
played the doorman in TNG "Time's Arrow Part I."

KLAG, LIEUTENANT
second in command, played by Brian Thompson, of the Klingon ship *Pagh* in TNG episode "A Matter of Honor."

KLASS, JUDY
author of Classic Trek novel *The Cry Of The Onlies.*

Klavdia III
planet on which Anya and Salia, born on Daled IV, have lived for 16 years in TNG episode "The Dauphin."

Kligat
Capellan weapon, much like a sharp-edged boomerang, seen in Classic episode "Friday's Child."

KLINE, RICHARD H.
director of photography on "Star Trek: The Motion Picture." His other credits include "The Andromeda Strain," "Battle For The Planet Of The Apes" and "King Kong" ('76).

Kling
also known as Klinzhai, the Klingon homeworld mentioned in TNG episode "Heart of Glory."

Klingon Death Ritual
involves opening the eyes of the dead person, lifting the head and loudly crying out, performed in TNG episode "Heart of Glory."

Klingon Oath
part of the Klingon marriage ceremony.

Klingon Pain Sticks
long rods which inflict pain in TNG episode "The Icarus Factor."

Klingon Sark
horse.

Klingon Tea Ceremony
ceremony during which Klingon love poetry is recited. The tea is said to be deadly to humans and has ill effects on Klingons as well. Pulaski and Worf share the tea, but Pulaski first takes an antidote to the poison in TNG episode "Up The Long Ladder."

Klingonese
the language of the Klingons, also known as Klingoni.

Klingons
alien race whose culture is based on a warrior code honoring strength, combat and ritual. They appear very violent and aggressive in Classic Trek but by the TNG era they are allies of the Federation, an alliance first introduced in "The Motion Picture." In Classic Trek, Klingons appear dark and swarthy but are later given more alien distinctions in the films and TNG, appearing with ridged foreheads and long hair.

KLOOG
a thrall, played by Mickey Morton, on Triskelion in Classic episode "The Gamesters of Triskelion."

KLOTHOS
name of a Klingon battlecruiser in animated episode "Time Trap."

KLUNIS, TOM
appeared in DS9 "A Man Alone."

Klystron IV
where Dax, at the time Curzon Dax, was allegedly responsible for the murder of a famous military commander in DS9 episode "Dax."

KNEPPER, ROB
played Wyatt Miller in TNG "Haven."

KNEUBUHL, JOHN
scriptwriter of Classic Trek "Bread and Circuses."

KNICKERBOCKER, THOMAS
played the gunman in TNG "Clues."

Knife of Kirom
knife, stained with the blood of the real Kahless, used to test the authenticity of Kahless in TNG episode "Rightful Heir."

KNIGHT, WILLIAM
played the singing crewman in Classic Trek "The Naked Time."

KNIGHT, WYATT
played a technician in TNG "Coming Of Age."

KNOWLAND, JOE
played the antique store owner in "The Voyage Home."

KOCH, KENNY
played the kissing crewman in TNG "The Naked Now."

**KODOS
THE EXECUTIONER**
also known as Anton Karidian, Kodos was the governor on Tarsus IV who invoked martial law during a famine and executed half the colonists, supposedly choosing people thought to be inferior, in order to save the rest. However a supply ship arrived just after the incident and Kodos was held morally responsible for the deaths. He was supposedly burned to death but actually escaped with his daughter, Lenore, and created the Karidian company of actors as a disguise. Kirk and Kevin Riley, who witnessed his entire family killed, were the only two witnesses left who could identify Kodos, since they were children on Tarsus when the incident occurred.

KOENIG, WALTER
starred as Pavel Chekov in Classic Trek during its second and third season. He also wrote the animated script "The Infinite Vulcan," and has starred in all the Trek movies. Born in Chicago, Illinois on September 4, 1936, Koenig grew up in Manhattan and attended Grinnell College in Iowa where he studied pre-med and performed in summer productions. He later transferred to U.C.L.A. where he graduated with a B.A. in psychology while studying theatre with Arthur Friedman. He later moved to New York where he worked as a hospital orderly, and did off Broadway work for two years. His TV credits include "Day In Court," "Mr. Novak," "The Great Adventure," "Gidget," "Jerrico," "The Lieutenant," "Ben Casey," "Combat," "The Great Adventure," "Ironside," "Mannix," "Medical Center," "The Men From Shiloh," "The Untouchables," "I, Spy," and "Alfred Hitchcock Presents" in an episode titled "Memo From Purgatory" written by Harlan Ellison. (Koenig and Ellison remained good friends after the show.) His role on Star Trek was not meant to be permanent at first. When George Takei took ten weeks off to star in the John Wayne movie "The Green Berets," however, Koenig's character got the lines originally written for Sulu. It wasn't until the series' third season that he was signed on as a permanent character. His favorite episodes include "Spectre of the Gun," "I, Mudd," and "The Trouble With Tribbles." After Trek was cancelled, he had bit roles in "Columbo" (with William Shatner,) "Goodbye Raggedy Ann" (with Martin Sheen and Mia Farrow) and "The Questor Tapes" (with Mike Farrell and produced by Gene Roddenberry.) He also appeared in two episodes of "The Starlost," created by Harlan Ellison. He did more stage work, appeared at many Trek conventions and began concentrating on writing and selling scripts to the TV series "Family," "Class of '65," "The Powers of Matthew Star," and the Saturday morning show "Land of the Lost." He now writes a comic book "Raver," for Malibu Comics. His recent acting appearances include a starring role in the film "Moontrap" (a film which may have a sequel,) and an appearance in the film "Deadly Honeymoon." His wife, son and daughter are actors as well. His son appeared as a semi-regular character, Boner, on the sitcom "Growing Pains" and was billed both as Josh A. Koenig and Andrew Koenig. His daughter, Danielle, appeared in two episodes of "Life Goes On," and the short lived series "The Faneilli Boys." His wife, Judy Levitt, appeared with him and actor Mark Lenard (Sarek, The Romulan Commander, etc.,) in a one act play. She also appeared in "The Voyage Home" as a doctor. Koenig also works as an acting teacher, and continues to write. His book *Chekov's Enterprise* was recently updated and re-released.

Kohms
term referring to the Asian-looking villager people in Classic episode "The Omega Glory."

KOHNERT, MARY
played Ensign Tess Allenby in TNG "Final Mission" and "The Loss."

Koinonia
planet on which the Koinonians wiped themselves out in a war, leaving a second native species of energy beings to live alone on the world in TNG episode "The Bonding."

KOL
Goss's second aid, who, along with the first aid, Arridor, is marooned in TNG episode "The Price."

KOLBE, WINRICH
director of TNG episodes "Where Silence Has Lease," "Pen Pals," "Up The Long Ladder," "Evolution," "The Bonding," "Allegiance," "Identity Crisis," "Darmok," "The Masterpiece Society," "Cost of Living," "Man of the People," "Birthright," "Rightful Heir" and of DS9 episodes "Past Prologue" and "Vortex."

Kolem
Romulan unit of measure mentioned in TNG episode "The Next Phase."

Kolinahr
Vulcan rite which supposedly purges all emotion from the participant and gives them total logic. Spock attempts to complete the rite successfully for two years on Gol on

Vulcan prior to "The Motion Picture" and fails.

KOLLOS, AMBASSADOR
member of the telepathic Medusan race who is transported in a box because his appearance drives humans insane in Classic episode "Is There In Truth No Beauty?" He appears as a creature made up of a kaleidoscope of multi-colored flashing lights.

KOLOTH, CAPTAIN
Klingon, played by William Campbell, whose ship visits Space Station K 7 in Classic episode "The Trouble With Tribbles."

KOLRAMI, SIRNA
Zakdornian Starfleet strategist, played by Roy Brocksmith, in TNG episode "Peak Performance."

Kolvoord Starburst
illegal and dangerous maneuver which killed Wesley's classmate when they and their friends decided to try it during graduation rehearsals in TNG episode "The First Duty."

KOMACK, JAMES
director of Classic Trek "A Piece Of The Action." A well known TV director, he also starred in the series "The Courtship Of Eddie's Father" (which he produced.)

KOMACK, ADMIRAL
head of Starfleet Command, played by Byron Morrow, who orders Kirk to go to Altair VI for the inauguration ceremonies instead of to

Vulcan in Classic episode "Amok Time."

KONMEL
Klingon lieutenant who dies trying to escape from the *Enterprise* brig in TNG episode "Heart of Glory."

KONSAV
Romulan lecturer silenced for his dissident statements mentioned in TNG episode "Face of the Enemy."

Koo-nut Kal-if-fee
Vulcan word for a marriage or a challenge in Classic episode "Amok Time."

KOPACHE, THOMAS
played Mirok in TNG "The Next Phase."

KOR, COMMANDER
Klingon commander, played by John Colicos, who tries to conquer Organia in Classic episode "Errand of Mercy." In the animated episode "Time Trap," he is the commander of the Klingon ship *Klothos.*

KORAK, GLIN
Gul Lemec's aid in TNG episode "Chain of Command."

KORAX
Captain Koloth's second, played by Michael Pataki, who starts a fight with Scotty on Space Station K 7 by insulting Kirk and the *Enterprise* in Classic episode "The Trouble With Tribbles."

KORBY, DR. ROGER
Christine Chapel's fiance who had been missing for

years before an android in his likeness is found on Exo III. It is discovered that the real Korby, an exobiologist and an expert in archeological medicine played by Michael Strong, is dead.

KOROB
warlock character, played by Theo Marcuse, on Pyris VII who is really a tiny crab-like creature killed by Sylvia in Classic episode "Catspaw."

KOROTH
leader of the monastery Klingons visit to conjure up a vision of Kahless in TNG episode "Rightful Heir."

KORRIS
leader, played by Vaughn Armstrong, of a rebel group of Klingons who dies fighting Worf in TNG episode "Heart of Glory."

KOSH, PAMELA
played Mrs. Carmichael in TNG "Time's Arrow Part II."

KOSINSKI
one of the Starfleet Corps of Engineers, played by Stanley Kamel, who is really a fraud in TNG episode "Where No One Has Gone Before."

Kostolain
home of Campio, Lwaxana Troi's fiance in TNG episode "Cost of Living."

KOVACK, NANCY
played Nona in Classic Trek "A Private Little War." Born in 1935, her credits include several TV shows of the 1960's as well as "Jason And The Argonauts"

and "Tarzan and the Valley Of Gold."

KOVAS, MAGDA
a short haired blonde android raised at a helium experimental station, played by Susan Denberg, who is one of Mudd's women in the Classic episode of the same name.

KOWAL, JON
played Gossett in Classic Trek "Mudd's Women." His credits include guest stints on "The Wackiest Ship In The Army" and "Voyage To The Bottom Of The Sea."

KRAG, INSPECTOR
member, played by Craig Richard Nelson, of the Tanugan security force who is ordered to take Riker into custody for the murder of Dr. Apgar in TNG episode "A Matter of Perspective."

KRAKO, JOJO
boss, played by Victor Tayback, of the southside territory on Iotia in Classic episode "A Piece of the Action."

KRAMER, JOEL
played a Klingon in "Star Trek: The Motion Picture."

KRAS
Klingon, played by Tige Andrews, who is trying to prevent Capella from joining the Federation in Classic episode "Friday's Child."

KRASNOWSKY, CAPTAIN
member, played by Bart Conrad, of Kirk's trial board

in Classic episode "Court Martial."

Krayton
name of the Ferengi ship captained by Tog in TNG episode "Menage A Troi."

Kreechta
Ferengi ship commanded by DaiMon Bractor in TNG episode "Peak Performance."

KRELL
Klingon agent, played by Ned Romeo, who arms the villagers in Classic episode "A Private Little War."

Kreos
Klingon colony world whose leader is Vagh in TNG episode "The Mind's Eye."

Krieger Waves
new source of power Dr. Apgar is working to harness at the Tanuga Research Station before he dies in TNG episode "A Matter of Perspective."

Krik'ta
Ferengi ship, commanded by DaiMon Bractor, which attacks the *Enterprise* in TNG episode "Peak Performance."

KRIKES, PETER
scriptwriter of "The Voyage Home."

Krios
world locked in a war with Valt Minor and home of the empathic metamorph Kamala in TNG episode "The Perfect Mate."

KRODAK
member of the planet Gideon, played by Gene Dynarski, who beams aboard the *Enterprise* in Classic episode "Mark of Gideon."

KROLA
security minister, played by Michael Ensign, of Malcoria III in TNG episode "First Contact."

KROTUS
mentioned by Garth as a famous ruler in Classic episode "Whom Gods Destroy."

Kroykah
the Vulcan term for silence used in Classic episode "Amok Time."

KRUGE
Klingon commander, played by Christopher Lloyd, who kills Kirk's son, David, and almost succeeds in killing Spock in "The Search For Spock."

KRYTON
one of Elaan's attendants, played by Tony Young, whose love for her causes him to turn traitor to the Klingons in order to stop her marriage to the ruler of Troyius. He ends up committing suicide in Classic episode "Elaan of Troyius."

KRZEMIAN, RICHARD
scriptwriter of TNG "The Last Outpost."

Ku'vat
a Klingon ship under the command of Morag patrolling near Starfleet Subspace Relay Station 47 in TNG episode "Aquiel."

KUDA, VING
author of the book *Ethics, Sophistry and the Alternate Universe* which Picard is reading in TNG episode "Captain's Holiday."

KUKULKAN
alien who visited Earth as a feathered serpent in the past and became the basis of many legends. He appears, played by James Doohan, in the animated episode "How Sharper Than A Serpent's Tooth."

KUNIVAS
Klingon, played by Robert Bauer, who dies in TNG episode "Heart of Glory."

KURAK
female Klingon warp field specialist who thinks Dr. Reyga's theories will never work in TNG episode "Suspicions."

KURI, COMMANDER
Klingon in the animated episode "Time Trap."

Kurlan Naikous Statue
rare, 1,200-year-old bowl with statues decorating its sides made by the extinct Kurlan race and given to Picard by Professor Galen in TNG episode "The Chase."

KURLAND, JAKE
young student, played by Stephen Gregory, who loses to Wesley for an opportunity to take the Academy entrance exam in TNG episode "Coming of Age."

KURN, COMMANDER
Worf's younger brother, played by Tony Todd, also

orphaned at Khitomer and raised by Lorgh.

KUSATSU, CLYDE
played Admiral Nakamura in TNG "The Measure of a Man."

KUSHELL
played by Albert Stratton, leader of the planet Streleb's Legation of Unity. He is searching for Okona, believed to have stolen Streleb's Jewel of Thesia, in TNG episode "The Outrageous Okona."

Kut'luch
Klingon assassin's ceremonial weapon in TNG episode "Sins of the Fathers."

KYLE, LIEUTENANT
British transporter chief, played by John Winston, who appeared in many Classic Trek episodes as well as "The Wrath of Khan."

Kyushu, U.S.S.
ship destroyed by the Borg at Wolf 359 in TNG episode "The Best of Both Worlds." Benjamin Sisko's ship in DS9 episode "Emissary" was also destroyed there.

Kzinti
alien race of felinoid beings who are eight feet tall and have two hearts in the animated episode "The Slaver Weapon." They will eat humans if given the opportunity.

L'Kor
head of the Klingons in the Carraya IV Romulan prison camp in TNG episode "Birthright."

L'Langon Mountains

high, desert range on Vulcan where children take their Kahs'wan tests as mentioned in animated episode "Yesteryear." Also the location of Vulcan's Forge.

L374 III

planet on which Commodore Decker left his crew, to protect them from a monolithic ship-eating machine, in Classic episode "The Doomsday Machine." The machine attacks the planet, however, leaving it in rubble.

La MURA, MARK

played John Doe in TNG "Transfigurations."

LA RUE, BARTELL

played the voice of the Guardian of Forever in Classic Trek "The City On The Edge Of Forever," the newscaster in "Patterns of Force" and the announcer on "Bread And Circuses."

Labarre, France

location of Picard's family estate and vineyard in TNG episode "Family."

Lactra VII

location of a gigantic zoo in which *Enterprise* members are confined in animated episode "The Eye of the Beholder."

Lacunar Amnesia

a type of selective amnesia the children of the Starnes expedition experience in Classic episode "And The Children Shall Lead."

LAFFERTY, MARCY

played Chief DeFalco on "Star Trek: The Motion Picture." She is married to William Shatner, with whom she also appeared in "T.J. Hooker" and in a stage play "Otherwise Engaged." Her other stage work includes "Cat On A Hot Tin Roof." She met Shatner while working on the set of "The Andersonville Trial." She and her husband also show horses.

LaFORGE, LIEUTENANT COMMANDER GEORDI

chief engineer of the *Enterprise*, played by LeVar Burton, in "The Next Generation." Born blind, he wears a special visor which enables his brain to detect objects in minute detail, allowing him to "see" better than humans. Geordi has trouble forming romantic relationships with women because he lacks confidence in himself but he is a genius in the engine room. He has saved the ship countless times because of his quick imagination and diligence. Geordi gets along with everyone well but has developed an actual friendship only with Data. Geordi's mother is a starship captain who disappeared in a seventh season episode. He has several siblings in his close knit family.

LAID, LAMONT

played the Indian boy in Classic Trek "The Paradise Syndrome."

LAKSO, EDWARD J.

scriptwriter of Classic Trek "And The Children Shall Lead." He also wrote for "The Guns of Will Sonnett," and the pilot for "The Pigeon."

LAL

Data's daughter, played by Hallie Todd, whom he constructs in TNG episode "The Offspring." Data creates her with an ability to feel emotion and use contractions (which Data claims he cannot do, although he can when mimicking someone else.) Lal dies from emotional overload when facing possible separation from her "father" by a man who wants to take her away to study her and Data cannot resurrect her. Lal means "beloved" in Hindi. The sexless, faceless version of the android was played by Leonard John Crofoot.

LAL

one of the Vians, played by Alan Bermann, who tortures Kirk, Spock and McCoy in Classic episode "The Empath."

Lalo, U.S.S.

freighter attacked by the Borg and never heard from again in TNG episode "The Best of Both Worlds." It is also mentioned in "We'll Always Have Paris," an episode which takes place before its destruction.

LALSINGH, REGINALD

played Captain Chandra in Classic Trek "Court Martial."

Lambda Field Generator

part of Dr. Apgar's work with Krieger wave equipment mentioned in TNG episode "A Matter of Perspective."

LAMBDIN, SUSANNE

writer of TNG story premise "Family."

LAMBERT, PAUL

played Melian in TNG "When The Bough Breaks," and Dr. Howard Clarke in "Devil's Due."

LAMEY, THAD

played the devil in TNG "Devil's Due."

LANDAU, LES

director of TNG "The Schizoid Man," Samaritan Snare," "The Survivors," "Deja Q," "Sins of the Father," "Sarek," "Family," "Future Imperfect," "Clues," "Night Terrors," "Half A Life," "Ensign Ro," "Unification Part I," "Conundrum," "Time's Arrow, Part I and II," "Chain of Command" and "Tapestry."

LANDER, DAVID L.

played a tactician in TNG "Peak Performance."

LANDERS, HARRY

played Dr. Coleman on Classic Trek "Turnabout Intruder." He was also a regular on the series "Ben Casey."

LANDO, JOE

played a shore patrolman in "The Voyage Home." Formerly a regular character on "All My Children," he currently plays Sully in the hit series "Dr. Quinn, Medicine Woman."

LANDON, YEOMAN MARTHA
Chekov's girlfriend, played by Celeste Yarnall, in Classic episode "The Apple."

LANDOR, ROSALYN
played Brenna O'Dell in TNG "Up The Long Ladder."

Landris II
archeology dig headed by Professor Mowray, which Picard wants to visit in TNG episode "Lessons."

LANDRU
ruler of the planet Beta III, played by Charles MacAulay, who is actually an image generated by the computer which has controlled the populace for six thousand years in Classic episode "The Return of the Archons."

LANDRY, KAREN
played Ajur in TNG "Captain's Holiday."

LANDSBURG, DAVID
scriptwriter of TNG "The Outrageous Okona."

LANE, BRIAN ALAN
scriptwriter of TNG "Elementary, Dear Data."

LANE, IVA
played one of the bridge crew in "Star Trek: The Motion Picture," and Zero Zero in TNG "11001001." Her movie credits include "10 to Midnight."

LANEL
medical staff person, played by Bebe Neuwirth, who demands Riker have sex with her before she'll help him escape in TNG episode "First Contact."

LANG, CHARLIE
played Duffy in TNG "Hollow Pursuits."

LANG, LIEUTENANT
gunnery officer, played by James Farley, who dies on Cestus III at the hand of the Gorns in Classic episode "Arena."

Lang Cycle Fusion Engines
propulsion system of the Promellian ship *Cleponji* in TNG episode "Booby Trap."

LANGFORD, DR.
archeologist from whom Picard has a standing invitation to join him at his dig in TNG episode "Rascals."

LANGOR
Brekkan salesperson, played by Kimberly Farr, trying to sell felicium to the Ornarans in TNG episode "Symbiosis."

LANSFORD, WILLIAM DOUGLAS
scriptwriter of TNG "Devil's Due."

LANSING, ROBERT
played Gary Seven in Classic Trek "Assignment: Earth." Other TV credits include "Gunsmoke," "One Step Beyond," "The Twilight Zone" (in an episode with Mariette Hartley,) and regular roles in "87th Precinct," "Twelve O'Clock High," "The Man

Who Never Was" and "Automan." Film credits include "The 4 D Man" and Empire of the Ants." He is currently a regular on "The New Kung Fu" series (starring David Carradine.)

Lantree, U.S.S.
class 6 supply ship, captained by L. Iso Tolaka, whose crew is exposed to Darwinian antibodies which cause them to age rapidly and die in TNG episode "Unnatural Selection."

Lapling
sand-burrowing creature, and the last of her species, owned by Fajo in TNG episode "The Most Toys."

Lappa IV
Ferengi world mentioned in TNG episode "Menage A Troi."

LARA
character in animated episode "Jihad."

LAREN, ENSIGN RO
see entry for Ro Laren.

LARGE, NORMAN
played Proconsul Neral in TNG "Unification Part I and II."

LaROUQUE, FREDERICK
character in TNG episode "Time's Arrow" who discovers Data has abilities surpassing normal humans'.

LARROQUETTE, JOHN
comedian who played Maltz in "The Search For Spock." His film credits include "Stripes," "Cat People," "Bare Essence,"

"The Last Ninja" and "Meatballs II." His first regular series was "Black Sheep Squadron" and later "Doctor's Hospital," but he is most famous for playing Dan Fielding in "Night Court." He also recently starred in his own TV series named after him.

LARS
drill thrall, played by Steve Sandor, specially assigned to Uhura in Classic episode "The Gamesters of Triskelion."

LARSON, MAJLISS
author of Classic Trek novel *Pawns and Symbols*.

LaSALANDRA, JOHN (S.M.E.)
music editor of TNG.

LaSalle, U.S.S.
ship which reports radiation anomalies in the Gamma Arigulon system in TNG episode "Reunion."

LASHLY, JAMES
played Ensign Kopf in TNG "Brothers" and appeared in DS9 episodes "The Passenger" and "Move Along Home."

LAST OUTPOST, The
first season TNG episode written by Richard Krzemian and Herbert Wright and directed by Richard Colla. The *Enterprise* and a Ferengi ship become trapped by the last outpost of the Tkon Empire. A gnome appears, challenging them to solve a riddle. Guest stars: Darryl Henriques, Armin Shimerman, Jake Dengel,

Tracy Walter and Mike Gomez.

LATHAL
representative, played by Robert Harper, of the Beta moon of Peliar Zel in TNG episode "The Host."

LATIMER
navigator, played by Ress Vaughn, on the Galileo and the first crewmember killed on Taurus II in Classic episode "The Galileo Seven."

Latinum, Gold Pressed
see entry for "credits."

LAURITSON, PETER
director and co-producer of TNG "The Inner Light."

LAUTER, ED
played Albert in TNG "The First Duty."

LAVIN, RICHARD
played one of the mediators in TNG "Justice."

Lavinius V
location of an ancient civilization destroyed by the Denevan parasites, mentioned in Classic episode "Operation: Annihilate!"

Lawgiver, First
played by Sid Haig, member Landru's brainwashing enforcement organization in Classic episode "The Return of the Archons." Anyone who does not cooperate is shot with a hollow tube-like weapon.

Lawmim Galactopedia
rare artifact owned by Fajo in TNG episode "The Most Toys."

LAWRENCE, J.A.
co-author of Star Trek 12 with James Blish, also her husband, and sole author of Classic novel *Mudd's Angels*.

LAWTON, YEOMAN TINA
played by Patricia McNulty, character turned into an iguana by Charlie in Classic episode "Charlie X."

LAZARUS
time traveler, played by Robert Brown, who has met his double from a negative universe. The two Lazarus are trying to kill one another in Classic episode "The Alternative Factor."

LAZEBNIK, PHILIP
scriptwriter of TNG "Devil's Due" and "Darmok."

LE GARDE, TOM & TED
twin actors who played the Hermans in Classic Trek "I, Mudd."

Le'Matya
deadly mountain creature native to Vulcan. It has poisonous teeth and claws in the animated episode "Yesteryear."

LEADER, TONY
director of Classic Trek "For The World Is Hollow And I Have Touched The Sky" and episodes of "Lost In Space."

LEDA
Harry Bernard's "adopted mother," played by Michele Marsh, in TNG episode "When The Bough Breaks."

LEDER, REUBEN
scriptwriter of TNG "The Perfect Mate."

LEDERMAN, BOB
director of TNG "I, Borg."

LEE, BILL CHO
played the male patient in TNG "Time's Arrow Part II."

LEE, EVERETT
played the cafe owner in "The Voyage Home."

LEE, STEPHEN
played Chorgon in TNG "The Vengeance Factor."

LEE, THELMA
played Kahlest in TNG "Sins of the Fathers."

LEECH, FELIX
played by Harvey Jason, assitant to Cyrus Redblock, a crime boss in the Dixon Hill scenario on the holodeck in TNG episode "The Big Goodbye."

LEFLER, ENSIGN ROBIN
junior officer, played by Ashley Judd, on the *Enterprise* and Wesley's friend in TNG episodes "The Game" and "Darmok."

LEGACY
fourth season TNG episode written by Joe Menosky and directed by Robert Scheerer. Tasha's sister, Ishara, comes aboard the *Enterprise* when the ship travels to Turkana IV to answer a distress signal. Data befriends her, only to discover she has ulterior motives behind her diplomacy. Guest stars: Beth Toussaint, Don Mirrault, Colm Meaney, Vladimir Velasco and Christopher Michael.

Legara IV
world for which Sarek hopes to negotiate a treaty and which he visits prior to coming aboard the *Enterprise* in TNG episode "Sarek."

Legarans
race which exists in a slimy residue at 150 degrees Celsius and for whom Sarek is negotiating a treaty in TNG episode "Sarek."

LEGATO, ROB
director of TNG "Menage A Troi" and "The Nth Degree" and visual effects supervisor on DS9.

LeGAULT, LANCE
played K'Temoc in TNG "The Emissary."

LEIDER, HARRIET
played Amarie in TNG "Unification Part II."

LEIGHTON, SHEILA
played Luma in Classic Trek "Spock's Brain." Her TV credits include "The Man From U.N.C.L.E."

LEIGHTON, DR. THOMAS
Kirk's friend, played by William Sargent, who sees the Karidian players perform and believes Anton is Kodos the Executioner. He is later murdered in Classic episode "The Conscience of the King."

LEIGHTON, MARTHA
wife, played by Natalie Norwick, of Dr. Thomas Leighton in Classic episode "The Conscience of the King."

LEITJEN, LIEUTENANT COMMANDER SUSANNA
officer, played by Maryann Plunkett, who met Geordi while aboard the *U.S.S. Victory*. Both are affected by a parasitical alien metamorphosis in TNG episode "Identity Crisis."

LEMANI, TANIA
played Kara in Classic Trek "Wolf In The Fold." Her TV credits include "The Man From U.N.C.L.E." and "The Wackiest Ship In The Army."

LEMEC, GUL
Cardassian representative in TNG episode "Chain of Command." He is not the one who captures Picard.

LEMLI, MR.
Enterprise officer, played by Roger Holloway, who appears in Classic episodes "Return to Tomorrow," "The Way to Eden" and "Turnabout Intruder."

LEMON, BEN
played Jev in TNG "Violations."

LENARD, MARK
played the Romulan Commander in Classic Trek "Balance of Terror" and the Klingon commander in "Star Trek: The Motion Picture." He is known, however, as Sarek in the Classic episode "Journey To Bable," the movies "The Search For Spock," "The Voyage Home" and "The Undiscovered Country," TNG episodes "Sarek," and "Unificiation Part I," and the animated "Yesteryear." Lenard was a stage actor before he was cast as Sarek, his first role on television. He later guest starred in various TV shows and movies and regularly appeared in "Here Comes the Brides" and "Planet of the Apes."

Lenarians
alien race which fires on the *Enterprise*, almost killing Picard, who has a near death experience with Q as his guide in TNG episode "Tapestry."

LEONE, MARIA
played one of the Ten Forward crew in TNG "The Offspring."

LEONG, PAGE
played April Anaya in TNG "The Nth Degree."

Lepton
substance which, combined with mesons, builds up and causes the wormhole to become unstable in TNG episode "The Price."

LESLIE, LIEUTENANT
officer, played by Eddie Paskey, who appears in many Classic episodes as an *Enterprise* relief helmsman, a participant on landing parties and as a security guard. (One of the few who survive.)

LESSING, ARNOLD
played a security guard in Classic Trek "The Changeling."

LESSONS
sixth season TNG episode written by Ronald Wilderson and Jean Louise Matthias and directed by Robert Wiemer. Picard and a stellar cartologist, Nella Daren, fall in love but find their romance interferes with their professional lives. They part as friends, hoping to see each other on shore leave, and Nella transfers to another ship. Guest star: Wendy Hughes.

LESTER, JEFF
played the FBI agent in "The Voyage Home." He played a regular role in "Walking Tall" and starred in the film "The Little Drummer Girl."

LESTER, JANICE
Kirk's old friend and lover, played by Sandra Smith, who exchanges bodies with him on Camus II in Classic episode "Turnabout Intruder." She is insane after deliberately murdering her science team by exposing them to radiation.

LESTRADE, INSPECTOR
infamous Victorian London lawman, played by Alan Shearman, who appears in a holodeck projection in TNG episode "Elementary, Dear Data."

LET THAT BE YOUR LAST BATTLEFIELD
written by Oliver Crawford and Lee Cronin and directed by Jud Taylor, this third season Classic Trek episode aired 1/10/69. The *Enterprise* picks up an alien named Lokai who is fleeing the planet Cheron. The man pursuing him, Bele, is of the same race, and yet because he is black on the right side and white on the left, he and others like him believe they are superior to Lokai's type who are black on the left side and white on the right. Guest stars: Lou Antonio and Frank Gorshin.

LETEK
Ferengi played by Armin Shimerman in TNG episode "The Last Outpost."

LETHE
a very hollow, unemotional woman, played by Suzanne Wasson, encountered on the Tantalus Penal colony in Classic episode "Dagger of the Mind."

LETTIAN
Aldean musician, played by Paul Lambert, who "adopted" Katie, a young girl from the *Enterprise* and encouraged her to seek music.

Leutscher Virus
compared to the nanites in TNG episode "Evolution."

Levetric Pulse
phaser energy level used against Data in TNG episode "Descent."

LEVITT, JUDY
a stage actress married to Walter Koenig, she played Doctor #2 in "The Voyage Home."

LEWIN, BOB (Robert)
scriptwriter of TNG "Datalore," "11001001," "The Arsenal of Freedom" and "Symbiosis."

LEWIS, SHARI
scriptwriter of Classic Trek "The Lights of Zetar" and famous for her puppeteering, especially with her sidekick Lamb Chops.

Lexington, U.S.S.
ship, commanded by Commodore Wesley, damaged severely by the M 5 computer in Classic episode "The Ultimate Computer."

LEYOR
Caldonian, played by Kevin Peter Hall, who is part of the Barzan negotiations in TNG episode "The Price."

LIATOR
played by Jay Louden, a member of the council of Edo looking into Wesley's violation of the law in TNG episode "Justice."

Library
place on Sarpeidon people visit to pick a past time in which they would like to live in Classic episode "All Our Yesterdays."

Lidugeal Gold
supposedly the purest form of gold known in the galaxy with which the Ferengi try to bribe Ambassador Briam in TNG episode "The Perfect Mate."

LIEUTENANT, SS
played by Ralph Maurer, man from whom Spock steals a police uniform in

Classic episode "Patterns of Force."

Ligana Sector
location four months away to which the *Ghandi* is sent on a terraforming mission in TNG episode "Second Chances."

LIGHTS OF ZETAR, THE
written by Jeremy Tarcher and Shari Lewis and directed by Herb Kenwith, this third season Classic Trek episode aired 1/31/69. The "Lights" are the mental energy of a group of aliens who take over Lt. Mira Romaine's body, Scotty's new love, after destroying all life forms and vast computer stores of knowledge on Memory Alpha. Guest stars: Jan Shutan, John Winston and Libby Erwin.

Ligillium, Ruins of
archeological site where the famous Zatteral Emerald is hidden in TNG episode "Devil's Due."

Ligon II
planet where inhabitants know the cure for Anchilles Fever, a disorder plaguing Styris IV in TNG episode "Code of Honor."

Ligos VII
planet where the Ferengi capture a Federation science team in TNG episode "Rascals."

LIKO
Mintakan, played by Ray Wise, who is saved by the *Enterprise* and returns to his people talking of worshipping "The Picard" in TNG episode "Who Watches The Watchers."

Lima Sierra System
location of a planet with an irregular orbit mentioned by Picard in TNG episode "Loud as a Whisper."

LIN, ENSIGN KENNY
Enterprise junior officer, played by veteran Trek actor Brian Tochi, in TNG episode "Night Terrors."

Linars
a bat-like creature that lives in caves on Seltris III in TNG episode "Chain of Command."

LINCOLN, ABRAHAM
Kirk's hero. An image of him, played by Lee Bergere, appears in Classic episode "The Savage Curtain."

LINCOLN, ROBERTA
Gary Seven's secretary, played by Teri Garr, who has no idea what her boss uses his powerful computers and transporters for in Classic episode "Assignment: Earth."

LINDEN, DON
child, played by Mark Robert Brown, in Classic episode "And The Children Shall Lead."

LINDESMITH, JOHN
played an Engineer in Classic Trek "The Paradise Syndrome."

LINDSEY, ELIZABETH
played Luisa Kim in TNG "Homesoil."

LINDSTROM
played by William Meader, a member of Kirk's trial board in Classic episode "Court Martial." Another Lindstrom, a sociologist played by Christopher

Held, stays behind on Beta III to help its people in "The Return of the Archons."

Linear Models of Viral Propagation
supposedly the first definitive book on its subject written by Dr. Katherine Pulaski and mentioned in TNG episode "Unnatural Selection."

LINEBACK, RICHARD
played Romas in TNG "Symbiosis." He also appears in DS9 "Dax."

LING
one of Khan's followers in Classic episode "Space Seed."

LINKE, DR.
one of the researchers, played by Jason Wingreen, killed by the Vians in Classic episode "The Empath."

LINVILLE, JOANNE
played the Romulan commander in Classic Trek "The Enterprise Incident." Her many TV credits include "Gunsmoke," "Dan August" and a starring role in the 1981 series "Behind the Screen." She has also appeared in the films "Secrets," "The Critical List," "The Users" and "The Seduction."

LIPTON, POLICE SERGEANT
security guard, played by Lincoln Demyan, at McKinley Rocket Base in Classic episode "Assignment: Earth."

Lirpa
deadly Vulcan weapon which is sharp and hatchet-like on one end and blunt on the other, like a club. Kirk and Spock fight with these weapons in Classic episode "Amok Time."

LISKA, STEPHEN
played Torg in "The Search For Spock."

Little Boy
Jahn's sidekick, played by John Megna, in Classic episode "Miri."

LIVINGSTON, DAVID
director of TNG "The Mind's Eye" and "Power Play" and line producer of the series. He also wrote and directed DS9 episode "The Nagus."

LIVINGSTON, HAROLD
scriptwriter for "Star Trek: The Motion Picture." Known for his TV work, he also wrote "Escape To Mindanao," and worked on "The Barbary Coast."

LIYANG
a member of the Kohm race about to execute a Yang in Classic episode "The Omega Glory."

LLOYD, CHRISTOPHER
played Kruge in "The Search For Spock." He is famous for his "Taxi" role as Reverend Jim from 1970 to '83, and for his professorial role in the "Back to the Future" films. He also appeared in the films "The Legend of the Lone Ranger," "Clue" and "To Be Or Not To Be."

LLOYD, NORMAN
guest starred in TNG episode "The Chase."

Lobes
Ferengi errogenous zone. Also a term the Ferengi frequently use as a synonym for strength, courage and masculinity as in, "I didn't think you had the lobes!"

LOCARNO, CADET FIRST CLASS NICHOLAS
leader, played by Duncan McNeill, of the Nova Squadron in TNG episode "The First Duty."

LOCHER, FELIX
played Robert Johnson in Classic Trek "The Deadly Years." His TV guest appearances include "The Man From U.N.C.L.E.," "Branded" and "One Step Beyond."

LOCKWOOD, GARY
played Gary Mitchell in Classic Trek "Where No Man Has Gone Before." Born in Van Nuys, CA in 1937, he got his start as a stunt man and Anthony Perkins' stand-in. He went on to star in the series "The Lieutenant" (produced by Gene Roddenberry,) and was a regular on "Follow The Sun." His films include "The Magic Sword" and "2001: A Space Odyssey." He was once married to actress Stefanie Powers.

LOCUTUS
name of the person Picard becomes when he is integrated with the Borg in TNG episode "The Best of Both Worlds."

LODGE, SUZANNE
played a serving girl in Classic Trek "Wolf In The Fold."

LOFTIN, GARY
stunt driver in Classic Trek "The City On The Edge Of Forever."

LOFTON, CIRROC
stars as Jake Sisko in DS9. Born in Los Angeles, Cirroc started acting at age 9 in the educational program "Agency for Instructional Technology" and appeared in commercials for McDonalds, Tropicana Orange Juice and Kellogg's Rice Crispies. His big break was an appearance in the movie "Beethoven." He aspires to be a doctor when he grows up and loves to play basketball. He lives with his sister and mother.

LOGAN
Enterprise engineer, played by Vyto Ruginis, who tries to take command in TNG episode "The Arsenal of Freedom."

LOKAI
native of the planet Cheron, played by Lou Antonio, where the inhabitants killed themselves in race wars mentioned in Classic episode "Let That Be Your Last Battlefield." Black on the left side and white on the right, he is pursued as a fugitive by Bele, also from Cheron and the only other native still living, who has reversed coloring.

London Kings
21st century baseball team which included a player who broke Joe DiMaggio's

hitting record, mentioned in TNG episode "The Big Goodbye."

LONELY AMONG US
first season TNG episode written by D.C. Fontana and Michael Halperin and directed by Cliff Bole. A cloud-like being takes over the computer and Picard. Guest stars: Colm Meaney, Kavi Raz and John Durbin.

LONG, ED
played Midro in Classic Trek "The Cloud Minders."

Lonka Pulsar
rotating neutron star to which the fake Picard brings the *Enterprise* as a test of the crew in TNG episode "Allegiance."

LOOMIS, ROD
played Paul Manheim in TNG "We'll Always Have Paris."

LOPEZ, PERRY
played Lt. Esteban Rodriquez in Classic Trek "Shore Leave." Born in 1931, his credits include "Voyage To The Bottom of the Sea" and "Hec Ramsey."

LOPEZ, ENSIGN
Enterprise junior officer criticized by a distracted Worf for incorrectly preparing the duty roster in TNG episode "Birthright."

LORA
woman, whose voice is played by Majel Berrett, to whom Harry Mudd gives his love potion in animated episode "Mudd's Planet."

LORCA, ISABELLE
played Gabrielle in TNG "We'll Always Have Paris."

LORE
Data's twin brother, also played by Brent Spiner, created before Data by Dr. Noonian Soong. Lore, who was given emotions but no conscience, is very cruel. He is first seen in "Datalore" and in several later TNG episodes.

LORELEI SIGNAL, The
written by Margaret Armen, this animated Classic Trek episode aired 9/29/73. Kirk, Spock, McCoy and a security man are imprisoned on a planet populated only by women and are drained of their energy causing them to age rapidly. An all-female landing party, with Uhura in command, rescues them. Guest voices: Majel Barrett (Theela) and Nichelle Nichols (Dara, Computer and Security Officer Davison.)

Loren III
only world located in the Kurlan sector which supports life, mentioned in TNG episode "The Chase."

Lorenze Cluster
location of the planet Minos in TNG episode "The Arsenal of Freedom." It is also said this star group can be seen from the planet Aucdet IX in "The Child."

LORGH
Klingon who raised Kurn, Worf's younger brother, after their parents were killed in the Khitomer Massacre mentioned in

TNG episode "Sins of the Fathers."

LORMER, JON
played Dr. Theodore Haskins in Classic Trek pilot "The Cage" and "The Menagerie," Tamar in "Return of the Archons" and Old Man in "For The World Is Hollow And I Have Touched The Sky." His other TV credits include "One Step Beyond," "Voyage To The Bottom Of The Sea" and "Perry Mason." His film credits include "Rally 'Round The Flag Boys," "Frankenstein," "Conspiracy of Terror," "The Golden Gate Murders" and "Creepshow."

Lornack Clan
people known to have massacred the Tralestas in TNG episode "The Vengeance Factor."

LORRAH, JEAN
science fiction author of several books including the Classic Trek novels *The Vulcan Academy Murders*, *The IDIC Epidemic*, and TNG novels *Survivors* and *Metamorphosis*.

LOS, TANA
injured fugitive who asks for political asylum on Deep Space 9 in DS9 episode "Past Prologue."

LOSIRA
Kalandan projection of a long dead Kalandan leader, played by Lee Meriwether, who severely injures Sulu with her deadly touch in Classic episode "That Which Survives."

LOSKENE, COMMANDER
heard but unseen commander of a Tholian ship who asks the *Enterprise*, which is on a rescue mission for the missing Captain Kirk, to leave their space immediately in Classic episode "The Tholian Web."

LOSS, The
fourth season TNG episode written by Hilary J. Bader, Alan J. Adler and Vanessa Greene, and directed by Chip Chalmers. Two-dimensional life forms, on their way toward a cosmic string fragment, catch the *Enterprise* in their path causing Troi to temporarily lose her empathic powers. Guest stars: Kim Braden, Whoopi Goldberg and Mary Kohnert.

LOU, CINDY
played the nurse in Classic Trek "Return To Tomorrow."

LOUD AS A WHISPER
second season TNG episode written by Jacqueline Zambrano and directed by Larry Shaw. Ambassador Riva, the great deaf mediator, is brought to Soleis IV to mediate a dispute between the world's peoples but the three member chorus through whom he communicates is accidentally killed and he is at a loss as to how to communicate on his own. Guest stars: Howie Seago, Marnie Mosiman, Thomas Oglesby and Leo Damian. Of note: Data translates sign language in this episode but sometimes makes the mis-

take of translating the words before the signer has "spoken" them.

LOUIS
Picard's old friend, played by Dennis Creaghan, who wants Picard to work with him on the Atlantis deep sea colonization project in TNG episode "Family."

LOUISE
Miri's friend who reaches maturity and succumbs to the virus that killed all the adults. She attacks Kirk and is killed by a phaser stun blast.

LOUVOIS, CAPTAIN PHILIPA
played by Amanda McBroom, the senior officer of Starbase 173 Judge Advocate General's office who prosecuted the *Stargazer* courtmartial ten years before and presides over the hearing concerning Data's sentience in TNG episode "The Measure of a Man."

LOVSKY, CELIA
played T'Pau in Classic Trek "Amok Time."

LOWRY/LOWRY-JOHN-SON, JUNIE
in charge of casting for TNG and DS9.

LUCAS, JOHN MEREDYTH
scriptwriter/director/producer who wrote Classic Trek episodes "The Changeling," "Patterns of Force," "Elaan Of Troyius" and "That Which Survives," directed "The Ultimate Computer," "The Enterprise Incident" and

"Elaan of Troyius," and produced the series' second season. He also directed "Planet of the Apes" and wrote for the TV series "Logan's Run" as well as the pilot for "City Beneath The Sea/One Hour To Doomsday."

LUCIA, CHIP
played Ambassador Ramid Ves Alkar in TNG "Man of the People."

LUCIEN
a satyr, played by James Doohan, in animated episode "The Majick's of Megas Tu" who appears on the *Enterprise* bridge. He is a magician who claims to love humans and has visited Earth.

LUCKINBILL, LAURENCE
played Sybok in "The Final Frontier." Born in 1934, his credits include "The Boys In The Band," "Winner Take All" and "The Lindbergh Kidnapping Case." He is married to actress Lucie Arnez.

Lucrovextitrin
toxic substance which can alter glass in TNG episode "Hollow Pursuits."

LUKE, KEYE
played Cory in Classic Trek "Whom Gods Destroy." Born in Canton, China in 1904, his credits include "The Painted Veil," many "Charlie Chan" films, several "Dr. Kildare" movies and the role of Kato in some "Green Hornet" serials. He appeared regularly in the TV series "Kentucky Jones," "Anna and the King," "Kung Fu" (1972-

1975,) and "Harry O" ('76.) He also played the Chinese man who had the gremlin in the movie "Gremlins."

LUM, BENJAMIN W.S.
played Jim Shimoda in TNG "The Naked Now."

LUMA
Eymorg, played by Sheila Leighton, of Sigma Draconis VI who is overpowered by Kirk and his landing party in Classic episode "Spock's Brain."

Lumar Cafe
where Beverly, Worf and Data are when the Rutian bomb goes off in TNG episode "The High Ground."

LUMO
Indian warrior, played by Peter Virgo, Jr., who rescues the drowned boy from the lake in Classic episode "The Paradise Syndrome."

LUNA, BARBARA
played Marlena Moreau in Classic Trek "Mirror, Mirror." Born in New York in 1939, her credits include "Mission: Impossible" and "Buck Rogers In The 25th Century" (in which she played Hawk's wife, Koori.) Her films include "Five Weeks in a Balloon" and "The Gatling Gun." She is the former wife of actors Doug McClure and Alan Arkin.

Lunar V
moon orbiting Angosia and the location of a penal colony housing super soldiers from a past war in TNG episode "The Hunted."

LUND, JORDAN
played Kulge in TNG "Redemption Part II."

LUNDIN, VICTOR
played a Klingon lieutenant in Classic Trek "Errand of Mercy." His credits include "Voyage To The Bottom Of The Sea."

LUPO, TOM
played a security guard in Classic Trek "The Alternative Factor."

Lura-mag
siren device used by the women of Taurus II to lure men in animated episode "The Lorelei Signal." They are not from the same Taurus II featured in "The Galileo Seven."

LURIAN, DaiMON
Ferengi renegade leader who tries to take over the *Enterprise* in TNG episode "Rascals."

LURRY
manager, played by Whit Bissell, of Space Station K 7 in Classic episode "The Trouble With Tribbles."

LURSA
played by Barbara March, a Klingon who, with her sister, is attempting to make an illegal sale on Deep Space 9 in episode "Past Prologue." Lursa also appears in TNG episode "Redemption, Part II."

LUTAN
the Primary of Ligon, played by Jessie Lawrence Ferguson, who kidnapped Tasha Yar in TNG episode "Code of Honor."

LUZ, FRANC
played Odan in TNG "The Host."

Lya III
planet from which Admiral Haden's transmission originates, mentioned in TNG episode "The Defector," and the destination of the *Enterprise* after leaving Angosia in "The Hunted."

Lya IV
planet Fajo orbits for half a day after kidnapping Data in TNG episode "The Most Toys."

Lya Station Alpha
where the *Enterprise* takes refuge from the Cardassian attack on Solarion IV in TNG episode "Ensign Ro."

LYNCH, HAL
played an air police sergeant in Classic Trek "Tomorrow Is Yesterday." His other TV credits include "Cannon."

LYNCH, KEN
played Chief Engineer Vanderberg in Classic Trek "Devil In The Dark." His credits include the films "Anatomy of a Murder," "Run, Simon, Run," "Poor Devil," "The Winds of War," and regular roles on "The Plainclothesman" and "McCloud."

LYNCH, PAUL
director of TNG "The Naked Now," "11001001," "Unnatural Selection" and "A Matter of Time" as well as DS9 episodes "A Man Alone," "Babel," "Q Less" and "The Passenger."

LYNCH, LT. COMMANDER LELAND T.
Enterprise engineer, played by Walker Boone, in TNG episode "Skin of Evil."

LYON, BOB
played a villager in Classic Trek "A Private Little War."

LYONS, GENE
played Ambassador Robert Fox in Classic Trek "A Taste of Armageddon." His other credits include "One Step Beyond" and a regular role on "Ironside."

Lyre, Vulcan
auto harp-type of instrument, also called a lytherette, which Spock plays in several episodes including "Charlie X" and "The Way To Eden."

Lysian Alliance
enemies of the Sartaarans. The *Enterprise* is told the Federation is at war with the Lysians in TNG episode "Conundrum."

Lytian System
location where Worf and Beverly rendezvous with the *Enterprise* after the two officers raid on the Cardassian base at Seltris III in TNG episode "Chain of Command."

M'BENGA, DR.
Enterprise doctor of African descent, and a specialist in Vulcan medicine, who appears in Classic episodes "A Private Little War" and "That Which Survives."

M'REL
Gowron's father who heads the Klingon high

council mentioned in TNG episode "Redemption."

M'RESS
felinoid alien bridge personnel/communications officer from the planet Cait in the Lynx system in the animated series. Majel Barrett provides the voice.

M'UMBHA
Uhura's mother mentioned in Classic episode "The Man Trap."

M-33 Galaxy
galaxy beyond Triangulum, 2.7 million light years from the Milky Way, mentioned in TNG episode "Where No One Has Gone Before." The Traveller accidentally propels the *Enterprise* to this galaxy.

M-4
hovering robot created by Flint in Classic episode "Requiem For Methuselah" to do all his chores and act as a security guard that can kill.

M-5 multitronic unit
computer designed by Dr. Richard Daystrom which takes over the *Enterprise* in Classic episode "The Ultimate Computer." James Doohan provides the voice until Kirk talks it into sentencing itself to death for murder and releasing control of the ship.

M-rays
Spock uses them to neutralize Apollo's force field holding the *Enterprise* in Classic episode "Who Mourns For Adonais?"

M-Zed V
false destination of the ship *Batris* mentioned in TNG episode "Heart of Glory." Actually a Federation outpost.

M113, planet
Professor Crater and his wife Nancy lived and studied archeological digs on this homeworld of the salt vampire in Classic episode "The Man Trap."

M113 creature
salt vampire in Classic episode "The Man Trap" that can take the form of anyone it sees, but actually looks like a hairy, elephant-nosed creature with suction cups on the ends of its fingers.

M24 Alpha
name of Triskelion's sun mentioned in Classic episode "The Gamesters of Triskelion."

M43 Alpha
name of the star around which the planets Ekos and Zeon orbit in Classic episode "Patterns of Force."

MA, TZI
played the biomechanical specialist in TNG "Samaritan Snare."

MAAB
Akaar's man, played by Michael Dante, who takes over when Akaar is killed by the Klingon, Kras in Classic episode "Friday's Child."

Mab Bu IV
giant, gaseous planet seen in TNG episode "Power Play," it's class M moon

holds a penal colony for Ux-Mal prisoners.

MacCAULEY, CHARLES
played Landru in Classic Trek "The Return of the Archons," and Jaris in "Wolf In The Fold." Other tv credits include "Griff" and "Shannon." Films include "A Case of Rape," "The Return of the World's Greatest Detective" and "The Munsters' Revenge."

MacDONALD, SCOTT
actor in DS9 "Captive Pursuit," he also guest-starred in TNG episode "Face of the Enemy."

MacDOUGAL, SARAH
Enterprise's chief engineer in TNG episode "The Naked Now" played by Brooke Bundy.

MACER, STERLING jr.
appeared in TNG episode "Birthright."

MACET, GUL
Cardassian, played by Marc Alaimo, who comes aboard the *Enterprise* to help search for Captain Benjamin Maxwell in TNG episode "The Wounded."

MacKENZIE, ARD'RIAN
cyberneticist and resident of Tau Cygna V, played by Eileen Seeley, who falls in love with Data in TNG episode "The Ensigns of Command."

MacLACHLEN, JANET
played Lt. Charlene Masters in Classic Trek "The Alternative Factor." TV credits include "Ghost Appearances," "Griff," and regular roles on "Love Thy

Neighbor," "Friends" and "All In The Family."

MADALONE, DENNIS

played Ramos in TNG "Heart of Glory," and Hedwick in TNG "Identity Crisis."

MADDEN, EDWARD

played a geologist in Classic Trek pilot "The Cage" ("The Menagerie,") and Technician Fisher in "The Enemy Within."

MADDOX, COMMANDER BRUCE

assistant chairman of robotics at the Daystrom Institute, played by Brian Brophy, who wants to take Data apart and see what makes him tick in TNG episode "The Measure of a Man."

MADELINE

secretary, played by Rhonda Aldrich, of Dixon Hill in the holodeck simulation in TNG episodes "Manhunt," "Clues," and "The Big Goodbye."

Madeline II

planet from which Lt. Commander Nella Daren says she bought a small keyboard. She plays it in a duet with Picard, playing his Resican flute, in TNG episode "Lessons."

MADISON

Regula I scientist working with Dr. Carol Marcus in "The Wrath of Khan."

MADRED, GUL

Cardassian on Seltris III who tortures Picard in TNG episode "Chain of Command." Jilorra is his daughter.

MAFFEI, BUCK

played the creature in Classic Trek "The Galileo Seven." He was also in the movie "Cheech And Chong's Nice Dreams."

MAGEE, TOM

played the Klingon monster in TNG "Devil's Due."

Magellan

Enterprise shuttlecraft from TNG. The shuttle is destroyed in an explosion in "The Outcast." In "Starship Mine," there is reference to a starship by this name.

Magnaspanner

Ensign Zweller uses this tool to tamper with the dom'jot table, a game like pool, in TNG episode "Tapestry,"

Magnesite-nitron tablets

McCoy has them in his medi-kit. When struck, they burn with a bright light as seen in Classic episode "Friday's Child."

Magnetometric-guided charges

type of "depth charge" used by the Borg in TNG episode "The Best of Both Worlds."

Maht-H'a

attack ship under the command of Captain Nu'Daq in TNG episode "The Chase."

MAISIE

series of androids created by Harry Mudd and played by twins Tamara and Starr Wilson in Classic episode "I, Mudd."

MAJICKS OF MEGAS-TU, The

written by Larry Brody, this animated Classic Trek episode aired 10/27/73. The *Enterprise* is caught in an energy whirlwind which carries it somewhere they cannot discover because the ship's instruments do not work. As they drift toward a nearby planet, a satyr appears on the bridge, calling himself Lucien and taking part of the crew down to the magic world of Megas-Tu. The natives become angry at Lucien for bringing strangers and put him on trial. Guest voices: James Doohan (Lucien,) Ed Bishop (Megan Prosecutor) and George Takei (voice.)

MAJOR, S.S.

officer of Ekos played by Gilbert Green in TNG episode "Patterns of Force."

MajQa

Klingon rite consisting of meditation followed by exposure to great heat, inducing hallucination and, it is hoped, a vision of the ancient fathers. In TNG episode "Birthright," it is mentioned that Worf underwent the rite as a child.

MAKEE, BLAISDELL

played Lt. Spinelli in Classic Trek "Space Seed," and Mr. Singh in "The Changeling." TV credits include "Iron Horse."

MAKERS, the

mysterious, now extinct, race who made the androids on Mudd's Planet in Classic episode "I, Mudd."

Makho Root

ugly root used in medicinal/magical healing by Nona, a Kanutu witch woman, on Kirk to cure him of the Mugato's poison in Classic episode "A Private Little War."

MAKORA

Sayana's boyfriend, played by David Soul, in Classic episode "The Apple."

Maktag

in TNG episode "New Ground," it is learned that Alexander, Worf's son, was born on the 23rd of this Klingon month on Stardate 43205.

Makus III

destination of the the *Enterprise* when delayed by the loss of the shuttlecraft in Classic episode "The Galileo 7." They are transporting medical supplies to Makus III.

Malad

transport ship in TNG episode "New Ground."

Malcoria III

world receiving first contact team from the *Enterprise* in TNG episode "First Contact." Malcoria's leader, Chancellor Durken, thinks that though his people are scientifically advanced, they are too traditional and closed to face alien contact. He plans to cover up the *Enterprise*'s visit.

MALENCON, ARTHUR

hydraulic specialist, played by Mario Roccuzzo, working on the terraforming project on Velara III when

the laser drill malfunctions, killing him in TNG episode "Home Soil."

Maleran System
home of Amanda Rogers' adoptive parents, Starfleet marine biologists, mentioned in TNG episode "True Q."

Maliamanda Tapestry
rare item owned by Fajo in TNG episode "The Most Toys."

Malkis IX
home of the Lairons, people who developed the written word before developing sign or spoken language, mentioned in TNG episode "Loud As A Whisper."

MALLON
in TNG episode "The Vengeance Factor," he is left in charge of the Hromi.

MALLORY, ENSIGN
a security officer, played by Jay Jones, killed by tripping over an exploding rock on Gamma Trianguli VI in Classic episode "The Apple."

MALTZ
Klingon, played by John Larroquette, who worked under Kruge and is the only survivor of the Klingon party that attacked the ship and people on Genesis in "The Search For Spock."

Malurian System
the four planets of Omega Cygni destroyed by Nomad after it deemed four billion inhabitants "imperfect biological units"

in Classic episode "The Changeling."

MAN ALONE, A
first season DS9 episode written by Michael Piller and Gerald Sanford and directed by Paul Lynch. Odo is accused of the murder of a Bajoran black marketeer on the Promenade. Guest stars: Rosalind Chao, Edward Lawrence Albert, Max Grodenchik, Peter Vogt, Aron Eisenerg, Stephen James Carver, Tom Klunis, Scott Trost, Patrick Cupo, Kathryn Graf, Hana Hatae and Diana Cignoni.

MAN OF THE PEOPLE
sixth season TNG episode written by Frank Abetemarco, and directed by Winrich Kolbe. An alien ambassador tries to use Troi as a receptacle for his evil thoughts and emotions, drastically changing Troi's personality. Guest stars: Chip Lucia, Susan Rench, Stephanie Erb, Rick Scarry, J.P. Hubbell, Lucy Boryer and George D. Wallace.

MAN TRAP, The
this first season Classic Trek, written by George Clayton Johnson and directed by Marc Daniels, aired 9/8/66. A creature referred to as a Salt Vampire morphs into human forms but actually looks like a fuzzy swamp beast with suction cups on its elongated fingers and a megaphone for a mouth. Guest stars: Jeanne Bal and Alfred Ryder. Of note: First introduction of Saurian Brandy and the phrase "Great Bird of the Galaxy" (which is how fans later

affectionately refer to Gene Roddenberry.)

Manark IV
home of "sandbats" which, when resting, appear to be rock crystals mentioned in Classic episode "The Empath."

MANCOUR, T.L.
author of TNG novel *Spartacus.*

MANDARIN BAILIFF
played by Cary-Hiroyuki, he assists Q at the *Enterprise's* trial in TNG episode "Encounter At Farpoint."

MANDEL, JOHNNY
stunt double for Sulu in Classic Trek "Mirror, Mirror."
MANDL, KURT
director of the Gardeners of Eden terraforming project on Valara III played by Walter Gotell in TNG episode "Home Soil."

MANHEIM, DR. PAUL
scientist who created an uncontrollable experiment with time on Vandor IV, played by Rod Loomisseen, in TNG episode "We'll Always Have Paris" and mentioned in "Time Squared."

MANHEIM, JANICE
Picard's old flame, married to Dr. Paul Manheim, who comes aboard the *Enterprise* in TNG episode "We'll Always Have Paris."

Manheim Effect
time distortion created by Dr. Paul Manheim on Vandor IV in TNG episode "We'll Always Have Paris."

MANHUNT
second season TNG episode written by Terry Devereaux and directed by Rob Bowman. Lwaxana Troi boards ship while experiencing "the phase," a kind of menopause that makes Betazoid woman highly sexed, and Picard hides on the holodeck in a Dixon Hill story. Guest stars: Majel Barrett, Rod Arrants, Carel Struycken, Rhonda Aldrich, Robert Costanzo, Mick Fleetwood, Wren T. Brown, Colm Meaney and Robert O'Reilly.

Manitoba Journal of Interplanetary Psychology
publication which contacts Deanna Troi for research purposes in TNG episode "The Price."

MANKIEWICZ, DON
scriptwriter of Classic Trek "Court Martial." Writing credits include "I Want To Live," "One Step Beyond" and "Ironside."

MANLEY, STEPHEN
played Spock at age 17 in "The Search For Spock." TV credits include regular roles on "Married: The First Year" and "Secret Of Midland Heights."

MANNERS, KIM
director of TNG episode "When The Bough Breaks."

MANNING, RICHARD
story editor of first and second season and scriptwriter of TNG "The Arsenal of Freedom," "Symbiosis," "The Schizoid Man," "The Emissary," "Shades of Gray,"

"Who Watches The Watchers," "Yesterday's Enterprise" and "Allegiance." He was co-producer of TNG's third season.

Mar Obscura Nebula
the *Enterprise* fires photon torpedoes into this dark area to illuminate it in TNG episode "In Theory."

MARA
a Klingon woman, Kang's wife and science officer, played by Susan Howard in Classic episode "Day of the Dove."

Marajeritus VI
inhabited by people known as Ulans in TNG episode "Manhunt."

MARCELINO, MARIO
played the communications officer on *U.S.S. Grissom* in "The Search For Spock." TV credits include a regular role on "Falcon Crest," and the film "Losin' It."

MARCH, BARBARA
played Lursa in TNG "Redemption Part I and II," and guest starred in DS9 "Past Prologue."

MARCH
scientist, played by Kevin Sullivan, on Regula I working with Dr. Carol Marcus in "The Wrath of Khan."

Marcoffian Snow Lizard
Q mentions that he could have taken this form instead of appearing human during his exile from the Continuum in TNG episode "Deja Q."

Marcos XII
planet to which the Gorgon wants the children to lead him. The monster plans to enslave the world's supposed millions of inhabitants in Classic episode "And The Children Shall Lead."

MARCUS, DR. CAROL
Kirk's past lover and head of the scientific team that invented Genesis on Regula I played by Bibi Besch in "The Wrath of Khan." She has brought up their son, David.

MARCUS, DR. DAVID
the son of Dr. Carol Marcus and James Kirk, he was instrumental in the development of the Genesis device in "The Wrath of Khan." Kruge kills him when he tries to protect Saavik and Spock in "The Search for Spock." He was played by Merritt Butrick.

MARCUS, CLAUDIUS
proconsul, played by Logan Ramsey, who presides over planet 892-IV's version of the Roman empire in Classic episode "Bread and Circuses."

Marcus II
Sten, a famous artist known to Spock, lived on this planet in Classic episode "Requiem For Methuselah." Flint might have been Sten.

MARCUSE, THEO
played Korob on Classic Trek "Catspaw." Born in 1920 and died in 1967, his TV credits include "Voyage To The Bottom Of The Sea" and "The Man From U.N.C.L.E." Films include "The Cincinnati Kid" and "Last Of The Secret Agent."

MARGAN
Ornaran leader who needs felicium in TNG episode "Symbiosis."

MARGOLIS, MARK
played Dr. Apgar in TNG "A Matter of Perspective."

Mariposa, S.S.
a DYO-500 class Earth ship, commanded by Captain Walter Granger, sent from Earth November 27, 2183 with the ultimate destination of Ficus Sector. It is mentioned in TNG episode "Up The Long Ladder."

Mariposa
class M planet in the Ficus Sector, one light year from the Bringloidi system, inhabited by a race of slowly dying clones in TNG episode "Up The Long Ladder." The Spanish word mariposa means "butterfly."

MARIYE, LILY
played the ops officer in DS9 "Emissary."

MARK OF GIDEON, The
written by George F. Slavin and Stanley Adams and directed by Jud Taylor, this third season Classic Trek episode aired 1/17/69. Kirk is unknowingly transported to a duplicate Enterprise and believes his crew has disappeared. He meets a mysterious woman apparently connected to the secretive planet Gideon, which the *Enterprise* was investigating. Guest stars: Sharon Acker, David Hurst,

Gene Dynarsky and Richard Derr.

MARKLE, STEPHEN
played Kover Tholl in TNG "Allegiance."

MARKO, PETER
played Gaetano in Classic Trek "The Galileo Seven."

MARLO, STEVE
played Zabo in Classic Trek "A Piece Of The Action." Credits include "Branded" and several other Westerns, including the films "The Young Captives" and "The Hanged Man."

Marlonia
mentioned by Guinan as the most beautiful planet in the quadrant in TNG episode "Rascals."

MARLOWE, SCOTT
played Keeve Falor in TNG "Ensign Ro."

MAROUK, SOVEREIGN
leader on Acamar III, played by Nancy Parsons, who tries to make peace with the Gatherers in TNG episode "The Vengeance Factor." Yuta, her chef, is a traitor.

MARPLE
unseen security guard in Classic episode "The Apple" who, on Gamma Trianguli VI, is killed when one of the natives bashes his head in with a club.

MARPLON
Landruite technician and member of the underground, played by Torin Thatcher in Classic episode "The Return of the

Archons," who helps Kirk and Spock stop the machine on Beta III.

MARQUEZ, LIEUTENANT

helps Lt. Commander Nella Daren coordinate the evacuation of the Bersallis III colonists in TNG episode "Lessons."

MARR, DR. KILA

Enterprise xenologist, played by Ellen Geer, who finds her son's journal, killed by the Chrystalline Entity on Omicron Theta, carried within Data in TNG episode "Silicon Avatar."

Marrab Sector

location of Devidia II mentioned in TNG episode "Time's Arrow." A ciliated life form from this world is found along with Data's head in a cave in San Francisco.

MARS, BRUCE

played Finnegan in Classic Trek "Shore Leave," and a police officer on "Assignment: Earth." His credits include "Voyage To The Bottom Of The Sea" and "Then Came Bronson."

Mars

fourth planet of Sol system. The *Enterprise* was constructed on this world at the Utopia Planecia shipyards.

Mars defense perimeter ships

automated ships mentioned in TNG episode "The Best of Both Worlds." Three are destroyed by the Borg.

Mars Toothpaste

advertised in a magazine on Planet 892-IV in Classic episode "Bread and Circuses."

MARSH, MICHELE

played Leda in TNG "When The Bough Breaks."

MARSHAK, SONDRA

author of Classic Trek novels *The Price of the Phoenix, The Fate of the Phoenix, The Prometheus Design, Triangle,* the nonfiction book *Shatner: Where No Man* and editor of *The New Voyages I* and *II* with Myrna Culbreath. She also co-wrote *Star Trek Lives!*

MARSHALL, BOOKER

played Dr. M'Benga in Classic Trek "A Private Little War" and in "That Which Survives." He is also a writer.

MARSHALL, DON

played Lt. Boma in Classic Trek "The Galileo Seven." He also starred in the TV series "Land of the Giants" and has appeared on other shows including "The Bionic Woman."

MARSHALL, JOAN

played Lt. Areel Shaw in Classic Trek "Court Martial."

MARSHALL, SARAH

played Dr. Janet Wallace in Classic Trek "The Deadly Years." She was a regular on "Miss Winslow and Son," guested on "Perry Mason," and has been in the films "Scruples," "The Bunker" and "The Letter."

MARSHALL, WILLIAM

played Dr. Richard Daystrom in Classic Trek "The Ultimate Computer." Born 1924, he is a Shakespearean actor whose film credits include "Blacula," "The Boston Strangler" and "Twilight's Last Gleaming." He had a regular role on "Rosetti and Ryan."

MARTA

Orion woman, played by Yvonne Craig, kept at the asylum on Elba II with Garth of Izar who kills her by forced exposure to Elba's poisoned atmosphere in Classic episode "Whom Gods Destroy."

MARTEL, ARLENE

played T'Pring in Classic Trek "Amok Time." She guest starred in such TV series as "Iron Horse," "The Man From U.N.C.L.E." and "Petrocelli," and in the films "The Adventures of Nick Carter," "Indict and Convict" and "Conspiracy of Terror." She was sometimes credited under the name Tasha Martel.

MARTIA

shapeshifting alien assassin played, as an adult, by Iman in "The Undiscovered Country." When she appears as a little girl, she is played by Katie Jane Johnson.

Martian Colonies, Fundamental Declaration of

mentioned in Classic episode "Court Martial" as a precedent-setting document in interstellar law. A Mars colony is mentioned

in TNG episode "The Drumhead" as the birthplace of Crewman First Class Simon Tarses.

Martian Colony III

home of Mira Romaine in Classic episode "The Lights of Zetar."

MARTIN, JEFFREY

played an electronic technician in "The Voyage Home."

MARTIN, MEADE

played an engineer in Classic Trek "The Changeling."

MARTIN, NAN

played Victoria Miller in TNG "Haven."

MARTIN, DR.

Enterprise medical doctor played by Rick Fitts in TNG episode "Violations."

MARTINE, ANGELA

specialist in Life Sciences, played by Barbara Baldavin, who married Robert Tomlinson just before he died in an accident on the *Enterprise* in Classic episode "Balance of Terror." She reappears in "Shore Leave."

MARVICK, DR. LAWRENCE

co-worker, played by David Frankham, infatuated with Miranda Jones in Classic episode "Is There In Truth No Beauty." Jealous of the Medusan Kollos, he attempts to kill him, but instead glimpses him which drives him insane. The doctor then takes the *Enterprise* beyond the galaxy energy barrier, nearly stranding them.

Masiform D

drug McCoy uses on Spock, making him sick to his stomach, after he is attacked by poison darts from a plant on Gamma Trianguli VI in Classic episode "The Apple."

MASON, DAN

played Accolan in TNG "When The Bough Breaks."

MASON, JOHN

producer and scriptwriter of TNG "Unnatural Selection."

MASON

one of the kidnapped *Enterprise* children in TNG episode "When The Bough Breaks."

MASSETT, PATRICK

played Duras in TNG "Sins of the Father" and "Reunion."

MASTERPIECE SOCIETY, the

fifth season TNG episode written by James Kahn, Adam Belanoff and Michael Piller and directed by Winrich Kolbe. A stellar core fragment is heading for a planet inhabited by human colonists who have constructed a utopian world and do not want outside interference. Their lives are in danger without the intervention of the *Enterprise* which in turn causes disruption and entices some colonists to leave. The changes will ultimately destroy the perfect society even though the stellar core fragment is

diverted. Guest stars: John Snyder, Dey Young, Ron Canada and Sheila Franklin.

MASTERS, LIEUTENANT CHARLENE

officer in charge of some engineering sections on the *Enterprise*, played by Janet MacLachlin in Classic episode "The Alternative Factor."

MATHESON, RICHARD

scriptwriter of Classic Trek "The Enemy Within." Born in 1926, he is a famous horror author who wrote scripts for "The Incredible Shrinking Man," "The Night Stalker" and "Ghost Appearances/Circle of Fear," as well as many print stories.

MATLOVSKY, ALISA

second assistant director in DS9 "Emissary."

MATLOVSKY, SAMUEL

composer of music in Classic Trek "I, Mudd." His other score credits include the movie "Fish Hawk."

MATSON, LIEUTENANT

crewmember in the rec room played by David Troy in Classic episode "The Conscience of the King" when Uhura sings "Beyond Antares" to Riley.

MATTER OF HONOR, a

second season TNG episode written by Wanda M. Haight, Gregory Amos and Burton Armus, and directed by Rob Bowman. In an officer exchange program, Riker is sent to serve on the Klingon ship *Pagh*. Then the captain decides to

attack the *Enterprise*. Guest stars: John Putch, Christopher Collins, Brian Thompson, Laura Drake, Colm Meaney and Peter Parros.

MATTER OF PERSPECTIVE, A

third season TNG episode written by Ed Zuckerman and directed by Cliff Bole. Riker is accused of murdering Dr. Apgar when the research station orbiting Tanuga IV explodes just as he beams off it to return to the *Enterprise*. Different versions of the events on the station are played out according to the testimony of different witnesses. Guest stars: Craig Richard Nelson, Gina Hecht, Mark Margolis, Juli Donald and Colm Meaney.

MATTER OF TIME, A

fifth season TNG episode written by Rick Berman and directed by Paul Lynch. A time traveler, Dr. Rasmussen, visits the *Enterprise* from the future, but is actually from the past, stealing future technology to sell for profit before it is actually discovered. Guest stars: Matt Frewer, Stefan Gierasch, Sheila Franklin and Shay Garner. Of note: This episode was supposedly written with Robin Williams in mind, but when he could not play the role Matt Frewer was hired. Robin Williams is a Star Trek fan and has always wanted to act in an episode.

Matter/Energy Scrambler

transporter-like device used by the Minarans in Classic episode "The Empath."

MATTHEW

child on the *Enterprise* in TNG episode "The Last Outpost."

MATTHEWS, ERIC

played one of the Edo children in TNG "Justice."

MATTHEWS, TODD

mentioned in TNG episode "The Royale" as the author of the novel *The Hotel Royale*.

MATTHEWS

one of the security officers, killed by Ruk, who accompany Kirk and Chapel to Exo III in Classic episode "What Are Little Girls Made Of."

MATTHIAS, JEAN LOUISE

scriptwriter for TNG "Imaginary Friend," "Lessons" and "Schisms."

MAURA

Lt. Aquiel Uhnari's dog in TNG episode "Aquiel."

MAURER, RALPH

played Bilar in Classic Trek "The Return of the Archons," and the SS Lieutenant in "Patterns of Force."

MAURISHKA

played Yeoman Zara Jamal in Classic Trek "Operation: Annihilate!"

MAVEK
attendant at the Tilonus Institute for Mental Disorders who insists Riker stabbed another man in TNG episode "Frame of Mind."

MAVIG
played by Deborah Downey, a young, blonde woman who wore her hair in a ponytail in Classic episode "The Way To Eden."

Maxia Zeta
site of a battle between the *Stargazer* and a Ferengi vessel mentioned in TNG episode "The Battle." It was supposedly the first Ferengi contact, though the ship's origin was unknown at the time.

MAXWELL, CHARLES
played Virgil Earp in Classic Trek "Spectre of the Gun." His TV credits include "I Led Three Lives" and "Branded."

MAXWELL, CAPTAIN BENJAMIN
Starfleet captain who lost his family to a Cardassian raid, played by Bob Gunton in TNG episode "The Wounded."

MAYAMA, MIKO
played Yeoman Tamura in Classic Trek "A Taste of Armageddon."

MAYBERRY, RUSS
director of TNG "Code of Honor."

MAYLOR, SEV
supposedly the 93-year-old mother of Ambassador Olcar in TNG episode "Man of the People."

MAYNARD, BIFF
played Ruffian in TNG "Elementary, Dear Data."

McAllister C5 Nebula
a gaseous cloud which hides an entire Cardiassian fleet in TNG episode "Chain of Command."

McBROOM, AMANDA
played Philipa Louvois in TNG "The Measure of a Man."

McCARTHY, JEFF
played Roga Danar in TNG "The Hunted."

McCARTNY, DENNIS
composer of incidental music in a dozen first season TNG episodes, and at least that many more during the second and third seasons. He also scored the main title theme for DS9 and the music for "Emissary."

McCAULEY, DANNY
assistant director on "Star Trek: The Motion Picture." His other directing credits include "Zorro: The Gay Blade," "Jinxed" and "Blue Thunder."

McCAY, BILL
author of TNG novel *Chains of Command.*

McCHESNEY, MART
played Armus in TNG "Skin of Evil," and Sheliak in TNG "The Ensigns of Command."

McCONNELL, JUDY
played Yeoman Tankris in Classic Trek "Wolf In The Fold." TV credits include "The Beverly Hillbillies," "Green Acres" and the movie "Gidget Gets Married."

McCORMICK, CAROLYN
played Minuet in TNG "11001001" and "Future Imperfect."

McCOY, JAMES L.
make-up artist on "The Search For Spock."

McCOY, MATT
played Devinoni Ral in TNG "The Price."

McCOY, JOANNA
unseen daughter of Dr. Leonard McCoy. Trained in the medical field, she communicates with her father often. In the animated episode "The Survivor," she is mentioned attending school on Cerberus.

McCOY, DR. LEONARD H.
ship's doctor in Classic Trek played by DeForest Kelley. "An old country doctor" from Georgia, nicknamed Bones, he is Kirk's good friend and Spock's friendly adversary. He is divorced and has a daughter named Joanna (who is never seen.) McCoy appears in TNG at age 137 in "Encounter At Farpoint," though his name is never officially spoken. Prior to "The Motion Picture," he tried to retire but Kirk had him called back to duty. A cynic with a good heart, he hates transporters (he's afraid of them.) He always gets some of the best lines, including his famous "I'm a doctor, not a fill in the blank" statements. In "Court Martial," the computer reads off his commendations as including "Legion of Honor, Awards of Valor, decorated by Starfleet Surgeons."

McCREADY, ED
actor and stunt man who played both the male and female creature in Classic Trek "Miri," an inmate in "Dagger of the Mind," an SS trooper in "Patterns of Force," Dr. Carter in "The Omega Glory" and the barber in "Spectre of the Gun." His other credits include "Today's FBI" and the film "Partners."

McCULLOUGH, ROBERT L.
producer, and scriptwriter of TNG "The Icarus Factor" and "Samaritan Snare."

McCUSKER, MARY
played the nurse in TNG "Evolution."

McDERMOTT, KEVIN
played the alien baseball player who goes up to bat in DS9 "Emissary."

McDONALD, CHRISTOPHER
played Castillo in TNG "Yesterday's Enterprise."

McDOUGALL, DON
director of Classic Trek "The Squire of Gothos." He has also directed episodes of "Ghost Appearances," "Planet of the Apes," "The Gemini Man" and "The Bionic Woman." He has also directed the films "The Aquarians," "The Heist" and "The Mark of Zorro."

McDUFF, COMMANDER KIERAN
identity assumed by a Sartaaran provocateur, played by Erich Anderson, to control the *Enterprise* and make them attack the Lysian Alliance in TNG episode "Conundrum."

McEVEETY, STEVEN
played the red-haired boy in Classic Trek "Miri." He is the son of director Vincent McEveety.

McEVEETY, VINCENT
director of Classic Trek episodes "Miri," "Dagger of the Mind," "Balance of Terror," "Patterns of Force," "The Omega Glory" and "Spectre of the Gun." He has also directed episodes of the TV series "Petrocelli," and the Disney films "Million Dollar Duck" and "Herbie Goes Bananas."

McFADDEN, GATES
stars as Dr. Beverly Crusher in TNG. Before landing the TNG role, the actress did stage work and studied dance. She attended Brandeis University where she graduated with a B.A. in theater arts, and studied acting under Jack LeCoq in Paris. She starred in several New York plays, and directed the choreography and puppet movement for the film "Labyrinth," and assisted in stage fantasy sequences for "Dreamchild." McFadden was dropped from TNG after the first season for reasons unknown to her, then was re-assigned the role in the third season. During the second season of TNG Diana Muldaur played the

ship's doctor, a completely different character from that of Beverly Crusher. During the year she was not on TNG, Gates had a small role in the film "The Hunt For Red October."

McGINNIS, SCOTT
played "Mr. Adventure" in "The Search For Spock." His TV credits include a regular role in "Operation: Petticoat," and the films "Survival of Dana" and "Joysticks."

McGIVERS, LIEUTENANT MARLA
ship's historian, played by Madlyn Rhue, who falls in love with Khan and ends up going into exile with him on Ceti Alpha V in Classic episode "Space Seed."

McGONAGLE, RICHARD
played Dr. Ja'dar in TNG "New Ground."

McGOWAN, OLIVER
played the caretaker in Classic Trek "Shore Leave."

McGREEVEY, MICHAEL
scriptwriter of DS9 "Babel."

McHURON, EVE
one of Mudd's women, played by Karen Steele, in Classic episode "Mudd's Women" who marries Ben Childress.

McILVAIN, RANDY
art director of DS9.

McINTYRE, DEBORAH
writer of TNG "The Neutral Zone." (The original story was written with Mona Glee.)

McINTYRE, JAMES
played Hali in TNG "Who Watches The Watchers."

McINTYRE, VONDA
author of Classic Trek novels *The First Adventure*, *The Entropy Effect*, *The Wrath of Khan*, *The Voyage Home* and *The Search For Spock*.

McKANE, BRENDAN
played a technician in TNG "Coming of Age."

McKinley, Earth Station
repair facility which orbits Earth in TNG episodes "Family" and "The Drumhead." The *Enterprise* goes here after suffering damage during an attack by the Borg.

McKinley Rocket Base
houses the rocket Gary Seven sabotages in Classic episode "Assignment: Earth."

McKINNEY
crewmember killed in an accident mentioned in TNG episode "Conspiracy."

McKNIGHT, ENSIGN
played by Pamela Winslow, an *Enterprise* officer in TNG episodes "Clues" and "In Theory."

McLEISTER, TOM
played Kolos in TNG "Q Less."

McLIAM, JOHN
played Fento in TNG "Who Watches The Watchers."

McLOWERY, FRANK
one of the Clanton gang in Classic episode "Spectre of

the Gun." This is also the name the people of Tombstone call Spock.

McLOWERY, TOM
member of the Clanton gang and the role given to McCoy by the Melkots in Classic episode "Spectre of the Gun."

McNALLY, KELLY ANN
played One One in TNG "11001001."

McNALLY, TERENCE
played B'Tardat in TNG "Half A Life."

McNAMARA, PATRICK J.
played Captain Taggert in TNG "Unnatural Selection."

McNARY, SHARON
Lt. McNary's wife in TNG episode "The Big Goodbye."

McNARY
Police Chief Dan Bell's lieutenant, played by Gary Armagnal, in a hologram simulation in TNG episode "The Big Goodbye."

McNEILL, ROBERT DUNCAN
played Nicholas Locarno in TNG "The First Duty."

McNULTY, PATRICIA
played Yeoman Tina Lawton in Classic Trek "Charlie X." Her other TV credits include a regular role on "The Tycoon."

McPHERSON
one of the "supermen" in Classic episode "Space Seed."

McTOSH, BILL
played a Klingon in "Star Trek: The Motion Picture."

MEA 3
native of Eminiar VII, played by Barbara Babcock, in Classic episode "A Taste of Armageddon."

MEADER, WILLIAM
played Space Command Representative Lindstrom in Classic Trek "Court Martial."

MEANEY, COLM
stars as Chief Miles Edward O'Brien in both TNG and DS9. Born in Dublin, Ireland, he appeared in the BBC programs "Z Cars" and "Strangers" before locating to New York in 1978. He worked off Broadway and in regional theatre before moving to Los Angeles in the mid-1980's to do film and TV work. His many credits include TV guest spots on "Moonlighting," "Remington Steele," "Tales From The Dark Side" and the pilot for "Dr. Quinn, Medicine Woman." His films include "Dick Tracy," "Come See The Paradise," "Die Hard II," "The Gambler III," "Far and Away" (in which he helped Tom Cruise with his accent,) "The Last of the Mohicans," "Under Seige" and "The Commitments." He was in the first three episodes of TNG, then took a role in the soap opera "One Life To Live" before finally getting the more permanent TNG role, although he does not appear in every episode. Meaney jumped at the chance to be transferred to

a starring role on DS9. He has a wife, Barbara, and a young daughter, Brenda, a Star Trek fan herself.

MEARS, YEOMAN
one of the seven aboard the shuttlecraft who survives the crash on Taurus II, and is played by Phyllis Douglas in Classic episode "The Galileo 7."

MEASURE OF A MAN, The
second season TNG episode written by Melinda M. Snodgrass and directed by Robert Scheerer. A cyberneticist, who believes Data to be an object and not a being, wants to take him apart to learn how to make more Datas. A trial ensues to prove that Data has rights as an individual and can deny this man's request to take him away from the *Enterprise*. Guest stars: Amanda McBroom, Clyde Kusatsu, Brian Brophy, Colm Meaney and Whoopi Goldberg. Of note: This episode got Melinda Snodgrass the attention of TNG's producers and more assignments. She ended up moving to Hollywood to become the series' executive script consultant for the third through fifth season.

Mecklinite
substance which interferes with the *Enterprise*'s sensors in TNG episode "Galaxy's Child."

Medal of Honor
medal which reminds Kirk of his real life as he is packing to leave the *Enterprise* and join his crew on

Omicron Ceti III. The shock of his remembrances throws off the spores' effect in Classic episode "This Side of Paradise."

Medallion
piece of jewerly containing a shapeshifting element that may be a distant "cousin" to Odo in DS9 episode "Vortex."

MEDIATORS
two Mediators, played by David Q. Combs and Richard Lavin, sentence Wesley to death on Rubicam III in TNG episode "Justice."

Medina
star system and location of Altec and Straleb in TNG episode "The Outrageous Okona."

MEDLOCK, MICHAEL A.
scriptwriter who wrote TNG "Second Chances."

Medusans
race which resembles a rainbow spectrum of lights. It is said their appearance drives humans insane. Medusans are telepaths and empaths. Kollos of Classic episode "Is There In Truth No Beauty?" is a Medusan.

MEERSON, STEVE
played "Fat Little Boy" in Classic Trek "Miri." Film credits include "The Boy In The Plastic Bubble," "Skag" and "The Cannonball Run."

Megas Tu
magical planet in animated episode "The Majicks of Megas Tu."

MEIER, JOHN
stunt double for William Shatner in "The Voyage Home." He also did work on the film "Cannery Row."

Mek'ba
name of the court trial Worf must go through to clear his father's name from treason in TNG episode "Sins of the Fathers."

Melakol
Romulan unit of pressure mentioned in TNG episodes "The Defector" and "The Next Phase."

MELAKON
in Classic episode "Patterns of Force," the deputy Fuhrer who is truly in charge. He is played by Skip Homeier (who also plays Dr. Sevrin in "The Way To Eden.")

Melanoid Slimeworm
insult Rondon calls Wesley in TNG episode "Coming of Age."

Melbourne, U.S.S.
one of the ships involved with the Borg at the same time as the *Saratoga* in Deep Space Nine's first episode "Emissary." It is also seen in TNG episode "11001001." The ship is offered to Riker in "The Best of Both Worlds."

Melkot
species mistrustful of strangers who test the *Enterprise* command crew by putting them through the motions of acting out the battle at the OK Corrall

in Classic episode "Spectre of the Gun."

MELL, JOSEPH
played the Orion trader in Classic Trek pilot "The Cage" (scenes of which appeared in the "The Menagerie" which was actually released.) Film credits include "City of Fear" and "The Delphi Bureau." He has also guest starred on the TV series "Adventures of Superman."

Mellis II
in TNG episode "Ship in a Bottle," this is the destination (in virtual reality) of Moriarty and Countess Bartholomew.

Mellitus
cloud creature of Alpha Majoris I mentioned in Classic episode "The Wolf In the Fold." It is solid at rest and gaseous in motion.

Melona IV
new Federation colony attacked by the Chrystalline Entity in TNG episode "Silicon Avatar."

Meltasion Asteroid Belt
area through which the *Enterprise* tows a 300 year old garbage scow leaking radiation to dump it in the Gamelan system in TNG episode "Final Mission."

Memory Alpha
central library storage and research facility which is damaged by "The Lights of Zetar" in the third season of Classic Trek. Mira Romaine goes to Memory Alpha at the end of the episode to help start restoring its computers' knowledge banks.

Mempa Sector
in TNG episode "Redemption," Gowron attacks Duras' supply bases located in this sector.

MENAGE A TROI
third season TNG episode written by Fred Bronson and Susan Sackett and directed by Rob Legato. The Ferengi kidnap Riker, Troi and Lwaxana while the *Enterprise* is on shore leave at Betazed. Guest stars: Majel Barrett, Frank Coresentino, Ethan Phillips, Peter Slutsker, Rudolph Willrich and Carel Struycken.

MENAGERIE, The (Part 1 and 2)
written by Gene Roddenberry, this first season Classic Trek episode aired 11/17/66 and 11/24/66. Part one was directed by Marc Daniels and part two by Robert Butler. Interspersed with scenes from Star Trek's original pilot "The Cage," this ingenious script brings back Captain Pike and sets Spock on an illegal journey to the off-limits world of Talos IV, a trip which reveals a lot of the history of the *Enterprise*. Guest stars, which include both those who appeared in "The Cage" as well as in the later sequel: Malachi Throne, Sean Kenney (Pike in wheelchair,) Julie Parrish, Jeffrey Hunter (original Pike,) John Hoyt, Susan Oliver, Majel Barrett (when she played Number One her stage name was M. Leigh Hudec,) Laurel Goodwin, Peter Duryea, Meg Wyllie and Jon

Lormer. Of note: The Keepers were all played by older women. The early Spock behaves uncharacteristically, smiling and yelling a lot because "The Cage" scenes were filmed before much was known about Vulcans and their behavior and philosophy. Leonard Nimoy notes that he was at a loss as to how to play his role opposite the brooding, stoic and standoffish Jeffrey Hunter (both characters, Pike and Spock, were too alike to allow for much contrast.) When William Shatner was brought in to play a more impulsive and brash young captain, everything clicked into place. This episode won the Hugo Award for Best Dramatic Presentation of 1966.

MENCHEN, LES
scriptwriter of TNG "The Outrageous Okona."

MENDAK, ADMIRAL
Romulan commander of the *D'Voris* in TNG episode "Data's Day." He was played by Alan Scarfe.

MENDEZ, COMMODORE JOSE I.
commander of Starbase 11 in Classic episodes "The Menagerie" and "The Cage." He was played by Malachi Throne.

MENDON, ENSIGN
Benzite junior officer, played by John Putch, on the *Enterprise* as part of an exchange program in TNG episode "A Matter of Honor."

MENDOZA, SETH
the Federation representative to Barzan in TNG episode "The Price." He is played by Castulo Guerra.

MENDROSSEN, KI
Chief of Sarek's staff, played by William Denis, who shields Sarek from others to hide Sarek's disease in TNG episode "Sarek."

MENGES, JAMES
played the jogger in "The Voyage Home."

MENOSKY, JOE
scriptwriter of TNG "Legacy," "Clues," "First Contact," "The Nth Degree," "In Theory," "Darmok," "Hero Worship," "Conundrum," "Time's Arrow Part I and II" "The Chase" and "Suspicions."

Menthars
in TNG episode "Booby Trap," dead race known to be very innovative at one time who built the booby traps in the debris of Orelious IX.

MENVILLE, CHUCK
scriptwriter of the animated episodes "Once Upon A Planet" (with Len Jenson) and "Practical Joker."

MENYUK, ERIC
played The Traveller in TNG "Where No One Has Gone Before" and "Remember Me."

Merak II
planet plagued by a disease that is destroying all its vegetation in Classic episode "The Cloud Minders." The *Enterprise*

goes to Ardana to get the zienite which will stop the spread of this scourge.

Merculite Rockets
Koras says the Klingons warded off the Ferengi with these weapons in TNG episode "Heart of Glory."

MERET, VICE PROCONSUL
Romulan high official defector in TNG episode "Face of the Enemy."

MERIK, CAPTAIN R.M.
commander of the *Beagle*, played by William Smithers, which the *Enterprise* finds empty and orbiting Planet 892 IV in Classic episode "Bread and Circuses." Merik, who has become Merikus, First Citizen of the Roman Empire, is killed by Claudius when he tries to help the *Enterprise* crew escape Claudius' prison.

MERIKUS
see entry for Merik, Captain R.M.

MERIWETHER, LEE
played Losira in Classic Trek "That Which Survives." Born in 1935, the former Miss America had regular roles on "The Time Tunnel," "The New Andy Griffith Show," "Mission: Impossible," and "Barnaby Jones." She also played Catwoman in the 1960's movie "Batman." Most recently, she has appeared in recent commecials for Uncle Ben's Rice among other products.

MERRIFIELD, RICHARD
played Technician Webb in Classic Trek "Tomorrow Is Yesterday."

MERRILL, TODD
played Gleason in TNG "The Best of Both Worlds Part II" and "Future Imperfect."

Merrimac, U.S.S.
ship that will transport Sarek and Perrin to Vulcan at the end of TNG episode "Sarek."

MERSON, RICHARD
played the pie man on TNG "Elementary, Dear Data."

Meruvian Tea
in TNG episode "The Child," Guinan makes this drink in Ten Forward.

MESEROLL, KENNETH
played McDowell in TNG "The Next Phase."

Meson
substance which, combined with leptons, builds up in the Barzan wormhole making it unstable in TNG episode "The Price."

Messalina System
destination of the *Enterprise* after TNG episode "Cost of Living."

Metagenic Weapon
genetic virus that can destroy an entire biosphere. These kinds of weapons are outlawed by the Federation because they are so deadly. It is believed the Cardassians have one in TNG episode "Chain of Command," but it is only a

lure to get Picard, Worf and Crusher to check it out.

METAMORPHOSIS
written by Gene L. Coon and directed by Ralph Senensky, this second season Classic Trek episode aired 11/10/67. In this alien love story, Kirk, Spock, McCoy and Nancy Hedford's shuttle is forced to land on an asteroid where they discover a marooned man, Zephram Cochrane, inventor of the warp drive, and a cloud-like creature he calls The Companion. Guest stars: Elinor Donahue and Glenn Corbett. Of note: Majel Barrett provides the voice for The Companion. A universal translator is used to communicate with the alien entity.

Metaphasic Shield
invented by Ferengi scientist Dr. Reyga, a type of force field which allows a ship to enter, unharmed, the core of a star. Reyga is killed for his theories in TNG episode "Suspicions."

Metaphysics, First Law of
philosophical theory which comes up on Spock's computer in "The Voyage Home" as he is reeducating himself. It states, simply, "Nothing unreal exists."

Metathalmus
Vulcan brain organ mentioned in TNG episode "Sarek."

METRONS
an advanced race of beings resembling young, angelic boys who can stop ships

with their minds and are encountered in Classic episode "Arena." The Metron we see is played by Carole Shelyne.

Mev Yap
Klingon for "that is enough" heard in TNG episode "Sins of the Father."

MEYER, NICHOLAS
director/scriptwriter. He directed "The Wrath of Khan" and "The Undiscovered Country" and co-wrote the scripts for "The Voyage Home" and "The Undiscovered Country." His other film scripts include "The Seven Percent Solution" and "Time After Time" as well as some movies made for TV.

MICHAEL, CHRISTOPHER
played Man #1 in TNG "Legacy."

MICHAELIAN, MICHAEL
scriptwriter of TNG "Too Short A Season."

MICHAELS, MICKEY S.
set decorator on DS9.

MICHELSON, HAROLD
production designer on "Star Trek: The Motion Picture." He also did work on the film "Mommie Dearest."

MICKEY, D.
character who kills the Bell Boy in TNG episode "The Royale." He is played by Gregory Beecroft.

Microbrain
inorganic but intelligent life form on Velara III

which declares war on the *Enterprise* in TNG episode "Home Soil."

Micromius
mentioned in TNG episode "11001001" as the location of a medical disaster which Dr. Crusher studied under Dr. Epstein.

Midos V
a world mentioned by the Kirk android in Classic episode "What Are Little Girls Made Of?" as the location of the first experiments involving Dr. Korby's androids.

MIDRO
troglyte, played by Garry Evans, in Classic episode "The Cloud Minders."

Mikat
Cardassian city were Gul Madred grew up mentioned in TNG episode "Chain of Command."

Mikulaks
race that donated tissue samples to help cure Correllium Fever on Nahmi IV in TNG episode "Hollow Pursuits."

Milan
transport ship carrying Worf's parents in TNG episode "New Ground."

MILES, BOB
actor and stunt man who played McCoy's double in Classic Trek "Miri" and played a Klingon in "The Trouble With Tribbles."

MILES, JOANNA
played Perrin in TNG "Sarek," and "Unification Part I."

Milika III
mentioned in TNG episode "Tapestry" as a world where Picard led an away team which saved an ambassador's life, a major event in his career.

MILKIS, EDWARD K.
assistant producer of Classic Trek's second season and the producer of season three as well as the producer of TNG. He also produced the series "Petrocelli," and the movies "Women In Chains" and "The Devil's Daughter."

MILLER, ALLAN
played the "Alien In The Bar" in "The Search For Spock." TV credits include regular roles on "AES Hudson Street," "Soap," "Nero Wolfe" and "Knots Landing." He also had guest roles on such shows as "Battlestar Galactica."

MILLER, STEPHEN
Wyatt Miller's elderly father in TNG episode "Haven." He was played by Robert Ellenstein.

MILLER, VICTORIA
Wyatt Miller's elderly mother in TNG episode "Haven." She was played by Nan Martin.

MILLER, WYATT
doctor who is engaged to Deanna in TNG episode "Haven." He left the *Enterprise* to save some Tarellian refugees dying from a plague. He was played by Rob Knepper.

MILLS, KEITH
scriptwriter of TNG "The Royale."

Milnos IV
mentioned as the world where Lt. Commander Nella Daren studied thermal geysers early in her career in TNG episode "Lessons."

Mimas
moon of Saturn where Wesley's Nova Squadron team is taken by an emergency transporter after evacuating them from their ships in TNG episode "The First Duty."

Minara
sun about to go nova. It has several satellites, including the world where Gem lives and the Vians homeworld in Classic episode "The Empath."

Minara II
second planet in the Minaran system and apparently the Vians homeworld in Classic episode "The Empath."

MIND'S EYE, The
fourth season TNG episode written by Ken Schafer and Rene Echevarria and directed by David Livingston. Geordi is kidnapped on his way to Risa and brainwashed by the Romulans, using his Visor, to kill a Klingon governor. Guest stars: Larry Dobkin, Edward Wiley, John Fleck, Colm Meaney and Denise Crosby.

Mind Meld
Vulcan technique of joining minds with another by placing their hands at various pressure points on the face of the person they are melding with. The minds join and thoughts can be exchanged as well as feeling and personality. Spock uses the meld for the first time in the Classic episode "Dagger of the Mind" when he joins minds with Van Gelder. He melds with McCoy in "Mirror, Mirror," Kirk in "The Paradise Syndrome" and "Requiem For Methuselah," and Kirk, Scotty and McCoy in "Spectre of the Gun." He uses the meld in the movie "The Wrath of Khan" to give McCoy his katra for safe-keeping. A meld restores him in "The Search for Spock." In "The Voyage Home" he melds with the humpback whale Gracie and ascertains that she is pregnant. In "The Undiscovered Country" he melds with Valeris to get information from her. Sarek melds with Kirk in "The Search For Spock," and with Picard in "Sarek." In short, a nifty Vulcan talent that makes for some good drama.

Mind-sifter
Klingon device mentioned in Classic episode "Errand of Mercy." Supposedly a way to empty a mind of valuable information, its side effects include brain damage.

Mind Sphere
in TNG episode "The Battle," a Ferengi mind control tool DaiMon Bok uses to convince Picard he is back on the *Stargazer*.

MINES, STEPHEN
played Specialist Robert Tomlinson in Classic Trek "Balance of Terror."

MINNERLY, LIEUTENANT
mentioned in TNG episode "Skin of Evil" as Tasha's martial arts opponent.

MINOR, MICHAEL
art director on "The Wrath of Khan." He has also done work for the Classic Trek series and on the movies "The Man Who Saw Tomorrow," and "Spacehunter: Adventures in the Forbidden Zone."

Minos
located in the Lorenze Cluster, planetary home of a humanoid race which sold weapons to both sides in the Ersalrope Wars mentioned in TNG episode "The Arsenal of Freedom. Their own weapons wiped them out.

Minos Corva
mentioned in TNG episode "Chain of Command" as a world fought over in the Federation/Cardassian war and eventually ceded to the Federation although the Cardassians still want it. Picard is tortured when he won't reveal Starfleet's defense plans for the world. It is 11 light years from McAllister C5 Nebula (see entry.)

Mintaka III
in TNG episode "Who Watches The Watchers," world inhabited by Vulcanoids. The world is again encountered in "Allegiance."

Mintakans
Vulcanoid inhabitants of the planet Mintaka III who

are at a primitive age in their development in TNG episode "Who Watches the Watchers."

MINUET
in TNG episode "11001001," an image, played by Carolyn McCormick, created by the Bynars to distract Riker.

Mira System
location of the planet Dytalix B in TNG episode "Conspiracy."

Miradorn
bad-tempered race in DS9 episode "Vortex."

MIRAMANEE
Indian woman, one of two who see Kirk emerge from the temple and believes he is a god. Later she and Kirk marry and she becomes pregnant with his child. She dies when her people shower her and Kirk with rocks in the belief that Kirk is a false god when he cannot make the beam come from the temple. Miramanee is played by Sabrina Scharf in Classic episode "This Side Of Paradise."

MIRANDA, JOHN
played a garbageman in "The Voyage Home." He has also appeared on the TV series "The Paper Chase."

MIRAT, PENNY
student from Rigel who studied at the Academy with Picard. She and Picard never had an affair but always wanted to. Picard gets a chance to change that when Q makes him

relive this episode in his life in TNG episode "Tapestry."

MIRI
this first season Classic Trek episode aired 10/27/66 and was directed by Vince McEveety and written by Adrian Spies. The *Enterprise* visits a planet where all the adults died, leaving behind children with a virus that makes them age one month for every 300 years. As the children enter puberty, they go insane and die. Guest stars: Kim Darby, Michael J. Pollard, Jim Goodwin (Farrell in several Trek episodes,) John Megna and Ed McCready. Of note: Several of the children in this episode are the children of cast members. Grace Lee Whitney's sons are included, as well as William Shatner's two older daughters, Leslie and Lisabeth, around 7 and 5 years old at the time. Director Vince McEveety's son Steven McEveety had the role of "red headed boy" while Dawn Roddenberry, Gene's daughter from his first marriage, played another extra.

MIRI
young girl played by Kim Darby in Classic episode "Miri." She is on the verge of adolescence, and contracts the aging disease. She helps Kirk find the other children so he can help them and develops a crush on him in the process.

MIRICH, ERNIE
played the waiter in TNG "Relics."

MIROK
Romulan science officer, played by Thomas Kopache, in TNG episode "The Next Phase."

MIRRAULT, DON
played Hayne in TNG "Legacy."

MIRREN, OLIANA
one of the students, played by Estee Chandler, competing with Wesley to take the Academy exam in TNG episode "Coming of Age."

MIRROR, MIRROR
written by Jerome Bixby and directed by Marc Daniels, this second season Classic Trek episode aired 10/6/67. Kirk, McCoy, Scott and Uhura are accidentally transported to a parallel universe where their crewmates are barbaric and the Enterprise is part of a violent empire. Meanwhile, their savage counterparts are transported aboard the real ship and all must find a way to get back to where they belong. Guest stars: Barbara Luna, Vic Perrin, Pete Kellett, Garth Pillsbury and John Winston. Of note: The savage Spock sports a slick beard, Sulu has a long, facial scar and the hots for Uhura, and Chekov screams. This episode was nominated for a Hugo Award for Best Dramatic Presentation of 1967.

MIRT
one of Oxmyx's hoods in Classic episode "A Piece of the Action." He was played by Jay Jones.

Mishiama Wrist Lock and Break

martial arts strategy Tasha mentions she wants to learn for the competition in TNG episode "Skin of Evil."

MITCHELL, DALLAS

played Tom Nellis in Classic Trek "Charlie X." TV credits include "Voyage To The Bottom Of The Sea." Films include "Any Second Now," "Hijack!" and "Tail Gunner Joe."

MITCHELL, JAMES X.

played Lt. Josephs in Classic Trek "Journey To Babel."

MITCHELL, V.E.

author of TNG novel *Imbalance*, and Classic Trek novels *Windows On A Lost World* and *The Enemy Unseen*.

MITCHELL, ADMIRAL

mentioned in TNG episode "Starship Mine" as an official Commander Hutchinson worked for in Starfleet.

MITCHELL, LIEUTENANT COMMANDER GARY

science officer of the *Enterprise* who experiences an electrical shock when the ship tries to cross the galaxy's energy barrier in Classic episode "Where No Man Has Gone Before." He is Kirk's best friend and attended Starfleet Academy with him. He is killed by Dr. Elizabeth Dehner when the heightened mental powers he gains from the shock cannot be controlled and he

turns evil. He was played by Gary Lockwood.

Mizar II

mentioned in TNG episode "Allegiance" as the homeworld of Kova Tholl which has been conquered six times in 300 years.

Mizarians

inhabitants of Mizar II who have been conquered six times in 300 years because they do not resist attack. This is how they've survived, as mentioned in TNG episode "Allegiance."

MLODINOW, LEONARD

story editor, and scriptwriter of TNG "The Dauphin."

Moab IV

name of the closed colony that has had no outside contact for over 200 years in TNG episode "The Masterpiece Society."

Module L 73

module affected by Eichner radiation in TNG episode "The Child." It carries a plasma plague that begins to mutate and grow after being exposed to the radiation.

MOFFAT, KATHERINE

played Etana in TNG "The Game."

MOGH

mentioned in TNG episode "Sins of the Fathers" as Worf and Kurn's father. He was denounced as a Romulan spy in the Khitomer massacre, where he died, but it was really Duras' father Ja'rod who was the traitor.

Mok'ba

Klingon exercises mentioned in TNG episodes "Birthright" and "Second Chances."

Molecular Cybernetics

Dr. Noonian Soong's specialty mentioned in TNG episode "The Schizoid Man."

Molybdenum Cobalt Alloy

substance out of which Data is made mentioned in TNG episode "The Most Toys."

MONAK, GARY

responsible for special effects on DS9.

Mondor

a Pakled ship in TNG episode "Samaritan Snare." Captained by Captain Grebnedlog, it has a few armaments and Romulan designed shields.

Monitor, U.S.S.

in TNG episode "The Defector," ship on its way to the Neutral Zone to help the *Enterprise* but it doesn't arrive in time.

MONROE, LIEUTENANT

Enterprise bridge officer, played by Jana Marie Hupp, killed in an explosion in TNG episode "Disaster" leaving Deanna in charge as the next highest ranking officer.

MONTAIGNE, LAWRENCE

played Decius in Classic Trek "Balance of Terror," and Stonn in "Amok Time." TV credits include "The Man From U.N.C.L.E.," "Voyage To The Bottom Of

The Sea" and "The Feather and Father Gang." Films include "The Underground Man" and "Deadly Blessings."

MONTALBAN, RICARDO

played Khan Noonian Singh in Classic Trek "Space Seed" and in the film "The Wrath of Khan." Born November 25th, 1920 in Mexico City, his credits in the U.S. include the films "Neptune's Daughter," "The Singing Nun" and "Conquest of the Planet of the Apes." His starring role in the "Fantasy Island" series and his Chrysler car commercials made him a household name.

MONTGOMERY

Enterprise security guard in Classic episode "The Doomsday Machine." He is attacked by Decker while escorting him to Sickbay. He was played by Jerry Catron.

MOORDIGAN, DAVE

played a Klingon in "Star Trek: The Motion Picture." Film credits include "48 Hours."

MOORE, RONALD D.

story editor and scriptwriter of TNG "The Bonding," "The Defector," "Yesterday's Enterprise," "Sins of the Father," "Family," "Reunion," "First Contact," "In Theory," "Redemption Part I and II," "Disaster," "The First Duty," "The Next Phase," "Relics," "Aquiel," "Tapestry," "The Chase," "Rightful Heir," "Descent" and "Chain of Command."

MOORE, ADMIRAL JAMES
officer who tells Picard of a distress call from the Ficus Sector in TNG episode "Up The Long Ladder."

MOOSEKIAN, DUKE
played Gillespie in TNG "Night Terrors."

MORAG, COMMANDER
Klingon commander of the *Ku'vat* patrolling the nearby Starfleet Subspace Relay Station 47 in TNG episode "Aquiel."

MORAN, W. REED
scriptwriter of TNG "Sins of the Father."

Mordan IV
planetary member of the Federation, headed by Karnas who kidnapped a Federation diplomatic party in TNG episode "Too Short A Season."

MORDOC
Ferengi in TNG episode "The Last Outpost." He was played by Jake Dengel.

MORDOCK
Benzite who is the first of his people to be accepted by Starfleet Academy in TNG episode "Coming of Age." He was played by John Putch, the same actor who played the Benzite Ensign Mendon in "A Matter of Honor." Wesley suspects the two characters are the same person.

Mordock Strategy
the Benzite Mordock becomes famous for this military theory at the Academy and greatly impresses Wesley in TNG episode "Coming of Age."

MORE TROUBLES, MORE TRIBBLES
written by David Gerrold, this animated Classic Trek episode aired 10/6/73 and features the return of Cyrano Jones, the tribbles, the Klingons, (including Captain Koloth) and a Glommer, the tribbles natrual enemy. In this story, instead of reproducing when they eat the tribbles just get bigger and bigger. Voices: David Gerrold (Korax,) James Doohan (Koloth) and Stanley Adams (Cyrano Jones.)

MOREAU, LIEUTENANT MARLENA
the captain's woman who works in the ship's chem labs in the mirror universe in Classic episode "Mirror, Mirror." She works in the ship's chem labs.

MORGA, TOM
played a Klingon in "Star Trek: The Motion Picture," and "the brute" in "The Undiscovered Country."

MORGAN, SEAN
played Lt. O'Neil in Classic Trek "The Return of the Archons," and "The Tholian Web." He also played Ensign Harper in "The Ultimate Computer," and the engineer in "The Paradise Syndrome." TV credits include "Voyage To The Bottom Of The Sea" and a regular role on "The Adventures of Ozzie and Harriet."

Morgana Quadrant
destination of the *Enterprise* after it leaves Tango Sierra in TNG episode "The Child" and mentioned as a destination in "Where Silence Has Lease."

Morgs
male species on Sigma Draconis in Classic episode "Spock's Brain." They are kept primitive by the women who will not let them have use of any technology. The leader of the Morgs is played by James Daris.

MORI, JEANNE
played the helmswoman on the *U.S.S. Grissom* in "The Search For Spock." Film credits include "Night Shift."

MORIARTY, PROFESSOR JAMES
first seen in TNG episode "Elementary, Dear Data," he is played by Daniel Davis. Sherlock Holme's famous adversary returns to the *Enterprise* via the holodeck in "Ship In A Bottle." He believes he can become a real person and not a simulation given the correct technology.

Morikun VII
world where Picard trained during his days at the Starfleet Academy mentioned in TNG episode "Tapestry."

MORLA
Kara's fiance who lives on Cantaba Street on Argelius II and is questioned about her murder in Classic episode "Wolf in the Fold."

He is played by Charles Dierkop.

Moropa
race which maintain a truce with the Bolians in TNG episode "Allegiance."

MORRIS, JOAN STUART
appeared in TNG episode "Suspicions."

MORRIS, LESLIE
played Reginod in TNG "Samaritan Snare."

MORRIS, PHIL
played Trainee Foster in "The Search For Spock." He is the son of Greg Morris who starred in "Mission: Impossible." Phil Morris starred in the new "Mission: Impossible" as Barney's son.

MORROW, BYRON
played Komack in Classic Trek "Amok Time" and Admiral Westervliet in "For The World Is Hollow And I Have Touched The Sky." TV credits include "Lost In Space," and "The Bionic Woman," and regular roles on "The New Breed" and "Executive Suite."

MORROW, ADMIRAL
officer who appears in "The Search For Spock" and is played by Robert Hooks.

MORSHOWER, GLENN
played Burke in TNG "Peak Performance."

Mortae
mining tool used by the troglytes in Classic episode "The Cloud Minders."

MORTON, MICKEY
played Kloog in Classic Trek "The Gamesters of

Triskelion." TV credits include "The Bionic Woman," "The Man From U.N.C.L.E." and "Iron Horse."

MORWAY, PROFESSOR
mentioned as an archeologist working at the Landris digs in TNG episode "Lessons."

MORWOOD, PETER
author of Classic Trek novel *Rules of Engagement.*

MOSER, DIANE
played a member of the Ten Forward crew in TNG "The Offspring."

MOSIMAN, MARNIE
played "woman" in TNG "Loud As A Whisper."

MOSLEY, DR. HAL
scientist on Penthara IV assisting the *Enterprise* in cooling the planet's atmosphere in TNG episode "A Matter of Time." He was played by Stefan Gierasch.

MOSS, ARNOLD
played Anton Karidian in Classic Trek "The Conscience of the King." Born Jan. 28, 1910 in Brooklyn, his TV credits include "The Man From U.N.C.L.E." and "The Girl From U.N.C.L.E." His film credits include "My Favorite Spy" and "Caper of the Golden Bulls."

MOSS, STEWART
played Joe Tormolen in Classic Trek "The Naked Time" and Hanar in "By Any Other Name." TV credits include a regular stint on "Fay" and guest spots on "Cannon." Film credits include "Live Again, Die Again," "Conspiracy of Terror" and "Women In White."

MOST TOYS, The
third season TNG episode written by Shari Goodhartz and directed by Timothy Bond. Kivas Fajo, a collector of rare items, kidnaps Data for his collection, but Data refuses to cooperate. Guest stars: Saul Rubinek, Jane Daly, Nehemiah Persoff and Colm Meaney.

MOT
Bolian barber who works in the *Enterprise* and appears in TNG episodes "Ensign Ro" and "Starship Mine." He is played by Ken Thorley.

MOVAR, GENERAL
Romulan officer under Commander Sela in TNG episode "Redemption." He was played by Nicholas Kepros.

MOVE ALONG HOME
first season DS9 episode written by Frederick Rappaport, Lisa Rich, Jeanne Carrigan Fauci and Michael Piller and directed by David Carson. Beings who call themselves the Waddi visit DS9 and introduce Quark to a new game. Unknown to Quark, however, his players are actually Sisko, Kira, Dax and Bashir who experience the life-threatening events of the game as if they are really happening. Guest stars: Clara Bryant, Joel Brooks and James Lashly.

MUDD, HARCOURT FENTON
swindler, liar, cheat and rogue encountered by the *Enterprise* in Classic episodes "Mudd's Women," "I, Mudd" and the animated "Mudd's Planet." Leo Francis Walsh is one of his aliases. He had a wife named Stella who apparently tormented him until he left her. He was played by Roger C. Carmel.

MUDD, STELLA
Harcourt Fenton Mudd's wife of whom he made an android duplicate in Classic episode "I, Mudd." She was played by Kay Elliott.

MUDD'S PASSION
written by Stephen Kandel, this animated Classic Trek episode aired 11/10/73. Yet another sequel to the Harry Mudd series. This time Mudd has a love potion which gets released on the *Enterprise* and affects the crew. It has a side-effect however. Once the potion has run its course, the victims go through a few hours of hating each other. Guest voices: Majel Barrett (M'Ress, Lora,) James Doohan (Lt. Arex, human miner,) Roger C. Carmel (Mudd) and Nichelle Nichols (female Ursinoid.)

MUDD'S WOMEN
first season Classic Trek written by Stephen Kandel and Gene Roddenberry and directed by Harvey Hart, this episode aired 10/13/66, and features the first appearance of Harry (Harcourt Fenton) Mudd (later seen in "I, Mudd.") Shuttling women to sell as brides to men on a mining colony on Rigel XII is only one of Mudd's jobs. He also possesses an illegal drug from Venus which exagerrates an individual's physical attractiveness. Guest stars: Roger C. Carmel, Karen Steele, Susan Denberg, Maggie Thrett, Gene Dynarski and Jim Goodwin (who appears as Farrell in "The Enemy Within," "Miri," and others.) Dilithium crystals are a big deal in this episode. Round playing cards are also featured when Eve McHuron (one of the brides to be) plays solitaire called Doublejack.

MUDIE, LEONARD
played a survivor in Classic Trek pilot "The Cage" and in "The Menagerie." Born in 1894 and died in 1965, his film credits include "The Mummy" ('32,) "Dark Victory" ('39) and "The Magnetic Monster" ('53.) TV credits include "Adventures of Superman."

Mudor V
planet on which the *Enterprise* just completed a mission at the beginning of TNG episode "Disaster."

Mugato
ape-like creature with white fur and a horn like a unicorn sticking out from the center of its forehead from planet Neural. One attacks Kirk in Classic episode "A Private Little War." Later, another one attacks Nona. They have poisonous fangs, mate for life and are very territorial. Kirk refers to it once as a Gumato, which could have

just been a slip of the tongue.

Muktok Plants

plant which sings or emits music. Riker and Troi planted one on Betazed when they met and which is still there, mentioned in TNG episode "Menage A Troi."

MULDAUR, DIANA

played Dr. Ann Mulhall in Classic Trek "Return To Tomorrow," Dr. Miranda Jones in "Is There In Truth No Beauty?" and Dr. Katherine Pulaski during the second season of TNG. She also had regular roles on "The Survivors," "McCloud," "Born Free," "The Tony Randall Show," "Hizzoner," "Fitz and Bones" and "L.A. Law." She has also guest starred in numerous TV series.

MULHALL, DR. ANNE

astrobiologist whose body is used by the entity Thalessa in Classic episode "Return To Tomorrow." She is played by Diana Muldaur.

MULL, PENTHOR

mentioned in TNG episode "The Vengeance Factor" as an Acamarian Gatherer who died because of Yuta's vengeance.

MULLENDORE, JOSEPH

composer of the score for Classic Trek "The Conscience of the King." He also scored episodes of "Lost In Space" and "Voyage To The Bottom Of The Sea."

MULRONEY, KIERAN

played Benzan in TNG "The Outrageous Okona."

Multitronics

technology used on the M 5 computer invented by Dr. Daystrom in Classic episode "The Ultimate Computer."

MURAMOTO, BETTY

played the scientist on TNG "Deja Q."

Murasaki 312

electromagnetic, quasar-like phenomenon the shuttlecraft Galileo is going to study when it is swept off course and crashes on Taurus II in Classic episode "The Galileo 7."

MURDOCK, GEORGE

played the god creature in "The Final Frontier" and Admiral Hanson in TNG "The Best of Both Worlds Part I and II."

MURDOCK, JOHN M.

played the beggar in "Time's Arrow Part I."

MURDOCK, KERMIT

played the prosecutor in Classic Trek "All Our Yesterdays." Film credits include "The Lonely Profession," "The Godchild" and "Captains and the Kings."

MURDOCK, M.S.

author of the Classic Trek novel Web of the Romulans.

Murinite

mineral found on Rigel IV. Henghist's knife is made of this material as mentioned in the Classic episode "Wolf In The Fold."

MUSKAT, JOYCE

scriptwriter of Classic Trek "The Empath."

Muskinseed Punch

Hahliian drink Lt. Uhnari enjoys in TNG episode "Aquiel."

MUSTIN, TOM

played an intern in "The Voyage Home."

MYERS

one of Geordi's diagnostic engineers in TNG episode "Hollow Pursuits."

N'Game Nebula

planet inhabited by the Paxans in TNG episode "Clues."

N'VEK, SUBCOMMANDER

second in command on the Romulan warbird Khazara who kidnaps Troi in TNG episode "Face of the Enemy." He is killed when his plot is discovered.

NAAB, CAPTAIN

captain of the Ajax mentioned in TNG episode "Tapestry."

NAFF, LYCIA

played Sonya Gomez in TNG "Q Who" and "Samaritan Snare."

NAGEL, ENSIGN

in TNG episode "Peak Performance," crewmember who accompanies Riker to the Hathaway and helps create the "false image" defense maneuver. She was played by Leslie Neale.

NAGILUM

alien scientist who studies life and death and captures the Enterprise in TNG episode "Where Silence Has Lease." He was played by Earl Boen.

NAGUS, The

first season DS9 episode written by Ira Steven Behr and David Livingston and directed by David Livingston. The Ferengi high ruler, the Nagus, visits Quark on DS9 in the hopes that the Ferengi can use the wormhole to do business in the Gamma Quadrant where their reputation does not precede them as it does in the Alpha Quadrant. Guest stars: Wallace Stevens, Max Grodenchik, Lou Wagner, Tiny Ron, Barry Gordon, Lee Arenberg and Aron Eisenerg.

Nagus, Grand

Ferengi high official who rules the race. In DS9 his name is Zek, played by Wallace Shawn.

Nahmi IV

world which has an outbreak of Correllium Fever in TNG episode "Hollow Pursuits."

NAKAMURA, ADMIRAL

commander of Starbase 173 in TNG episode "The Measure of a Man," played by Clyde Kusatsu.

NAKED NOW, The

first Season TNG episode written by John D.F. Black and J. Michael Bingham and directed by Paul Lynch. In a story very similar to the Classic episode

"The Naked Time," the *Enterprise* encounters the Psi 2000 virus from another ship, the *Tsiolkovsky*, which causes victims to lose all inhibitions. Guest stars include: Brooke Bundy, Benjamin W.S. Lum, Michael Rider, David Renan, Skp Stellrecht and Kenny Koch. Of note: Tasha manages to successfully seduce Data and it apparently has a very positive effect on both of them. In this episode, an image on the computer screen appears: A picture of a bird with nacelles wearing a Starfleet shirt with insignia. Could this be the Great Bird?

NAKED TIME, The

first season Classic Trek episode written by John D.F. Black and directed by Marc Daniels which aired 9/29/66. An alien virus infects the crew and exposes their most private longings. This plot was reused in a first season Next Generation episode called "The Naked Now." Guest stars: Bruce Hyde and Stewart Moss. Lieutenant Kevin Riley makes his first appearance later returning in "Conscience of the King." Nurse Christine Chapel (Majel Barrett) also makes her first appearance of many. Spock cries, Sulu chases people with a sword and Kirk professes an almost psychotic love for his ship.

NALDER, REGGIE

played Shras in Classic Trek "Journey To Babel." Film credits include: "The Dead Don't Die," "Salem's Lot" and "The Devil and Max Devlin." He has also done TV guest appearances on shows such as "The Man From U.N.C.L.E."

NALEE, ELAINE

played the female Klingon in TNG "Hide And Q."

Nanites

little robots created by Wesley who run amok on the *Enterprise* in TNG episode "Evolution."

NAPIER, CHARLES

played Adam in Classic Trek "The Way to Eden." He had regular starring roles on the TV series "Outlaws" and "The Oregon Trail." Film credits include "Wacko" ('82).

NARADZAY, JOSEPH

played First Sergeant USMC in "The Voyage Home."

NARDINO, GARY

executive producer of "The Search For Spock" and "The Undiscovered Country."

Narenda III

Klingon outpost mentioned as having been destroyed in an alternate timeline in TNG episode "Yesterday's Enterprise."

NARSU, ADMIRAL UTTAN

superior officer to Captain Shumar on the *Exeter* in TNG episode "Power Play."

NASH, JENNIFER

played Meribor in TNG "The Inner Light."

NATIRA

high priestess of Yonada in Classic episode "For The World Is Hollow And I Have Touched The Sky." She and McCoy fall in love and want to marry. She was played by Kate Woodville.

NAYROCK, PRIME MINISTER

in TNG episode "The Hunted," the leader of the Angosians. He was played by James Cromwell.

Nazreldine

mentioned as the *Enterprise*'s last stop in TNG episode "The Icarus Factor" where a crewman picks up the flu.

NEALE, LESLIE

played Nagel in TNG "Peak Performance."

Nebula Class Starship

ships of this class include the *Phoenix* and the *Sutherland* which appeared in TNG episodes "The Wounded" and "Redemption" in that order.

NECHAYEV, VICE ADMIRAL ALINA

in TNG episode "Chain of Command" she allows Picard to take a commando team into Cardassian space. She also appears in "Descent."

Neck Pinch

Vulcan neck pinch which can render a victim unconscious. To perform this stunt, the side of the neck is pinched, supposedly stopping the blood flow. Also known as a Vulcan nerve pinch.

NEEDHAM, HAL

actor/director/stuntman who played Mitchell's double in Classic Trek "Where No Man Has Gone Before." Born in 1931, his directing credits include "Smokey and the Bandit," "The Cannonball Run" and "Megaforce."

Negatron Hydrocoils

a drop of jelly-like substance which make robotic muscles work like real muscles in the android bodies Sargon, Henoch and Thalessa are constructing in Classic episode "Return To Tomorrow."

NEIL

a member of the team trying to steal trilithium from the *Enterprise* in TNG episode "Starship Mine."

Neinmann

mentioned in TNG episode "When The Bough Breaks" as a lost civilization, much like Atlantis, which disappeared on Xerxes VII.

Nel

in TNG episode "Violations," telepathic rapist Jev previously visited this world.

Nel Bato System

mentioned in TNG episode "The Most Toys" as a place where Jovis might have gone.

NELLEN

silent aide to Admiral Satie in TNG episode "The Drumhead." She was played by Ann Shea.

NELLIS, TOM
an *Enterprise* crewman in Classic episode "Charlie X." He was played by Dallas Mitchell.

NELSON, CAROLYN
played Yeoman Atkins in Classic Trek "The Deadly Years." Film credits include: "Man On A String," "Freedom" and "Memorial Day."

NELSON, GENE
director of Classic Trek "The Gamesters of Triskelion." Born in 1920 he also worked as an actor. He has directed the movies "Kissin' Cousins" and "Washington Behind Closed Doors" as well as episodes of "Get Christie Love!" and "The Wackiest Ship In The Army."

Nelvana III
in TNG episode "The Defector," Jarok says the Romulans are building a base on this world so they can have an advantage in a first strike attack against the Federation.

Nenebek
miner Captain Dirgo's shuttle in TNG episode "Final Mission."

NEPTUNE, PETER
played Aron in TNG "The Dauphin."

Neptune Bath Salts
advertised in a magazine on Planet 892 IV in Classic episode "Bread and Circuses."

NERAL
Romulan proconsul when Picard last visited the Romulan homeworld mentioned in TNG episode "Unification."

Nervala IV
earthquake-prone world on which a duplicate Riker is stranded for eight years in TNG episode "Second Chances."

NERYS, MAJOR KIRA
regular character in "Deep Space Nine" played by Nana Visitor. She is a Bajoran who grew up fighting the Cardassians. A young woman whose mistrust of others' motives has made her both strong and naive, she became an underground terrorist at a very early age but quit when she didn't agree with their tactics. Although she works for the Federation she doesn't agree with every decision they make. A capable pilot, her fighting abilities are equal to a man's and she has proven herself capable of commanding DS9 when Sisko is away. Despite her violent nature, she is a woman of compassion and intellect but who has a lot of trouble relating to others on a personal level. She hates the Cardassians, although she understands her view is prejudiced since not all Cardassians are represented by the evil few in charge.

Nestorial III
in TNG episode "Time's Arrow," the planet where Guinan was living when picked up by the *Enterprise* to begin running Ten Forward.

NESVIG, COLONEL
head of McKinley Rocket Base who captures Kirk and Spock in Classic episode "Assignment: Earth." He was played by Morgan Jones.

Neural
planet of hill people and villagers who used to be peaceful but are learning about weapons and killing due to Klingon interference in Classic episode "A Private Little War."

Neural Field
weapon the Kelvans use to paralyze their opponents in Classic episode "By Any Other Name."

Neural Neutralizer
machine which can empty the mind and is used on the Tantalus penal colony in Classic episode "Dagger of the Mind." The device appears to be much like the Klingon mind-sifter (see entry.)

Neural Paralyzer
drug McCoy gives Kirk when he is fighting Spock on Vulcan in Classic episode "Amok Time." It puts the body in a death-like state.

Neural Scanners
in TNG episode "Future Imperfect," Riker is told the Romulans used these machines on him to find out everything about him.

Neutral Zone, Romulan
area of space that is a no man's land of sorts. Federation and Romulan ships agree not to cross it,

protecting their territories from each other.

Neutrino Beacon
device used to find Geordi in TNG episode "The Enemy."

Neutrino Beam
used in TNG episode "A Matter of Honor" to remove ship-eating parasites from the *Enterprise* and the *Pagh*.

Neutronium
mentioned in Classic episode "The Doomsday Machine" as the element used to make the hull of the out-of-control weapon.

NEUWIRTH, BEBE
played Lanel in TNG "First Contact." She is best known for her recurring role in "Cheers" and has done both theatrical films and TV.

New Berlin
Federation colony which thinks it's being attacked by the Borg when Ferengi ships show up in TNG episode "Descent."

NEW GROUND
fifth season TNG episode written by Stuart and Sara Charno and Grant Rosenberg and directed by Robert Scheerer. Worf's son, Alexander, comes to live with Worf on board the ship. Meanwhile, the *Enterprise* is to participate in an experiment involving a new means of propulsion called a Soliton Wave. Guest stars: Brian Bonsall, Georgia Brown, Jennifer Edwards and Richard McGonagle.

New Manhattan
located on Beth Delta I mentioned in TNG episode "Evolution."

New Martim Vaz
aquatic city on Earth mentioned in TNG episode "The Survivors."

New Paris
colony suffering from a plague. The *Enterprise* is en route there when the *Galileo* is lost in Classic episode "The Galileo 7."

New Providence
colony mentioned in TNG episode "The Best of Both Worlds" as located on Jouret IV.

New United Nations
referred to by Data in TNG episode "Encounter At Farpoint" as having been active since 2036.

NEWLAND, JOHN
director of Classic Trek "Errand of Mercy." He hosted and directed the series "One Step Beyond" and directed episodes of "The Man From U.N.C.L.E." and many other 1960's shows.

NEWMAN, WILLIAM
played Kalin Trose in TNG "The Host."

NEWMAR, JULIE
played Eleen in Classic Trek "Friday's Child." Born in 1935, her TV credits include "Batman" (she played Catwoman,) "The Twilight Zone," "The Bionic Woman" and "My Living Doll." Her film credits include "Seven Brides For Seven Brothers" and "McKenna's Gold."

NEXT PHASE, The
fifth season TNG episode written by Ronald D. Moore and directed by David Carson. It appears that Ro and Geordi are killed when they return from a rescue mission but they have actually phased into another space where they can see the crew but the crew cannot see them. Guest stars: Michelle Forbes, Thomas Kopache, Susanna Thompson, Kenneth Meseroll, Shelly Leverington and Brian Cousins.

Ni'pok
Klingon word meaning "deja vu" in TNG episode "Cause and Effect."

NIBOR
Ferengi who plays chess with Riker in TNG episode "Menage A Troi." He was played by Peter Slutsker.

NICHOLS, NICHELLE
starred as Uhura in Classic Trek and all the movies, and provided the voice for Uhura and many other characters in the animated series. Born in Robbins, Illinois, she has done stage work, writing, singing and dancing. She was twice nominated for the Sara Siddon Award as best actress of the year for her work in the plays "Kicks & Co." and "The Blacks." She also toured as a vocalist with Duke Ellington and the Lionel Hampton bands. Her TV credits before Trek include "The Lieutenant" and "CBS Repertory Theatre." When she was on "The Lieutenant," she met and had a love affair with Gene Roddenberry, but they had parted as friends before she landed her role as Uhura. She almost quit Trek after its first season because of her lack of lines but met Martin Luther King Jr. who told her that she had to stay on because her character was treated as an equal by her shipmates, providing a great role model for blacks and black women. Her film credits include "Mister Buddwing," "Three For The Wedding," "Truck Turner," "Made In Paris," "Porgy and Bess" (with Sammy Davis, Jr.) and "Doctor, You've Got To Be Kidding." One of her more recent films is "The Supernaturals." She has made frequent appearances at Star Trek conventions, sung at many night clubs and released an album, "Dark Side Of The Moon." She is also involved in the recruitment of minorities for NASA. She recently sold her memoirs *Beyond Uhura* to Putnam. She also sold an idea for a science fiction novel which she is currently writing. In her spare time she paints, sculpts, designs clothing and writes poetry (some of which was published in the magazine *All About Star Trek Fan Clubs* during the late 1970's.)

NICKSON, JULIA
played Lian T'Su in TNG "The Arsenal of Freedom."

Nigala IV, Station
the destination of the *Enterprise* in "Deja Q."

NIGHT TERRORS
fourth season TNG episode written by Shari Goodhartz, Pamela Douglas and Jeri Taylor and directed by Les Landau. The crew experiences dream deprivation which makes them hallucinate while stranded in Tyken's Rift, a tear in space. Troi may resolve their dire straits if she can communicate with the only survivor of the *Brittain*, a comatose Betazoid man. Guest stars: Rosalind Chao, John Vickery, Duke Moosekian, Colm Meaney, Deborah Taylor, Lanei Chapman, Brian Tochi and Craig Hurley.

Night-Blooming Throgni
mentioned in TNG episode "Angel One" as a Klingon plant that has an odor like the virus plaguing the ship.

NILREM
medical personnel working at the hospital Riker is taken to on Malcoria III in TNG episode "First Contact."

Nimbus III
planet of Galactic Peace in "The Final Frontier." It is on this world that Sybok takes his hostages, one human, one Klingon, one Romulan, to lure the *Enterprise* (or any starship) into his clutches so he can use it to seek ShaKaRee.

NIMOY, ADAM
director of TNG episodes "Rascals" and "Timescape." He has a degree in law and is the son of actor/direc-

tor/writer/producer Leonard Nimoy.

NIMOY, LEONARD

actor/writer/director/producer who starred as Mr. Spock in Star Trek, all the movies, played the voice of Spock in the animated series, and an older Spock in TNG "Unification." He also directed "The Search For Spock," and directed and co-wrote "The Voyage Home." Nimoy is also responsible for inventing the Vulcan salute, the Vulcan neck pinch (with the help of Shatner) and the Vulcan mind meld. Born March 26, 1931 in Boston, he married actress Sandi Zober in 1954. They have two children, Julie and Adam (who went on to direct two episodes of TNG.) He studied acting under Jeff Corey (who played Plasus of "The Cloud Minders.) In the early part of his career, Nimoy also taught and worked in a pet shop and as a movie theater usher. His first roles, other than on the stage, include "Zombies of the Stratosphere," "Queen For A Day" and "Kid Monk Baroni." He also had walk-on and bit parts in movies such as "Them!" His TV roles included small stints on "Rawhide," "The Virginian," "The Outer Limits," "The Twilight Zone," "Profiles In Courage," "Dr. Kildare," "The Lieutenant," "Sea Hunt" and "The Man From U.N.C.L.E." (with Shatner) not all of them starring roles. After Trek was cancelled, Nimoy landed the starring role as Paris in

"Mission: Impossible" where he remained for two years. He was offered roles in other series but declined them. He hosted the long-running series "In Search Of," and "Lights, Camera, Action!" and did Broadway work, playing Tevye in "Fiddler on the Roof," Holmes in the play "Sherlock Holmes," and Dr. Martin Dysart in "Equus." He appeared on many game shows, including "The 20,000 Dollar Pyramid" with Shatner. He appeared in the films "Catlow" (in which he has a semi-nude scene, mostly in shadow,) "The Alpha Caper" and "The Missing Are Deadly" all while going to Antioch college where he finally obtained a Masters in education. He also produced several albums on which he sang hit songs of the 1960's much to his embarrassment today (his voice is weak.) He wrote several poetry books, and the autobiography of his early Trek days called *I Am Not Spock*. He also starred in the remake of "Invasion of the Body Snatchers," and following that, starred in his one-man play "Vincent" (which he also wrote and directed.) Nimoy refused to sign on as Spock for "Star Trek: The Motion Picture" until he came to an agreement with Paramount to receive royalties on the merchandising of his likeness. Spock was a popular face, and Nimoy received no money for any merchandising after the series. He finally got a $2.5 million settlement from

Paramount as part of his agreement to play Spock in the film. He also starred in the film "Seizure" around the same time. Though Nimoy denies it now, he was the one who came up with the idea to kill Spock in "The Wrath of Khan." He was tired of the role and didn't think it was furthering his career. Now that he's changed his mind, he denies any culpability in the "killing" of Spock. He had some more great roles in the 1980's, including "A Woman Called Golda," and the mini-series "Marco Polo." He has also directed the feature films "Three Men and A Baby," "The Good Mother" and "Funny About Love." During the filming of "The Voyage Home," Nimoy met his second wife, Susan Bay. They are currently married and living in Los Angeles. (Bay, a studio production executive, recently had a small part in an episode of DS9.) His first wife Sandi, from whom he separated in 1986 and then divorced, has appeared on some TV talk shows discussing their long marriage and quick divorce. She claims she had no warning and to this day they do not speak. Nimoy, in his turn, discussed the divorce on "The Whoopie Goldberg Show," explaining that the marriage had been rocky for many years, but that he was waiting for his children to "grow old and die" before he took on the difficult task of breaking up with his wife of over 30 years. His most recent starring role (other than Trek) is in the 1991 film

"Never Forget" which he also produced. He is currently working on possible future stage and television projects with William Shatner. The two, who have stayed in touch since the 1960's and have developed a close friendship, recently successfully toured the country in a two-man show discussing their Star Trek years. Of Shatner's directing on "The Final Frontier," Nimoy professes only admiration. Though the movie was not as successful as the other Trek movies, Nimoy blames a poor script for its luke-warm reception, the same reason, he says, for his own flop, "Funny About Love." When not acting or directing Nimoy's hobbies include photography and writing.

NIMS, SHARI

played Sayana in Classic Trek "The Apple."

Nitrium

in TNG episode "Cost of Living," the *Enterprise* involuntarily picks up parasites that feed off this substance and disable the ship.

NIVEN, LARRY

scriptwriter of the animated episode "The Slaver Weapon." He is a well known science fiction writer and co-author of several bestsellers with Jerry Pournelle such as *The Mote In God's Eye* and *Lucifer's Hammer* among others. He won the Hugo for his novel *Ringworld*, which spurred many sequels. The Kzin characters in the animated episode are an alien race he invented in his novels.

NOEL, DR. HELEN

psychiatrist who investigates the Tantalus penal colony with Kirk. He is forced by the neural neutralizer to fall in love with her in Classic episode "Dagger of the Mind." She is played by Marianna Hill.

NOG

young Ferengi who is Jake Sisko's friend on DS9. He is the son of Rom and Quark's nephew. He is played by Aron Eisenerg.

Nomad

machine that was once an Earth space probe but, through an accident, merged with a machine called Tan Ru in Classic episode "The Changeling." Its mission, to secure and sterilize soil samples, changed to "seek out and sterlize biological life forms" as a result. The voice of Nomad is Vic Perrin's.

Nome

a part of Vulcan philosophy mentioned in Classic episode "The Savage Curtain" as meaning "All."

NONA

Kanutu woman who has great knowledge (or magical powers) in healing and heals Kirk's Mugato bite with a Makho root. She is Tyree's wife but has her eye on Kirk. She dies when she is stabbed with her own knife by the villagers. She was played by Nancy Kovack.

Noranium Alloy

substance found on Gamma Hromi II at the Gatherer's camp in TNG episode "The Vengeance Factor."

NORED, LIEUTENANT ANNE

in animated episode "The Survivor," an *Enterprise* security woman engaged to Carter Winston. Her voice is Nichelle Nichols'.

Norep

drug Dr. Crusher uses on Warren in TNG episode "Who Watches the Watchers" without result. Dr. Crusher also uses this drug, referred to as "noreph" when trying to save Tasha in "Skin of Evil."

NORESS, DR. SUSAN

said to be the creator of the plasma plague held in module L 73 in TNG episode "The Child."

Norkan Outposts

site of a massacre for which Admiral Jarok is responsible, mentioned in TNG episode "The Defector."

NORLAND, VICTORIA

played Daras in Classic Trek "Patterns of Force." TV credits include "The Man From U.N.C.L.E."

NORMAN

the only coordinator of the androids on Mudd's planet in Classic episode "I, Mudd." He is played by Richard Tatro.

Norphin V

mentioned in TNG episode "Relics" as a beauti-

ful retirement world for former Starfleet officers.

Norsicans

three thugs who attacked Cadet Picard and pierced his heart with a knife as mentioned in TNG episode "Samaritan Snare" and who are seen in "Tapestry."

NORTON, JIM

played Einstein in TNG "The Nth Degree" and "Descent."

NORWICK, NATALIE

played Martha Leighton in Classic Trek "The Conscience of the King."

Nova Squadron

name of Wesley's cadet group in TNG episode "The First Duty."

Novachron

Wesley tells Guinan he and everyone else thinks she's from this world in TNG episode "The Child."

NOVAK, FRANK

played the businessman in DS9 "Babel."

NOWELL, DAVID

camera operator on "The Search For Spock."

NTH DEGREE, The

fourth season TNG episode written by Joe Menosky and directed by Robert Legato. Reginald Barclay is back after having been exposed to an alien probe that elevates his intelligence to near omnipotence. He takes control of the ship to increase the warp capacity in the engines and creates a distortion in space. Guest stars: Dwight Schultz, Saxon

Trainor, Jim Norton, Page Leong and David Coburn.

NU'DAQ, CAPTAIN

Klingon officer commanding the attack ship *Maht H'a* in TNG episode "The Chase."

Null G Ward

mentioned in TNG episode "Yesterday's Enterprise" as the place to which Dr. Selar is ordered.

Number 4 Shield

shield protecting the starboard side of the ship and that always seems to go out first.

NUMBER ONE

first officer of the *Enterprise* under Captain Pike in Classic pilot "The Cage" and "The Menagerie." She was played by Majel Barrett under the name M. Leigh Hudec.

NUMBER ONE

name Picard often calls Riker in TNG.

Numerian

Ambassador Olcar of TNG episode "Man of the People" is a member of this empathic species, whose powers work only within their own race.

NURIA

leader of the primitive Vulcans on Mintaka in TNG episode "Who Watches The Watchers" who thinks Picard and his crew are gods. She was played by Kathryn Leigh Scott.

Nus'ra

Tilonus IV blade used for ceremonial bartering. Worf accidentally cuts Riker with one in TNG episode "Frame of Mind."

NUYEN, FRANCE

played Elaan in Classic Trek "Elaan of Troyius." Born in 1939, her credits include "South Pacific," "A Girl Named Tamiko," "Battle for the Planet of the Apes" and a regular role on "St. Elsewhere." She is married to actor Robert Culp.

O'BRIAN

mentioned as an officer Mudd captures, but who is never seen in Classic episode "I, Mudd."

O'BRIEN, JOYCELYN

played Mitana Haro in TNG episode "Allegiance."

O'BRIEN, KEIKO ISHIKAWA

recurring character in "The Next Generation" and "Deep Space 9." She is married to Miles O'Brien and they have a young daughter, Molly. A botanist aboard the *Enterprise* in TNG, on DS9 she teaches the diverse group of children living at the station. She is played by Rosalind Chao.

O'BRIEN, OPS CHIEF MILES EDWARD

a regular on "Deep Space 9" and a recurring character on "The Next Generation." Miles, played by Colm Meaney, is married to Keiko and they have a small daughter, Molly (played by Hana Hatae.) He served aboard the *U.S.S.*

Rutledge under Captain Benjamin Maxwell, where he fought against the Cardassians and has traumatic memories of when he was forced to kill one. He has a deep seated prejudice against them. He met Keiko Ishikawa after joining the *Enterprise* crew. He loves gambling, is a wizard with hardware and an excellent technician. On DS9 he has settled down somewhat, a devoted family man and a valued worker.

O'BRIEN, MOLLY

young daughter of Keiko and Miles O'Brien and played by Hana Hatae. She has appeared in a TNG episode and a few DS9 episodes in very small roles. She is preschool age at the beginning of DS9's run. She was born literally into the hands of Worf when no doctor was available to aid the laboring Keiko.

O'CONNEL, STEVE

young boy in Classic episode "And The Children Shall Lead" whose parents are influenced to commit suicide by the Gorgon. He is played by Caesar Belli.

O'CONNELL, WILLIAM

played Thelev in Classic Trek "Journey To Babel." His other credits include the film "The Dead Don't Die" ('72).

O'CONNOR, TERRANCE

played Chief Ross in "Star Trek: The Motion Picture." TV credits include "Barnaby Jones."

O'CONNOR, TIM

played Briam in TNG episode "The Perfect Mate."

O'DELL, BRENNA

the real leader of the Bringloidi colony in the Ficus Sector whose father is Danilo O'Dell, in TNG episode "Up The Long Ladder." She is played by Rosalyn Landor.

O'DELL, DANILO

puppet leader whose daughter, Brenna, is the real ruler of the Bringloidi colony in TNG episode "Up The Long Ladder." His title is Shan'a'kee. He is played by Barrie Ingham.

O'FERREN, MARTY

mentioned in the Dixon Hill scenario in TNG episode "Manhunt" as having been "greased."

O'HERLIHY, MICHAEL

director of Classic Trek "Tomorrow Is Yesterday." Born in Ireland in 1929, his credits include the Disney films such as "The Fighting Prince of Donegal" ('66) and "The One And Only Genuine Original Family Band" ('68). TV directing credits include episodes of "Today's FBI" and "The Guns of Will Sonnett."

O'HERLIHY, LIEUTENANT

character killed on Cestus III by the Gorns in Classic episode "Arena." He was played by Jerry Ayers.

O'KUN, LAN

scriptwriter of TNG story "Haven."

O'NEIL, LIEUTENANT

one of the officers "absorbed" with Sulu, in the first landing party sent to Beta III in Classic episode "The Return of the Archons." He was played by Sean Morgan who also plays the transporter officer in "The Tholian Web."

O'NEILL, AMY

played Annette in TNG "Evolution" but all of her scenes were cut.

O'NEILL, TRICIA

played Captain Rachel Garrett on TNG "Yesterday's Enterprise" and "Suspicions."

O'NEILL, ENSIGN

member of the landing party searching on the wrong world for the crashed shuttle in Classic episode "The Galileo Seven."

O'REILLY, ROBERT

played Kuzo in TNG "Manhunt," and Gowron in "Redemption Part I and II" and "Rightful Heir."

O'SHEA, CAPTAIN

captain of the *Huron* in animated episode "The Pirates of Orion."

O.K. Corral

famous gunfight scene between the Clantons and the Earps, set up by the Melkotians for Kirk, Spock, McCoy and Scotty to relive in Classic episode "Spectre of the Gun."

Oath

Klingon term for marriage.

Obelisk
structure in Classic episode "The Paradise Syndrome" supposedly built by the Preservers as an asteroid deflector. Kirk falls inside it when his communicator inadvertently replicates the sound code that opens it up.

Obi VI
world mentioned in TNG episode "The Child" where Dr. Susan Nuress tested a virus similar to the plasma plague.

Obie System
where the plasma plague contained in Module L 73 was developed by Dr. Susan Noress as mentioned in the TNG episode "The Child."

OBSESSION
written by Art Wallace and directed by Ralph Senensky, this second season Classic Trek episode aired 12/15/67. A vampiric cloud creature Kirk once encountered on Tycho IV, where it killed Garrivick, his friend and captain, is rediscovered on Argus X. Kirk becomes obsessed with destroying it. Guest stars: Stephen Brooks and Jerry Ayers.

Oceanus IV
in TNG episode "The Game," the *Enterprise* is en route to this world on a diplomatic mission.

OCETT, GUL
female Cardassian in command of two warships in TNG episode "The Chase." She attacks the *Enterprise* as soon as she thinks she has the last clue to Professor

Galen's micropaleontology mystery.

ODAN, AMBASSADOR
Trill who falls in love with Dr. Crusher while hosted in his male body, played by Franc Luz, in TNG episode "The Host." (See entry on Trills.) He is a symbiote being whose true form looks like a slug. He comes aboard to mediate a dispute between Peliar Zel's moons, Alpha and Beta. His new female body, Kareel, is played by Nicole Orth-Pallavicini.

Odet IX
planet visited by the *Enterprise* and mentioned in TNG episode "The Child."

Odin, S.S.
freighter of which Captain Ramsey is in command when it crashes into Asphia in TNG episode "Angel One."

ODO, SECURITY CHIEF
shapechanging alien, the only one of his race, who is a regular on "Deep Space 9." He doesn't know what race he is because he was raised by Bajorans. He is played by Rene Auberjonois. Odo was found 50 years before the DS9 series begins in a spacecraft found drifting near the Denorios Belt near Bajor but has no memory of how he got there. Once a day, Odo must change from his humanoid form to his true form, a liquid, to sleep. His bed is a bucket. When the Cardassians were in charge of DS9, they made Odo into a sort of circus act, forcing him to shapechange to entertain

them. He worked as security for the Cardassians on the station as well, though he had no loyalties toward them. Under the Federation, he is the chief of security, working for Sisko.

ODONA
young woman from Gideon who befriends Kirk on the fake *Enterprise* in Classic episode "Mark of Gideon." She has contracted Vegan Choriomeningitis from Kirk's blood which is deadly to her species. This was done to her on purpose to test whether or not Gideons are susceptible to the disease, which will later be used for population control. Odona was played by Sharon Acker.

OFFZEL, MARK
artist who sculpted a vase Fajo owns mentioned in TNG episode "The Most Toys."

OFFENHOUSE, RALPH
wealthy, fifty-five year old man whose body was preserved in cryonic suspension in TNG episode "The Neutral Zone." He is revived and played by Peter Mark Richman.

OFFSPRING, The
third season TNG episode written by Rene Echevarria and directed by Jonathan Frakes. Data creates his own child, Lal, whom he allows to choose her own form and race. She choses to be a human female but the emotions involved with becoming human are so trying that they destroy

her, coming to a head when a Starfleet official wants to take her away from Data to study her, a move her relative youth cannot handle. Guest stars: Hallie Todd, Nicolas Coster, Judyann Elder, Leonard John Crowfoot, Diane Moser, Hayne Bayle, Maria Leone and James G. Becker.

OGAWA, NURSE ALYSSA
assists Dr. Crusher in sickbay in various TNG episodes. She is played by Patti Yasutake.

OGLESBY, THOMAS
played the scholar in TNG "Loud As A Whisper."

OGLETHORPE, VISCOUNT
man to whom the Countess Bartholomew compares Picard in TNG episode "Ship In A Bottle."

OJI
a Mintakan and young daughter of Liko. She was played by Pamela Segall in TNG episode "Who Watches the Watchers."

OKONA, CAPTAIN THADDIUN
captain of the freightor *Erstwhile* in TNG episode "The Outrageous Okona." He was played by William O. Campbell.

OKRAND, MARC
Vulcan language translator in "Star Trek: The Wrath of Khan."

OKUDA, MICHAEL
technical consultant and scenic art supervisor for TNG. He created a lot of the

ship models, and in "Unification," ships designed by Okuda, Greg Jein and Robert McCall all appear, many of them formerly featured in Star Trek movies and brought out from storage.

Okudagram
name of the computer graphic displays on the *Enterprise*. Obviously, this word is a tribute to TNG's technical consultant, Michael Okuda.

OLCAR, AMBASSADOR VAS
Numerian diplomat who keeps himself young by putting his negative thoughts into another person he chooses as a receptacle. This practice prematurely ages and kills his assistant, Sev. He tries to do the same to Troi, but fails. When a second attempt to get another woman to be his psychic receptacle fails, he suddenly ages rapidly and dies. He appears in TNG episode "Man of the People."

OLIVER, SUSAN
played Vina in Classic Trek pilot "The Cage" and "The Menagerie." Born in 1937, her TV credits include a regular role on "Peyton Place," and guest roles on "The Man From U.N.C.L.E.," "Alias Smith and Jones" and "Circle of Fear." Film credits include "Green Eyed Blonde" ('57) and "Looking For Love" ('64).

OMAG
Ferengi played by William Batiani in TNG episode "Unification."

Omaha Air Base
where Captain John Christopher is from in Classic episode "Tomorrow Is Yesterday."

Omega Cygni
the Malurian system is located here as mentioned in Classic episode "The Changeling."

OMEGA GLORY, The
written by Gene Roddenberry and directed by Vince McEveety, this second season Classic Trek episode aired 3/1/68. On the planet Omega IV, Captain Ronald Tracey of the *U.S.S. Exeter* remains the only survivor of a virus which the rest of his landing party brought back to his ship. The planet acts as a natural immunity to the virus and he also believes it holds the secret to extended life. Kirk and Spock must stop his interference with the native society, a society which parallels American origins and is in the middle of a civil war. Guest stars: Morgan Woodward, Roy Jensen, Irene Kelley, David L. Ross, Eddie Paskey, Ed McCready, Lloyd Kino and Morgan Farley.

Omega IV
planet where the Yangs and Kohms are fighting a civil war, aided by Captain Ronald Tracey in Classic episode "The Omega Glory." The native inhabitants have developed a culture surprisingly parallel to American culture on Earth, down to a battered American flag.

Omega Sagitta 12 System
location of the Coalition of Medina in TNG episode "The Outrageous Okona."

Omicron Ceti III
where an agricultural colony lived under spore influence and amid deadly Berthold Rays in Classic episode "This Side of Paradise."

Omicron Delta Region
location of the shore leave world in Classic episode "Shore Leave."

Omicron IV
mentioned by Gary Seven as a world that was almost destroyed by nuclear arms in Classic episode "Assignment: Earth." He compares Earth to this world.

Omicron Pascal
the *Enterprise* stayed here in TNG episode "11001001."

Omicron Theta IV
mentioned in TNG episode "Datalore" as the world where Dr. Soong lived at the time he created Data and Lore.

ONCE UPON A PLANET
written by Len Jenson and Chuck Menville, this animated Classic Trek episode aired 11/3/73. The crew return to the "Shore Leave" planet which seems to have gone out of control and produces harmful illusions. Guest voices: James Doohan (Lt. Arex, Gabler, White Rabbit,) Majel Barrett (Lt. M'Ress,) George Takei (computer) and Nichelle Nichols (Alice.)

ONE OF OUR PLANETS IS MISSING
written by Marc Daniels, this animated Classic Trek episode aired 9/22/73. A giant planet-eating cloud threatens heavily populated planets. The *Enterprise* makes a journey through its "insides" and Spock finally manages to communicate with it through a Vulcan mind meld. The cloud understands it is killing people and agrees to leave the galaxy and return to its "home." Guest voices: all the original cast. James Doohan supplies the voice for Lt. Arex.

Oneamisu Sector
where the Braslota system is located in TNG episode "Peak Performance."

Onizuka
an *Enterprise* shuttlepod seen in TNG episodes "The Ensigns of Command" and "The Mind's Eye." The shuttle was named for one of the astronauts who died on the *Challenger* space shuttle.

Onkians
Romulan temperature measurement mentioned in TNG episode "The Defector."

Oomox
a word for Ferengi pleasure. Giving someone oomox means you give them great pleasure as mentioned in TNG episode "Menage A Troi."

OPAKA, KAI
spiritual leader of Bajor. She shows Sisko the celestial orb which takes him

back to his past to relive meeting his wife.

OPATASHU, DAVID
played Anan 7 in Classic Trek "A Taste Of Armageddon." Born in 1918, his TV credits include "The Man From U.N.C.L.E.," "Voyage To The Bottom Of The Sea," "The Bionic Woman," and regular roles on "Bonino" and "The Secret Empire." Film credits include: "Exodus" ('60) and "Tarzan And The Valley Of Gold" ('66). He also did theater work.

Operation Support Services
a branch of Starfleet which runs the Federation's starbases, mentioned in TNG episode "11001001."

OPERATION: ANNIHILATE!
written by Stephen W. Carabatsos and directed by Herschel Daugherty, this final first season Classic Trek episode aired 4/13/67. Mass insanity seems to have overtaken the inhabitants of Deneva. The *Enterprise* investigates and finds that horrible aliens which resemble flying, flat, rubbery pancakes have invaded the world. Kirk's only brother, George Samuel Kirk, dies along with his wife Aurelean. Their son, Peter, survives. Guest stars: Dave Armstrong, Craig Hundley, Joan Swift and Maurishka Taliferro. Of note: In this episode the Vulcan inner eyelid is revealed.

Ophiuchus VI
where Harry Mudd was headed with his "women" in Classic episode "Mudd's Women" before taking the side trip with the *Enterprise* to Rigel XII.

Opraline
destination of the *Enterprise* after it leaves Ornara in TNG episode "Symbiosis."

Ops
the command center is referred to as Ops on "Deep Space 9." On TNG the station often manned by Data is referred to as Ops.

Oracle
name of the computer which runs the world of Yonada in Classic episode "For The World Is Hollow And I Have Touched The Sky." It uses an implant at the temple to control its populace.

ORANGE, DAVID
played the "sleepy" Klingon in "The Final Frontier."

Ordek Nebula
the Wogneers live here in TNG episode "Allegiance."

Orelious IX
in TNG episode "Booby Trap," this world was destroyed during a war between the Promellians and the Menthars.

Organia
planet over which the Klingons and the Federation are fighting in Classic episode "Errand of Mercy." The Organians who inhabit it are actually advanced life forms of pure energy who are disgusted by the fighting between the two races.

Organian Peace Treaty
when the Organians in Classic episode "Errand of Mercy" have had enough of the fighting between the Federation and the Klingons, they impose this treaty: If the fighting continues, the Organians will intervene rendering all weapons useless on both sides.

ORIEGA, STAN
mentioned in TNG episode "The Outrageous Okona" as a 23rd century comedian who joked about quantum mathematics.

Orientine Acid
element in animated episode "The Survivor" which eats through everything except the crystal container it is kept in.

Orion
planet known for its green Orion slave women, who are said to be irresistible to men. A neutral world located in the Rigel system, it is mentioned in Classic episodes "The Menagerie," "What Are Little Girls Made Of?" (Dr. Korby worked on an immunization project with information from Orion ruins,) "Journey To Babel," (in a reference to Orion smugglers; Thelev, an Andorian, is actually an Orion agent,) "Whom Gods Destroy" (Marta is an Orion) and several animated episodes including "The Pirates of Orion."

Orion Trader
character seen in Captain Pike's fantasy in Classic episode "The Menagerie." He was played by Joseph Mell.

Orion Wing Slugs
Lwaxana refers to these creatures, saying she would rather eat them than face Tog in TNG episode "Menage A Troi."

ORMENY, TOM
played the Klingon first officer in TNG episode "Redemption Part I."

Ornara
located in the Delos System, this world thinks it suffers from a chronic disease for which they need felicium but are actually drug addicts in TNG episode "Symbiosis."

Ornaran Plague
mentioned in TNG episode "Symbiosis" as the disease from the Ornaran claim they are suffering, when in actuality their world was cured of the disease 200 years before. Their symptoms are actually those of drug addiction.

ORTA
leader of a Bajoran resistance group. He speaks with a voice box and is disfigured because of Cardassian tortures in TNG episode "Ensign Ro." He was played by Jeffrey Hayenga.

ORTEGA, JIMMY
played Torres in TNG "Encounter At Farpoint."

ORTH-PALLAVICINI, NICOLE

played Kareel in TNG episode "The Host."

ORTIZ, ENSIGN

mentioned as a replacement violin player for Data in TNG episode "The Ensigns of Command."

ORTON

administrator of Arkaria in TNG episode "Starship Mine" who is working with the mercenaries trying to steal trilithum from the *Enterprise.*

OSBORNE, LIEUTENANT

head of security on the *Enterprise* in Classic episode "The Devil In The Dark." He is also a member of the landing party in "A Taste of Armageddon."

Oskoid

a type of Betazed food served by Lwaxana in TNG episode "Menage A Troi." It is served with sap.

OSWALD, GERD

director of Classic Trek episodes "The Conscience of the King" and "The Alternative Factor." Born in 1916, he was a child actor before becoming a director. His TV directing credits include "The Outer Limits," "Bonanza" and "Voyage To The Bottom Of The Sea." He also directed the films "A Kiss Before Dying" ('56) and "Agent For Harm" ('56).

Otar II

the destination of the *Enterprise*'s at the end of TNG episode "The Offspring."

OUTCAST, The

fifth season TNG episode written by Jeri Taylor and directed by Robert Scheerer. Riker falls for a hermaphrodite-like alien whose world forbids its inhabitants from favoring themselves as one gender or another. This alien, however, feels very feminine when she's with Riker, a fact which causes her people to take her away against her will to be "corrected" despite Riker's protests. Guest stars: Melinda Culea, Callan White and Megan Cole.

Outpost 23

hidden Starfleet base mentioned in TNG episode "Future Imperfect."

Outpost Delta 05

located in the Neutral Zone, this outpost was destroyed in TNG episode "The Neutral Zone." In "Q Who" it is hinted that the outpost was destroyed by the Borg.

Outpost Sera VI

outpost near the Neutral Zone in TNG episode "The Defector."

Outpost Seran T1

Dr. Leah Brahms worked here designing a dilithium crystal chamber as mentioned in TNG episode "Booby Trap."

Outposts

planets which can travel through space made by the ancient, dead Tkon Empire. One was named the Delphi Ardu in TNG episode "The Last Outpost."

OUTRAGEOUS OKONA, The

second season TNG episode written by Les Menchen, Lance Dickson, David Landsburg and Burton Armus and directed by Robert Becker. Captain Okona, pursued by the warring planets Atlek and Streleb, is granted immunity by the *Enterprise* while Data gets a lesson in humor from Guinan. Guest stars: William O. Campbell, Doublas Rowe, Albert Stratton and Joe Piscopo.

OVERDIEK, DIANE

production coordinator of TNG.

Overseer

all powerful deity worshipped by the Mintakans in TNG episode "Who Watches the Watchers."

OVERTON, FRANK

played Elias Sandoval in Classic Trek "This Side Of Paradise." His TV credits include a regular role on "Twelve O'Clock High," and guest star roles on "Perry Mason" and "One Step Beyond." Film credits include "The Last Mile" ('59).

Owan Eggs

type of food mentioned in TNG episode "Time Squared." Pulaski and Geordi don't like them.

OXMYX, BELA

one of the bosses in Classic episode "A Piece of the Action." He runs the northside territory and is played by Anthony Caruso.

OZABA, DR.

one of the researchers who disappeared from the research station on Minara II in Classic episode "The Empath." He dies after the Vians apparently torture him. He was played by David Roberts.

OZOLS-GRAHAM, VENITA

first assistant director on DS9 "Emissary."

P'rang

Klingon ship following the *Enterprise* in TNG episode "The Emissary."

Pacara VI

world where Troi was attending a neuropsychology seminar when Romulan Subcommander N'Vek abducted her in TNG episode "Face of the Enemy."

Pacifica

the *Enterprise* is en route to this ocean planet in TNG episode "Conspiracy." In "Manhunt" it is referred to as a conference planet.

Pagh

Riker serves on this Klingon ship as part of an officer exchange program in TNG episode "A Matter of Honor." It is commanded by Captain Kargan. It also appears in "Sins of the Fathers."

Pakleds

humanoid race in TNG episode "Samaritan Snare." They want to tap the *Enterprise*'s computers, having stolen from others, including the Klingons and Romulans, in the past.

PALAMAS, CAROLYN
A and A officer of the *Enterprise* who joins the landing party in Classic episode "Who Mourns For Adonais?" She falls in love with Apollo but betrays him to save the ship. She was played by Leslie Parrish.

Pallas 14 System
from animated episode "One Of Our Planets Is Missing," this system contains Alondra, Bezaride and Mantilles and is located on the fringe of the galaxy. Alondra is destroyed by a cosmic cloud that ingests it for food/energy.

PALMER, CHARLES
played a Vulcan litterbearer in Classic Trek "Amok Time." His credits include "Little Gloria: Happy At Last" ('82).

PALMER, DR.
member of the Mintakan station who escapes with Riker in TNG episode "Who Watchers The Watchers."

PALMER, LIEUTENANT
communications officer who relieves Uhura in Classic episodes "The Doomsday Machine" and "The Way To Eden." She is played by Elizabeth Rogers.

Pandro
located in the Garo VII system and homeworld of Commander Ari bn Bem as mentioned in animated episode "Bem." This world is very advanced in medical technology.

Par Lenor
one of the Ferengi representatives of the Ferengi Trade Mission who sneaks aboard the *Enterprise* in TNG episode "The Perfect Mate." He was played by Max Grodenchik.

PARADISE SYNDROME, The
written by Margaret Armen and directed by Jud Taylor, this third season Classic Trek episode aired 10/4/68. On an idyllic planet, Kirk inadvertantly activates an alien device, falls through the ground door, and is knocked unconscious. Meanwhile, an asteroid is hurtling toward the world, populated by peaceful American Indian-type people. The Enterprise, unable to find Kirk, is forced to leave him behind and attempt to destroy the asteroid, a move which disables the ship. Kirk lives on the world with the native people for about two months while suffering total amnesia. He even marries a woman named Miramanee. (It is the first time Kirk is known to marry. The second time occurs prior to The Motion Picture when Kirk marries Vice Admiral Lori Ciani in a contractual marriage that lasts temporarily. Lori later dies in a transporter malfunction.) Guest stars: Sabrina Scharf, Rudy Solari, Richard Hale, Sean Morgan and Lamont Laird. Of note: There is a fairly intense mind meld between Kirk and Spock at the end of the episode.

Parallax Colony
colony on Shereleus VI which has mud baths, jugglers, dancers and other interesting entertainments. Lwaxana Troi recreates this world on the holodeck in TNG episode "Cost of Living."

PARDEK, SENATOR
Romulan statesman in TNG episode "Unification." He was supposedly working with Spock on peace between the Romulans and the Federation but was really a spy for the Romulan government. He was played by Malachi Throne.

PARKER, SACHI
played Krola in TNG episode "First Contact."

Parliament
destination of *Enterprise* in TNG episode "Lonely Among Us." It is a planet comparable to Babel and belongs to the Federation.

PARMEN
leader of the Platonians who is dying from a simple cut which became infected in Classic episode "Plato's Stepchildren." When McCoy cures him, he wants to keep him on Platonius as their doctor. He was played by Liam Sullivan.

Parrises Squares
Tasha and Worf play this game in TNG episode "11001001."

PARRISH, JULIE
played Miss Piper in Classic Trek "The Menagerie." TV credits include a regular role on "Good Morning,

World." Film credits include: "The Time Machine" ('78), "When She Was Bad..." ('70) and "The Devil And Max Devlin" ('81).

PARRISH, LESLIE
played Lt. Carolyn Palamas in Classic Trek "Who Mourns For Adonais?" Film credits include "Li'l Abner" ('59) and "Banyon." TV credits include "Perry Mason" and "The Man from U.N.C.L.E."

PARROS, PETER
played the tactics officer in TNG "A Matter of Honor."

Parrot's Claw Case
mentioned in TNG episode "Manhunt" as a Dixon Hill case on the holodeck.

PARSONS, LINDSLEY JR.
executive in charge of production on "Star Trek: The Motion Picture." He also worked on the films "Al Capone" and "The Purple Gang."

PARSONS, NANCY
played Marouk in TNG "The Vengeance Factor."

Parsteel
in TNG episode "The Measure of a Man," Data bends a rod made of this substance. It has a tensile strength of 40 kilobars.

Parthus
green vegetable from Acamar III. Yuta cooks with it in TNG episode "The Vengeance Factor."

Particle Fountain
experimental mining technology used at Tyrus VIIA in TNG episode "Quality of Life."

PARTON, REGINA
stunt double for Nona in Classic Trek "A Private Little War."

PARTRIDGE, DEREK
played Dionyd in Classic Trek "Plato's Stepchildren." His film credits include "The Ivory Ape" and "Savage Harvest."

Parvenium System
system being scanned by the *Enterprise* when they encounter the Kataan probe in TNG episode "The Inner Light."

PASKEY, EDDIE
played Lt. Leslie in Classic Trek "The Conscience Of The King," "The Return of the Archons," "This Side of Paradise," "The Alternative Factor" and "The Omega Glory." He also played a security guard in "Where No Man Has Gone Before" and an Eminiar guard in "A Taste Of Armageddon."

PASSENGER, The
first season DS9 episode written by Morgan Gendel, Robert Hewitt Wolfe and Michael Piller and directed by Paul Lynch. An alien named Vantakar, who was guilty of using his science illegally and was sought as a murderer, is found dead but his entity takes over Bashir. Meanwhile, Odo must contend with a Starfleet security officer he is ordered to work with. Guest stars: Caitlin Brown,

James Lashly, Christopher Collins and James Harper.

PAST PROLOGUE
first season DS9 episode written by Kathryn Powell and directed by Winrich Kolbe. A Bajoran terrorist and a member of the group to which Kira used to belong boards DS9 asking for asylum from the Cardassians. The terrorist however, continues to wage war against the Cardassians, and when Kira refuses to help him murder people, he tells her she is not a true patriot. They fight when she tries to stop him. Guest stars: Jeffrey Nordling, Andrew Robinson, Gwynyth Walsh, Barbara March, Susan Bay, Vaughn Armstrong and Richard Ryder.

Pasta a la Fiarella
food Geordi serves to Worf on DS9 in TNG episode "Birthright," but the replicators make it taste wrong. Worf, however, loves it.

PATAKH
a Romulan who survives the crash on the Galorndon Core and needs a transfusion of ribosomes from Worf, who refuses in TNG episode "The Enemy." He is played by Steve Rankin.

PATAKI, MICHAEL
played the Klingon Korax in Classic Trek "The Trouble With Tribbles" and Karnas in TNG "Too Short A Season." His TV credits include a regular role on "Paul Sand in Friends and Lovers," "Get

Christie Love!" "The Amazing Spiderman" and "Phyl And Mickey" as well as guest roles in "Voyage To The Bottom Of The Sea" and others. Film credits include "Dead And Buried" and "Sweet Sixteen."

Patches
Jeremy Aster's calico cat who disappears in TNG episode "The Bonding."

PATRICK, CHRISTIAN
played the transporter technician in Classic Trek "The Alternative Factor."

PATRICK, RANDALL
played crewman #1 in TNG "Evolution."

PATTERNS OF FORCE
written by John Meredyth Lucas and directed by Vince McEveety, this second season Classic Trek episode aired 2/16/68. On the planet Ekos, a Nazi-like culture has developed due to the interference of cultural observer John Gill. Gill acts as Fuhrer of the planet but turns out to be drugged, his image used as a puppet by a more evil man, Melakon. Kirk and Spock must try to stop Ekos from warring against another planet, Zeon. Guest stars: David Brian, Skip Homeier, Richard Evans, Valora Norland, William Wintersole, Patrick Horgan, Ralph Maurer and Gilbert Green.

PAUL, BARBARA
author of Classic Trek novel *The Three- Minute Universe*.

Paulson Nebula
in TNG episode "The Best of Both Worlds," the *Enterprise* enters this nebula to avoid the Borg. The nebula consists of 82 percent dilithium hydroxyls, magnesium and chromium.

PAVLIK, ENSIGN
Enterprise junior officer in TNG episodes "Galaxy's Child" and "Disaster." She is played by Jana Marie Hupp.

Paxans
xenophobic race encountered in TNG episode "Clues." They cause a memory loss in the *Enterprise* crew so the race will not be discovered by other people. They also contemplate destroying the ship if this tactic does not work.

PAZ, JOE
played a Vulcan litterbearer in Classic Trek "Amok Time." He also appears in the 1959 movie "Never Steal Anything Small."

PEAK PERFORMANCE
second season TNG episode written by David Kemper and directed by Robert Scheerer. The *Enterprise* is involved in war games with the *Hathaway* that turn real when a Ferengi vessel arrives. Guest stars: Roy Brocksmith, Armin Shimerman, Leslie Neale, Glenn Morshower and David L. Lander.

PECHEUR, SIERRA
played T'Pel in TNG episode "Data's Day."

PECK, ED
played Colonel Fellini in Classic Trek "Tomorrow Is Yesterday." He also played Officer Kirk in the TV series "Happy Days," and acted in "Major Dell Conway Of The Flyter Tigers," "The Super" and "Semi-Tough." He was in the 1982 movie "Zoot Suit."

PEDDLER
hologram salesman, created by the Minosians, who peddles weapons in TNG episode "The Arsenal of Freedom." He was played by Vincent Schiavelli.

PEEK, RUSS
played a Vulcan executioner in Classic Trek "Amok Time."

PEEPLES, SAMUEL A.
scriptwriter of Classic Trek "Where No Man Has Gone Before" and the animated episode "Beyond The Farthest Star." He also scripted episodes for "The Girl From U.N.C.L.E." and "Rawhide" as well as the move script of the Roddenberry produced "Spectre." He wrote and produced the 1978 film "A Real American Hero."

PEEPLES, ENSIGN
Enterprise junior officer who appears in TNG episode "Night Terrors." He was played by Craig Hurley.

Pegos Minor System
Manheim's distress signal is relayed to this system in TNG episode "We'll Always Have Paris."

Peliar Zel
governed by Leka Trion, the world has two moons, Alpha and Beta, who require Ambassador Odan to mediate for them in TNG episode "The Host."

Pelius V
destination of the *Enterprise* in TNG episode "11001001."

PEN PALS
second season TNG episode written by Melinda M. Snodgrass and Hannah Louise Shearer and directed by Winrich Kolbe. Data hears a distress signal from a child and breaks the Prime Directive to help save her life. Guest stars: Nicholas Cascone, Nikki Cox, Ann Gillespie, Whitney Rydbeck and Colm Meaney.

PENDLETON, CHIEF
mentioned as an *Enterprise* communications officer in TNG episode "Aquiel."

PENN, LEO
director of Classic Trek "The Enemy Within." He has also directed for the TV shows "The Bionic Woman," "Lost In Space," "Remington Steele" and "Voyage To The Bottom Of The Sea."

Pentarus III
world with a moon on which the shuttle *Nenemic* crashes in TNG episode "The Final Mission."

Pentarus V
where Picard is headed to mediate a miners' dispute in TNG episode "The Final Mission."

Penthara IV
in TNG episode "A Matter of Time," an asteroid hits this world causing the temperature to lower significantly. The *Enterprise* reverses the damages.

PENTHOR MUL
Gatherer leader who died 50 years before TNG episode "The Vengeance Factor."

PERFECT MATE, The
fifth season TNG episode written by Rene Echevarria, Reuben Leder and Michael Piller and directed by Cliff Bole. The Kriosian ambassador's peace offering to Valt Minor turns out to be a metamorph being named Kamala, who can adjust herself to be the perfect mate for any man. She comes out of stasis, however, before her scheduled time and falls in love with Picard. Once metamorphed into his perfect mate, she cannot change, but pretends to so she can fulfill her duty to Valt Minor. Guest stars: Famke Janssen, Tim O'Connor, Max Grodenchik, Mickey Cottrell, Michael Snyder, April Grace, David Paul Needles, Roger Rignack and Charles Gunning.

Pergium
one of the minerals mined on Janius VI in Classic episode "Devil in the Dark."

Pericules
species of Ferengi flower, the Zan Periculi species, native to Lappa IV. Tog gives some to Lwaxana while trying to woo her in

TNG episode "Menage A Troi."

PERKINS, JACK
played Master of the Games in Classic Trek "Bread And Circuses." His TV guest appearances include "Hart To Hart" and "The Young Rebels." Film credits include: "Killer Bees" ('74) and "Night Shift" ('82).

PERNA, DAVE
stunt double for Spock in Classic Trek "Amok Time" and "A Private Little War."

PERRIN, VIC
played the voice of Balok in Classic Trek "The Corbomite Maneuver," the Metron's voice in "Arena," Nomad's voice in "The Changeling," and Tharn in "Mirror, Mirror." He was in the 1969 film "Dragnet," the 1975 films "The Abduction of Saint Anne," and "The UFO Incident." He has guest starred on such TV shows as "Perry Mason."

PERRIN
Sarek's wife in TNG episode "Sarek" and "Unification." She is human, as was his first wife Amanda. She is played by Joanna Miles.

PERRY, JOYCE
scriptwriter of the animated episode "The Time Trap."

PERRY, ROD
played the security officer in "Star Trek: The Motion Picture." His TV credits include a regular role in "SWAT." He has also appeared in the 1974 movie "The Autobiography of

Miss Jane Pittman" and the 1974 film "Trapped Beneath The Sea."

PERRY, JO

scriptwriter of TNG episode "Reunion" with Thomas Perry, Drew Deighan, Ronald D. Moore and Brannon Braga.

PERRY, ROGER

played Captain John Christopher in Classic Trek "Tomorrow Is Yesterday." He has guest starred on the TV shows "The Bionic Woman" and "Barnaby Jones," and has had regular roles on such series as "Harrington And Son," "Arrest And Trial," "The Facts of Life" and "Falcon Crest." He is married to Joanne Worley of "Laugh In" fame.

PERRY, THOMAS

scriptwriter of TNG episode "Reunion" with Jo Perry, Drew Deighan, Ronald D. Moore and Brannon Braga.

Persephone V

planet from which Admiral Mark Jameson is picked up in TNG episode "Too Short A Season."

PERSOFF, NEHEMIAH

played Toff in TNG episode "The Most Toys."

Personnel Officer

in Classic episode "Court Martial," she testifies against Kirk. She was played by Nancy Wong.

PETERMAN, DONALD

director of photography in "The Voyage Home." He's also worked on the films "King of the Mountain," "Rich and Famous," "Kiss Me Goodbye" and "Flashdance."

PETERMAN, KEITH

camera operator on "The Voyage Home."

PETERS, BROCK

played Admiral Cartwright in "The Voyage Home" and "The Undiscovered Country." Born in 1927, his film credits include the 1959 "Porgy And Bess," the 1962 "To Kill A Mockingbird" and the 1973 "Soylent Green." He has also appeared on "The Girl From U.N.C.L.E." and "The Bionic Woman."

PETERS, GREGG

assistant producer of Classic Trek season three.

PETERSON, CASSANDRA

played Maggie in "The Voyage Home." She is the assistant who barges in on Scotty and McCoy as they are about to give the polymer plant manager the matrix for transparent aluminum. She is most famous for playing Elvira, Mistress of the Dark.

PETERSON, VIDAL

played D'Tan in TNG episode "Unification Part II."

PETIET, CHRISTOPHER

played "boy" in TNG "The High Ground."

PETRI, LORD

ambassador of Troyius in Classic episode "Elaan of Troyius." Elaan stabs Petri who swears not to have anything to do with her, forcing Kirk to take over in teaching her "manners." He was played by Jay Robinson.

PETTYJOHN, ANGELIQUE

played Shahna in Classic Trek "The Gamesters of Triskelion." Her TV credits include "Batman" and "The Man From U.N.C.L.E." She made many convention appearances in her Shahna costume in the 1980's and often worked in Las Vegas. She died of cancer in 1991.

PEVNEY, JOSEPH

director of Classic Trek "Arena," "The Return of the Archons," "A Taste of Armageddon," "Devil In The Dark," "The City On The Edge Of Forever," "Amok Time," "The Apple," "Catspaw," "Journey To Babel," "Friday's Child," "The Deadly Years," "Wolf In The Fold," "The Trouble With Tribbles" and "The Immunity Syndrome." Born in 1920 in New York, he worked in vaudeville before becoming a TV actor. His directing credits include the 1951 movie "Air Cadet," the 1956 "Away All Boats" and the 1966 "The Night of the Grizzly." TV directing credits include "Petrocelli."

Phase, The

menopause for female Betazeds. During this "phase" their sex drive is increased four times over. Lwaxana Troi is at the height of her Phase in TNG episode "Manhunt."

Phase 7 Survey

in TNG episode "Relics," this kind of survey is conducted by the *Enterprise* on the Dyson sphere.

Phase Inverter

tool used by Geordi in TNG episode "Time Squared" to get information from a shuttlepod's logs. The device is also mentioned in "The Next Phase."

Phase One Search

Enterprise search conducted in Classic episode "Court Martial" to find Finney. This type of search presupposes a person is hurt or sick and cannot answer. It does not presume the person is intentionally eluding the search, which Finney was doing.

Phaser

ship's weapons which look like lasers but can be put on stun or disintegrate modes. Hand phasers have several different settings and come in a phaser gun form, pistol form (hand phaser type 2) and the little box form (hand phaser type 1.) Phasers do not seem to have changed much throughout the different series, although the hand phasers take on slightly different shapes.

Phaser Coolant

pink gas in Classic episode "Balance of Terror" which kills Tomlinson.

Phaser Range

a target range on the holodeck which appears in TNG episode "A Matter of Honor."

Pheban System
in TNG episode "A Matter of Honor," the *Pagh* undergoes undesignated maneuvers here.

Phelan System
in TNG episode "The Outcast," the destination of the *Enterprise* to negotiate a trade agreement.

PHELPS, WIN
director of TNG episode "Symbiosis."

PHILANA
Parmen's wife in Classic episode "Plato's Stepchildren." She is 2300 years old but stopped aging at 30. She was played by Barbara Babcock.

PHILIPS, ROBERT
played the Orion space officer in Classic Trek pilot "The Cage" and "The Menagerie." TV credits include "Planet of the Apes," and the films "Yuma," "The Gun And The Pulpit" and "The Ultimate Imposter."

PHILLIPS, ETHAN
played Dr. Farek on TNG episode "Menage A Troi."

PHILLIPS, FRED B.
make up artist on Classic Trek as well as "Star Trek: The Motion Picture." He also worked as a make up artist on the series "Stoney Burke."

PHILLIPS, JANNA
make up artist on "Star Trek: The Motion Picture." She is the daughter of Fred Phillips.

PHILLIPS, MICHELLE
played Jenice Manheim in TNG "We'll Always Have Paris." She is a well known actress who has done much television and film work.

PHILLIPS, RALPH
scriptwriter of TNG episode "Suddenly Human."

PHILLIPS, WILLIAM F.
associate producer on "The Wrath of Khan." He has also worked on the films "Richie Brockelman," "The Night Rider" and "Listen To Your Heart."

PHILLIPS, ASTROBIOLOGIST
recommended as a member of the landing party on Alpha Carinai II by both Kirk and the M-5 computer in Classic episode "The Ultimate Computer."

Phoenix, U.S.S.
Nebula class starship NCC-55420 captained by Benjamin Maxwell in TNG episode "The Vengeance Factor."

Phoenix Cluster
in TNG episode "The Game," the *Enterprise* is conducting scientific studies here.

Photon Torpedoes
projectiles which the *Enterprise* has the capablity of using to defend itself. They look like large blasts of light and explode on impact.

Phylos
planet where the *Enterprise* encounters Dr. Keniclius in animated episode "The Infinite Vulcan." Its natives are plant-like people.

Phyrox Plague
ravaged Cor Caroli V as mentioned in TNG episode "Allegiance."

Pi
Romulan scout vessel which crashed on the Galorndon Core uses this code name in TNG episode "The Enemy."

Piano Player
one of the holodeck band in TNG episode "11001001" played by Jack Sheldon.

PICARD, CAPTAIN JEAN-LUC
captain of the *Enterprise* in "The Next Generation." He is played by Patrick Stewart. His serial number is SP 937 215. His parents are Yvette and Maurice Gessard Picard and he has a brother, Robert. Prior to duty on the *Enterprise*, Picard served 22 years on the *Stargazer*. Born in Paris, France his hobbies include history and archeology. He also likes to practice on the Resican flute he brought back with him in the episode "The Inner Light." He likes to read detective fiction, is a drama fan (especially of Shakespeare) and has been known to take an art class (part of the plot in "A Matter of Perspective.") A fair man and a decisive leader, he is very good friends with Dr. Crusher, with whom he has breakfast every morning. Another close friend is Guinan, to whom he can reveal indecision, pain and his personal opinions, traits a captain cannot or should not reveal to his crew. He likes caviar and Earl Grey tea. He has an artificial heart because he was stabbed by Norsicans while at the Academy (seen in "Tapestry.") He also loves horseback riding (he owns his own saddle) and won a running marathon at the Academy when he was a cadet. He is also a good fencer. He quarters are on deck 9, #3601.

PICARD, MARIE
Picard's sister-in-law who has a son named Rene, in TNG episode "Family." She is played by Samantha Eggar.

PICARD, MAURICE
Picard's father who appears in TNG episode "Tapestry."

PICARD, RENE
Picard's nephew, son of Robert and Marie Picard. He wants to go to the stars, like his uncle, in TNG episode "Family." He is played by David Tristan Birken.

PICARD, ROBERT
Picard's older brother seen in TNG episode "Family." A farmer and vineyard owner, he is married to Marie, and has a son, Rene. He was played by Jeremy Kemp.

PICARD, MAMAN
old woman who appears in TNG episode "Where No One Has Gone Before" to serve Picard tea when the *Enterprise* goes into the Beyond. She was played by Herta Ware.

PICARD, YVETTE GESSARD

Picard's mother. See entry for Picard, Maman.

PIE MAN

played by Richard Merson, he appears in TNG episode "Elementary, Dear Data."

PIKE, DONALD

stunt coordinator on "The Undiscovered Country."

PIKE, CAPTAIN CHRISTOPHER

captain of the *Enterprise* seen in the first Classic pilot "The Cage" and played by Jeffrey Hunter. He is from Mojave, CA and once had a horse named Tango. He wanted to leave the *Enterprise* because he was tired, and ended up retiring horribly scarred for life when he tried to rescue some cadets and was exposed to radiation. The scarred Pike was played by Sean Kenney. He is taken to Talos IV by Spock so he can live with Vina, with whom he fell in love in "The Cage," and not be encumbered by his useless body. He is mentioned as having been assassinated by Kirk in the Mirror universe in "Mirror, Mirror."

Pike

shuttlepod 12 from the *Enterprise* that explodes in TNG episode "The Most Toys." It is named after Captain Christopher Pike.

PILLAR, GARY

played Yutan in Classic Trek "A Private Little War."

PILLER, MICHAEL

executive producer on "The Next Generation," and creator/executive producer of "Deep Space 9." He wrote the script for DS9 "Emissary," "A Man Alone," "Captive Pursuit," "The Passenger" and the story for "Move Along Home." He also wrote the TNG scripts "Evolution," "Booby Trap," "The Enemy," "The Best Of Both Worlds Part I and II," "First Contact," "Ensign Ro," "Unification Part I and II," "The Masterpiece Society," "The Perfect Mate" and "Time's Arrow Part I." Piller attended the Julliard School of Music and worked for CBS news. He also wrote and produced for the TV series "Simon And Simon," "Cagney and Lacey," "Probe" and "Miami Vice."

PILLSBURY, GARTH

played Wilson in Classic Trek "Mirror, Mirror" and a prisoner in "The Cloud Minders."

Piloris Asteroid Field

metal parasites consuming the *Enterprise* are brought here in TNG episode "Cost of Living."

PINE, PHILIP

played Colonel Green in Classic Trek "The Savage Curtain." Born in 1925, his TV credits include "Barnaby Jones" and "Voyage To The Bottom Of The Sea." He had a regular role on "The Blue Knight," and appeared in the 1959 film "The Big Fisherman."

PINSON, ALLEN

played the police man in Classic Trek "Bread and Circuses."

PIPER, DR.

doctor on board the *Enterprise* in second Classic pilot "Where No Man Has Gone Before." He was played by Paul Fix.

PIPER, MISS

assistant to Commodore Mendez in Classic episode "The Menagerie." She was played by Julie Parrish.

PIRATES OF ORION, The

written by Howard Weinstein, this animated Classic Trek episode aired 9/7/74. Spock comes down with a deadly illness, and the only cure is on Beta Canopis, four days away. To save time, they plan to rendezvous with another ship, the *Huron*, which will have picked up the cure, but the *Huron* is attacked before the meeting. The *Enterprise* tracks down the Orion ship that attacked and stole the *Huron's* cargo, and attempt to retrieve the drug in time to save Spock's life.

PISCOPO, JOE

actor/comedian who played the Comic in TNG "The Outrageous Okona." He is best known for his regular stint on "Saturday Night Live." He has appeared in films and commercials.

PISTONE, MARTIN

played Starfleet Controller in "The Voyage Home."

Plak Tow

Vulcan word for the blood fever mentioned in Classic episode "Amok Time." It usually appears with the pon farr.

PLAKSON, SUZIE

played Lt. Selar in TNG "Unnatural Selection" and K'Ehleyr in "The Emissary" and "Reunion."

Planet Q

where the *Enterprise* picks up the Karidian players. Dr. Tom Leighton lived there with his wife before he was murdered in Classic episode "The Conscience of the King."

Plasma Plague

mentioned in TNG episode "The Child" as a disease with several different strains being studied on Aucdet IX so antidotes can be created. A cure must be found to stop a plague on Rachelis.

PLASUS

high advisor to the city in the sky, Stratos, in Classic episode "The Cloud Minders." He has a daughter, Droxine. He was played by Jeff Corey.

PLATO'S STEPCHILDREN

written by Meyer Dolinsky and directed by David Alexander, this third season Classic Trek episode aired 11/22/68. After receiving a distress signal, an *Enterprise* away team beams down to find a planet inhabited by a small group of people with incredible mind powers and long lives who do not have a doctor. They attempt to force McCoy to stay with them by using mind-control on Kirk and Spock and torturing them. Guest stars: Michael Dunn, Liam Sullivan, Barbara Babcock, Ted Scott and Derek Partridge. Of note: Spock sings "Maiden Wine," and Kirk and Uhura kiss in what is supposedly the first interracial kiss shown on TV. Consequently, the episode was originally banned by some network affiliate stations.

Platonius
planet where the seemingly ageless Platonians, who came there from Sandara, live. They lived on Earth before moving to Platonius.

Pleasure Haven
where Picard vacations on Rise in TNG episode "Captain's Holiday."

Pleiades Cluster
a group of seven stars (the seven sisters) in the Taurus constellation. The *Enterprise* is mapping in this area of space before they are diverted to Velara III in TNG episode "Home Soil."

Plomeek Soup
a Vulcan dish Chapel brings to Spock's quarters in Classic episode "Amok Time." Supposedly humans find it vile.

PLUMMER, CHRISTOPHER
played General Chang in "The Undiscovered Country." Born in

Montreal in 1927, his career spans TV, film and stage. His most famous roles were in "The Sound of Music," "International Velvet," "Somewhere In Time," "The Return of the Pink Panther" and "Dragnet." His daughter, Amanda, is also a successful actress.

PLUNKETT, MARYANN
played Commander Susanna Leitjen in TNG episode "Identity Crisis."

POLA
young boy from the *Enterprise* in TNG episode "The Last Outpost."

Police Special
type of gun Sulu finds on the recreation planet in Classic episode "Shore Leave."

Policeman
character who catches Kirk and Spock with stolen clothing in Classic episode "The City On The Edge Of Forever." Kirk gives him the famous mechanical rice picker story when trying to explain why Spock's ears are pointed. He was played by Hal Baylor.

POLITE, CHARLENE
played Vanna in Classic Trek "The Cloud Minders." She also starred in the 1971 film "Love Hate Love."

POLLACK, NAOMI
played Lt. Rahda in Classic Trek "That Which Survives," and an indian woman in "The Paradise Syndrome."

POLLACK, REGINALD MURRAY
an Earth artist from the 20th century whose work appears in Flint's home in Classic episode "Requiem For Methuselah."

POLLARD, MICHAEL J.
played Jahn in Classic Trek "Miri." Born in 1939, his TV credits include "Lost In Space." His films include the 1967 "Bonnie and Clyde," the 1972 film "Dirty Little Billy," and "Melvin and Howard."

Pollux IV
four billion-year-old Earth-like world Apollo inhabits in Classic episode "Who Mourns For Adonais?"

Pollux V
mentioned in Classic episode "Who Mourns For Adonais?" as a planet devoid of intelligent life but habitable.

POMPET
name of a member of the team trying to steal trilithium in TNG episode "Starship Mine."

Pon Farr
a madness endured by Vulcans once every seven years. When afflicted, they must mate or die. Spock suffers from pon farr in Classic episode "Amok Time."

Porman V
where Picard, Crusher and Worf go in a shuttlecraft en route to Seltris III in TNG episode "Chain of Command."

PORTAL, The
protector of the Delphi Ardu in TNG episode "The Last Outpost." He is played by Darryl Henriques.

PORTER, BRETT
played General Stex in "The Undiscovered Country."

Positronic Theory
robots in Isaac Asimov's books have positronic brains which allow them to think, learn and react like humans. This term is borrowed, with permission, from Asimov's robot books to describe Data's brain. It is mentioned in TNG episode "Datalore" and "The Measure of a Man" among others.

Poteen
Bringloidi's like this Earth-brewed alcoholic beverage in TNG episode "Up The Long Ladder."

Potemkin, U.S.S.
starship that plays war games with the *Enterprise* in Classic episode "The Ultimate Computer." It is also mentioned in "Turnabout Intruder" and the animated episode "The Pirates of Orion." In TNG, Riker served as a Lieutenant aboard this starship as mentioned in "Peak Performance."

POTENZA, VADIA
played Spock at age 13 in "The Search For Spock."

POTTS, CLIFF
played Admiral Kennelly in TNG episode "Ensign Ro."

POTTS, JAKE
in TNG episode "Brothers," he plays a practical joke on his brother which endangers his brother's life. He was played by Cory Danziger.

POTTS, WILLIE
in TNG episode "Brothers," his life is endangered when his brother Jake plays a practical joke on him. He was played by Adam Ryen.

POVILL, JON
associate producer on "Star Trek: The Motion Picture" and scriptwriter of TNG "The Child."

POWELL, KATHRYN
scriptwriter of DS9 "Past Prologue."

POWELL, SUSAN
played Marla Aster in TNG "The Bonding."

POWELL BLAIR, WILLIAM
played a Cardassian officer in DS9 "Emissary."

POWER, STEPHEN
played the chanting Monk in DS9 "Emissary."

POWER PLAY
fifth season TNG episode written by Paul Ruben, Maurice Hurley, Rene Balcer, Herbert J. Wright and Brannon Braga and directed by David Livingston. Troi, O'Brien and Data are possessed by prisoners from an alien moon and take command of the *Enterprise* by taking hostages in Ten Forward. Speaking through the officers, the prisoners demand their fellow prisoners be released from the moon where they have existed as energy forms for 500 years. Guest stars: Rosalind Chao, Michelle Forbes and Colm Meaney.

POWERS, KATHRYN
scriptwriter of TNG "Code of Honor."

PRACTICAL JOKER
written by Chuck Menville, this animated Classic Trek episode aired 9/21/74. The *Enterprise* hides in a cloud to avoid a Romulan attack, only to have the cloud invade their humidity system. All sorts of strange things occur as a result: The food processors screw up, forks bend and Spock gets black rings around his eyes while looking into a viewer. Guest voices: James Doohan (Arex, Romulan Commander, Crewman) and Majel Barrett (M'Ress.)

Praetor
title of the Romulan's leader.

Praxillus
Dr. Timicin unsuccessfully attempts his theory for helium ignition on this star in TNG episode "Half A Life."

PRENDERGAST, GERARD
played Bjorn Benson in TNG "Homesoil."

Preservers, The
race of beings who seeded many worlds with humanoid species, which may be an answer to Hodgkins law of parallel development (since there are so many planets containing human life in the galaxy.) They built the obelisk on the planet Amerind in Classic episode "The Paradise Syndrome." No one has ever seen or met a Preserver.

PRESTON, PETER
a young engineering technician who is killed in Khan's first attack in "The Wrath of Khan." He is mentioned in the novelization as being Scotty's nephew. He is mourned as a hero because he died in an attempt to saves others. He was played by Ike Eisenman.

PRICE, The
third season TNG episode written by Hannah Louise Shearer and directed by Robert Scheerer. The *Enterprise* hosts a delegation convened to negotiate for rights to the Barzan wormhole, which turns out to be useless after all. Guest stars: Matt McCoy, Elizabeth Hoffman, Castulo Guerra, Scott Thomson, Kevin Peter Hall, Dan Shor and Colm Meaney.

PRIETO, BEN
in TNG episode "Skin of Evil," he was the pilot of shuttlepod 13 who is almost killed when the ship crashed on Veigra II. He was played by Raymond Forchion.

Prime Directive
also known as General Order Number One, it forbids anyone from interfering with the natural development of an alien civilization. It is often violated when danger to the alien people or the Federation itself is imminent although at times even that is not considered a good enough reason to interfere.

Primmin
Starfleet security officer who comes to DS9 to work with Odo (much to Odo's irritation) in DS9 episode "The Passenger." He is played by James Lashly.

PRINE, ANDREW
guest starred in TNG episode "Frame of Mind."

Priority 2 Signal
used in TNG episode "Chain of Command" by Jellicoe to notify Admiral Nechayev that Picard has been captured by the Cardassians on Seltris III.

Priority A
distress call on channel 1 used in Classic episode "The Trouble With Tribbles." It puts a whole quadrant on alert.

Procedure Q
used in Classic episode "Bread and Circuses," it cautions that the planet is extremely hostile and the landing party should beam down fully armed.

Proconsul
title for a Romulan head of state in TNG episode "Unification."

Progenitors, The
supposedly built the Custodian on Aldea as seen in TNG episode "When The Bough Breaks."

Progressive Encryption Lock
state of the art device for communicating in code in TNG episode "Unification."

PROHASKA, JANOS
played the Horta in Classic Trek "Devil In The Dark" and the Mugato in "A Private Little War." He has played monsters on many TV shows including "Lost In Space," "The Outer Limits" and "Voyage To The Bottom Of The Sea." He regularly played a bear on "The Andy Griffith Show."

PROKOP, PAUL
played a guard in Classic Trek "Mirror, Mirror."

Promellians
ancient beings who fought a war with the Menthars. The *Clepjoni*, encountered in TNG episode "Booby Trap," is a Promellian battlecruiser which was caught in a Menthar booby trap amid the debris of the destroyed world Orelious IX.

Promenade
level of DS9 where Quark's bar and gambling casino are located, as well as other shops and food venders.

Promethean Quartz
Vash's orange crystal, which she brought back from the Gamma Quadrant in DS9 episode "Q Less," looks like this substance according to one of the DS9 personnel.

PROSTITUTE
appears on the holodeck "Holmes" simulation in TNG episode "Elementary, Dear Data." She was played by Diz White.

Proto Star Cloud
location, near Tanuga, where the *Enterprise* is headed in TNG episode "A Matter of Perspective."

Protodynoplaser
medical tool that stabilizes John's immune system in TNG episode "Transfigurations."

Providers
aliens who run the "games" on Triskelion in Classic episode "The Gamesters of Triskelion." They have evolved until they are mere brains contained in a glass case. They bet on the outcome of the games which is their entertainment.

Proximity Detectors
used by the gangs on Turkana IV to warn of approaching enemies in TNG episode "Legacy."

Psi 2000
planet visited by the *Enterprise* in Classic episode "The Naked Time." It contains a virus that causes people's deepest desires and personas to surface. The *Enterprise* encounters this virus again in TNG episode "The Naked Now," calling it the Psi 2000 Virus.

Psychotech
mentioned in Classic episode "Wolf in the Fold" as someone who is trained to run a psychotricorder.

Psychotricorder
device which can play back a person's actions from the past. One is going to be used on Scotty in Classic episode "Wolf In The Fold," but the psychotech is killed.

Psychotronic Stability Examination
Troi gives Data this test in TNG episode "The Schizoid Man" when Picard suspects something is wrong with him.

PULASKI, DR. KATHERINE
chief medical officer of the *Enterprise* during "The Next Generation's" second season, played by Diana Muldaur. She previously served aboard the *U.S.S. Repulse*. She wrote a book, *Linear Models of Viral Propatation* (see entry), has been married three times and had an affair with Kyle Riker. She likes to argue emotions with Data, play poker and is fascinated by Worf.

PULFORD, DON
stunt double for Kirk in "The Final Frontier."

Punishment Zone
a forbidden zone on Rubicam III chosen randomly by the Mediators. Trespassing into this area is punishable by death.

PUTCH, JOHN
played Mendon in TNG "A Matter of Honor."

PXK Reactor
used on Janus VI as a power source in Classic episode "Devil In The Dark." The Horta steals its main circulating pump, causing the power to go out.

PYNE, FRANCINE
played the younger Nancy Crater in Classic Trek "The Man Trap."

Pyris VII
class M planet where Kirk and crew meet Sylvia and Korob in Classic episode "Catspaw."

Pyrocytes, Blood
substance which causes allergic reactions in other people in TNG episode "The Price."

Q, Planet
where the *Enterprise* picks up the Karidian players in Classic episode "The Conscience of the King." See entry for "Planet Q."

Q
supposedly omnipotent being, and Picard's nemesis, who troubles the *Enterprise* with his strange sense of humor and jokes, often causing them harm in the process. He appears in many TNG episodes and one DS9 episode to date. He has said he is a Klingon at heart and his I.Q. level is 2005. He comes from a somewhere called the Q continuum and supposedly knows Guinan from another time. He is played by John DeLancie.

Q Continuum
unknown place (or dimension) where the omnipotent Q beings exist. See entry for "Q."

Q LESS

first season DS9 episode written by Robert Hewitt Wolfe and Hannah Louise Shearer and directed by Paul Lynch. Vash arrives on the station with some rare archeological relics at the same time as Q who purposely annoys Sisko. Guest stars: John deLancie, Jennifer Hetrick, Van Epperson, Tom McLeister and Laura Cameron.

Q PID

fourth season TNG episode written by Randee Russell and Ira Steven Behr and directed by Cliff Bole. Q reappears and involves Picard and some of his officers in a Robin Hood scenario, making Picard play Robin and Vash play Maid Marion. Guest stars: John deLancie, Jennifer Hetrick, Clive Revill and Joi Staton.

Q WHO

second season TNG episode written by Maurice Hurley and directed by Rob Bowman. Q sends the *Enterprise* far into an unexplored region of the galaxy where they have their first encounter with the destructive Borg race. Guest stars: John deLancie, Whoopi Goldberg, Lycia Naff and Colm Meaney.

Q'Maire

Talarian warship captained by Endar in TNG episode "Suddenly Human."

Q.E. II

cruise ship from the 20th century. The letters stand for Queen Elizabeth. Offenhouse compares this

ship to the *Enterprise* in TNG episode "The Neutral Zone."

Q2

another Q being with great powers and omnipotence. He appears in TNG episode "Deja Q" and is played by Corbin Bernsen.

Qapla

Klingon word meaning "success." It is used in TNG episodes "Sins of the Father" and "Aquiel."

Quadra Sigma III

in TNG episode "Hide and Q," world on which a mining accident occured.

Quadrant 904

where the *Enterprise* is travelling when they discover Gothos in Classic episode "The Squire of Gothos."

Quadratanium

another element from which Data and Lore were made mentioned in TNG episode "Datalore."

Quadrotriticale

a four lobed, hybrid grain stored on Space Station K 7 for Sherman's planet in Classic episode "The Trouble With Tribbles."

QUAICE, DR. DALEN

Beverly Crusher's mentor under whom she served her residency on Delos IV. He is about to retire when the *Enterprise* picks him up at Starbase 133 in TNG episode "Remember Me." He wife, Patricia, had just died. He was played by Bill Erwin.

QUALITY OF LIFE, The

sixth season TNG episode written by Naren Shankar and directed by Jonathan Frakes. Dr. Farallon's project involving exocomp robots is suspected by Data, who believes the exocomps act as independent life forms and should have the right not to be forced into deadly situations. Guest star: Ellen Bry.

Qualor II

in TNG episode "Unification," location of the orbital surplus depot Zed 15.

Quantum Filament

in TNG episode "Disaster," the *Enterprise* hits a quantum filament in space, supposedly a very rare thing to happen.

Quantum Singularity

supposedly Romulan ships' source of power mentioned in TNG episode "Face of the Enemy" and "Timescape."

QUARK

regular character on "Deep Space Nine" played by Armin Shimerman. A greedy Ferengi, he runs the bar and gambling casino on the Promenade level of DS9 with his brother Rom, whose son Nog is also a regular character. Quark also runs DS9's holosuites, where any fantasy can be played out. He has shown himself to be a coward on a number of occasions, but has also shown some guilt for actions which might cause harm to another. He and Odo openly quarrel but are also tentative

friends. He has an obvious lust for Dax and sometimes even Kira. While Dax likes the Ferengi and finds the race amusing and entertaining, (she has been known to play cards and gamble with them) Kira has threatened Quark's life on a number of occasions should he ever touch her.

Quatloos

monetary unit used by the Triskelions for betting on the games in Classic episode "The Gamesters of Triskelion."

Quazulu VII

Wesley and his friends picked up a virus here that infects the *Enterprise* in TNG episode "Angel One."

Questar M17

negative star which pulls the *Enterprise* toward it in animated episode "Beyond The Farthest Star."

Quin'lat

ancient Klingon city referred to by Kahless in TNG episode "Rightful Heir."

QUINN, AMIRAL GREGORY

Starfleet admiral who appears in TNG episodes "Coming of Age" and "Conspiracy." He is possessed by parasites and is the only Starfleet officer to survive such an infliction. He was played by Ward Costello.

QUINTEROS, ORFIL

commander of Starbase 74. He helped design the Galaxy class ships mentioned in TNG episode

"11001001." He was played by Gene Dynarski.

Quintotriticale
a mutation of quadrotriti-cale (see entry), a five lobed plant, resistant to most disease, developed for Sherman's Planet in animated episode "More Tribbles, More Troubles."

QUIST, GERALD
make up artist on TNG.

Quol
Ferengi who appears in TNG episode "The Perfect Mate." He is played by Michael Snyder.

R'uustai
Klingon ritual that translates to "The Bonding." It can make those who are not related, brothers. Jeremy Aster and Worf share this ceremony after the death of Jeremy's mother, Marla Aster, in TNG episode "The Bonding."

RABO
hunter from Mintaka in TNG episode "Who Watches the Watchers."

Rachelis System
in TNG episode "The Child," inhabitants of this system are suffering from a deadly plague.

RAD, TONGO
one of the gang in Classic episode "The Way To Eden." He is the son of a Catullan ambassador. He was played by Victor Brandt.

Radans
jewels from Troyius which are actually raw dilithium in Classic episode "Elaan of Troyius."

RADLEY, LIZ
video consultant on DS9.

RADUE
in TNG episode "When The Bough Breaks," he is the Aldean leader who does not believe his race is dying from radiation exposure. He was played by Jerry Hardin.

RAEL
Scalosian leader in love with Deela, but because of his sterility he must allow her to marry another in order to bear children and help save their dying race. He is played by Jason Evers in Classic episode "Wink of an Eye."

RAGER, ENSIGN
Enteprise bridge officer in TNG episodes "Night Terrors," "Relics" and "Schisms." She was played by Lanei Chapman.

Rahm Izad system
system mentioned by Dr. Crusher as where the missing clue for the micropale-ontology mystery can be found. It turns out to be a false clue in TNG episode "The Chase."

RAKAL, MAJOR
Romulan in the Tal Shiar security service killed by the Romulan underground in TNG episode "Face of the Enemy." Troi impersonates her.

Rakar
world, located in the Gamma Quadrant, whose inhabitants are looking for the convict Crodon in DS9 episode "Vortex."

RAL, DEVINONI
representative hired by the Chrysalians to negotiate in the Barzan wormhole affair in TNG episode "The Price." He is 41 and is one fourth Betazoid and an empath. He was born in Brussels as part of the European Alliance and has lived since age 19 on Hurkos III.

RALSTON, GILBERT
scriptwriter of Classic Trek episode "Who Mourns For Adonais?"

RALSTON, KEN
visual effects supervisor on "The Voyage Home."

RAMART, CAPTAIN
captain of the *Antares* which discovered Charlie in Classic episode "Charlie X." Later, Charlie destroys the ship with his mind powers. Ramart is played by Charles J. Stewart.

Ramatis III
mediator on Riva's home-world in TNG episode "Loud As A Whisper."

RAMOS
Enterprise security officer who dies in TNG episode "Heart of Glory." He was played by Dennis Madalone.

RAMSAY, TODD
film editor on "Star Trek: The Motion Picture." He also worked on the films

"The Thing" and "Escape From New York."

RAMSEY, ANN ELIZABETH
played Clancy in TNG episodes "Elementary, Dear Data" and "The Emissary."

RAMSEY, LOGAN
played Claudius Marcus in Classic Trek episode "Bread and Circuses." Born in 1921, his TV appearances include "Petrocelli," "The Man From U.N.C.L.E.," "Alias Smith and Jones" and a regular role on the series "On The Rocks."

RAMSEY, CAPTAIN
in TNG episode "Angel One," he and his crew are fugitives on Angel One. His ship, the *S.S. Odin* , crashed on Asphia.

RAMUS, NICK
played the helmsman on the *USS Saratoga* in "The Voyage Home." He had regular roles on "Falcon Crest" and "The Chisholms" and appeared in the film "Windwalker."

Rana IV
in TNG episode "The Survivor," the Husnock attacked and killed all 11,000 people on this world except one. It is mentioned that a tasty tea grew wild on the planet before it was destroyed.

RAND, YEOMAN JANICE
Kirk's personal yeoman during first season Classic Trek, played by Grace Lee Whitney. Rand also returns in "The Motion Picture" as the transporter chief. She has a cameo in "The Search

For Spock," and is one of Sulu's bridge crew, Commander Rand, in "The Undiscovered Country." In first season Trek, she appeared to have a crush on Kirk. Kirk liked her, too, but fought the feelings because he was "married" to his ship.

RANDOLPH, LIEUTENANT NANCY
navigator aboard the ship *Ariel* in animated episode "Eye of the Beholder."

RANKIN, STEVE
played Patakh in TNG episode "The Enemy." He also played a Cardassian officer in DS9 episode "Emissary."

Rapakh Unguhr
a kind of Klingon measles cured by a ritualistic fasting mentioned in TNG episode "Up The Long Ladder."

Rape Gang
mentioned as a part of Yar's past. On her home-world of Turkana IV, she was pursued by rape gangs, but survived, as seen in TNG episode "Where No One Has Gone Before."

RAPELYE, MARY LINDA
played Irini Galliulin in Classic Trek episode "The Way To Eden."

RAPPAPORT, FREDERICK
scriptwriter of DS9 episode "Move Along Home."

RASCALS
sixth season TNG episode written by Allison Heck, Ward Botsford, Diana Dru Botsford and Michael Piller and directed by Adam Nimoy. Picard, Guinan, Ro and Keiko are on a shuttle which passes through a strange cloud nearly causing it to break up. As they are beamed aboard the *Enterprise*, the cloud affects their bodies, making them age backwards suddenly. All appear on the *Enterprise* in pre-adolescent bodies but with their adult memories intact. Meanwhile, the Ferengi invade the ship and try to take over. Guest stars: David Tristan Birkin, Brian Bonsalld and Michael Snyder. Of note: Adam Nimoy, Leonard Nimoy's son, makes his TNG directorial debut with this episode.

RASHELLA
in TNG episode "When The Bough Breaks," she is an Aldean and an aide to Radu. She adopts Alexander, one of the children kidnapped from the *Enterprise*. She was played by Brenda Strong.

RASMUSSEN, BERLINGOFF
a thief who claims to be from the future but is really from the past trying to get future technology to sell in the past. He was played by Matt Frewer in TNG episode "A Matter of Time."

RASULALA, THALMUS
played Captain Donald Varley in TNG episode "Contagion."

RATA
Ferengi science officer aboard Bok's ship in TNG episode "The Battle." He was played by Robert Towers.

Rator III
planet located in the Neutral Zone in animated episode "The Survivor."

RAWLINGS, ALICE
played Jamie Finney in Classic Trek episode "Court Martial."

RAWLINGS, PHIL
unit production manager on "Star Trek: The Motion Picture." He also worked on the 1959 film "Al Capone."

RAWLINS
an *Enterprise* geologist chosen for the Alpha Carinae II landing party by Kirk in Classic episode "The Ultimate Computer."

RAYBURN
one of the numerous *Enterprise* security personnel killed on duty. Rayburn dies at the hand of Ruk on Exo III in Classic episode "What Are Little Girls Made Of?" He was played by Budd Albright.

RAYMOND, GUY
played the trader/bartender in Classic Trek "The Trouble With Tribbles." He had a regular role on "Ichabod And Me" and "90 Bristol Court" and appeared in the films "Queen of the Stardust Ballroom" and "4D Man."

RAYMOND, CLARE
housewife from the 20th century who died of an embolism and was put into cryonic freeze at age 35 in TNG episode "The Neutral Zone." She is revived in the 24th century. She had two sons when she died, Eddie and Tommy, aged 8 and 5. She was played by Gracie Harrison.

RAYMOND, EDDIE AND TOMMY
sons of Clare Raymond mentioned in TNG episode "The Neutral Zone." They were born in Secaucus, New Jersey.

RAYMOND, THOMAS
Clare Raymond's descendent on Earth in the 24th century as mentioned in TNG episode "The Neutral Zone."

RAYMONE, KIRK
played Duur in Classic Trek "Friday's Child" and the Cloud Guide in "The Cloud Minders."

Rayna VI
in TNG episode "Q Who," Sonya is said to be from this world.

RAZ, KAVI
played Singh in TNG episode "Lonely Among Us."

Ready Room
Picard's office off the *Enterprise* bridge furnished with two chairs, a couch and a fish tank embedded in the wall. It also contains a food replicator as well as a model of his old ship, the *Stargazer*.

REALM OF FEAR
sixth season TNG episode written by Brannon Braga and directed by Cliff Bole. Barclay returns to help solve the mystery of why the crew is missing from a derelict ship. The trans-

porter, which he fears, holds the clues. Guest stars: Dwight Schultz, Colm Meaney, Patti Yasutake, Renata Scott and Thomas Belgrey.

REARDON, CRAIG
make up artist on DS9.

REASON, RHODES
played Flavius in Classic Trek "Bread and Circuses." He was born in Berlin in 1928 and has a twin brother, Rex. He had regular TV roles on the series "White Hunter" and "Bus Stop." His films credits include "Jungle Heat" and "King Kong Escapes."

REAVES, MICHAEL
scriptwriter of TNG episode "Where No One Has Gone Before."

Reclar
Cardassian warship under command of Gul Lemec in TNG episode "Chain of Command." It is later caught in an antimatter mine booby trap.

Records Officer
Lieutenant Commander Ben Finney's official title in Classic episode "Court Martial." See entry for Finney, Ben.

RECTOR, JEFF AND JERRY
played aliens in TNG episode "Allegiance."

Red Alert
emergency alert requiring all officers to go to their posts.

Red Hour
time of mad partying and rioting on Landru's world, Beta III, in Classic episode "The Return of the Archons." The *Enterprise* landing party, in search of their lost crew, beams down when the Red Hour is being observed. Red Hour occurs on Festival Day once a year from six p.m. until dawn.

REDBLOCK, CYRUS
crime boss in Picard's 1941 San Francisco holodeck program. He was played by Lawrence Tierney.

REDDIN, JAN
played a crewmember in Classic Trek "Space Seed."

REDEMPTION I
fourth season TNG episode, the first of a two-part story, written by Ronald D. Moore and directed by Cliff Bole. The *Enterprise* travels to the Klingon homeworld where Picard will see Gowron ascend the throne and Worf and his brother try to restore their father's good name. The Duras family, however, threatens to destroy all good feelings between the Klingons and the Federation, allying with the Romulans in an attempt to undermine Gowron. Guest stars: Robert O'Reilly, Tony Todd, Whoopi Goldberg, Barbara March, Gwynyth Walsh, Ben Slack, Nicholas Kepros, J.D. Cullum, Tom Ormeny, Clifton Jones and Denise Crosby.

REDEMPTION II
fifth season TNG episode, the second of a two part story, written by Ronald D. Moore and directed by David Carson. Sela, Tasha's daughter, launches a Romulan attack against the Federation, and Worf's restoration of his father's good name may be what saves Gowron. Guest stars: Denise Crosby, Robert O'Reilly, Tony Todd, Whoopi Goldberg, Barbara March, Gwynyth Walsh, J.D. Cullum, Michael G. Hagerty, Timothy Carhart, Fran Bennett, Nicholas Kepros, Jordan Lund and Stephen James Carver.

Redjack
nickname Sybo calls the Jack The Ripper entity, the same name it was called while on Earth. She picks up this knowledge through her psychic talents in Classic episode "Wolf In The Fold."

REENA
see entry for Kapec, Reena. (Rayna is an alternative spelling.)

REEVES-STEVENS, JUDITH AND GARFIELD
writing team who authored Classic Trek novels *Prime Directive* and *Memory Prime.*

Reflection Therapy
therapy Riker undergoes at the Tilonus Institute for Mental Disorders in TNG episode "Frame of Mind." His friends appear in his imagination as aspects of himself, not real people, and Suna tries to convince

him the *Enterprise* never existed.

REGA, STANO
23rd century comedian who jokes about quantum mechanics mentioned in TNG episode "The Outrageous Okona."

Regalian Ox
in TNG episode "The Schizoid Man," Dr. Graves claims to be "healthy as a Regalian ox."

REGER
owner of a rooming house on Landru's planet, Beta III, in Classic episode "The Return of the Archons." He has a daughter named Tula and is a member of the underground. He was played by Harry Townes.

REGINOD
engineer of the *Mondor*, a Pakled vessel in TNG episode "Samaritan Snare." He was played by Leslie Morris.

Regulan Blood Worms
animal to which the Klingon Korax compares humans in Classic episode "The Trouble With Tribbles." David Gerrold actually did a more thorough creation of these horrible creatures in an unsold script. They are worms which enter a person's blood stream and drink their blood. They are extremely contagious and invisible (according to the preliminary script.)

Regulation 6.57
Starfleet regulation that states: "At least two officers shall be present during any

treaty or contract negotiation" as mentioned in TNG episode "When The Bough Breaks."

REIMERS, ED
played Admiral Fitzpatrick in Classic Trek "The Trouble With Tribbles." He was the announcer on the quiz show "Do You Trust Your Wife?" and is famous for doing Allstate commercials (the "good hands" guy.)

REINHARDT, RAY
played Admiral Aaron in TNG episode "Conspiracy."

Rejac Crystal
another rarity in Kivas Fajo's collection in TNG episode "The Most Toys."

Rekkags
in TNG episode "Man of the People," this race is at war with the Cironeans. Their mediator is to be Ambassador Olcar.

RELICS
sixth season TNG episode written by Ronald D. Moore and directed by Alexander Singer. Scotty from Classic Trek is discovered in stasis in a transporter beam on board a ship that has crashed into a Dyson sphere. When the *Enterprise* enters the sphere, they become trapped and Scotty and Geordi must figure out a way, on a nearly useless ship, to save them. Guest stars: James Doohan, Lanei Chapman, Erick Weiss, Stacie Foster and Ernie Mirich.

Relva VII
where Wesley took his Academy entrance exam. It houses a Federation starbase as seen in TNG episode "Coming of Age."

REMEMBER ME
fourth season TNG episode written by Lee Sheldon and directed by Cliff Bole. Because of Wesley's static warp field experiments, Beverly disappears into a reality which grows smaller and smaller. The Traveler returns to help Wesley and Geordi establish a gate through which they can rescue her. Guest stars: Eric Menyuk, Bill Erwin and Colm Meaney.

REMMICK, DEXTER
head investigator of the Starfleet conspiracy in TNG episode "Conspiracy." He also appears in "Coming of Age." While working in the General Inspector's office he is taken over by Parasites and later dies. He was played by Robert Schenkkan.

Remmler Array
in TNG episode "Starship Mine," site off Arkaria where the *Enterprise* docks for their baryon sweep.

Remus
twin world of Romulus, the Romulan homeworld, mentioned in Classic episode "Balance of Terror."

REN, SURMAK
Bajoran medical assistant who helps solve the problem of the aphasia plague on DS9 in "Babel."

RENAN, DAVID
played Conn in TNG episode "The Naked Now."

RENCH, SUSAN
played Ramid Sev Maylor in TNG episode "Man of the People."

Renegade, U.S.S.
a frigate in TNG episode "Conspiracy." Its captain was Tryla Scott who became infested with the Parasites.

Replicas
see entry for Androids.

Replicative Fading
a cloning term which refers to a process during which errors double with the creation of each new being, leading to an aboral mal clone as seen in TNG episode "Up The Long Ladder."

Replicator
also known as a food processor in old Trek language. A non-food replicator can also reproduce items such as clothing and jewelry.

Republic, U.S.S.
Kirk and Finney served together on this ship as mentioned in Classic episode "Court Martial." They were good friends until Kirk reported Finney for negligence for leaving a circuit open that could have destroyed the ship. Finney was reprimanded by the *Republic*'s captain and put at the bottom of the promotion list, a punishment for which Finney blamed Kirk.

Repulse, U.S.S.
seen in TNG episodes "The Child" and "Unnatural Selection," this ship is an Excelsior class ship, NCC 2524 commanded by Captain Taggart. Dr. Pulaski comes aboard to serve on the *Enterprise* straight off this ship.

Repulsor Beam
mentioned in TNG episode "The Naked Now" as a reconfigured tractor beam. It is also called a pressor beam.

REQUIEM FOR METHUSELAH
written by Jerome Bixby and directed by Murray Golden, this third season Classic Trek episode aired 2/14/69. A plague called Rigellian fever is affecting the *Enterprise* crew and they need vast amounts of Ryetalyn to combat it. Holberg 917G is the nearest planet with deposits of Ryetalyn and when the *Enterprise* arrives they discover it habitated by a man named Flint and his ward, Reena Kapec. Kirk falls in love with Reena, only to find out she is an advanced android form built by Flint who wants a companion who will not age. Flint has a rare body chemistry that makes him virtually immortal and all his other wives have died. Guest stars: James Daly, Louise Sorel and John Buonomo. Of note: This episode shows Spock's aptitude for the piano.

RESCHER, GAYNE
director of photography in "The Wrath of Khan." Her

film credits include "Claudine" and "Rachel Rachel."

Research Station 75

an outpost on the Federation/Romulan border where the *Enterprise* picks up Ensign DeSeve, who had defected to the Romulans twenty years before. It is seen in TNG episode "Face of the Enemy."

Resican Flute

flute Picard brought back with him from Kataan, where he spent a life in virtual reality in TNG episode "The Inner Light." In "Lessons," he plays a duet on it with Nella Daren.

Resonance Tissue Scan

medical device which can find infections. It is used by Dr. Crusher on Geordi in TNG episode "Schisms."

RETURN OF THE ARCHONS, The

written by Boris Sobelman and Gene Roddenberry and directed by Joseph Pevney, this first season Classic Trek episode aired 2/9/67. On a world where "absorbed" people are controlled by a computer called Landru, the Enterprise searches for the lost members of the crew of the *Archon*. Guest stars: Harry Townes, Torin Thatcher, Charles Macauley, Christopher Held, Brioni Farrell, Jon Lormer, Morgan Farley, Sid Haig, Ralph Maurer, Eddie Paskey and Sean Morgan. Of note: Kirk breaks the Prime Directive in this episode, but defends his actions by saying that it

applies only to healthy, growing societies. It is also revealed in this episode that Spock sleeps with his eyes open.

RETURN TO TOMORROW

written by John Kingsbridge and directed by Ralph Senensky, this second season Classic Trek episode aired 2/9/68. The Enterprise picks up a communication from deep under the earth of the dead planet Arret and discovers three energy beings from an extinct civilization still alive. The beings appropriate Kirk, Spock, and Dr. Anne Mulhall's bodies in order to create robot bodies for themselves using their vast knowledge and the *Enterprise*'s facilities. Spock's entity, however, decides to keep Spock's body and will kill Spock's essence and anyone else who gets in his way. Guest star: Diana Muldaur. Of note: James Doohan provides the voice of Sargon.

REUNION

fourth season TNG episode written by Thomas Perry, Jo Perry, Ronald D. Moore, Drew Deighan and Brannon Braga and directed by Jonathan Frakes. Worf meets his son, Alexander, for the first time, and Picard tries to find out which of two Klingons has been poisoning the Klingon High Commander. Guest stars: Suzie Plakson, Charles Cooper, Patrick Massett, Robert O'Reilly, Jon Steuer, Michael Rider, April Grace,

Basil Wallace and Mirron E. Willis.

REX

played by Rod Arrants in TNG episode "Manhunt," he runs Rex's Bar in the holo simulation of Dixon Hill. He and Dixon Hill team up to capture Marty O'Ferren and send him to jail.

REYGA, DR.

in TNG episode "Suspicions" he is the Ferengi scientist who builds a device that can shield ships from the heat in the center of a star. He is killed for his discovery by Dr. Jo'Bril.

RHADA, LIEUTENANT

Enterprise helmsman who takes Sulu's place after he joins the landing party in Classic episode "That Which Survives." She was played by Naomi Pollack.

RHODES, MICHAEL

director of TNG episode "Angel One."

RHUE, MADLYN

played Lt. Marla McGivers in Classic Trek "Space Seed." Born in 1934, her TV appearances include "The Guns of Will Sonnett," "The Man From U.N.C.L.E." and "Ghost Appearances," as well as a regular role on "Bracken's World," "Executive Suite," "Fame" and "Days of our Lives." Film credits include "Operation Petticoat" and "It's A Mad, Mad, Mad, Mad World." She has been struggling with multiple sclerosis for many years, but continues to act in TV movies,

appearing at times as a character in a wheel chair.

RICE, PAUL

the captain of the *U.S.S. Drake* who dies and is replicated by Echo Papa 607 (see entry) in TNG episode "The Arsenal of Freedom."

RICH, LISA

scriptwriter of DS9 episode "Move Along Home."

RICHARDS, CHET

scriptwriter of Classic Trek episode "The Tholian Web."

RICHARDS, MICHAEL

scriptwriter of Classic Trek episodes "That Which Survives" and "The Way To Eden." His name is also a psuedonym for another writer.

RICHEY, COLONEL STEPHEN

one of the people who was trapped and died 283 years before at the Hotel Royale in TNG episode "The Royale." He was commander of an early NASA ship, the *Charybdis*. He lived in the alien-made Royale for 38 years before his death.

RICHMAN, PETER MARK

played Ralph Offenhouse in TNG episode "The Neutral Zone."

RICHMOND, BRANSCOMBE

played the Klingon gunner in "The Search For Spock." A regular in "Hawaiian Heat," his film credits include "Death Moon," "Damien: The Leper Priest" and "The Mystic Warrior."

Richter Scale of Culture

scale for rating the development of societies. A B rating is equivalent to Earth in 1485. A G rating is equivalent to Earth in 2030, as mentioned in Classic epiosdes "Errand of Mercy" and "Spock's Brain."

RIDER, MICHAEL

played the transporter chief in TNG episodes "The Naked Now," "Code of Honor," "Haven" and "Reunion."

RIEHLE, RICHARD

played Batal in TNG episode "The Inner Light."

Rigel Cup, The

great honor won by the Nova Squadron, Wesley's team, in TNG episode "The First Duty."

Rigel II

world McCoy mentions in Classic episode "Shore Leave." He remembers a cabaret there and two girls, who instantly show up and flank him.

Rigel IV

Hengist, administrator of Argelius II, is from this world as mentioned in Classic episode "Wolf In The Fold."

Rigel V

mentioned as the homeworld of beings who have a body chemistry not unlike Vulcans. A drug from this world is used on Spock when he gives his father, Sarek, a transfusion in Classic episode "Journey To Babel."

Rigel VII

site of a fight between Captain Pike and a Rigellian in Classic pilot "The Cage." One of these Rigellians appears in "The Gamesters of Triskelion."

Rigel XII

planet the *Enterprise* visits to pick up some dilithium in Classic episode "Mudd's Women." It is a mining world with dust storms and high winds.

Rigellian Fever

a contagious disease plaguing the *Enterprise* in Classic episode "Requiem For Methuselah." Ryetalyn is the only known antidote and Holberg 917G, Flint's planet, has deposits of it. By the end of the episode, nearly the entire crew has the disease and three people have died of it.

Rigellian Kassaba Fever

McCoy tells the Kelvans that Spock is suffering from this disease, much like malaria. He says Spock will die if he isn't treated soon in Classic episode "By Any Other Name."

Rigellian Phaser Rifles

the Gatherers use these weapons on Gamma Hromi II in TNG episode "The Vengeance Factor."

RIGHTFUL HEIR

sixth season TNG episode written by Ronald D. Moore and James E. Brooks and directed by Winrich Kolbe. Worf begins questioning his Klingon beliefs, and travels to Boreth, the site of a Klingon temple.

Worf undergoes ritual and ceremony there in an attempt to have a vision of Kahless, when suddenly Kahless actually appears. He has been cloned from residual cells left over from the actual Kahless, but believes he is the real Kahless. Guest stars: Kevin Conway and Robert O'Reilly.

RIGNACK, ROGER

played one of the miners in TNG episode "The Perfect Mate."

RIKER, COMMANDER WILLIAM THOMAS

first officer of the *Enterprise* in "The Next Generation" and played by Jonathan Frakes. Often called "Number One" by Picard, he is not only second in command, but commands the away team missions from the ship. He was born in Valdez, Alaska to Kyle Riker and was supposedly 32 years old by the fourth season of TNG. His mother died when he was very young so he never knew her. He and Deanna Troi were once lovers, when he was a psychology student and junior officer, but are now only friends. He came to serve aboard the *Enterprise* when it picked him up at Farpoint Station in "Encounter At Farpoint." His quarters are located on Deck 8, 0912. He has been offered command of his own ship several times and turned it down because he enjoys working on the *Enterprise* too much. Riker's code is "Theta Alpha 2737 Blue, Enable." He served as first officer under Captain

DeSoto on the *Hood*. He is a master poker player.

RIKER, JEAN LUC

in TNG episode "Future Imperfect," Riker is told he has a son, Jean Luc but it is an illusion.

RIKER, KYLE

William Riker's father, played by Mitchell Ryan, who appeared in TNG episode "The Icarus Factor." He and Will Riker had not seen each other for fifteen years prior to this episode. He is a civilian adviser to Starfleet. He was the only survivor in Starfleet's conflict with the Tholians.

RIKER, LIEUTENANT THOMAS

in TNG episode "Second Chances," a second Riker is discovered, who has been stranded on Nervala IV eight years before by a transporter accident that split Riker into two people. He is not a clone, but a real person who still has deep feelings for Troi, since he spent eight years stranded, pining after her. He consummates his love with an affair with Troi, takes on his legal middle name, and resumes his career by joining the crew of the *Ghandi*.

RILEY, LIEUTENANT KEVIN

an *Enterprise* navigator who appeared in Classic episodes "The Naked Time" and "The Conscience of the King." He is an energetic young man with a great sense of humor. He was born on Tarsus IV where Kodos the Executioner

killed his entire family. An Irishman, and very proud of it, he was brilliantly played by Bruce Hyde.

Rings of Tautee
Q mentions that Amanda could walk on these because she is all powerful in TNG episode "True Q."

Rio Grande
one of the runabouts on DS9 in "Emissary."

RIORDAN, DANIEL
played Rondon in TNG episode "Coming of Age."

RIPPY, LEON
played Sonny Clemons in TNG episode "The Neutral Zone."

Risa
a resort world, very like a paradise, in TNG episode "Captain's Holiday." The Tox Uthat (see entry) is located here. Weapons are not permitted on this world.

Rishium Cheese Pastry
Commander Hutchison serves this at his party on Arkaria in TNG episode "Starship Mine."

RIVA, AMBASSADOR
deaf mediator from Ramatis III in TNG episode "Loud As A Whisper." He was played by Howie Seago.

RIVAN
one of the council of Edo who comes aboard the *Enterprise* and see Edo's "god" in TNG episode "Justice." She was played by Brenda Bakke.

RIXX, CAPTAIN
commander of the *Thomas Paine* who had met Picard before at an Altarian conference in TNG episode "Conspiracy." He was played by Michael Berryman.

RIZZO, ENSIGN
Enterprise officer killed on Tycho IV by the vampire cloud in Classic episode "Obsession." He was played by Jerry Ayers.

RO LAREN, ENSIGN
Bajoran who is responsible for the deaths of eight people while on a landing party because she disobeyed orders. She was imprisoned for her crime, as mentioned in TNG episode "Ensign Ro." After getting out of prison she joined the *Enterprise*. She likes to draw, grew up in a refugee camp, and hates the Cardassians because they tortured and killed her father in front of her when she was seven. She also appears in the episodes "Conundrum," "Violations," "Rascals," "Disaster" and "The Next Phase." She was played by Michelle Forbes. The part of Kira on DS9 was originally written for Ro Laren, but Forbes had other plans.

ROARKE, ADAM
played C.P.O. Garrison in Classic Trek pilot "The Cage." He had a regular role on the TV series "The Keegans" and guest starred on such shows as "The Man From U.N.C.L.E."

Robbiana
Dermal Optic Test
pyschological test McCoy gives Kirk/Janice in Classic episode "Turnabout Intruder" because of Kirk's strange behavior.

ROBERTS, DAVID
played Dr. Ozaba in Classic Trek episode "The Empath." His TV appearances include "The Feather And Father Gang," "The Man From U.N.C.L.E." and "Branded." His films include "The Challenge," "Return To Earth" and "The Winds of War."

ROBERTS, JEREMY
played an *Excelsior* officer in "The Voyage Home."

ROBERTS, TED
scriptwriter of TNG episode "Half A Life."

ROBINSON, ANDREW
appeared in DS9 "Past Prologue."

ROBINSON, JAY
played Lord Petri in Classic Trek episode "Elaan of Troyius." Born in 1930 in New York, his TV appearances include "Planet of the Apes" and "Voyagers!" and the films "The Robe" and "Shampoo."

ROCCO, TONY
played a Klingon in "Star Trek: The Motion Picture."

ROCHA,
LIEUTENANT KEITH
commander of the Starfleet Subspace Relay Station 47 in TNG episode "Aquiel." He had an excellent record but went crazy and tried to kill Aquiel.

Instead, he kills himself and Aquiel becomes a suspect in his murder. He turns out not to be the real person, but a coalescent organism that took on his form.

ROCKOW, JILL
make up artist on DS9.

RODDENBERRY, GENE
creator/producer/writer of the Star Trek series and concept, as well as "The Next Generation." Born in El Paso, TX, in 1921, he died on October 24, 1991. He grew up with one brother and one sister. His full name is Wesley Eugene Roddenberry. (He based the character of Wesley Crusher on the character he wanted to be as a child. In Classic Trek, Commodore Wesley is also a tribute to his name.) His scripts include Classic Trek episodes "The Cage," "Charlie X," "Mudd's Women," "The Menagerie Part I and II," "The Return of the Archons," "A Private Little War," "The Omega Glory," "Bread and Circuses," "Assignment: Earth," "The Savage Curtain" and "Turnabout Intruder." He also wrote TNG episodes "Encounter At Farpoint," "Hide and Q" and "Datalore" and the novel *Star Trek: The Motion Picture*. Roddenberry was a WW II pilot and a Los Angeles police officer before becoming a writer. He wrote speeches for the chief of police and poetry, some of which was published in *The New York Times*. He began writing for TV shows such as "Have Gun Will Travel,"

"Highway Patrol," "Dragnet," "The Virginian," "Alias Smith And Jones," "Naked City," "Dr. Kildare," "Two Faces West," "June Allyson Show," "The Detectives," "Highway Patrol" and "West Point Story," many of which were written under the pen name Robert Wesley. He also created the series "The Lieutenant." He created the pilots for "Genesis II," "Spectre," "Planet Earth" and "The Questor Tapes" and produced the movie "Pretty Maids All In A Row." He was married at the time of his death to his second wife, Majel Barrett, with whom he had a son, Gene, Jr., nicknamed "Rod." With his first wife, Eileen, he has two daughters, Darlene Incopero and Dawn Compton. Roddenberry was given, by the fans and cast, the affectionate nickname Great Bird of the Galaxy. (This phrase was used in the first episode, "The Man Trap.") He was a noted speaker who toured college campuses and conventions bringing with him copies of "The Cage" and the famous Star Trek blooper reel. The first writer ever nominated for a Star on Hollywood Boulevard, the ceremony was held on Sept. 4, 1985. The star is number 1,810 and located at 6683 Hollywood Blvd. A building on the Paramount lot is also named after Gene. He suffered several strokes during his last years with TNG before dying of a heart attack in 1991 at the age of 70. Of Gene's vision, Rick Berman says, "Gene felt strongly about the goodness of mankind. He knew there were rotten things also, but he liked to think of the future where wonderful things would continue and man could enhance the quality of his life."

RODENT
homeless man who is killed by a phaser he stole from McCoy in Classic episode "The City On The Edge Of Forever." He was played by John Harmon.

Rodinium
hardest known substance used to shield outposts, though the Romulan attacks pulverize it in Classic episode "Balance of Terror."

RODRIQUEZ, MARCO
played Paul Rice in TNG episode "The Arsenal of Freedom" and Glen Telle in "The Wounded."

RODRIQUEZ, PERCY
played Commodore Stone in Classic Trek episode "Court Martial." Born in 1924, his TV appearances include "Tarzan" and "Planet of the Apes," as well as a regular role on "Peyton Place," "The Silent Force" and "Executive Suite." He also appeared in Roddenberry's "Genesis II."

RODRIQUEZ, LIEUTENANT ESTEBAN
Angela Martine Teller's friend on the recreation planet in Classic episode "Shore Leave." He was played by Jerry Lopez.

ROEBUCK, DANIEL
played Romulan #1 in TNG episode "Unification Part I and II."

ROEVES, MAURICE
appeared in TNG episode "The Chase."

ROGERS, ELIZABETH
played Lt. Palmer in Classic Trek episodes "The Doomsday Machine" and "The Way To Eden." Her film credits include "Something Evil" and "An Officer and a Gentleman."

ROGERS, AMANDA
young woman who interns aboard the *Enterprise* but who is actually, according to Q, a member of the Q Continuum. The Q Continuum killed her biological parents and she was adopted and raised by humans. She has had strange powers all her life, but hid them, not understanding what she was. She decides to join the Q Continuum, determined to do good with her powers. Amanda was played by Olivia D'Abo in TNG episode "True Q."

ROJAN
Kelvan in charge of the expedition to invade the Milky Way in Classic episode "By Any Other Name." He was born in intergalactic space, so has never known his homeworld in the Andromeda galaxy. He has taken human form, though his actual shape is large with many tentacles. He was played by Warren Stevens. (See entry on Kelvans.)

ROJAY
companion of Devinoni Ral in TNG episode "The Price."

Rokeg Blood Pie
one of Worf's favorite Klingon dishes mentioned in TNG episode "Family."

ROLFE, SAM
scriptwriter of TNG episode "The Vengeance Factor." He also wrote DS9 episode "Vortex."

ROLLMAN, ADMIRAL
Kira calls her in an attempt to go over Sisko's head in DS9 episode "Past Prologue." She was played by Susan Bay (Leonard Nimoy's wife.)

ROLLS, DANA KRAMER
author of Classic Trek novel *Home Is The Hunter*.

ROM
Quark's brother who has a recurring role on DS9. He is rather weasel-like and cowardly. He has a son named Nog.

ROMAINE, JACQUES
mentioned Mira Romaine's father in Classic episode "The Lights of Zetar." He is a retired Starfleet engineer.

ROMAINE, LIEUTENANT MIRA
she is supervising the transfer of equipment to Memory Alpha, via the *Enterprise*, when Scotty falls in love with her in Classic episode "The Lights of Zetar." Her parents are Jacques and Lydia Romaine. She was played by Jan Shutan.

ROMAINE, LYDIA
mentioned in Classic episode "The Lights of Zetar" as Mira Romaine's mother.

ROMAN, RON
scriptwriter of TNG episode "Booby Trap."

ROMANIS, GEORGE
composer of incidental music for TNG episode "Too Short A Season."

ROMAS
felicium addicted Ornaran seen in TNG episode "Symbiosis." He was played by Richard Lineback.

Romboi Dronegar Sector 006
location of the Pakled vessel when it signals the *Enterprise* in TNG episode "Samaritan Snare."

ROMERO, NED
played Krell in Classic Trek episode "A Private Little War." His TV appearances include regular roles on "The D.A." and "Dan August." Film credits include "Winchester 73," "I Will Fight No More Forever" and the 1984 miniseries "George Washington."

Romii
sun in the Romulan system mentioned in Classic episode "Balance of Terror."

Romulan Ale
Kirk gets some of this blue drink from McCoy for his birthday in "The Wrath of Khan." It is also served to the Klingons in "The Undiscovered Country." It is mentioned as not reproducable by the *Enterprise*

replicators in TNG episode "The Defector."

ROMULAN COMMANDER
commander of the Bird of Prey warship which attacks outposts using a cloaking device in Classic episode "Balance of Terror." He destroys his ship rather than allowing himself to be taken prisoner. He was played by Mark Lenard.

Romulan Empire
nation of Romulans and enemies of the Federation. This empire changes little from Classic Trek through TNG and DS9. They continue to be enemies of the Federation, a very warlike, territorial race of beings who trust few other races.

Romulan Execution
involves torture before death mentioned in Classic episode "The Enterprise Incident."

ROMULAN FEMALE COMMANDER
commands a flagship of three Romulan vessels which surround the *Enterprise* and demand its surrender. Her strong attraction to Spock causes her downfall. The *Enterprise* takes her prisoner. She is played by Joanne Linville.

Romulan Neutral Zone
see entry for Neutral Zone.

Romulan War
referred to in Classic episode "Balance of Terror" as a war fought 100 years before. The ships were less advanced and neither side saw the other's face. The

struggle resulted in the establishment of the famous Neutral Zone. Entry into the Neutral Zone could start a war.

Romulans
a pointy-eared race who resemble Vulcans and are, in fact, their distant cousins. They are militaristic, but beyond that little is known about them. They appear in both Classic Trek and "The Next Generation." In "Unification," Spock is working hard on bringing about peace between the Federation and the Romulans, apparently a very difficult task.

Romulus
twin to Remus, the double planet homeworld of the Romulans. The secondary star of the binary Romulan sun is also sometimes called Romulus by the Federation. In TNG episode "The Defector," Jarok, a Romulan, mentions the firefalls of Gal'Gathong and the Apnex Sea on this world.

RON, TINY
appeared in the DS9 episode "The Nagus."

RONDELL, R.A.
stunt coordinator on "The Voyage Home."

RONDON
in TNG episode "Coming of Age," he is a Zaldan who insults Wesley. He was played by Daniel Riordon.

ROOT, STEPHEN
played K'Vada in TNG episode "Unification Part I and II."

ROSE, CHRISTINE
appeared in TNG episode "Birthright."

ROSE, MARGOT
played Eline in TNG episode "The Inner Light."

ROSE
one of the children kidnapped from the *Enterprise* in TNG episode "When The Bough Breaks."

ROSENBERG, GRANT
scriptwriter of TNG episode "New Ground."

ROSENMAN, LEONARD
composer of the score for "The Voyage Home." He also wrote the music for "Rebel Without A Cause," "Beneath The Planet Of The Apes," "Lord of the Rings" and the unsold pilot for "Alexander The Great" (starring William Shatner.) He was born Sept. 7, 1924.

ROSS, DAVID L.
actor/extra who played a security guard in Classic Trek episodes "Miri," "The Return of the Archons," "The Trouble With Tribbles," "Turnabout Intruder" Galloway in "A Taste of Armageddon," "The City On The Edge Of Forever" and "The Omega Glory," Lt. Johnson in "Day of the Dove" and the transporter officer in "The Galileo Seven."

ROSS, JANE
played Tamoon in Classic Trek episode "The Gamesters of Triskelion."

ROSS, STEVEN
producer of "The Final Frontier."

ROSS, CHIEF
Enterprise officer in "The Motion Picture." He was played by Terrance O'Connor.

ROSS, YEOMAN TERESA
appears in Classic episode "The Squire of Gothos" and was played by Venita Wolf.

ROSSA, ADMIRAL CONNAUGHT
Jeremiah Rossa's human grandmother in TNG episode "Suddenly Human." She was played by Barbara Townsend.

ROSSA, JEREMIAH
human boy found on board a Talarian ship in TNG episode "Suddenly Human." He had been missing for ten years after the Talarians raided the colony on Galen IV. He was assimilated into Talarian society and loves his Talarian adoptive father, Endar. He goes by the name Jono and does not want to return to Earth or his human heritage, stabbing Captain Picard to prove to him that he is no longer human. Admiral Connaught Rossa is his grandmother. He was played by Chad Allen.

ROSSILLI, PAUL
played the Klingon Kerla in "The Undiscovered Country."

Rostrum
beam on Statos to which prisoners are tied in Classic episode "The Cloud Minders." When the prisoner answers a question wrong, a painful beam of light enters the prisoner.

Rousseau V
in TNG episode "The Dauphin," Wesley takes Salia here via the holodeck. This broken world is held together by neutrino clouds that sing.

ROWE, DOUGLAS
played Debin in TNG episode "The Outrageous Okona."

ROWE, STEPHEN M.
music editor in DS9.

ROWE, LIEUTENANT
security officer in Classic episode "I, Mudd." He is played by Mike Howden.

ROYALE, The
second season TNG episode written by Keith Mills and directed by Cliff Bole. Data, Riker and Worf become trapped in a hotel that is taken from the novel *The Royale* and made real by aliens on Theta VIII. There they find the wreckage of a NASA shuttle. Guest stars: Noble Willingham, Sam Anderson, Jill Jacobsen, Leo Garcia, Gregory Beecroft and Colm Meaney.

Royale, The
a hotel and casino, in TNG episode "The Royale," built to resemble a hotel out of a pulp fiction book called *The Royale*. The place was created by aliens on Theta VIII as a home for Colonel Stephen Richey who was taken from his ship, *The Charybdis*.

ROYGAS, MICHAEL
played Lt. Cleary in "Star Trek: The Motion Picture."

ROYKIRK, JACKSON
creator of Nomad or, at least, the person Nomad thinks is its creator in Classic episode "The Changeling." He did create the original Nomad probe, a machine supposedly capable of independent thought.

ROZHENKO, ALEXANDER
Worf's son. See entry for Alexander.

ROZHENKO, SERGEY AND HELENA
Worf's adoptive parents who adopted him after his parents died on Khitomer. They are Russian natives but raised Worf on the farm world Gault. They are seen in TNG episode "Family" and played by Theodore Bikel and Georgia Brown.

Ruah IV
mentioned as a class M world Professor Galen recently visited in TNG episode "The Chase."

RUBEN, PAUL
scriptwriter of TNG episode "Power Play."

RUBENSTEIN, PAUL
played one of the garbagemen in "The Voyage Home." He had a regular role in the series "Working Stiffs." His film credits include "Contract On Cherry Street," "The Last American Virgin" and "Getting Physical."

RUBENSTEIN, SCOTT
story editor of TNG's second season, and

scriptwriter of TNG episode "The Dauphin."

Rubicam III
paradise-like homeworld of the Edo in TNG episode "Justice."

RUBIN, RICHARD
property master in "Star Trek: The Motion Picture."

Rubindium Crystals
seen in Classic episode "Patterns of Force" as part of the subcutaneous transponders Kirk and Spock have embedded in their arms.

RUBINEK, SAUL
played Kivas Fajo in TNG episode "The Most Toys."

RUDMAN, COMMANDER
mentioned in TNG episode "Birthright" as an officer aboard the *Merrimac*.

RUGG, JIM
special effects coordinator for Classic Trek.

RUGINIS, VYTO
played Logan in TNG episode "The Arsenal of Freedom."

RUK
very tall, male android and one of Dr. Korby's helpers in Classic episode "What Are Little Girls Made Of?" Created by the "old ones" of Exo III, he was the only one of the old androids left when Dr. Korby arrived. He was played by Ted Cassidy.

Runabout
a shuttle capable of warp drive used in both TNG and DS9. Runabouts on DS9

look small, but in TNG episode "Timescape" it had a conference room, bunk sections and an aft engineering section.

RUSH, MARVIN V.
director of TNG episode "The Host" and director of photography on TNG.

RUSKIN, JOSEPH
played Galt in Classic Trek episode "The Gamesters of Triskelion." His TV credits include "Voyage To The Bottom Of The Sea," "Planet of the Apes" and "The Bionic Woman." Film credits include "Panache," "Captain America" and "The Munsters' Revenge."

RUSS
one of the engineers who beams aboard the *Constellation* with Kirk in Classic episode "The Doomsday Machine." He is played by Tim Burns.

RUSSELL, MARK
played a Vulcan litterbearer in Classic Trek episode "Amok Time."

RUSSELL, MAURI
actor who played a Vulcan bell and banner carrier in Classic Trek episode "Amok Time."

RUSSELL, RANDEE
scriptwriter of TNG episode "Qpid."

RUSSELL, DR. TOBY
in TNG episode "Ethics," she is a neurologist who comes aboard the *Enterprise* to help treat Worf. She tries an experimental technique on him that had pre-

viously failed. She was played by Caroline Kava.

RUSSELL
an *Enterprise* engineer in TNG episode "The Tin Man."

Russhton Infection
mentioned in TNG episode "The Bonding" as the disease Jeremy Aster's father died of five years before.

RUSSO, BARRY
played Lt. Commander Giotto in Classic Trek episode "The Devil In The Dark" and Commodore Wesley in "The Ultimate Computer."

RUTH
Kirk's old flame who appears to him on the shore leave planet in Classic episode "Shore Leave." She is played by Shirley Bonne.

Rutia IV
in TNG episode "The High Ground," the home world of the Ansata and the Rutians, who are fighting each other. The Ansata believe the Federation is aiding the Rutians, which is why they kidnap Dr. Crusher and Picard.

Rutledge, U.S.S.
Chief O'Brien served aboard this ship under the command of Benjamin Maxwell in TNG episode "The Wounded."

RUTTER, GEORGE A.
script supervisor of Classic Trek.

RYAN, MITCHELL
played Kyle Riker (Riker's father) in TNG episode "The Icarus Factor."

RYAN, LIEUTENANT
he takes over the helm for Sulu in Classic episode "The Naked Time."

RYDBECK, WHITNEY
played Alans in TNG episode "Pen Pals."

RYDER, ALFRED
played Professor Robert Crater in Classic Trek episode "The Man Trap." His TV credits include "Voyage To The Bottom Of The Sea" and "One Step Beyond."

RYDER, RICHARD
played a Bajoran deputy in DS9 episodes "Past Prologue" and "A Man Alone."

RYEN, ADAM
played Willie in TNG episode "Brothers."

Ryetalyn
only known cure for Rigellian fever which plagues the *Enterprise* in Classic episode "Requiem For Methuselah." A deposit is found on Holberg 197G, Flint's planet. It has to be pure to effectively cure the fever.

RYUSAKI, KIMBERLY L.
stand-in in the film "The Search For Spock."

SABAROFF, ROBERT
scriptwriter of Classic Trek episode "The Immunity Syndrome" and TNG episodes "Home Soil" and "Conspiracy."

SABRE, RICHARD
hair stylist on DS9.

SACKETT, SUSAN
assistant to Gene Roddenberry on "Star Trek: The Motion Picture" and all the other movies as well as "The Next Generation." She wrote the TNG scripts "Menage A Troi" and "The Game" and is also the author of *The Making of Star Trek: The Motion Picture* with Gene Roddenberry, and the books *Letters To Star Trek* and *Star Trek Speaks*. She nominated Gene Roddenberry's name to the Walk of Fame committee for a star on Hollywood Boulevard, which they awarded him.

SACKMAN, GERRY
incidental music composer for TNG.

SAGE, DAVID
played Tarmin in TNG episode "Violations."

SAGE, WILLARD
played Thann in Classic Trek episode "The Empath." His TV credits include "The Man From U.N.C.L.E.," "Voyage To The Bottom Of The Sea," "Perry Mason" and "The Young Rebels." His films include the 1959 "Timbuktoo" and the 1971 "A Step Out Of Line."

SAKAR OF VULCAN
mentioned in Classic episode "The Ultimate Computer" by Dr. Daystrom as a genius along the lines of Einstein.

Sakharov
Pulaski uses this *Enterprise* shuttle in TNG episode "Unnatural Selection." Picard and Wesley use it in "Samaritan Snare."

SAKKATH
Sarek's Vulcan assistant in TNG episode "Sarek." He helps to shield Sarek's emotions and enhance his mental discipline. He is played by Rocco Sisto.

Sakuro's Disease
the disease Nancy Hedford is suffering from in Classic episode "Metamorphosis." It resembles leukemia and exists on Epsilon Canaris III. It is deadly unless properly treated.

SALIA
an allasomorph and a shapeshifter whose form is pure light. She has lived on Klavdia III for her entire life, 16 years, and is the future leader of Daled IV. She is played by Jamie Hubbard in TNG episode "The Dauphin."

SALISH
medicine chief who fights Kirk in Classic episode "The Paradise Syndrome." He is supposed to know how to make the asteriod deflector work in the obelisk but his predecessor died before he could learn how. He is in love with Miramanee. Rudy Solari plays him.

SALLIN, ROBERT
producer of "The Wrath of Khan."

Salt Vampire
name for the M115 creature in Classic episode "The

Man Trap." It is the last of its kind and is killed at the end of the episode when it tries to feed on Kirk by sucking out all his body's salt through his face. Sharon Gimpel played this horrible creature.

Saltzgadum
a material, one of five such substances, that can alter glass as mentioned in TNG episode "Hollow Pursuits."

SAM
ship's officer who is in the gymnasium when Kirk tries to teach Charlie about wrestling in Classic episode "Charlie X." When Sam laughs at Charlie, Charlie makes him disappear. The Thasians later return him to the ship.

SAMARITAN SNARE
second season TNG episode written by Robert L. McCullough and directed by Les Landau. Picard is forced to have surgery on his artificial heart that could kill him and Geordi is kidnapped by a Pakled vessel. Guest stars: Christopher Collins, Lycia Naff, Leslie Morris, Daniel Banzali and Tzi Ma.

SAMPSON, ROBERT
played Sar 6 in Classic Trek episode "A Taste of Armageddon." His TV credits include "Voyage To The Bottom Of The Sea" as well as regular roles on "Bridget Loves Bernie" and "Falcon Crest." Films include the "Fear No Evil" ('68), the "Shell Game" ('75) and the 1984 film "The Jerk, Too."

SAMURAI
Japanese warrior Sulu thinks about on the recreation planet in Classic episode "Shore Leave." When the warrior appears, he attacks Sulu and others. He is played by Sebastian Tom.

San Francisco Navy Yard
mentioned in animated episode "The Counter Clock Incident" as where the original components for the *Enterprise* were built.

SANCHEZ, RALPH
scriptwriter of TNG episode "Home Soil."

SANCHEZ, DR.
medical officer on the *Enterprise* mentioned in Classic episode "That Which Survives." He does the autopsy on Ensign Wyatt who was killed by Losira's touch.

Sanction
Ornaran freighter destroyed when its control coil malfunctions in TNG episode "Symbiosis."

Sandara
original home of the Platonians mentioned in Classic episode "Plato's Stepchildren." Its sun went nova.

Sandbats of Maynark IV
mentioned in Classic episode "The Empath" as creatures who look like rock crystals when at rest.

SANDOR, STEVE
played Lars in Classic Trek "The Gamesters of

Triskelion." He had a regular role in "Amy Prentiss" (1974-'75) and guest starred on "Alias Smith and Jones." Film credits include "The Young Country," "Stryker" and "Fire and Ice."

SANDOVAL, ELIAS
the leader of the colony on Omicron Ceti III who is affected by the spores. When the spores leave him he wants to move to another world and start over. He is played by Frank Overton.

SANDS, SERENA
played a Talosian in Classic Trek pilot "The Cage" and "The Menagerie."

SANFORD, GERALD
scriptwriter of DS9 episode "A Man Alone."

Saplin
mentioned in Classic episode "The Apple" as a substance comparable to what tips the poison thorns of the Gamma Trianguli VI pod plant. The Saplin thorns, however, are a thousand times more deadly.

SAR, GALEK
in TNG episode "The Booby Trap," he was captain of the Promellian battlecruiser *Cleponji*. He is played by Albert Hall.

Sar 6
Anan 7's aide in Classic episode "A Taste of Armageddon." He is played by Robert Sampson.

Saratoga, U.S.S.
ship seen in "The Voyage Home." This ship is also the

ship Benjamin Sisko, commander of DS9, served on as first officer under the command of a Vulcan, Captain Storil. Storil dies when the ship is attacked by the Borg at Wolf 359, along wtih Sisko's wife, Jennifer. Sisko escapes the ship with his son, Jake, in a shuttle as seen in a flashback in DS9 episode "The Emissary."

SAREK, AMBASSADOR

Spock's father in Classic Trek episode "Journey To Babel" who also appears in "The Search For Spock," "The Voyage Home" and "The Undiscovered Country" as well as in TNG episodes "Sarek" and "Unification." He was married to a human, Amanda Grayson, in Classic Trek and the movies, and to another human woman, Perrin, in TNG. An astrophysicist, he acts as a Vulcan ambassador to many different worlds, often working for the Federation. In Classic Trek he is 102.437 years old. (Vulcans' normal life span is 250 years.) He stopped talking to Spock for 17 years after Spock chose a Starfleet career over one of distinguished repute working and teaching at the Vulcan Science Academy. Both Sarek and Spock have t-negative blood. In "The Final Frontier," Spock encounters his older brother, Sybok, previously unknown in the Vulcan's biography. Spock intimates the Sarek was once married, when he was very young, to a Vulcan princess but apparently the marriage

was dissolved. In "Sarek," Sarek is suffering from Bendii syndrome, a Vulcan form of Alzheimer's which causes a breakdown in his Vulcan mental disciplines, making his emotions uncontrollable. There is no cure for this disease and Sarek dies from it in "Unification." Sarek is played by Mark Lenard.

SAREK

third season TNG episode written by Peter S. Beagle, Marc Cushman and Jake Jacobs and directed by Les Landau. Spock's father, Ambassador Sarek, comes aboard the *Enterprise* to meet with a reclusive alien race, the Legarans. He is suffering, however, from a rare Vulcan disease, Bendii Syndrome, that affects the brain and makes him unable to control his emotions. His telepathic output, as a result, affects those around him. There is no cure for the disease and it eventually kills him. Guest stars: Mark Lenard, Joanna Miles, William Denis, Rocco Sisto, John H. Francis and Colm Meaney. Of note: The music recital in this episode contains a sextet (not a quartet) by Brahms, not Mozart, as misstated in the script.

SARGENT, JOSEPH

director of the Classic Trek episode "The Corbomite Maneuver." Born in 1925, his work includes "The Man From U.N.C.L.E." and the films "Colossus: The Forbin Project" and "McArthur." He won an Emmy in 1973 for "The Marcus-Nelson Murders" in

which he portrayed the character of Kojak.

SARGENT, WILLIAM

played Dr. Thomas Leighton in the Classic Trek episode "The Conscience of the King." He also made guest appearances in TV shows such as "The Immortal," "Barnaby Jones" and "The Man From U.N.C.L.E."

SARGON

one of three energy beings that survived for millenniums after a devastating war on Arret 500,000 years before. His wife is Thalassa. Henoch, the third survivor, was Sargon's enemy. Sargon uses Kirk's body to move around in Classic episode "Return To Tomorrow" and James Doohan's voice to speak.

SARJENKA

Dremian girl who calls for help on a transmitter. Data picks up her distress signal and breaks the prime directive to help her and her world from being destroyed by massive seismic activity. Dr. Pulaski clears her memory of the *Enterprise* and Data from her mind. She has parents and brothers who are unseen. She appears in TNG episode "Pen Pals" and is played by Nikki Cox.

SARLATTE, BOB

played the waiter in "The Voyage Home."

Sarona VIII

destination of the *Enterprise* in TNG episode "We'll Always Have Paris." They planned to take shore

leave there before they were diverted to Vandor IV.

Sarpeidon

world whose sun is going nova. All the inhabitants have escaped into their world's past through the atavachron in Classic episode "All Our Yesterdays."

Sartaarans

a reptilian-like race and long time enemies of the Lysian Alliance as seen in TNG episode "Conundrum."

Sarthong V

in TNG episode "Captain's Holiday," Vash says she wants to visit the archeological ruins here but Sarthongians don't like trespassers.

SASEK

name Spock gives himself when he claims to be the son of Sasek and T'Pel in animated episode "Yesteryear" when goes back in time to meet himself.

Sasheer

name of a Kelvin flower made of crystals that grow very quickly and mentioned by Kelinda in Classic episode "By Any Other Name."

SATAK, CAPTAIN

name of the commander of the Vulcan ship *Intrepid*, lost with all hands when it encountered the galactic amoeba in Classic episode "The Immunity Syndrome."

SATELK, CAPTAIN

Vulcan who is on the inquest panel looking into the death of Cadet Joshua Albert in TNG episode "The First Duty." He is played by Richard Fancy.

SATIE, ADMIRAL NORAH

she investigates the sabotage to the *Enterprise* warp core and believes there is an alien infiltration. Her investigation becomes a witch hunt as she obsesses on everyone's darker motives in TNG episode "The Drumhead." Her father was Judge Aron Satie, a famous Federation judge. She is played by Jean Simmons.

SATTLER

a member of the team trying to steal trilithium from the *Enterprise* in TNG episode "Starship Mine." He is killed by the baryon sweep.

Saurian Brandy

McCoy's favorite drink as seen throughout the Classic series. Kirk seems to like it too; his negative self demands this kind of brandy from McCoy in "The Enemy Within." It is served in Ten Forward on TNG.

Saurian Virus

Dramia II was hit by this virus which McCoy cured nineteen years before in animated episode "The Albatross."

SAVAGE CURTAIN, The

written by Gene Roddenberry and Arthur Heinemann and directed by Herschel Daugherty, this third season Classic Trek episode aired 3/7/69. The *Enterprise* is surveying a planet where there is thought to be no intelligent life when suddenly a patch of Earth-like conditions appears on the planet, and Abraham Lincoln beams aboard. Lincoln invites them back down to the planet where Kirk, Spock and McCoy meet up with Surak of ancient Vulcan lore, and four notorious villians, Colonel Green, Kahless, Genghis Khan and Zora, and are ordered by a rock creature, Yarnek, to fight it out to the death. Guest stars: Phillip Pine, Carol Daniels Dement, Lee Bergere, Barry Atwater, Nathan Jung, Robert Herron and Arell Blanton.

SAVAR, DAMIRAL

Vulcan Starfleet officer controlled by parasites in TNG episode "Conspiracy."

SAVIOLA, CAMILLE

appeared in DS9 episode "Emissary."

SAWAYA, GEORGE

played Chief Humbolt in Classic Trek episode "The Menagerie" and Second Klingon Lt. in "Errand of Mercy." TV credits include "Perry Mason," "Branded," "The Man From U.N.C.L.E" and "Barnaby Jones." Film credits include "Moon of the Wolf," "The Red Badge Of Courage" and "Dead Men Don't Wear Plaid."

SAXE, CARL

stunt double for Korob in Classic Trek episode "Catspaw."

SAYANA

young woman of Gamma Trianguli IV who is in love with Makora in Classic episode "The Apple." She is played by Shari Nims.

Scalos

planet located in an outer quadrant of the galaxy where a beautiful city is all that is left of the dying inhabitants' civilization in Classic episode "Wink of an Eye." Radiation killed the world's children and left the adult males sterile. The few remaining survivors try to kidnap fertile men from the *Enterprise* to impregnate their women when the ship answers their distress call. They are also difficult to detect, since they live in an accelerated time frame compared to the *Enterprise* crew. The substance responsible for the Scalosians' acceleration, and later, some of the *Enterprise* crew, is found in the water on Scalos. (Also see entry on Deela.)

SCANLAN, JOSEPH L.

director of TNG episode "The Big Goodbye," "Skin of Evil" and "Time Squared."

SCARABELLI, MICHELE

played Jenna D'Sora in TNG episode "In Theory."

SCARFE, ALAN

played Mendak in TNG episode "Data's Day" and appeared in "Birthright."

SCHAFER, KEN

scriptwriter of TNG episode "The Mind's Eye."

SCHAFFER, SHARON

stunt woman who appeared in "The Voyage Home."

SCHALLERT, WILLIAM

played Nilz Baris in Classic Trek episode "The Trouble With Tribbles." He has been a familiar face on TV and recently was a regular on the sitcom "The Torkelsons."

SCHARF, SABRINA

played Miramanee in Classic Trek episode "The Paradise Syndrome." She has also made guest appearances on such TV shows as "Hunter" and "The Man From U.N.C.L.E."

SCHEERER, ROBERT

director of TNG episodes "The Measure Of A Man," "Peak Performance," "The Price," "The Defector," "Tin Man," "Legacy," "New Ground," "The Outcast" and "True Q."

SCHENKKAN, ROBERT

played Dexter Remmick in TNG episodes "Coming of Age" and "Conspiracy."

SCHIAVELLI, VINCENT

played the Peddler in TNG episode "The Arsenal of Freedom."

SCHIFFER, PAUL

scriptwriter of TNG episode "Conundrum."

SCHISMS

sixth season TNG episode written by Brannon Braga, Ronald Wilkerson, Jean

Matthias and directed by Robert Wiemer. Riker has not been sleeping well while other crewmembers, including Worf, are having strange reactions to things, such as barber scissors. It is discovered that aliens from another dimension are kidnapping, experimenting on and torturing crewmembers while they sleep.

SCHIZOID MAN, The
second season TNG episode written by Hans Beimler, Richard Manning and Tracy Torme and directed by Les Landau. The dying Dr. Ira Graves transfers his personality into Data. Guest stars: W. Morgan Sheppard, Barbara Alyn Woods and Suzie Plakson.

SCHKOLNICK, BARRY M.
scriptwriter of TNG episode "Conundrum."

SCHMERER, JAMES
scriptwriter of the animated episode "The Survivor." His other writing credits include the series "Chase."

SCHMIDT, FOLKERT
played a doctor in TNG episode "Contagion."

SCHMIDT, GEORGIA
played a Talosian in Classic Trek pilot "The Cage" and "The Menagerie." Film credits include "A Killing Affair" ('77) and "Terror at Alcatraz" ('82).

SCHMITTER
a miner on Janus VI killed by the Horta in Classic episode "Devil In The Dark." He is played by Biff Elliott.

SCHNEIDER, PAUL
scriptwriter of Classic Trek episodes "Balance of Terror," "The Squire of Gothos" and the animated "The Terratin Incident."

SCHOENBRUN, MICHAEL P.
unit production manager of "The Search For Spock."

SCHOFIELD, SANDY
author of DS9 novels and the pen name for the married science fiction writing/editing team Kristine Kathryn Rusch and Dean Wesley Smith. Kristine Rusch currently edits *The Magazine of Fantasy & Science Fiction* and has several horror and fantasy novels published. Dean Smith is the current publisher of the magazine *Pulphouse*.

SCHOLAR, YANG
old man who is keeper of the records on Omega in Classic episode "The Omega Glory." Among the documents are a United States constitution, a Bible and an American flag. He is played by Morgan Farley.

SCHONE, REINER
played Esoqq in TNG episode "Allegiance."

SCHUCK, JOHN
played the Klingon ambassador in "The Voyage Home" and "The Undiscovered Country." Born in 1944, his TV work includes roles on the series "McMillan and Wife," "Holmes and Yoyo," "Turnabout" and "The Odd Couple." He was also in the movies "M*A*S*H" and

"Earthbound." He is also the ex-husband of Susan Bay (see entry for Bay) who is Leonard Nimoy's wife.

SCHULTZ, DWIGHT
played Lt. Reginald Barclay in TNG episodes "Hollow Pursuits," "The Nth Degree," "Realm of Fear" and "Ship In A Bottle." He has also appeared in many TV movies.

SCHULTZ, JOEL
played a Klingon in "Star Trek: The Motion Picture."

SCORZA, PHILIP A.
scriptwriter of TNG episode "Disaster."

SCOTT, JUDSON
played Joachim in "The Wrath of Khan" and guest starred as Sobi in TNG episode "Symbiosis." He was unbilled in the movie due to a misunderstanding between his agent and the studio. He also starred in the short-lived TV series "The Phoenix" and appeared in the film "I, The Jury" ('82).

SCOTT, RENATA
played an admiral in TNG episode "Realm of Fear."

SCOTT, TED
played Eraclitus in Classic Trek episode "Plato's Stepchildren."

SCOTT, CAPTAIN TRYLA
captain of the *Renegade* who was controlled by parasites in TNG episode "Conspiracy." She is played by Ursaline Bryant.

SCOTT, LT. COMMANDER MONTGOMERY
chief engineer on the *Enterprise* in Classic Trek. The resident miracle worker, he always seems to be able to call up more power out of the ship's maxed-out engines. He is played by James Doohan. Scotty, which is the nickname his friends use, had a nephew, Peter Preston, who died in "The Wrath of Khan." Born in Aberdeen, Scotland, his serial number is SE197514. He likes to read technical manuals for recreation. He appears in TNG "Relics," awakened after being held in stasis by a transporter beam for 75 years.

SCOTTER, DICK
played Painter in Classic Trek episode "This Side of Paradise."

SEAGO, HOWIE
played Riva in TNG episode "Loud As A Whisper."

SEALES, FRANKLYN
played a bridge crewman in "Star Trek: The Motion Picture" and had a recurring role on "Silver Spoons." Film credits include "Beulah Land" and "Southern Comfort."

SECOND CHANCES
sixth season TNG episode written by Rene Echevarria and Michael A. Medlock and directed by LeVar Burton. The *Enterprise* discovers a duplicate Riker who has been stranded, through a transporter accident, for eight years on Nervala IV. He is Riker in every way, a complete

being, but still in love with Troi. Guest star: Mae Jemison.

Sector 108
in TNG episode "Where Silence Has Lease," this sector is located in the Void.

Sector 21305
where the *Enterprise* conducts surveys in TNG episode "Ensign Ro."

Sector 21459
where the Rahm Izad system is located, and where Crusher believes Professor Galen's micropaleontology clue can be found in TNG episode "The Chase."

Sector 21947
on the border of Talarian space in TNG episode "Suddenly Human."

Sector 23
region closest to the Neutral Zone as mentioned in TNG episode "The Measure of a Man." Philipa Louvois is the representative of this region's JAG office.

Sector 2520
near the Klingon-Federation border mentioned in TNG episode "Aquiel."

Sector 30
located in the Neutral Zone as mentioned in TNG episode "The Neutral Zone." The Federation had two outposts which were destroyed in this sector.

Sector 31
in TNG episode "The Neutral Zone," this sector had two outposts with

which all communication was lost on Stardate 41903.2. It is located near the Neutral Zone.

Sector 37628
destination of the *Enterprise* in TNG episode "Ethics."

Sector 396
the Selimi Asteroid Belt is located here in TNG episode "The Offspring."

Sector 39J
location of the Gamma 7A system. It is in this system that the *Intrepid* is destroyed by the galactic amoeba in Classic episode "The Immunity Syndrome." The *Enterprise* later meets up with the amoeba here and destroys it.

Sector 63
in TNG episode "Conspiracy," the *Horatio* was destroyed here.

Sector 9569
in TNG episode "Transfigurations" the *Enterprise* meets the Zalkonian ship here.

Sector 001
Earth's sector mentioned in TNG episodes "The Best of Both Worlds" and "Time's Arrow."

Security Guards
the *Enterprise* has many and they appear in dozens of episodes. Often called "red shirts" by the fans of Trek, they often do not last long. They are the first to be killed on landing parties, etc.

SEEL, CHARLES
played Ed in Classic Trek episode "Spectre of the Gun." His TV credits include "One Step Beyond," "The Guns of Will Sonnett" and "Griff." He also had a regular role as Barney on "Gunsmoke" and another regular role on "The Road West." He also appeared in the 1983 film "Duel."

SEELEY, EILEEN
played Ard'rian Mackenzie in TNG episode "The Ensigns of Command."

SEGALL, PAMELA
played Oji in TNG episode "Who Watches The Watchers."

Sehlat
Vulcan animal which resembles a giant teddy bear with six inch fangs. Spock had one for a pet, named I'Chaya, according to Amanda in Classic episode "Journey To Babel." I'Chaya dies while defending Spock during his Kaswan in animated episode "Yesteryear."

SELA, COMMANDER
half-Romulan daughter of Tasha Yar, played by Denise Crosby, who brainwashes Geordi in TNG episode "The Mind's Eye," aids Klingon rebels in "Redemption" and captures Picard, Spock and Data in "Unification."

SELAR, LIEUTENANT
Enterprise medical officer who is Vulcan. She appears in TNG episode "The Schizoid Man," "Tapestry," "Remember Me" and "Yesterday's Enterprise."

She is played by Suzie Plakson.

Selay
planet located in the Beta Renor system which is inhabited by reptile people who eat live prey. They are at war with Antica, a neighboring world, in TNG episode "Lonely Among Us."

SELBURG, DAVID
played Whalen in TNG episode "The Big Goodbye" and appeared in "Frame of Mind."

Selcundi Drema Sector
sector whose systems are plagued with seismic disturbances in TNG episode "Pen Pals."

SELEK
Vulcan name Spock gives himself when he meets his young self on Vulcan in animated episode "Yesteryear." He claims to be a cousin to the family, the son of Sasak and T'Pel.

Seleya, Mount
Mount Seleya, located on Vulcan, is a special place for mysticism and healing which can be reached by climbing an endless curve of stairs carved into the mountain's side. It is also where people bring the katras of their loved ones to the Hall of Thought. Seleya is seen in "The Search For Spock." It is here that a Vulcan priestess rejoins Spock's body with his katra, (the katra was held by McCoy,) at the end of the film. It is at the temple at the top of this mountain where they give Spock

the white monk's robe with a hood which he wears throughout his healing and on into "The Voyage Home." He regains his uniform by the end of "The Voyage Home."

Selgninaem
substance that can alter glass, one of five such substances, mentioned in TNG episode "Hollow Pursuits."

Selimi Asteroid Belt
in TNG episode "The Offspring," the *Enterprise* is en route to this location to chart the area.

SELMON, KAROLE
played Yareena in TNG episode "Code of Honor."

Selodis IV Convention for the Treatment of Prisoners of War
mentioned in TNG episode "Chain of Command." Picard demands his rights under this treaty when the Cardassians capture him, but they do not abide by the convention.

SELSBY, HARVE
played a guard in Classic Trek episode "The Cloud Minders." He was in the 1978 movie "Sergeant Matlovich vs. The US Air Force."

Seltris III
where Picard is captured by Cardassians while attempting to ascertain if it is the location of a secret underground base in TNG episode "Chain of Command."

Senate, Angosian
in TNG episode "The Hunted," this group is responsible for the decison to isolate the Angosian veterans left over from the Tarsian War.

SENENSKY, RALPH
director of Classic Trek episodes "This Side of Paradise," "Metamorphosis," "Obsession," "Return To Tomorrow," "Bread and Circuses," "Is There In Truth No Beauty?" and "The Tholian Web." TV directorial credits include episodes of "Planet of the Apes." Films include "A Dream For Christmas," "Death Cruise" and "The New Adventures of Heidi."

Sensor Web
Miranda Jones wears one of these which allows her to "see" and move about without aid in Classic episode "Is There In Truth No Beauty?" She is blind, but the web allows her to ascertain the shapes of objects and the distance they are from her body.

Sentinel Minor IV
destination of the *Lalo* when it was attacked by the Borg in TNG episode "The Best of Both Worlds."

Sentinels
the guards in Stratos city are called sentinels in Classic episode "The Cloud Minders."

Septimis Minor
in TNG episode "The Ensigns of Command," the *Artemis* was en route to

this location but ended up on Tau Cygna V.

SEPTIMUS
a former senator of Planet 892 IV in Classic episode "Bread And Circuses." He is an older man who leads the worshippers of the Son. He is played by Ian Wolfe.

Servo
Gary Seven's weapon which resembles a pen in Classic episode "Assignment: Earth."

SETAL, SUBLIEDUTENANT
false name used by Romulan Admiral Jarok in TNG episode "The Defector."

SETI, MR
the barber's assistant on the *Enterprise* in TNG episode "Schisms."

Setlik III
O'Brien killed a Cardassian on this world, which was massacred by Cardassians in TNG episode "The Wounded."

SETZNICK, ALBIE
played the juggler in TNG episode "Cost Of Living."

SEURAT, PILAR
played Sybo in Classic Trek episode "Wolf In The Fold." TV credits include "The Man From U.N.C.L.E." and "Voyage To The Bottom Of The Sea."

SEVEN, GARY
20th century Terran who was born on another planet and a member of a highly advanced, secret society interested in helping Earth survive its nuclear age and

develop into a peaceful society. He is also known as Supervisor 194. His 20th century human assistant, inadvertantly drawn into his mission, is Roberta Lincoln. In Classic episode "Assignment: Earth," is it intimated at the end that the two will marry. Gary is played by Robert Lansing.

SEVRIN, DR.
leader of a group of space hippies in Classic episode "The Way To Eden." Once an engineer in acoustics, electronics and communications on Tiburon, he is a carrier of Sythococcus Navae, a disease contagious to indigenous peoples of primitive worlds. He dies when he eats poisoned fruit on the so-called Eden world. He is played by Skip Homeier.

SEYMOUR, CAROLYN
guest starred in TNG episode "Face of the Enemy" and played Toras in TNG episode "Contagion" and Mirasta Yale in "First Contact."

SHADES OF GRAY
second season TNG episode written by Maurice Hurley, Hans Beimer and Richard Manning and directed by Rob Bowman. A parasite invades Riker's body and to save him Pulaski must stimulate the memory center of his mind, forcing him to relive in flashbacks certain periods of his life. Guest star: Colm Meaney.

SHAHNA
Kirk's drill thrall who is to teach him the games in

Classic episode "The Gamesters of Triskelion." She is actually from Triskelion, born as a slave. Her mother was killed in the games. She is played by Angelique Pettyjohn.

ShaKaRee

home of the god Sybok says he seeks and to whom he has a personal channel. He searches for ShaKaRee using the *Enterprise* in "The Final Frontier." ShaKaRee turns out to be a dead world imprisoning an evil, omnipotent being.

SHANKAR, NAREN

scriptwriter of TNG episodes "The First Duty," "Face of the Enemy," "Suspicions" and "The Quality of Life." He also wrote the DS9 episode "Babel" and worked as the science consultant on TNG and DS9.

SHANKLIN, DOUGLAS ALAN

played a prison guard in "The Search For Spock."

SHANTHI, FLEET ADMIRAL

she orders Picard to command the blockage fleet on the Romulan-Klingon border in the Klingon civil war in TNG episode "Redemption." She is played by Fran Bennett.

SHAREE, KEITH

author of TNG novel *Gulliver's Fugitives*.

SHATNER, LESLIE

extra in Classic Trek episode "Miri" when she was around age seven. She

is the eldest daughter of William Shatner.

SHATNER, LISABETH

extra in Classic Trek episode "Miri" when she was around age five. She also wrote the book *The Making of Star Trek V*. She has worked on other projects with her father, William Shatner, and did some writing for the show "T.J. Hooker."

SHATNER, MELANIE

played Kirk's yeoman in "The Final Frontier." She is the youngest of William Shatner's three daughters and has also done a car commercial, which had a Star Trek theme, with her father. Her other TV credits include "T.J. Hooker."

SHATNER, WILLIAM

starred as Captain James Tiberius Kirk in "Star Trek," the subsequent six movies, in the animated series and directed the fifth Trek movie, "The Final Frontier." He also had a cameo appearance as Kirk on the sitcom "Mork and Mindy." Born March 22, 1931 in Montreal, Canada, Shatner intended to follow in his father's footsteps and take over the family company. He studied business in college, but his problems with math caused him to start studying acting. He moved to New York in 1956 and landed jobs on stage as well as in live television. His first film, "The Brothers Karamazov," in which he played Alexei Karamozov, received critical praise in 1957. For his stage and screen work in the late

fifties and early sixties, Shatner won critical acclaim for just about everything he did, winning numerous acting awards. He single-handedly saved the play "The World of Suzie Wong" from turning into a disaster by playing it as a comedy when audiences started walking out. Because of his imaginative performance, the play was not cancelled but went on to a successful, two year run on Broadway. He starred in the films "The Intruder" (also called "I Hate Your Guts!" and "Shame") and "Judgement At Nuremberg." He did two very famous "Twilight Zone" episodes before acting in the Star Trek pilot "Where No Man Has Gone Before" in 1965. The series ran three years and was a bittersweet experience for Shatner. During the series, he was going through many emotional ups and downs: He was in the process of separating from his first wife, Gloria, and he was also concerned that it had not been the right decision to work in Hollywood on a television series when his dream had actually been the pursuit of film and theatre. Gaining fame, recognition and noteriety did not necessarily mean success to him. When Star Trek was cancelled he was forced to take almost any role he could get just to pay the bills. During this time he starred in such films as "White Comanche," "Sole Survivor," "Pray For The Wildcats" and "The Andersonville Trial" (where he met his second

wife, Marcy Lafferty.) He made many guest appearances on TV shows of the 1970's such as "The Sixth Sense," "Barnaby Jones," "The Magician," "The Six Million Dollar Man," "Police Woman," "Columbo," "Mission: Impossible" and dozens of game shows including several appearances on "The 20,000 Dollar Pyramid" with Leonard Nimoy. He did some stage work as well, such as "Otherwise Engaged" (starring with his wife Marcy Lafferty, see entry.) When the Star Trek movies were made, he found new financial success. He was hesitant, at first, upon hearing that Nimoy would be directing the third movie; unsure of how their professional relationship would affect their personal one. But their friendship strengthened and survived, and of Nimoy's directing Shatner says, "Leonard is an outstanding director, very sure of himself but also receptive to ideas." Shatner finally got the chance to direct his own Star Trek movie, "The Final Frontier." Prior to the movie, he became the star of the series "T.J. Hooker" and had directed some of its episodes. The show lasted four seasons, mostly on the strength of Shatner's popularity, since the series was not especially notable in any other way. Leonard Nimoy guest starred in one episode, however, reuniting him with Shatner for the first time outside of their Star Trek roles. Shatner now hosts the very popular

"Rescue 911" series, which has run, to date, for four years. He also co-wrote, with Ron Goulart, the action science fiction novels *Techwar*, *Techlords* and *Techlab*, with more novels in the series scheduled to be published. The books have been sold to Universal for a possible movie and TV series. Shatner will direct the series and Greg Evigan will star. Also currently in progress is a play called "Believe" (based on a novel by Shatner and Michael Tobias) which William Shatner and Leonard Nimoy are working on together. They are also interested in producing movie projects together and recently toured the USA in a two man show discussing their Star Trek days. In 1993, Shatner's memoirs were finally released, *Star Trek Memories*. These are not his first. The book, *Shatner: Where No Man*, (co-written by Shatner, Sondra Marshak and Myrna Culbreath) came out in the early 1980's, but has never been re-released. Shatner, unhappy with the book, bought all reprint rights and buried it. He continues to work hard, as an actor, writer, director and producer, has a great love of horses and rides in professional horse shows in his spare time. He has three daughters, Leslie, Lisabeth and Melanie. Despite earlier set backs during the 1970's, he has enjoyed continuing success, much of it due to the cult popularity of "Star Trek," and much of it to his own energy and spirit. Of

Star Trek, he says, "It's been something that has given me great opportunities that I wouldn't have had otherwise." His star on Hollywood Boulevard is only one of the many awards he has received for his work.

SHAW, LARRY
director of TNG episode "Loud As A Whisper."

SHAW, KATIK
in TNG episode "The High Ground," he is a Rutian waiter attacked by the Ansata. It turns out he was probably the person who set off the bomb, and is a terrorist himself. He is played by Marc Buckland.

SHAW, LIEUTENANT AREEL
an old lover of Kirk's, she is a lawyer in the judge advocate's office on Starbase 11 who is hired to prosecute him in Classic episode "Court Martial." She is played by Joan Marshall.

SHAWN, WALLACE
played Zek in DS9 episode "The Nagus."

SHEA, ANN
played Nellen in TNG episode "The Drumhead."

SHEA, LIEUTENANT
Enterprise officer who is tortured by the Kelvans when they reduce him into a block of white powder and threaten to crush him. He is played by Carl Byrd in Classic episode "By Any Other Name."

SHEARER, HANNAH LOUISE
scriptwriter of TNG episodes "When The Bough Breaks," "Skin of Evil," "We'll Always Have Paris," "Pen Pals" and "The Price." She also wrote the DS9 story "Q Less."

SHEARMAN, ALAN
played Inspector Lestrade in TNG episode "Elementary, Dear Data."

SHEGOG, CLIFFORD
played a Klingon officer in "The Undiscovered Country."

SHELBY, LIEUTENANT COMMANDER
Starfleet tactical officer who helps the *Enterprise* fight the Borg in TNG episode "The Best of Both Worlds." She is played by Elizabeth Dennehy.

SHELDON, JACK
played the piano player in TNG episode "11001001."

SHELDON, LEE
scriptwriter of TNG episode "Remember Me."

Sheliak Corporate
group of beings who are crystalline in appearance and have refused contact with the Federation for 111 years. They do not see humanity as an intelligent race, merely an "infestation." In TNG episode "The Ensigns of Command," they threaten to destroy the colony on Tau Cygna V.

Sheliak Vessel
this ship is en route to Tau Cygna when Picard stops it in TNG episode "The

Ensigns of Command." The Sheliak commander of the ship is played by Mart McChesney.

Shelius
location of the Sheliak Corporate in TNG episode "The Ensigns of Command."

SHELYNE, CAROLE
played the Metron in Classic Trek episode "Arena." TV credits also include "The Man From U.N.C.L.E."

SHEPARD, DODIE
costume designer for "The Final Frontier" and "The Undiscovered Country."

SHEPHERD, JIM
stunt double for Thelev in Classic Trek episode "Journey To Babel."

SHEPPARD, W. MORGAN
played Dr. Ira Graves in TNG "The Schizoid Man."

Sherman's Planet
located near Space Station K 7 in Classic episode "The Trouble With Tribbles" and the animated episode "More Tribbles, More Troubles." Both the Federation and the Klingon Empire claim rights to this world, which will go to whoever can best develop it, according to the precepts of the Organian Peace Treaty. It suffers from a famine in the animated episode.

SHERVEN, JUDI
played a nurse in Classic Trek episode "Wolf In The Fold."

Shika Maru
ship which first encounters the "Children of Tama" in TNG episode "Darmok." It is commanded by Captain Silvestri.

ShiKahr
Vulcan city where Spock was raised. It is seen in the animated episode "Yesteryear."

SHIMERMAN, ARMIN
stars as the Ferengi bartender Quark in "Deep Space 9." Born in Lakewood, New Jersey, he was 17 when he moved to Los Angeles, not to act but to practice law. He got into acting, however, when he joined a drama group, and moved to New York where he starred in productions on Broadway. His TV credits include "Beauty and the Beast," as well as appearances in "L.A. Law," "Who's The Boss?" "Married With Children," "Alien Nation" and "Cop Rock" as well as a recurring role in "Brooklyn Bridge." He had many appearances in "The Next Generation," including unbilled performances as voices or aliens. His TNG credits include: Letek in "The Last Outpost," the voice of the "wedding box" in "Haven" and Bractor in "Peak Performance." The make up team for both TNG and DS9, responsible for the Ferengi make up, won an Emmy for their work.

SHIMODA, JIM
in TNG episode "The Naked Now," he is the assistant chief of engineering who removed all the chips

from the computer. He was played by Benjamin W.S. Lum.

SHIP IN A BOTTLE
sixth season TNG episode written by Rene Echevarria and directed by Alexander Singer. Barclay returns, this time to fix a malfunctioning holodeck, only to discover a secret memory file that includes Professor Moriarty who appears to have achieved consciousness. Moriarty wants to figure out a way to leave the holodeck with out disintegrating and takes over the ship in an attempt to make Data and others work on a solution. Guest stars: Daniel Davis, Dwight Schultz and Stephanie Beacham.

Shireleus VI
the Parallax Colony in TNG episode "Cost of Living" is located here.

SHIRRIFF, CATHIE
played Valkris in "The Search For Spock." Her other roles include "Today's FBI" and co-host of "Ripley's Believe It Or Not." Film credits include "Friendships, Secrets and Lies," "She's Dressed To Kill" and "One Shoe Makes it Murder."

SHOR, DAN
played Dr. Arridor in TNG episode "The Price."

SHORE LEAVE
written by award winning science fiction author Theodore Sturgeon, this first season Classic Trek episode was directed by Robert Sparr and aired 12/29/66. It involves a

world where your thoughts and wishes can become real and, in some cases, dangerous. Guest stars: Barbara Baldavin (who appeared in "Balance of Terror,") Emily Banks, Oliver McGowan, Perry Lopez, Bruce Mars and Shirley Bonne. Of note: Theodore Sturgeon based this plot on a short story he wrote titled "Case and the Dreamer." In one scene of this episode, you can see a collar on the terribly "vicious" tiger.

Shore Leave Planet
on this world, whatever you think or wish for can come to life, since it is a planet embedded with sensors that can read or overhear your desires. It is run by the Caretaker, a friendly old man who appears human in Classic episode "Shore Leave."

SHRAS
an Andorian ambassador to the Babel Conference in Classic episode "Journey To Babel." He is played by Reggie Nalder.

SHUGRUE, ROBERT F.
film editor on "The Search For Spock." He also worked with Harve Bennett on "The Gemini Man."

SHUTAN, JAN
played Lt. Mira Romaine in Classic Trek episode "The Lights of Zetar." Film credits include "Message To My Daughter," "Senior Year" and "This House Possessed." She was also a regular in "Sons and Daughters."

Shuttle 10
shuttle from the U.S.S. Repulse which brings Pulaski on board the Enterprise in TNG episode "The Child."

Shuttle 6
Q takes this shuttle in TNG episode "Q Who."

Shuttlecraft
small spacecraft on the Enterprise which can comfortably seat seven. In Classic Trek the Enterprise has two, the Galileo and the Columbus. In the animated series, it has one called the Copernicus. In TNG, the Enterprise has both shuttlecraft and runabouts of various names including the El Baz, Onizuka, Pike, Sakharov, Magellan, Feynman, Hawking, Goddard, Fermi, Famen, Cousteau, Aries and the Justman.

Shuttlecraft 13
destroyed by Armus on Veigra II in TNG episode "Skin of Evil."

Sickbay
ship's hospital overseen by Dr. McCoy in Classic Trek and Dr. Crusher in TNG. It is headed by Dr. Pulaski in TNG's second season only. It is the most protected area of the ship.

Sierra VI, Outpost
this outpost tracks the Romulan ship heading for the borders of the Federation in TNG episode "The Defector."

Sigma Draconis
G9 type star with nine planets where the ship that

took Spock's brain ends up in the Classic episode of the same name.

Sigma Draconis III
another inhabited world of the Sigma Draconis system, with a technology rating of 3, equivalent to Earth's development in 1485. It is mentioned in Classic episode "Spock's Brain."

Sigma Draconis IV
a world in the Sigma Draconis system with a G rating, equivalent to Earth's 2030 technology. This world is scanned in Classic episode "Spock's Brain."

Sigma Draconis VI
an ice world in the Sigma Draconis system where the Morgs live. The Eymorgs of "Spock's Brain" live under the surface with advanced technology, but no knowledge of how it works. A computer runs their society.

Sigma Draconis VII
planet in the Sigma Draconis system mentioned in Classic episode "Spock's Brain."

Sigma Erani System
in TNG episode "The Most Toys," this system is mentioned as the only source of hytritium.

Sigman Survivor
a mining accident survivor played by Elaine Nalee in TNG episode "Hide and Q."

SIKKING, JAMES B.
played Captain Styles in "The Search For Spock." He has been a regular in the TV series "Turnabout," "Hill Street Blues" and "Doogie Houser, M.D" and has guest starred in numerous series and TV movies. He also appeared in the 1983 film "The Star Chamber."

Silarian Sector
location of the dead world Kataan in TNG episode "The Inner Light."

SILICON AVATAR
fifth season TNG episode written by Lawrence V. Conley, Nancy Bond, Peter Allan Fields and Jeri Taylor and directed by Cliff Bole. The return of the Crystalline entity occurs while Dr. Kila Marr, whose son was killed by the creature, is on board the *Enterprise*. Under the auspices of studying it, she deliberately murders it just as the *Enterprise* crew might be on the verge of learning how to communicate with it to get it to voluntarily stop destroying worlds. Guest stars: Ellen Geer and Susan Diol. Of note: Dr. Marr holds her tricorder upsidedown during a conversation with Data.

SILVER, SPIKE
stunt man in "The Voyage Home."

SIMMONS, JEAN
played Admiral Nora Satie in TNG episode "The Drumhead."

Simoco III
in TNG episode "Conundrum," a technician strains her shoulder while diving off the Cliffs of Heaven located on this world in a Holodeck simulation.

SIMPSON, BILLY
played voice of young Spock in the animated "Yesteryear."

SIMPSON, JONATHAN
played young Sarek in "The Final Frontier."

SINGER, ALEXANDER
director of TNG episodes "Relics" and "Ship In A Bottle."

SINGER, RAYMOND
played the young doctor in "The Voyage Home." His TV credits include "Remington Steele," "The Feather and Father Gang," "Operation Petticoat" (on which he was a regular) and "Mama Malone." He also appeared in the 1983 film "The Entity."

SINGH, REGINALD LAL
played Board Officer Chandra in Classic Trek episode "Court Martial."

SINGH, KHAN NOONIAN
a superman, the result of genetic enhancement, who came to power on Earth briefly during the Eugenics Wars of the late 1990s. He is found by the *Enterprise* on a sleeper ship, the *Botany Bay*, along with eighty of his people, and is awakened into the 23rd century. He attempts to take control of the *Enterprise* and when he fails, Kirk condemns him to exile on Ceti Alpha V. *Enterprise* officer Marla McGivers goes with him to be his wife. Ricardo Montalban played Khan in Classic episode "Space Seed" and in the film "The Wrath of Khan."

SINGH, LIEUTENANT
an *Enterprise* crewmember who is briefly in charge of Nomad in Classic episode "The Changeling." He is played by Blaisdell Makee.

SINGH
Enterprise engineer killed by the cloud creature in TNG episode "Lonely Among Us." He is played by Kavi Raz.

SINS OF THE FATHER
third season TNG episode written by Ronald D. Moore, W. Reed Moran, Drew Deighan and directed by Les Landau. Worf and his younger brother challange a ruling against their dead father, who is thought to have been involved in high treason, in the Klingon high courts. Guest stars: Tony Todd, Charles Cooper, Patrick Massett, Thelma Lee and Teddy Davis.

SIRAH
Cloud William's Yang woman on Omega in Classic episode "The Omega Glory." She is played by Irene Kelley.

Sirius IX
in the animated episode "Mudd's Passion," Mudd relocated here with the money he made from selling Starfleet Academy to the people of Ilyra VI.

Sirrie IV
the vase owned by Fajo in TNG episode "The Most Toys" was carved by Mark Off'Zel on this world.

SIRTIS, MARINA
stars as Counselor Deanna Troi in "The Next Generation." Born on March 29, 1964, she is a British actress of Greek descent, who worked in England before coming to Hollywood. Six months after arriving, she landed the Trek series. She only had a six month visa and it was running out when she got the call that she had the job. She originally auditioned three times for the part of Tasha Yar when the producers decided to have her read for the part of Troi. While working in England, her roles included British TV and musical theatre. She appeared in the films "The Wicked Lady," (with Faye Dunaway) and "Deathwish III" (with Charles Bronson.) She is a soccer fan, (her brother is a professional soccer player) and an avid animal rights activist. Marina is married and lives in Los Angeles.

**SISKO,
COMMANDER BENJAMIN**
commander of Deep Space Nine and played by Avery Brooks. He had a wife, Jennifer, who died at Wolf 359 when the Borg attacked the *U.S.S. Saratoga* on which he served as first officer. His son, Jake, lives with him on DS9 and it is obvious that Sisko is a highly devoted parent. Sisko is a likeable man who has few prejudices, save against the Borg who killed his wife. A firm leader who does not allow his orders to be questioned, he is also open minded and fair. He has great compassion for

the Bajorans and what they have gone through at the hands of the Cardassians. He himself was discovered to be the "emissary" the Bajorans were waiting for, who would help them solve the riddle of the Bajoran Orbs they worship, which can tell some people their future. Before commanding DS9 Sisko worked for three years at the Mars Utopia Planetia Shipyards where the *Enterprise* was built. Ben's best friend is Dax whom he knew when Dax was Curzon. Now that "he" is Jadzia, he has some trouble with the fact that he's a beautiful, young female, but still talks about old times with his old friend, whose memories are retained within Jadzia. Sisko is one of the only people who has held communication with the aliens living within the wormhole that leads to the Gamma Quadrant. It is because of him that ships now have safe passage through the wormhole.

SISKO, JAKE
Benjamin Sisko's son who survived the Borg attack and lives with his dad, commander of DS9, on the station, and attends the school there, taught by Keiko O'Brien. His best friend is Nog, Rom's son and Quark's nephew. They enjoy hanging out on a balcony, their legs swinging over the side, watching all the people on DS9 come and go (especially the girls.) Jake, at fourteen, gets into some trouble, but is really a good kid, guided by intelligence and conscience, and

has a very strong bond with his father. Jake is played by Cirroc Loften.

SISTO, ROCCO
played Sakkath in TNG episode "Sarek."

**SITO,
CADET SECOND CLASS**
Bajoran female cadet in Wesley's Nova Squadron in TNG episode "The First Duty." She is played by Shannon Fill.

SKIN OF EVIL
first season TNG episode written by Joseph Stefano and Hannah Louise Shearer and directed by Joseph L. Scanlan. An evil being with great power causes a shuttle with Deanna Troi on board to crash on its world, Vagra II. When the *Enterprise* crew comes to Troi's rescue, the slimey creature, named Armus, kills Tasha Yar. It is the first time in the series that a major player is killed and the crew mourns her death for a long time. Guest stars: Walker Boone, Brad Zerbst, Raymond Forchion, Mart McChesney and Ron Gans (voice of Armus.) A blooper in this episode has Geordi dropping his phaser into Armus, then in the next scene he has it back in his hands.

SKORR
planet with winged humanoids in the animated episode "Jihad."

SKY, KATHLEEN
author of Classic Trek novels *Vulcan!* and *Death's Angel.*

SLACK, BEN
played K'Tal in "Redemption Part I."

SLATER, CHRISTIAN
played a Starfleet officer in "The Undiscovered Country." As a Star Trek fan, he asked for this cameo role. His film credits, which are numerous, include "Pump Up The Volume," "Heathers," "Kuffs," "Young Guns II" and "True Romance."

Slaver Weapon
see entry for "Slaver Weapon, The."

SLAVER WEAPON
written by reknowned science fiction author Larry Niven, this animated Classic Trek episode aired 12/15/73. A Slaver stasis box found on the planet Kzin is being shuttled to Starbase 25 for inspection. Spock, Uhura and Sulu are on board the *Copernicus* with the box en route to the Starbase when they get readings from a nearby planet that another stasis box is there. They investigate and discover Kzin there who takes them prisoner. In the box is a Slaver weapon that talks and has settings none of them understand. The weapon finally self destructs.

SLAVIN, GEORGE F.
scriptwriter of Classic Trek episode "The Mark Of Gideon." He also wrote the script for the 1959 film "Son of Robin Hood."

Slingshot Effect
the *Enterprise* uses this power source to travel backward and forward in

time in Classic episode "Tomorrow Is Yesterday" and in "The Voyage Home." They use the gravitational pull of a star to sling them at high warp speed through time.

SLOYAN, JAMES
played Admiral Jarok in TNG episode "The Defector."

SLUTSKER, PETER
played Nibor in TNG episode "Menage A Troi" and appeared in "Suspicions."

Small Boy
the boy who assists Kirk and Spock in Classic episode "A Piece of the Action" and is played by Sheldon Collins.

SMITH, EVE
played the elderly patient in "The Voyage Home."

SMITH, FRANK OWEN
played Curzon in DS9 episode "Emissary."

SMITH, FRED G.
played a policeman in TNG episode "The High Ground."

SMITH, K.L.
played a Klingon in Classic Trek "Elaan of Troyius." Film credits include "Battle of the Coral Sea," "Incident in San Francisco" and "The Delphi Bureau."

SMITH, KEITH
director of photography for Classic Trek episode "By Any Other Name."

SMITH, KURTWOOD
played the Federation president in "Star Trek VI: The Undiscovered Country."

SMITH, PATRICIA
played Sara Kingsley in TNG episode "Unnatural Selection."

SMITH, SANDRA
played Dr. Janice Lester in Classic Trek episode "Turnabout Intruder." She had a regular role on the TV series the "The Interns" and also appeared in "Iron Horse."

SMITH, YEOMAN
a yeoman Kirk keeps calling Jones in Classic episode "Where No Man Has Gone Before." She is played by Andrea Dromm.

SMITHERS, WILLIAM
played Merikus or Captain R.M. Merik in Classic Trek episode "Bread and Circuses." His TV credits include "Voyage To The Bottom Of The Sea," "Barnaby Jones" and regular roles in "Peyton Place," "Executive Suite" and "Dallas."

SNODGRASS, MELINDA M.
scriptwriter (and story editor/executive script consultant for fourth and fifth seasons) for TNG episodes "The Measure Of A Man," "Pen Pals," "Up The Long Ladder," "The Ensigns of Command" and "The High Ground." A science fiction novelist, she is also the author of the Classic Trek novel *The Tears of the Singers*.

SNYDER, JOHN
played Bochra in TNG episode "The Enem" and Aaron Conor in "The Masterpiece Society."

SNYDER, MICHAEL
played a Starfleet communications officer in "The Voyage Home." He also played Quol in TNG episode "The Perfect Mate" and appeared in "Rascals."

SOBELMAN, BORIS
scriptwriter of Classic Trek episode "The Return Of The Archons." Other writing credits include "The Man From U.N.C.L.E."

SOBI
leader of the Brekkan sales team who is trapped on the *Sanction*, and who is brought aboard the *Enterprise* in TNG episode "Symbiosis." He is played by Judson Scott.

SOBLE, RON
played Wyatt Earp in Classic Trek episode "Spectre of the Gun." TV credits include a regular role on "The Monroes" and appearances in the films "The Daughters of Joshua Cabe," "The Beast Within" and "The Mystic Warrior."

SOFAER, ABRAHAM
played the Thasian in Classic Trek episode "Charlie X" and the Melkotian voice in "Spectre of the Gun." Born Oct. 1, 1896 in Burma, he has been acting in the U.S. since the fifties. Film credits include the 1951 movie "Quo Vadis," "Captain Sinbad"('63) and "Journey to the Center of Time."

SOHL, JERRY
scriptwriter of Classic Trek episodes "The Corbomite Maneuver," "This Side Of Paradise" and "Whom Gods Destroy." A science fiction novelist who has written *The Time Dissolvers* and *The Odious Ones* . He also wrote under the pen name Nathan Butler (see entry.)

Solar System L370
ingested by the device in Classic episode "The Doomsday Machine."

SOLARI, RUDY
played Salish in Classic Trek episode "The Paradise Syndrome." TV credits include "The Bionic Woman" and "Voyage To The Bottom Of The Sea." He also had regular roles on "The Wackiest Ship In The Army," "Garrison's Gorillas" and "Redigo." He appeared in the 1982 film "The Boss's Son."

Solarion IV
Federation colony attacked by the Cardassians but who made it look like the Bajorans did it in TNG episode "Ensign Ro."

Soleis V
in TNG episode "Loud As A Whisper," this planet houses two warring groups of a race called the Solari. Riva is sent to help them.

SOLIS
Enterprise bridge officer in TNG episode "The Arsenal of Freedom." He is played by George de la Pena.

Solition Wave

new propulsion method invented by Dr. Jidar in TNG episode "New Ground" which doesn't work.

SOLOK, DaiMON

this Ferengi gives Picard, Worf and Crusher passage on his ship to Seltris III in TNG episode "Chain of Command."

SOLOMON, GERALD

hair stylist on DS9.

SOLOW, HERBERT F.

executive in charge of production for seasons one and two of "Star Trek." He also worked on the films "Heatwave!" "Get Crazy" and the TV series "The Man From Atlantis."

Son, The

the son of God and the deity the people of planet 892 IV worship. Kirk mistakenly thinks they mean their planet's "sun" in Classic episode "Bread And Circuses."

SONAK

Kirk's new Vulcan science officer who is going to meet him on the *Enterprise* in "The Motion Picture." He dies at the beginning of the film in a terrible transporter accident along with Admiral Lori Ciani.

SONGI, CHAIRMAN

head of Gamelan V in TNG episode "Final Mission." She was played by Kim Hamilton.

Sonic Disruptor Field

Klingon invention that acts as a door on the brigs of Romulan ships as mentioned in Classic episode "The Enterprise Incident."

Sonic Separator

medical device McCoy uses to put Spock's brain back in its rightful place in Classic episode "Spock's Brain."

SOONG, DR. NOONIAN

father and creator of Data and Lore as seen in TNG episode "Datalore" among others. Soong created Data in his own image. He was played by Brent Spiner.

SOREL, LOUISE

played Reena (or Rayna) Kapec in Classic Trek episode "Requiem For Methuselah." Her TV credits include "Iron Horse," "The Survivors" (in which she was a regular,) "The Don Rickles Show," "The Curse of Dracula" and "Ladies Man." She also appeared in the 1982 film "Airplane II: The Sequel."

SOREN

a member of the androgenous race, the J'naii, she thinks of herself as female which is against the law on her world. She has an affair with Riker in TNG episode "The Outcast." She is played by Melinda Culea.

SORENSEN, PAUL

played a merchantship captain in "The Search For Spock." TV credits include "Iron Horse," "The Guns of Will Sonnett" and "Barnaby Jones."

SORENSON, CINDY

played Furry Animal in TNG episode "The Dauphin."

SOUL, DAVID

played Makora in Classic Trek episode "The Apple." Born August 28, 1943, he was the star of the TV series "Here Come The Brides," "Owen Marshall, Counselor At Law," "Starsky and Hutch," "Casablanca" and "The Yellow Rose." He has also starred in numerous TV movies and had a hit single song in the late seventies, "Don't Give Up On Us."

SOVAK

Ferengi on Risa who is looking for the Tox Uthat and thinks Picard and Vash can lead him there. He is played by Max Grodenchik in TNG episode "Captain's Holiday."

SOWARDS, JACK B.

scriptwriter of "The Wrath of Khan." He also wrote the TNG episode "Where Silence Has Lease" and the films "Deliver Us From Evil," "Cry Panic," "Death Cruise" and "Desperate Woman" as well as episodes of "Barnaby Jones."

Space Normal Speed

slower than the speed of light (which is also known as impulse power) mentioned in Classic episode "The Galileo Seven."

SPACE SEED

written by Gene L. Coon and Carey Wilbur and directed by Marc Daniels, this first season Classic Trek episode aired 2/16/67. The Enterprise encounters a sleeper ship, the *S.S. Botany Bay* from the late 1990's and awaken the people on board only to have them
take over the *Enterprise* and threaten the crews' lives. This episode led to the movie sequel, *Star Trek II: The Wrath of Khan.* Guest stars: Ricardo Montalban, Madlyn Rhue, Blaisdell Makee, Mark Tobin and John Winston. Of note: Chekov does not appear in this episode but in the movie Khan recognizes him from the past.

SPANO, CHARLES A. Jr.

co-author of Classic novel *Spock Messiah!*

SPARKS, DANA

played a weapons officer in TNG episode "Contagion."

SPARR, ROBERT

director of Classic Trek episode "Shore Leave." He also directed episodes of "Voyage To The Bottom Of The Sea."

SPECTRE OF THE GUN

written by Lee Cronin and directed by Vince McEveety, this third season Classic Trek episode aired 10/25/68. Finding a Melkot buoy in space that warns them away, the *Enterprise* crew insists on a meeting with the aliens on their mission of peace and find themselves victims of a great illusion wherein Kirk, Spock, McCoy, Scotty and Chekov are the Clanton gang who must fight the Earps and Doc Holliday. The only problem is, history dictates that the Clanton gang will lose and no matter how hard they try to escape the strange, half-built town or reason with its inhabitants, they find themselves at a face-off at

the O.K. Corral. Guest stars: Bonnie Beecher, Rex Holman, Ron Soble, Charles Maxwell, Sam Gilman, Bill Zuckert, Charles Seel, Ed McReady and Gregg Palmer. Of note: James Doohan provides the voice for the Melkot buoy.

Spectro Readings

used by the *Enterprise* to detect disease and contamination on alien worlds. It is mentioned in Classic episode "The Naked Time."

SPELLERBERG, LANCE

played the transporter chief in TNG episode "We'll Always Have Paris" and Ensign Herbert in "The Icarus Factor."

SPENCER, JIM

played the air policeman in the Classic Trek episode "Tomorrow Is Yesterday."

Spican Flame Gems

Cyrano Jones tries to sell these on Space Station K 7 in Classic episode "The Trouble With Tribbles." He is still selling them in the animated episode "More Tribbles, More Troubles."

SPIELBERG, DAVID

actor who guest starred in TNG episode "Starship Mine."

SPIES, ADRIAN

scriptwriter of Classic Trek episode "Miri." He also wrote for the TV show "The Man From U.N.C.L.E." and the films "Hauser's Memory," "The Family Kovack" and "Hanging By a Thread."

SPINELLI, LIEUTENANT

Enterprise navigator seen on the bridge in Classic episode "Space Seed." He is played by Blaisdell Makee.

SPINER, BRENT

stars as Commander Data on "The Next Generation." He also plays Lore, Data's brother, and Dr. Noonian Soong, Data's creator. Because of the nature of his character, he has played several multiple roles on TNG. Born in Houstan, TX, Spiner did a lot of acting work on and off Broadway and even drove a cab for six months when he was just starting out. He hates the fact that he can still hear his Texas accent in the voice of Data when he watches the show. He watched the original Star Trek series when he was in college (which perhaps hints at his age, which he does not like to divulge,) but says his hero when he was young was Jock Mahoney, the Range Rider. He does, however, believe in beings from other planets. Interested in comedy, he appeared in "The Little Shop Of Horrors" at the Westwood Playhouse in Los Angeles. His film credits include "Stardust Memories" as well as some TV movies. He has also guest starred on "The Twilight Zone," "Hill Street Blues," "Cheers" and "Night Court."

SPINRAD, NORMAN

scriptwriter of Classic Trek episode "The Doomsday Machine." A science fiction novelist who has penned such titles as *The Void Captain's Tale, The Iron Dream, Bug Jack Barron* and others, he currently has a review and science fiction criticism column in the magazine *Asimov's SF.* He also sells his short stories to various magazines, and has been nominated for, and won, many writing awards.

Spiny Lobefish

served at the Tilonus Institute for Mental Disorders to Riker in TNG episode "Frame of Mind." Riker does not like it.

SPOCK, COMMANDER

first officer of the *Enterprise* and the ship's science officer who starts out as Lt. Commander in the show's first season and is Captain Spock by the second Trek film, later becoming an ambassador in TNG. He is played by Leonard Nimoy. Spock is half Vulcan, half human, and was raised by his parents, Amanda Grayson and Sarek on Vulcan. He had a pet sehlat (see entry) named I'Chaya when he was a child. His service record, as quoted from Classic episode "Court Martial," reads: Serial # S179 276 SP, rank: Commander, commendations: Vulcan Scientific Legion of Honor, Award of Valor and twice decorated by Starfleet Command. He has adopted his Vulcan heritage but finds it often difficult to come to terms with his human half. He is reserved, claims he has no emotions (though he is often really suppressing them) and is a vegetarian. In Classic episode, "The Cage," he was only a lieutenant when he served under Pike. Spock has an A 7 computer rating, meaning he has very strong computer capabilities. He can memorize things in an instant, calculate odds while performing other, non-related tasks and is a genius at math, science and computer programming. He also appears interested in literature, and quotes often from literary works by humans. He plays the Vulcan lyre (and many other musical instruments, including the piano) with great skill. He had not spoken to his father for 17 years prior to "Journey To Babel," and was betrothed to a woman, when they were both seven years old, named T'Pring. T'Pring divorces Spock during their "wedding" when Spock was in the midst of pon farr (see entry.) He never married again during the series, although in the 24th century Picard mentioned attending Spock's wedding when he was a cadet at the Academy. At the beginning of the original series, Spock had been in service to Starfleet for 15 years and has served 11 years on board the *Enterprise*. Spock shows an unswerving loyalty to Captain Kirk and despite Spock's aloof nature, they become "brothers" (according to Spock in "Whom Gods Destroy,") and "family" (as mentioned in "The Final Frontier.") McCoy and Spock often spar verbally, but are actually good friends as well. Spock even refers to Kirk as "T'hy'la" (see entry) in the novelization of "The Motion

Picture" by Gene Roddenberry. Spock has had a lot of experiences, including dying and coming back to life (in "The Wrath of Khan," and "The Search For Spock" respectively.) Over the years his devotion to emotional discipline has relaxed, allowing him to reveal very deep emotions and a quick sense of humor.

SPOCK, MIRROR

seen in Classic episode "Mirror, Mirror," this Spock is less compassionate but no less intelligent. Also played by Leonard Nimoy, he is not afraid to show anger, and though he, too, is a scientist, he has few loyalties to the Empire he serves, and to the Captain Kirk for which he works. He inflicts pain upon Transporter Chief Kyle for a supposed error committed during the act of beaming up the landing party. He also sports a beard and mustache and a more rugged appearance than that of the real Spock. Kirk appeals to him to try to change the future of his "Empire" at the end of the episode, and Spock's reply is that he will think about it.

SPOCK'S BRAIN

written by Lee Cronin and directed by Marc Daniels, this third season Classic Trek episode aired 9/20/68. A woman is transported aboard the *Enterprise*, attacks the crew and surgically removes Spock's brain while the rest of the crew is unconscious. Kirk and the crew trace her advanced

ship to a world populated by all women where they find Spock's brain in time to return it to Spock before he dies. Guest stars: Marj Dusay, James Daris and Sheila Leighton. Of note: This episode also helped supply the plot for an x-rated parody film, only it wasn't Spock's brain which was stolen.

Spores

plants found on Omicron Ceti III which can enter a human's system and heal any illness but also makes an individual placid and lazy. Violent emotions will overcome and destroy the spores in the human (or Vulcan) system as seen in Classic episode "This Side of Paradise."

SPOT

Data's cat. Spot does not get along well with Riker. He likes to jump on Data's keyboard when he is working at the computer. He eats Feline Supplement 127.

SQUIRE OF GOTHOS, The

first season Classic Trek episode written by Paul Schneider and directed by Don McDougall. It aired 1/12/67 and involves a powerful creature, Trelane, who captures the *Enterprise* crew to "toy" with them. Guest stars: William Campbell, Richard Carlyle, Michael Barrier and Venita Wolf. Of note: William Campbell returns later as Koloth in "The Trouble With Tribbles." Also, Campbell dislocates his shoulder in a fight with Kirk (you can see this toward the end where he ends up not using the

arm at all and holding it close to his side.) The voices of Trelane's parents are Barbara Babcock (who guest stars in "A Taste of Armageddon" and "Plato's Stepchildren") and James Doohan.

St. Louis Academy

dance school Dr. Crusher attended and mentions in TNG episode "Data's Day."

Stacius Trade Guild

Fajo belongs to this guild in TNG episode "The Most Toys."

STADER, PAUL

stuntman in Classic Trek episode "Bread And Circuses."

Star Cluster NGC 321

where Eminiar and Vendikar are located in Classic episode "A Taste of Armageddon."

Star Desert

part of space with few stars. The *Enterprise* encounters Gothos in a star desert as mentioned in Classic episode "The Squire of Gothos."

Star Station Earhart

where Picard, as a cadet, was stabbed through the heart by Narsicans as mentioned in TNG episode "Tapestry" and "Samaritan Snare."

Star Station India

in TNG episode "Unnatural Selection," the *Enterprise* is en route here when they receive a message from the *Lantree*.

Star System 611

Landru's planet, Beta II, is located here as mentioned in Classic episode "Return of the Archons."

STAR TREK: THE MOTION PICTURE

this first feature length film of the Classic Star Trek series had a record breaking premiere at theaters in December, 1979. Directed by Robert Wise, it reunites the old crew of the *Enterprise* after a separation of over two years since their original five year mission ended. Spock lives on Vulcan while attempting to achieve Kolinahr at the Gol temple and Kirk has become an unhappy desk bound admiral. McCoy is in retirement on Earth, but all are called back to pilot the *Enterprise* on a mission to discover the mystery of a cloud that is destroying ships and planets. The cloud, a machine entity calling itself Vejur, is actually what remains of the Voyager One spacecraft launched from Earth in the late twentieth century. The craft apparently entered a machine-dominated universe, encountered an intelligence that reprogrammed it and sent it back on a new mission to seek out and destroy inferior, non-machine infestations. The *Enterprise* crew rushes to stop it. Guest stars include: Stephen Collins and Persis Khambatta, as well as brief appearances by previous Trek stars Grace Lee Whitney (reprising her role as Rand) and Mark Lenard (playing the Klingon captain.) Of note: Marcy

Lafferty, William Shatner's wife, also appears. Gene Roddenberry returns as producer, and science fiction author Alan Dean Foster created the story, which was in turn scripted by Harold Livingston. The special effects team of Douglas Trumbull and John Dykstra, along with the musical score by Jerry Goldsmith, made the movie a landmark epic in the industry. The movie broke both production cost records (with a budget of over $40 million budget spent) and box office totals. Though pronounced too long and boring by many fans, the film remains a Classic with added footage augmenting the video release.

STAR TREK II: THE WRATH OF KHAN

released in 1982, and directed by newcomer Nicolas Meyer, this movie details the characters in their later years, and pays little if any homage to "The Motion Picture." It is, instead, a sequel to an episode from the original series, "Space Seed." The antagonist is Khan, who has escaped from exile and is seeking out Kirk to take his revenge. Kirk is now serving as a desk bound admiral. Spock is an instructor, using the docked *Enterprise*, under his command, to educate his trainees. While Kirk is on board inspecting a new group of cadets, the emergency call comes in to investigate distress signals from a science team on Regula I. The Enterprise is the only closest ship and

Spock ends up turning over command to Kirk. Once in flight, they discover that Khan has appropriated a valuable device containing a Genesis Wave which can obliterate entire planets and then create new life in their wake. While battling Khan's insanity, the Enterprise becomes the target for the terrible device. Spock gives his life to save the day and the movie ends with a funeral service for the heroic Vulcan. Though many people consider this movie to be "real" Trek, accurate in areas of characterization, and involving a people-oriented plot which was one of the things that made Trek work, demands for Spock's return in a third movie were made worldwide. Guest stars include some famous names: Bibi Besch, Merritt Butrick, Paul Winfield, Kirstie Alley, Ricardo Montalban and Ike Eisenmann. John Winston reprises his role from the series as Kyle, and Teresa Victor, Leonard Nimoy's long time assistant from the original series, provides the voice of the Bridge. Harve Bennett was the film's executive producer as well as the writer (with Jack B. Sowards.) James Horner scored the film and Lucasfilm's Industrial Light and Magic team directed the special effects. This film's budget was substantially less than The Motion Picture's, but it also broke box office receipt records on opening day. It remains critically and financially the most successful of all the Trek movies.

STAR TREK III: THE SEARCH FOR SPOCK

in Leonard Nimoy's feature directorial debut, the characters put their lives and careers on the line to recover Spock's body and "katra," only to discover the Genesis Wave has somehow given Spock life. Spock goes through a rapid aging process (from babyhood to adulthood) as the crew battle vengeful Klingons on their way to save him. The *Enterprise* is destroyed and Klingons murder Kirk's son in the battle. Kirk, who has disobeyed Starfleet orders, faces a court martial, but they recover Spock, discover McCoy has been the receptacle for his "katra" all along and end up on Vulcan where a high priestess performs a kind of psychic surgery that puts Spock's "katra" back in its place. The end is bittersweet, with a Spock who has little memory of his friends, and fans called immediately for a sequel. Guest stars include James B. Sikking, Miguel Ferrer, Merritt Butrick, Robin Curtis, Christopher Lloyd, John Larroquette and Robert Hooks. Grace Lee Whitney returns in a cameo appearance and Mark Lenard returns as Sarek. Musical score was written by James Horner. Harve Bennett wrote the script and produced the film with Gary Nardino. Special effects were produced by Industrial Light and Magic.

STAR TREK IV: THE VOYAGE HOME

again directed by Leonard Nimoy, this fourth Trek movie is the third in the so-called "Wrath of Khan" trilogy, giving fans the sequel to "The Search For Spock" which they so adamantly demanded. It was released during Christmas of 1986. The crew, flying from Vulcan back to Earth to face criminal charges, are hurtled back in time to Earth's 20th century to capture a humpback whale in order to save a future Earth from a probe which is disrupting the atmosphere when it doesn't get an answer to its summons. The probe is apparently calling out to humpback whales, which are extinct in the 23rd century. The crew find their whales, George and Gracie, at a water park near San Francisco and Chekov runs into trouble when he is caught aboard the air craft carrier *Enterprise*. They all get out alive, however, and hurtle forward in time with the whales in the cargo bay of a Klingon ship to save Earth. They are then put on trial but the charges are dropped against everyone but Kirk, whose punishment is to be reduced in rank to captain. Guest stars include: Jane Wyatt as Amanda, Mark Lenard as Sarek, Catherine Hicks, Robin Curtis, Robert Ellenstein and John Schuck. Majel Barrett returns as Dr. Chapel and there is an appearance by Grace Lee Whitney. Though the plot of this movie sounds somewhat ridiculous, fans loved it and it proved to be the second highest grossing Trek film, after "The Wrath of Khan." Executive producer: Ralph Winter. Screenplay: Steve Meerson, Peter Krikes, Harve Bennett and Nicholas Meyer. Story by: Leonard Nimoy and Harve Bennett. Music: Leonard Rosenman. Producer: Harve Bennett. Director of photography: Don Peterman.

STAR TREK V: THE FINAL FRONTIER

directed by William Shatner, this June 1989 release introduces Spock's half brother Sybok, who journeys to Nimbus III, the planet of intergalactic peace, to recruit followers in his quest to locate ShaKaRee, a god with whom he says he has contact. To fulfill his quest, he kidnaps the *Enterprise* and crew, imprisons Kirk, Spock and McCoy, and heads to the center of the galaxy. This movie has some interesting aspects, though many fans consider it inconsistent with the Star Trek universe (mainly because Spock's brother pops up like the proverbial Vulcan inner eyelid.) The best parts of this movie, however, are the characters, their actions and their sense of humor. In no other movie does the crew relate so much like a family, a result of their deep faith in, and experiences with each other. Uhura and Scotty appear to have developed a very close relationship, and Spock has greatly mellowed since his "The Voyage Home" problems

with assimilating his human half. Melanie Shatner, William Shatner's daughter, plays yeoman to his captain. Guest stars: Laurence Luckinbill and David Warner. Executive producer: Ralph Winter. Producer: Harve Bennett. Special visual effects: Brad Ferren. Story by: William Shatner, Harve Bennett and David Loughery. Script by: David Loughery. Music: Jerry Goldsmith.

STAR TREK VI: THE UNDISCOVERED COUNTRY

directed by Nicholas Meyer, this December 1991 film is dark, with an unmistakable claustrophobic feeling as it follows Spock on a Sherlock Holmes-type investagation into the assassination of a high Klingon commander, and follows the journey of Kirk and McCoy as when they are sentenced to a cold, Klingon prison world, wrongly convicted of the assassination. There they meet a shapechanger who says she can help them escape. Guest stars: Iman, Christopher Plummer, David Warner, Michael Dorn, Kim Cattrall, Rene Auberjonois, Kurtwood Smith and Brock Peters. Christian Slater has a cameo, as does Grace Lee Whitney, who plays Commander Rand on Sulu's ship, *Excelsior*. This movie tried to tie in with "The Next Generation," and in fact, the references to Khitomer do accomplish that. Executive producer: Leonard Nimoy. Producers: Ralph Winter and Steven

Charles Jaffe. Written by: Nicholas Meyer and Denny Martin Flinn (screenplay,) Leonard Nimoy, Lawrence Konner and Mark Rosenthal (story.) Music: Cliff Eidelman.

Starbase 10

commanded by Commodore Stocker as mentioned in Classic episode "The Deadly Years." It is located near Gamma Hydra IV and the Neutral Zone.

Starbase 103

in TNG episode "The Arsenal of Freedom," the saucer section separates from the ship and is ordered to head to this base.

Starbase 105

mentioned in TNG episode "Yesterday's Enterprise."

Starbase 11

visited by the *Enterprise* in Classic episodes "Court Martial" and "The Menagerie."

Starbase 112

where the *Enterprise* picks up supplies for Tagra IV in TNG episode "True Q."

Starbase 118

the *Enterprise* is to pick up personnel on this base in TNG episode "A Fistful of Datas."

Starbase 12

located on a planet in the Gamma 400 system as mentioned in Classic episode "Space Seed." Also mentioned as being nearest to the planet Pollux in

"Where No Man Has Gone Before." In TNG episode "Captain's Holiday" the *Enterprise* is en route here after dropping Picard off on Risa. This starbase is also where an unexplained evacuation took place in TNG episode "Conspiracy."

Starbase 121

in TNG episode "Hollow Pursuits," Geordi tells Picard the ship needs to be bio-decontaminated to rid the ship of invidium. He suggests they go to Starbase 121.

Starbase 123

in TNG episode "The Tin Man," this base detects two Romulan cruisers on their way to Beta Stromgren.

Starbase 133

the *Enterprise's* destination after they leave Rana IV in TNG episode "The Survivor."

Starbase 14

in TNG episode "Code of Honor," a subspace message comes from here telling the *Enterprise* the extent of a plague which has hit Styris IV.

Starbase 152

destination of the *Enterprise* for inspection and repairs after leaving Beta Stromgren in TNG episode "The Tin Man."

Starbase 153

in TNG episode "The Emissary," K'Ehleyr is from here.

Starbase 157

the *Lalo's* distress signal was received by this base in

TNG episode "The Best of Both Worlds."

Starbase 173
located on the border of the Neutral Zone, this is a new post commanded by Admiral Nakamura. It mentioned in TNG episodes "The Measure of a Man," and "Q Who."

Starbase 179
Ensign Mendon is picked up by the *Enterprise* from here in TNG episode "A Matter of Honor."

Starbase 185
mentioned in TNG episode "Q Who" as being two years, seven months, three days and 18 hours away at maximum warp from where the Borg are.

Starbase 2
located between Beta Aurigae and Camus II. The *Enterprise* is headed here in Classic episode "Turnabout Intruder."

Starbase 211
the *Phoenix* returns here after Captain Maxwell has been relieved of command in TNG episode "The Wounded."

Starbase 212
where Lt. Uhnari will be taken, mentioned also as Starbase 12, in TNG episode "Aquiel."

Starbase 214
where Rasmussen is taken in TNG episode "A Matter of Time."

Starbase 218
Nella Daren and Nurse Beck come aboard ship

from here in TNG episode "Lessons."

Starbase 22
ship's destination in animated episode "How Sharper Than A Serpent's Tooth."

Starbase 220
the *Enterprise*'s destination in TNG episode "Night Terrors."

Starbase 23
Dr. Crusher is to meet Admiral Brooks here before a formal Starfleet inquiry into Dr. Reyga's death in TNG episode "Suspicions." Also mentioned as being nearest to the Arachna supernova in animated episode "The Terratin Incident."

Starbase 234
Fleet Admiral Brackett relays a message from here to the *Enterprise* about Spock's defection to the Romulans in TNG episode "Unification."

Starbase 24
where Kahlest was brought by the *Intrepid* after the Khitomer Massacre in TNG episode "Sins of the Fathers."

Starbase 25
where the shuttle *Copernicus* is headed in animated episode "The Slaver Weapon."

Starbase 260
the *Enterprise*'s destination in TNG episode "In Theory."

Starbase 27
near Omicron Ceti III mentioned in Classic episode "This Side of Paradise."

Starbase 29
in TNG episode "Frame of Mind," Admiral Budron of this base supposedly denied that Riker was a Starfleet officer.

Starbase 301
destination of the *Enterprise* in TNG episode "Conundrum."

Starbase 313
the *Enterprise* picks up scientific materials from here to take to the Guernica Colony in TNG episode "Galaxy's Child."

Starbase 324
Admiral Hanson arrives here to discuss strategy on the Borg threat with Starfleet Command.

Starbase 336
this base received the SOS from the T'Ong in TNG episode "The Emissary."

Starbase 343
in TNG episode "The Vengeance Factor," the *Enterprise* takes shore leave here after seeing to the Gatherer treaty.

Starbase 39 Sierre
in TNG episode "The Neutral Zone," Picard takes humans from an Earth satellite to this base.

Starbase 4
base near Triacus where the *Enterprise* is headed in Classic episode "And The Children Shall Lead." This is also the *Enterprise*'s desti-

nation at the end of "Let That Be Your Last Battlefield."

Starbase 416
Willie Potts is to be taken here for emergency treatment in TNG episode "Brothers."

Starbase 440
where the *Enterprise* takes the Ullian historian delegation in TNG episode "Violations."

Starbase 45
Admiral Jameson's last medical was taken here in TNG episode "Too Short A Season."

Starbase 513
this starbase lost contact with the *Vico* in TNG episode "Hero Worship."

Starbase 515
Wesley is travelling here to take his Academy exam in TNG episode "Samaritan Snare."

Starbase 55
Enterprise destination in TNG episode "Relics."

Starbase 6
destination of the *Enterprise* before it is diverted to Sector 39J to find the *Intrepid* in Classic episode "The Immunity Syndrome." Also mentioned as a destination in TNG episode "The Schizoid Man."

Starbase 67
destination of the *Enterprise* for repairs in TNG episode "Disaster."

Starbase 718

a meeting is held here to discuss the destroyed outposts in the Neutral Zone in TNG episode "The Neutral Zone."

Starbase 73

the *Enterprise* makes stops here in TNG episodes "Up The Long Ladder" and "Time Squared." Riker gets some Owan eggs (see entry) here. Worf meets his parents there in "Reunion."

Starbase 74

it orbits Tarsus III where the Bynars take over the *Enterprise* in TNG episode "11001001."

Starbase 83

in TNG episode "Q Who," the *Enterprise* sets a course here after encountering the Borg.

Starbase 84

after leaving the Klingon ship *Kartag* in TNG episode "Heart of Glory," the *Enterprise* heads here.

Starbase 9

where the ship was headed in Classic episode "Tomorrow Is Yesterday." Also mentioned in "Catspaw."

Starbase 97

mentioned by Hutchinson as being an "awful place" in TNG episode "Starship Mine."

Starbase Armus 9

in TNG episode "Datalore," Picard is to takes the *Enterprise* here for upgrading.

Starbase G6

in TNG episode "Hide and Q," Troi was dropped off here to catch a shuttle home.

Starbase Montgomery

Kyle Riker boards the *Enterprise* from this station in TNG episode "The Icarus Factor."

Starbase Scylla 515

a branch of Starfleet Academy is located here in TNG episode "Samaritan Snare."

Starbase Zendi 9

located in the Zendi Sabu sector, the *Stargazer* is headed here in TNG episode "The Battle."

Stardate

consisting of four numerals (the year) along with one or two after a decimal (or point) mark. In TNG it consists of 5 numerals and one numeral after the point. The one (or two) numerals after the point supposedly denotes the time.

Stardrive

another term for warp drive.

Starfleet

also known as Starfleet Command, they run defense and exploration missions for the Federation. They answer only to the Federation.

Starfleet Academy

where Starfleet hopefuls learn about life in space. The Academy is in San Francisco, California, and has apparently very high standards students must meet in order to graduate.

Starfleet Cybernetics Journal

in TNG episode "Birthright," Dr. Bashir wants to write an article for this publication on Data's newly discovered ability to dream.

Starfleet Orders

there are many. General order number one is also known as the Prime Directive, and forbids interference in naturally developing alien societies. According to Classic episode "The Doomsday Machine," order #104, section B, paragraph IA states: "In the absence of the commanding officer, the highest ranking officer, even if not of that ship's command, may take command." In section C, it reads: "The highest ranking officer may be relieved if medically or psychologically unfit to command." Starfleet order #2 prohibits Starfleet officers from taking the life of intelligent beings.

Stargazer, U.S.S.

Picard's first command. Jack Crusher served as his first officer and died when Picard sent him on an away team. The ship was lost at Maxia Zeta, then was presented by the Ferengi nine years later to Picard in the Zendi Sabu system in TNG episode "The Battle."

Starithium Ore

ore which interferes with Vash's sensor readings on Risa in TNG episode "Captain's Holiday."

STARNES, PROFESSOR

led the science expedition on Triacus and commits suicide through the Gorgon's influence. He leaves behind a son, Tommy. He was played by James Wellman.

STARNES, TOMMY

the oldest of the surviving children from Triacus, influenced by the Gorgon in Classic episode "And The Children Shall Lead." He is played by Craig Hundley.

STARSHIP MINE

this sixth season TNG episode was written by Morgan Gendel and directed by Cliff Bole. The *Enterprise* is docked at the Remmler Array to go through a cleansing sweep to rid the ship of baryon particles. All personnel are transported off the vessel, since the sweep is harmful to life, but Picard goes back at the last minute to retrieve his personal saddle in the hopes that on leave he can go horseback riding. Just as he is about to leave he realizes he is not alone. There is a group of thieves on board who are stealing trilithium from the ship to sell to terrorists on the black market. Guest star David Spielberg.

Starships

in Classic Trek, the fleet includes: The *Constellation* NCC 1017 (destroyed in "The Doomsday Machine,") the *Constitution* NCC 1700, the *Defiant* NCC 1764 (destroyed in "The

Tholian Web,") the *Enterprise* NCC 1701, the *Excalibur* NCC 1664 (destroyed by the M5 computer in "The Ultimate Computer,") the *Exeter* NCC 1672, the *Farragut* NCC 1647 (Kirk first served aboard this ship), the *Hood* NCC 1703, the *Intrepid* NCC 1631 (all Vulcan ship, destroyed by the galactic amoeba in "The Immunity Syndrome,") the *Lexington* NCC 1709, the *Potemkin* NCC 1702, the *Republic* NCC 1373 and the *Yorktown* NCC 1717.

STATIER, MARY
stunt double for Edith in Classic Trek episode "The City On The Edge Of Forever."

Station Nigala IV
destination of the *Enterprise* in TNG episode "Deja Q."

Station Salem I
this station is the locale for a preamble to war in TNG episode "The Enemy."

STATON, JOI
played a servant in TNG episode "QPid."

STEELE, KAREN
played Eve McHuron in Classic Trek episode "Mudd's Women." Her TV credits include: "Voyage To The Bottom Of The Sea," "Branded" and "The Wackiest Ship In The Army." She also appeared in the 1959 film "Ride Lonesome."

STEELE, TOM
stunt man in Classic Trek episode "Bread And Circuses."

Steelplast
a material mentioned in TNG episode "Too Short A Season." It can be cut by phasers.

STEFANO, JOSEPH
scriptwriter of TNG episode "Skin of Evil."

STEIN, MARY
played the alien nurse in TNG "Time's Arrow Part II."

STEINER, FRED
composer for dozens of episodes of Classic Trek, all seasons, as well as for the "The Next Generation." He also wrote music for the series "Lost In Space" and the well known "Perry Mason" theme.

Stellar Core Fragment
a dense chunk of star matter that threatens Moab IV in TNG episode "The Masterpiece Society."

STELLRECHT, SKIP
played an engineering crewman in TNG episode "The Naked Now."

STEN
artist mentioned in Classic episode "Requiem For Methuselah." Flint owns some of his work.

Sterilite
used during surgery to prevent infection as mentioned in Classic episode "A Private Little War."

STERNBACH, RICK
senior illustrator/technical consultant on DS9.

STEUER, JON
played Alexander in TNG episode "Reunion."

STEVEN, CARL
played Spock, age 9, in "The Search For Spock." He has also appeared in the 1982 movie "Rosie: The Rosemary Clooney Appearances" and the 1983 "Wait Till Your Mother Gets Home!"

STEVENS, WARREN
played Rojan in Classic Trek episode "By Any Other Name." Born in 1919, his films include the 1956 "Forbidden Planet." He has made guest appearances on the TV series "I, Spy," "Griff" and "Voyage To The Bottom Of The Sea" as well as a regular role on "Tales of the 77th Bengal Lancers," "The Richard Boone Show," "Bracken's World" and "Behind The Screen."

STEWART, BRYAN
scriptwriter of TNG episode "Family." (He helped write the premise.)

STEWART, CHARLES J.
played Captain Ramart in Classic Trek episode "Charlie X."

STEWART, PATRICK
stars as Captain Jean Luc Picard in "The Next Generation." Stewart was born on July 13 in the English town of Mirfield. He appeared in such BBC productions as "I, Claudius," "Smiley's People" and "Tinker, Tailor, Soldier, Spy." He was also in the American made films "Dune," "Excalibur" and "Lifeforce." He has done a lot of stage work, and is considered one of the leading talents on the British stage where he's played such notable characters as Shylock, Henry IV, Leontes, King John, Titus and Andronicus. Stewart has also done directing on TNG, including the episodes "Hero Worship," "In Theory" and "A Fistful of Datas." Stewart was very surprised to learn, in 1992, that *TV Guide* readers voted him "sexiest man of the year." He only wished it happened before he lost his hair at the age of 19. He's worn wigs most of his life, but the Star Trek producers decided he looked fine without and apparently that didn't deter the voters either. He lives in Los Angeles. Stewart's son, Daniel Stewart, appeared with him in the episode "The Inner Light" as his (and Kamin's) son Batai.

STIERS, DAVID OGDEN
played Dr. Timicin in TNG episode "Half A Life." He is best known for his role on the TV comedy "M*A*S*H."

STILES, LIEUTENANT ANDREW
an *Enterprise* navigator seen in Classic episode "Balance of Terror." He is a bigot who hates the Romulans because they killed his father. He soon learns to hate Spock when he finds out Romulans and Vulcans are very much alike, until he learns his hatred is irrational when Spock saves his life. He was played by Paul Comi.

STILLWELL, ERIC
scriptwriter of TNG episode "Yesterday's Enterprise."

STIMSON, VIOLA

played the lady in the tour on "The Voyage Home."

Stovo Kor

Klingon afterlife where Kahless is mentioned in TNG episode "Rightful Heir."

STOCKER, COMMODORE GEORGE

he takes over command of the *Enterprise* from Kirk when Kirk, due to accelerated aging, can no longer function as captain. He is inept at command, and needs to be pulled out of a dilemma with the Romulans when Kirk recovers in Classic episode "The Deadly Years." Stocker is played by Charles Drake.

Stokaline

in Classic episode "By Any Other Name," McCoy gives this to Spock to cure his faked Rigellian Kassaba fever. Stokaline is actually a vitamin compound.

STONE, COMMODORE

port master of Starbase 11 in Classic episode "Court Martial." He heads Kirk's trial board. He is played by Percy Rodriguez.

STONN

T'Pring's preferred Vulcan champion, before she ends up choosing Kirk to fight Spock, in Classic episode "Amok Time." T'Pring wants to divorce Spock so she can marry Stonn. Stonn is played by Lawrence Montaigne.

STRANGIS, GREG

creative consultant on TNG.

Strategema

in TNG episode "Peak Performance," this is a three-dimensional electronic tabletop game of skill.

Stratos

the cloud city that floats high above Ardana as seen in Classic episode "The Cloud Minders." The city's inhabitants devote themselves to art and education and violence is unheard of. Stratos subsidizes itself on the hard, blue collar labor of Ardana's "lower class" citizens, the Troglytes. The city is sustained by anti-gravity elevation.

STRATTON, ALBERT

played Kushell in TNG episode "The Outrageous Okona."

Streleb

located in the Medina system. It has a neighbor, Altec, from whom they are divided. They believe Captain Okona stole the Jewel of Thesia in TNG episode "The Outrageous Okona."

Streleb ship

captained by Kushell and seen in TNG episode "The Outrageous Okona."

STRINGER, KEN

second assistant director on "The Search For Spock."

Strnad

in TNG episode "Justice," mentioned as a new Federation colony located near Rubicam.

STRONG, BRENDA

played Rashella in TNG episode "When The Bough Breaks."

STRONG, MICHAEL

played Dr. Roger Korby in Classic Trek episode "What Are Little Girls Made Of?" His TV credits include "Planet of the Apes," "The Man From U.N.C.L.E.," "Cannon" and "Barnaby Jones." Film credits include "Vanished," "Queen of the Stardust Ballroom" and "This Year's Blonde."

STRUYCKEN, CAREL

Mr. Homn in TNG episodes "Haven," "Manhunt," "Menage A Troi," "Half A Life" and "Cost Of Living." His other roles include the giant in "Twin Peaks" and Lurch in the films "The Addams Family" and "Addams Family Values."

STUART, NORMAN

played the Vulcan Master in "Star Trek: The Motion Picture." He also appeared in the 1977 movie "79 Park Avenue."

STUBBS, DR. PAUL

he is an astrophysicist studying the Kavis Alpha explosion in TNG episode "Evolution." He is a fan of baseball. Ken Jenkins plays him.

STURGEON, THEODORE

scriptwriter of Classic Trek episodes "Shore Leave" and "Amok Time." He was born in 1918 and died on May 8, 1987. He is a well known science fiction writer who wrote such novels as the Hugo award winning *More*

Than Human as well as *The Dreaming Jewels, Venus Plus X* and many more. His story "Case and the Dreamer" is the one upon which "Shore Leave" is based. He has many wonderful short story collections, and has won numerous writing awards.

STURGEON

an *Enterprise* crewman killed by the salt vampire (the M113 creature) in Classic episode "The Man Trap."

Styris IV

this world is plagued by Anchilles Fever in TNG episode "Code of Honor."

Styrolite

sterile barrier that resembles thick, clear plastic seen in TNG episode "Unnatural Selection."

Subhadar

a Tarsian War rank to which Danar is promoted as mentioned in TNG episode "The Hunted."

Sublight Speed

attained using impulse power and mentioned in Classic episode "Elaan of Troyius." (see also "Space normal speed.")

Subspace Radio

used to talk to ships and places far away. Often the *Enterprise* is out of range even for this extended communication. It uses a warp effect so the sound waves can travel even faster than ships in warp.

Subspace Relay Station 194

in TNG episode "Aquiel," Station 47 receives this station's communications load.

Subspace Relay Station 47

Starfleet installation near the Klingon border where Aquiel Uhnari and Keith Rocha are assigned in TNG episode "Aquiel."

SUDDENLY HUMAN

fourth season TNG episode written by John Whelpley, Jeri Taylor and Ralph Phillips and directed by Gabrielle Beaumont. The *Enterprise* encounters a Talarian freighter with five boys on board, one of whom is human and has been missing for years when his world was attacked by Talarians. His rescue suddenly puts in the position of having to leave the only family he's ever known to regain his human heritage. Guest stars: Chad Allen, Sherman Howard and Barbara Townsend.

SULLIVAN, KEVIN

played March in "The Wrath of Khan."

SULLIVAN, LIAM

played Parmen in Classic Trek episode "Plato's Stepchildren." TV credits include "Voyage To The Bottom Of The Sea" and "Lost In Space." He also had a regular role on "The Monroes." Film credits include the 1979 "The Best Place To Be" and the 1984 "Ernie Kovaks: Between the Laughter."

SULLIVAN, SUSAN J.

played the woman in the transporter in "Star Trek: The Motion Picture."

SULU, HIKARU

the *Enterprise* helmsman, he ends up captain of the *Excelsior* by the sixth film, "The Undiscovered Country." Sulu can pilot anything, is fascinated by botany, old guns and fencing. His ancestry is Japanese, and he exhibits a great love for life. He is good friends with Chekov (they took shore leave together in "The Final Frontier.") He was underused in the series and so his character is less developed than the rest of the crew. He is played by George Takei. In the mirror universe, Sulu is a very sinister man with a long scar down the side of his face. He has aspirations to be captain of the *Enterprise* one day, even if he has to kill to do so and has a "thing" for Uhura.

SUMMERS, JARON

scriptwriter of TNG episode "The Child."

SUMMERS, JERRY

stunt double for Chekov in Classic Trek episode "The Trouble With Tribbles."

Sun Tzu

mentioned in TNG episode "The Last Outpost" as a Chinese oracle. One of its strategies, still taught in Starfleet, is "He will triumph who knows when to fight and when not to fight."

SUNA

person responsible for Riker's hallucinations in TNG episode "Frame of Mind." He is a scientist working with Tilonus IV rebels trying to get secret information from Riker's mind using a neurosomatic process.

SUNAD

Zalkonian in command of a ship that threatens the *Enterprise* in TNG episode "Transfigurations." He is played by Charles Dennis.

SUPERA, MAX

played Patterson on TNG episode "Disaster."

Supervisor 194

Gary Seven's title in Classic episode "Assignment: Earth." (See entry for Seven, Gary.)

SURAK

the legendary Vulcan who brought ultimate peace through logic to the Vulcan society thousands of years before. He was a great philosopher. An image of him is conjured up by Yarnek in Classic episode "The Savage Curtain." He is played by Barry Atwater.

Surata IV

in TNG episode "Shades of Gray," Riker is infected by microbes from this world.

Survey on Cygnian Respiratory Disease

name of the tape Nurse Chapel used to threaten Ensign Garrovick into eating. She says McCoy's voice is on the tape, ordering Garrovick to eat in Classic episode "The Immunity Syndrome."

SURVIVOR, The

written by James Schmerer, this animated Classic Trek episode aired 10/13/73. The *Enterprise* rescues a man, Carter Winston, who has been missing for five years. Winston is really a Vendorian, however, an alien which can assume the form of other humans. He assumes the form of Kirk and orders the ship into the neutral zone. A battle with the Romulans ensues. Guest voices: Ted Knight (Carter Winston/Allen,) Nichelle Nichols (Lt. Anne Nored,) Majel Barratt (Lt. M'Ress, computer) and James Doohan (Romulan Commander/Gabler.)

SURVIVORS, The

third season TNG episode written by Michael Wagner and directed by Les Landau. 11,000 inhabitants of Delta Rana IV have been wiped out, except for two humans, an older couple, who have mysteriously survived. Troi is going insane from hearing music in her mind, which is connected to the survivors. Guest stars: John Anderson and Anne Haney.

SUSPICIONS

sixth season TNG episode written by Joe Menosky and Naren Shankar and directed by Cliff Bole. Dr. Crusher is relieved of duty and about to be tried for violating medical ethics for conducting an illegal autopsy on a Ferengi scientist who was responsible for a metaphasic field discovery and committed suicide on board the ship. She believed he was murdered but the autopsy reveals nothing and the Ferengi are furious. Guest stars: Peter Slutsker, James Horan, Joan Stuart Morris and Tricia O'Neil.

SUTHERLAND, KEITH
voice of young Sepec in animated "Yesteryear."

Sutherland, U.S.S.
Data briefly commands this ship during the Klingon civil war in TNG episode "Redemption." Its first officer is Christopher Hobson.

SUTTER, CLARA
Ensign Daniel Sutter's daughter who encounters her imaginary friend in the flesh in TNG episode "Imaginary Friend." Her friend, Isabella, is actually an alien studying the crew. Clara is played by Noley Thornton.

Suvin IV
location of an archeological dig mentioned in TNG episode "Rascals." Dr. Langford and his team have offered Picard an open invitation to join them at the dig.

Swahili
the native language of the United States of Africa in the 23rd century. Uhura is Bantu and speaks Swahili fluently in Classic episode "Man Trap."

SWANSON, JANDI
played Katie in TNG episode "When The Bough Breaks."

SWENSEN, EDITHE
scriptwriter of TNG episode "Imaginary Friend."

SWENSON
Yar is supposed to compete against him in the ship's martial arts tournament but she dies in TNG episode "Skin of Evil."

SWETOW, JOEL
played Gul Jasal in DS9 "Emissary."

SWIFT, JOAN
played Aurelean Kirk in Classic Trek episode "Operation: Annihilate!"

SYBO
wife of Prefect Jaris of Argelius II. An empath, she forms a psychic link with the Jack The Ripper entity during a kind of seance in order to find out more about it in Classic episode "Wolf In The Fold." She dies when the entity kills her. Sybo is played by Pilar Seurat.

SYBOK
Spock's older half brother, slipped into Spock's personal history in the film "The Final Frontier." Played by Laurence Luckinbill, Sybok is searching for the legendary ShaKaRee, and claims to have a personal, mental channel to the mystical Vulcan god. He gathers followers interested in peace using a special Vulcan mind control on them, beginning his quest on Nimbus III, the planet of

Galactic Peace. Sybok renounced logic and left his homeworld of Vulcan decades before the film. Spock says he barely knew him. When he thinks he's found ShaKaRee, it turns out to be a prison housing an omnipotent, evil entity, and Sybok gives his own life to try to kill it and save the *Enterprise*. Before dying, he transfers his katra to Spock.

SYLVIA
blond woman Chekov meets in the Melkot simulation of the gunfight at O.K. Corral. She was played by Bonnie Beecher. Another Sylvia, played by Antoinette Bower, appears human but in her native form is actually a crab-like, frail creature in "Catspaw." She is ultimately destroyed by her own warped powers.

Symbalene Blood Burn
a swift-acting plague mentioned in Classic episode "The Changeling."

SYMBIOSIS
first season TNG episode written by Robert Lewin, Hans Beimler and Richard Manning, and directed by Wi Phelps. Ornara and Brekka are two worlds involved in a trade dispute which the *Enterprise* is trying to solve. It is learned, however, that the Brekkians are selling useless drugs for profit to the Ornarans who are addicted to them and believe they need them to keep from succumbing to a terrible disease. Guest stars: Merritt Butrick, Judson Scott, Kimberly Farr and Richard

Lineback. Of note: both Merritt and Judson had major roles in "The Wrath of Khan." Merritt played David Marcus, Kirk's son. Judson was Khan's protege, Joachim.

Synchronic Meter
tool used to check out the transporter in Classic episode "The Enemy Within."

Synthehol
drinks in Ten Forward aboard the TNG *Enterprise* are made of this substance. It is non-alcoholic and was invented by the Ferengi.

SYRUS, DR.
doctor at the Tilonus IV medical asylum who tells Riker he fell and hit his head in TNG episode "Frame of Mind."

System J 25
in TNG episode "Q Who" the *Enterprise* first sees the Borg here. It is 7,000 lightyears away from their position when Q causes the ship to materialize here.

System L374B
where the planet-eating device is when the *Enterprise* encounters it in Classic episode "The Doomsday Machine."

Sythococcus Novae
a deadly, bacillus strain which Dr. Sevrin carrys in Classic episode "The Way To Eden." Primitive people on a world which has not known this disease can catch it very quickly and die if they are not immunized. All Federation citizens are immunized, so Dr.

Sevrin can move freely among them, but he is a murderer if he sets foot on a new world that has not known the disease. It was discovered in the 21st century and an immunization vaccine was discovered by Dr. J. Pearce.

T'Acog
the Batris destroyed this ship in TNG episode "Heart of Glory."

T'BOK, COMMANDER
Romulan commander who helps Picard in TNG episode "The Neutral Zone." He is played by Marc Alaimo.

T'hy'la
Vulcan term of friendship defined in Roddenberry's novel *Star Trek: The Motion Picture*. It can mean, depending on the context, "friend, brother, or lover." Spock uses this term in his mind to describe his relationship with Kirk. On a talk show, William Shatner mispronounced it as t-ha'la. Some fans have been known to pronounce it t-hee-a. It is actually pronounced t-high-la. It is a popular word with fans and often appears in fan fiction, but the word, Roddenberry's invention, has never been used on screen.

T'JON
an Ornaran who is captain of the *Sanction* in TNG episode "Symbiosis." He is played by Merritt Butrick.

T'Kon Empire
they ruled the galaxy 600,000 years ago. Their

leftover outposts are encountered in TNG episode "The Last Outpost."

T'lli Beta
the *Enterprise* encounters these two dimensional life forms while en route to this world in TNG episode "The Loss."

T'Ong
Klingon ship, class D 7, commanded by Captain K'Temoc. Its crew had been in cryonic suspension for 75 years.

T'PAN, DR.
director of the Vulcan Science Academy who is married to a human, Dr. Christopher, in TNG episode "Suspicions."

T'PAU
Vulcan matriarch who turns out to also be Spock's grandmother in Classic episode "Amok Time." She is the only person to ever turn down a seat on the Federation High Council. She is played by Celia Lovsky. Also the name of a Vulcan ship dismantled and left at Qualor II in TNG episode "Unification."

T'PEL, AMBASSADOR
secretly a Romulan, Subcommander Selok, who is posing as a Vulcan in TNG episode "Data's Day." In "The Drumhead," Admiral Satie accuses Picard of being in league with her spy mission. She is played by Sierra Pecheur.

T'PEL
Spock mentions her as his mother when he pretends

to be Selek in animated episode "Yesteryear."

T'PRING
Spock's betrothed. They were promised to each other in a ceremony at the age of seven on Vulcan. Spock is drawn to return to her when he enters pon farr in Classic episode "Amok Time." She, however, does not want Spock. She wants Stonn, and challenges Spock for the right to divorce. This means Stonn must fight Spock, but T'Pring chooses Kirk as her champion instead, forcing the two friends to fight to the death. T'Pring is played by Arlene Martel.

T'SHALIK
in TNG episode "Coming of Age," she is a Vulcan girl from another ship who takes the Academy Exam with Wesley. She is played by Tasia Valenza.

T'SU, LIAN
an *Enterprise* ensign tested by Geordi in TNG episode "The Arsenal of Freedom." She is played by Julia Nickson.

T 9 Converter
in TNG episode "The Last Outpost," this is an energy system stolen by the Ferengi from Gamma Tauri.

T negative
blood type of both Spock and his father Sarek and mentioned in Classic episode "Journey To Babel."

T Tauri type star system
single star with only one satellite, which is extremely rare according to Data in TNG episode "Clues."

TAAR
Ferengi leader, (his title was DaiMon) who fought Picard at Delphi Ardu in TNG episode "The Last Outpost." He is played by Mike Gomez.

Tachyon Web
one of these is erected between the blockading Starfleet ships in TNG episode "Redemption."

TAGGART, CAPTAIN
commander of the *Repulse*, the ship Pulaski served on before coming to the *Enterprise*, and mentioned in TNG episode "Unnatural Selection." Taggart is played by J. Patrick McNamara.

Tagra IV
the *Enterprise* is carrying relief supplies to a colony on this world when they pick up Amanda Rogers in TNG episode "True Q."

Tagus III
Federation world with famous, billion year old ruins mentioned in TNG episode "Q Pid." The Tagians have closed off their world to outsiders.

TAJOR, GLIN
Cardassian aide of Gul Lemec in TNG episode "Chain of Command."

TAKAKI, RUSSELL
played Madison in "The Wrath of Khan."

Takaran

race which can simulate death in TNG episode "Suspicions." They have bluish skin.

TAKEI, GEORGE

starred as Lt. Hikaru Sulu in "Star Trek" and all the movies (in which his rank rose to Captain,) as well as the voice of Sulu in the animated series. Born in Boyle Heights, Los Angeles, his family was forced to relocate to Japanese detention camps in Arkansas and Tule Lake, California during World War II. Although only a small child at the time, the traumatic experience affected him for years afterwards. He graduated from UCLA with a theater arts degree and made his debut on "Playhouse 90." His TV credits include "Hawaiian Eye," "Perry Mason," "Alcoa Premiere," "Checkmate," "The Islanders," "The Wackiest Ship In The Army," "Mr. Novak," "The John Forsythe Show," "I, Spy," "Bob Hope Chrysler Theatre," "Felony Squad," "Bracken's World," "Ironside," "Mr. Roberts," "My Three Sons," "It Takes A Thief," "Voyage To The Bottom Of The Sea," "The Twilight Zone," "Kung Fu," "The Six Million Dollar Man," "Baa Baa Black Sheep," "Chico and the Man," "Hawaii Five-0," "Miami Vice" and the PBS movie "Year of the Dragon." He first appears in Star Trek in the second pilot, "Where No Man Has Gone Before." He also appeared in "Mission: Impossible" during the

filming of Trek, and in the movie "Green Berets." His other film credits include "A Majority of One," "Ice Palace," "Red Line 7000," "Hell To Eternity," "An American Dream," "Walk Don't Run," "Never So Few," "Josie's Castle," "The Loudmouth," "The Young Divorcees Pt 109," "Which Way To The Front," and most recently, "Return From The River Kwai" and "Prisoners of the Sun." Always politically active during his career, Takei ran for the Los Angeles city council but came in second. He has also co-written a novel, *Mirror Friend, Mirror Foe* with science fiction author Robert Asprin. He also loves to run and has competed in many long-distance marathons.

TAKEMURA, DAVID

visual effects associate on TNG.

TAL, SUBCOMMANDER

the Romulan Commander's second officer in Classic episode "The Enterprise Incident." He is played by Jack Donner.

Tal Shiar

greatly feared Romulan intelligence agency with a lot of power over the Romulan military. In TNG episode "Face of the Enemy," Troi masquerades as Major Rakal of the Tal Shiar.

Tal Shaya

Vulcan form of execution which involves quickly breaking the neck of a victim. It is the way the

Tellarite Gav dies in Classic episode "Journey To Babel."

Talarians

humanoid and warlike, Talarians attacked Galen IV ten years before the *Enterprise* encounters a ship with a human teenage survivor from the colony on board. The Talarians are suspicious, wear gloves around strangers, and are very family oriented. The human boy, who has been adopted by the captain of the ship, Jeremiah Rossa, does not want to return to his own kind. A Talarian freighter, the *Batris*, is stolen by Klingon rebels and is destroyed in "Heart of Glory."

Talos IV

one of eleven planets circling a binary star, it is the home of the Talosians, beings with super mental powers in Classic episode "The Menagerie." The Talosians moved underground when their surface world could no longer support them. They keep a zoo full of various creatures on this world including a female human named Vina. After Pike visited this world, it was declared off-limits to all under General Order #7, an order that carries the death penalty if disobeyed.

TALUNO, KAI

the Bajoran predecessor to Kai Opaka in TNG episode "Emissary." Two centuries earlier, when he was in the region of the Denorios Belt (where most of the Bajoran Orbs were found) he was stranded in space and

claimed the "heavens opened up and swallowed him."

Tama, Children of

race of beings whose communication involves metaphor and allusion, making it very difficult for the Federation to communicate with them in TNG episode "Darmok."

TAMAR

a member of the underground movement on Landru's planet who is killed by the lawgivers in Classic episode "The Return of the Archons." He is played by Jon Lormer (who also appeared in "For The World Is Hollow And I Have Touched The Sky.")

TAMOON

drill thrall on Triskelion assigned to Chekov in Classic episode "The Gamesters of Triskelion." She was played by Jane Ross.

TAMURA, YEOMAN

member of the landing party to Eminiar in Classic episode "A Taste of Armageddon." She was played by Miko Mayama.

Tan Ru

the machine Nomad met and joined together with in space in Classic episode "The Changeling."

Tango

name of Pike's horse he left behind in the city of Mojave, California and seen in Classic episode "The Menagerie."

Tango Sierra
located in the Rachelis system, this is a Federation medical facility mentioned in TNG episode "The Child."

TANKRIS, YEOMAN
an *Enterprise* recorder at Scotty's hearing in Classic episode "Wolf In The Fold." She was played by Judy McConnell.

Tantalus Field
dangerous weapon found in Kirk's quarters in the mirror universe in Classic episode "Mirror, Mirror." It can spy on and make a person disappear or die with the touch of a button.

Tantalus Penal Colony
hospital for the violently mentally ill headed by Dr. Tristan Adams and his associate, Dr. Simon Van Gelder. Dr. Adams invents a neural neutralizer which can brainwash patients, but starts using it to control others and make them obedient only to him. He uses it on Dr. Van Gelder in Classic episode "Dagger of the Mind," as well as on Kirk.

Tantalus V
location of the Tantalus Penal Colony in Classic episode "Dagger of the Mind."

Tanuga IV
location of the Tanuga Research Station. The Tanugans, who are humanoid, have a rule that men are guilty until proven innocent. The Tanuga Research Station which orbits the planet

explodes in TNG episode "A Matter of Perspective."

Tao Classical Music
Rishon Uxbridge composes this type of music in TNG episode "The Survivors."

Taos Lightning
type of whiskey served in Tombstone in Classic episode "Spectre of the Gun."

TAPESTRY
sixth season TNG episode written by Ronald D. Moore and directed by Les Landau. When Picard is knocked unconscious, while Crusher works desperately to save his life, he finds himself standing in a room filled with light. Q, wearing long robes, approaches him, and tells him he is in the afterlife. Picard is forced to relive segments of his life at Q's behest and finds himself back at the Academy when he was stabbed through the heart by Narsicans. Because he is reliving the episode with full foreknowledge, things happen differently, but he learns that without some of his brash decisions, he would not be the man he is today. Guest stars: John deLancie and Ned Vaughn.

TARAS, SUBCOMMANDER
she commands the Romulan ship *Harkona* in TNG episode "Contagion." She is played by Carolyn Seymour.

TARBOLDE, PHINEAS
author of the poem "Nightingale Woman" from which Gary Mitchell quotes in Classic episode "Where No Man Has Gone Before."

TARBUCK, BARBARA
played Leka in TNG episode "The Host."

Tarchannan III
home of parasites which have infected Geordi and Susanna Leitjen in TNG episode "Identity Crisis."

TARCHER, JEREMY
scriptwriter of Classic Trek episode "The Lights of Zetar" (with Shari Lewis.)

Tarella
where the people from planet Haven are from. They are survivors of a biological war that happened on Tarella many years before in TNG episode "Haven."

Targ
Klingon animal Worf once had as a pet when he was a child. It is mentioned in TNG episode "Where No One Has Gone Before."

TARK
father of the dancer, Kara, who was killed by the Jack the Ripper entity in Classic episode "Wolf In The Fold." He is an Argelian and is played by Joseph Bernard.

Tarkesian Razor Beast
Guinan uses this phrase in TNG episode "Rascals." When she is reverted to her child form, she wants to jump up and down on the bed like one of these beasts.

TARMIN
an Ullian historian going to Kaldra IV via the *Enterprise* in TNG episode "Violations." He is a mind rapist and is played by David Sage.

Tarod IX
in TNG episode "The Neutral Zone," this outpost on the Romulan border was destroyed.

TARRANT, NEWELL
played a CDO in "The Voyage Home."

TARRIGAN, ENSIGN
Enterprise security officer in TNG episode "Rightful Heir."

Tarsec Apertif
tricky concoction Guinan makes in Ten Forward in TNG episode "Time's Arrow."

TARSES, SIMON
medical technician on the *Enterprise* whose grandfather was a Romulan which makes the prejudiced Admiral Satie suspect him of treason in TNG episode "The Drumhead." He was played by Spencer Garrett.

Tarsian War
for this war, the Angosians altered their soldiers biologically to fight for them, then abandoned them in prison camps in TNG episode "The Hunted."

Tarsus III
Starbase 74 is located here, where the *Enterprise* was located when the Bynars stole her in TNG episode "11001001."

Tarsus IV
it was on this world that Kodos the Executioner murdered half the population, (4,000 less desireable colonists) so that the rest of the colony could live during a famine. Kirk and Kevin Riley were children at the time and witnesses of the atrocity as mentioned in Classic episode "The Conscience of the King."

Tartares V
mentioned as the location of some newly discovered ancient ruins. Q tells Vash she should go there in DS9 episode "Q Less."

TARVER, MILT
played a scientist in TNG episode "Time's Arrow Part I and II."

Tasmeen
Vulcan month mentioned in animated episode "Yesteryear." In an alternate timeline, Spock died on the 20th of this month during his Kaswan.

Tasva Egg
the Cardassian Gul Madred gives one of these to Picard, whom he has nearly tortured to death in TNG episode "Chain of Command." It is moving and still alive but Picard eats it anyway.

TATE, NICK
played Dirgo in TNG episode "Final Mission."

TATRO, RICHARD
played Norman in Classic Trek episode "I, Mudd."

Tau Alpha C
Riker thinks the Traveler is from here in TNG episode "Where No One Has Gone Before."

Tau Ceti
star near which the *Enterprise* used the Cochrane deacceleration maneuver to outwit a Romulan ship. This event is mentioned by Spock to Garth in Classic episode "Whom Gods Destroy."

Tau Ceti III
in TNG episode "Conspiracy" Picard first met Walker Keel here in a bar.

Tau Cygna V
the crew of the *Artemis* settled here in TNG episode "The Ensigns of Command." This world, located in the Delor Belt, is bombarded by hyperonic radiation and is owned by the Sheliak Corporate. The colony has a population of 15,253.

Taurus II
where the shuttlecraft *Galileo* crash lands in Classic episode "The Galileo Seven." The natives are large, furry humanoids who attack the shuttle crew and kill several of them. This planet is also used in the animated episode "The Lorelei Signal" as a planet whose inhabitants lure men to their world so they can drain them of their emotions. The men then age rapidly and die.

TAVA, DR.
medical aide at the hospital Riker is taken to on Malcoria in TNG episode "First Contact." Sachi Parker plays Tava.

TAYAR
Borg killed by the away team on Ohniaka III in TNG episode "Descent."

TAYBACK, VIC
played Jojo Krako in Classic Trek "A Piece of the Action." He was a regular on the TV series "Griff," "Khan" and "Alice" and his film credits include "Bullitt" and "The Choirboys." The owner of race horses, he died in the early 1990's.

TAYLOR, DEBORAH
played Zaheva in TNG episode "Night Terrors."

TAYLOR, JERI
scriptwriter of TNG story for the episodes "Descent," "Aquiel," "Final Mission," "The Wounded," "Night Terrors," "The Drumhead," "Silicon Avatar," "Unification Part I," "Violations," "The Outcast" and "Time's Arrow." Taylor also wrote the novelizaton of *Unification.*

TAYLOR, JUD
director of Classic Trek episodes "The Paradise Syndrome," "Wink of an Eye," "Let That Be Your Last Battlefield," "The Mark of Gideon" and "The Cloud Minders." His other directing credits include episodes of "The Guns of Will Sonnett," "The Man From U.N.C.L.E" and the films "Future Cop" and "Return To Earth."

TAYLOR, KEITH
played Jahn's friend in Classic Trek episode "Miri." He also guest starred in "Lost In Space" and was a regular on "McKeever and the Colonel."

TAYLOR, MARK L.
played Haritath in TNG episode "The Ensigns of Command."

TAYLOR, DR. GILLIAN
an expert on whales and a marine biologist who works at the Cetacean Institute in Sausalito in "The Voyage Home." She works for Bob Briggs, who transports the whales to the sea in the middle of the night without notifying her in order to set them free. She helps Kirk and Spock find the whales and transport them to the 23rd century. She tags along and becomes a new resident of the 23rd century, immediately finding work on a science vessel as a marine biologist.

TAYNA
Dr. Apgar's assistant in TNG episode "A Matter of Perspective" who claims Riker tried to rape her. She is played by Juli Donald.

Tchar
prince of the Skorr in Classic episode "Jihad." The Skorr are avian-like creatures. Skorr steals his own people's valuable relic in the hopes of starting a religious war.

Teacher, The
machine placed over the head of an individual which instantly gives them

all knowledge contained within the computer brain that runs Sigma Draconis VI in Classic episode "Spock's Brain." The knowledge is only temporary, however. The Eymorg, Kara, uses it when she steals Spock's brain.

TEER
title of a leader of the Ten Tribes on Capella IV in Classic episode "Friday's Child." The original Teer was Akaar, but he was killed and replaced by Maab, who was then killed and replaced by Eleen's newborn son, Leonard James Akaar.

Telemetry Probe
device shot into the galactic amoeba by the *Enterprise* to gather more information in Classic episode "The Immunity Syndrome."

Tellarites
aggressive species with pig-like faces. They are members of the Federation and appear in Classic episodes "Journey To Babel" and "Whom Gods Destroy." A Tellarite ship is caught in the Delta Triangle in animated episode "Time Trap."

TELLE, GLIN
a Cardassian member of a delegation on the *Enterprise* in TNG episode "The Wounded." He is played by Marco Rodriquez.

Tellun Star System
on the border of Klingon space, this system contains Troyius and Elas, two warring worlds who are to make peace when the Dohlman of Elas, Elaan, and the leader of Troyius marry in Classic episode "Elaan of Troyius."

Tellurian Spices
Andorians want to bid for these spices owned by Fajo in TNG episode "The Most Toys."

TEMAREK
he tastes a drink Marouk offers Brull in TNG episode "The Vengeance Factor." He is played by Elkanah J. Burns.

TEMPLE, NURSE
Enterprise nurse in TNG episode "Transfigurations." She is played by Patti Tippo.

TEMPLEMAN, S.A.
played John Bates in TNG episode "The Defector."

Temporal Rift
a time displacement.

Ten Forward
bar and lounge on the TNG *Enterprise* where the crew can relax while off duty and be served synthenol drinks as well as exotic foods.

TEPO
one of the lesser bosses on Iotia in Classic episode "A Piece of the Action."

TERKIM
Guinan's uncle, her mother's brother. Guinan says he was the family misfit but the only one in the family with a sense of humor in TNG episode "Hollow Pursuits."

Terra Ten
an original Earth colony sent to colonize a distant world and mentioned in animated episode "The Terratin Incident." The world "Terra Ten" has been, over the years, changed to "Terratin."

Terraform Command
Federation agency mentioned in TNG episode "Home Soil."

TERRATIN INCIDENT, The
written by Paul Schneider, this animated Classic Trek episode aired 11/17/73. After the *Enterprise* is hit by a bolt of energy from a planet orbiting the star Cepheus, the crew begins to shrink. A tiny city on the planet is responsible for the attack, and the transporter is the key to restoring the crew. Guest voice: James Doohan (Lt. Arex, Mendant of the Terratins.)

Terratins
people of the original Terra Ten Earth colony who colonized a world they call Terratin. Spiroid waves are responsible for shrinking them to the point that other ships could never find them. They built their own miniature cities, but are on an unstable planet and must now be moved in animated episode "The Terratin Incident."

TERRELL, CAPTAIN CLARK
commander of the *Reliant* when it is taken over by Khan in "The Wrath of Khan." Chekov is his first officer. He kills himself when the parasite in his brain tries to force him to shoot Kirk. He was played by Paul Winfield.

Territorial Annex of the Tholian Assembly
what the Tholians call the unknown region of space into which the **Enterprise** and the **Defiant** have travelled. They claim the area as their territory.

Tessin III
an asteriod threatens this world in TNG episode "Cost of Living."

Tetralubisol
the white, liquid poison Lenore uses to try to kill Kevin Riley in Classic episode "The Conscience of the King."

Tetryons
subatomic particles which pass through Dr. Reyga's shield in TNG episode "Suspicions."

TEXAS
name of a man from Texas who is in the Royale in TNG episode "The Royale." He is played by Noble Willingham.

THALASSA
an energy entity, one of three who have survived for thousands of years after a war destroyed her world in Classic episode "Return To Tomorrow." She is Sargon's wife. She enters the body of Dr. Anne Mulhall in order to build an android body for herself. Anne Mulhall is played by Diana Muldaur.

Thalium Compound

compound found in Mintakan strata disrupts sensor probes in TNG episode "Who Watches The Watchers."

Thalos VII

mentioned in TNG episode "The Dauphin" as the "home of Thalian chocolate mousse."

Thandaus V

mentioned in TNG episode "Loud As A Whisper" as a world where the people are born with no limbs.

THANN

one of the Vians who tortures Kirk, Spock and McCoy in Classic episode "The Empath." He is played by Willard Sage.

THARN

leader of the Halkans in Classic episode "Mirror, Mirror." He refuses the *Enterprise* permission to mine dilithium on Halka. He is played by Vic Perrin.

Thasian

an alien entity, one of many, who rescued Charlie Evans from his crashed ship on their world, Thasus, in Classic episode "Charlie X." They are energy beings with great mental powers. The Thasian who appears on the bridge to take Charlie away is played by Abraham Sofaer.

THAT WHICH SURVIVES

written by John Meredyth Lucas and Michael Richards and directed by Herb Wallerstein, this third season Classic Trek episode aired 1/24/69. When Kirk, McCoy, Sulu and D'Amato beam down to investigate a Class M planet riddled with earthquakes, they find it inhabited by Losira, a woman whose touch can kill life. Guest stars: Lee Meriwether, Naomi Pollack, Arthur Batanides, Brad Forrest, Kenneth Washington and Booker Marshall. Of note: This is Dr. M'Benga's second appearance.

THATCHER, KIRK

actor/associate producer/musician who appeared as the punk on the bus in "The Voyage Home." He wrote the song "I Hate You" which is loudly playing on the tape player on the bus. He was also the associate producer of "The Voyage Home." Kirk is British Ex-Prime Minister Margaret Thatcher's son and the creator/producer/writer of the popular sitcom "Dinosaurs!"

THATCHER, TORIN

played Marplon in Classic Trek episode "The Return of the Archons." Torin was born in Bombay on Jan. 15, 1905 and died in 1981. He was a teacher before he took up acting. His roles include the films "Great Expectations," "The Seventh Voyage of Sinbad" and "Mutiny on the Bounty." TV credits include "Lost In Space," "Voyage To The Bottom Of The Sea," "One Step Beyond" and "The Guns of Will Sonnett."

THE CHILD

second season TNG episode written by Jaron Summers, Jon Povill and Maurice Hurley and directed by Rob Bowman. New chief of surgery Kate Pulaski comes aboard the *Enterprise* to replace Dr. Crusher for a season, and Troi becomes mysteriously pregnant by an energy alien. Her gestation lasts two days and the alien boy who is born ages extraordinarily rapidly. Guest stars: Seymour Cassel, R.J. Williams, Dawn Arnemann, Zachary Benjamin and Dore Keller. Whoopi Goldberg appears for the first time as Guinan.

THE NEUTRAL ZONE

first season TNG episode written by Maurice Hurley, Deborah McIntyre and Mona Glee and directed by James L. Conway. Three 20th century humans in cryonic suspension are discovered on an old Earth satellite. They are brought aboard the *Enterprise* as the ship heads to a meeting with the Romulans to try to find out why Earth outposts are being mysteriously destroyed. Guest stars: Marc Alaimo, Anthony James, Leon Rippy and Gracie Harrison. In this episode Clare Raymond's family tree includes references to the TV series Dr. Who, M*A*S*H and Gilligan's Island.

THEELA

leader of the females on Taurus II in animated episode "The Lorelei Signal." Majel Barrett plays her voice.

THEI

Romulan subcommander in TNG episode "The Neutral Zone." He is played by Anthony James.

THEISS, WILLIAM WARE

costume designer for "Star Trek." He also did work on the films "Heart Like A Wheel" and is the costume supervisor on "The Next Generation."

THELEV

an Andorian who is actually an Orion spy in Classic episode "Journey To Babel." He is the murderer of the Tellarite Gav and stabs Kirk in the back during a fight in the ship's corridor. He commits suicide through slow poisoning when he is caught. He is played by William O'Connell.

Thelka IV

Picard mentions that a dessert he is especially fond of is made on this world. He wants Nella to try it some time in TNG episode "Lessons."

Thelusian Flu

a mild flu that, when mixed with a plague causes accelerated aging in TNG episode "Unnatural Selection."

Theragen

a Klingon nerve gas that, when diluted with alcohol by McCoy, is the cure for the madness that plagues the *Enterprise* when it is trapped in Tholian space in Classic episode "The Tholian Web."

Thermoconcrete

used for building temporary shelters for landing parties, it is also used by McCoy to bandage the wounded Horta in Classic episode "The Devil in the Dark."

Theta Cygni XII

this world's inhabitants were destroyed by the flying, rubbery parasites on Deneva in Classic episode "Operation Annihilate!" They also attacked Ingraham B two years before reaching Deneva.

Theta VII

this planet is waiting for the *Enterprise* to deliver medical supplies to them, but the *Enterprise* is delayed when it goes after the vampire cloud in Classic episode "Obsession."

Theta VIII

the *Charybdis* was taken here in TNG episode "The Royale." It is located in the Theta 116 system. The atmosphere contains nitrogen, methane, liquid neon and ammonia tornadoes and the temperature remains at 291 degrees centigrade.

THIS SIDE OF PARADISE

written by D.C. Fontana and Nathan Butler and directed by Ralph Senensky, this first season Classic Trek episode aired 3/2/67. On the planet Omicron Ceti III, spores from an alien plant protect the colony inhabitants from deadly Berthold rays but also gives them an extreme feeling of peace and harmony that makes

them never want to leave the world. The spores infect the *Enterprise* crew, causing everyone abandons the ship to go live on the planet. Guest stars: Eddie Paskey, Jill Ireland, Frank Overton and Grant Woods. Of note: The late Jill Ireland's husband, Charles Bronson, was on the set to make sure Leila's love scenes with Spock did not get out of hand.

THOLIAN WEB, The

written by Judy Burns and Chet Richards and directed by Ralph Senensky, this third season Classic Trek episode aired 11/15/68. The *Enterprise* finds the missing ship *Defiant* in a part of space that is unstable. They board to investigate and discover that the ship is phasing out into another dimension. Kirk stays behind as the transporter malfunctions, then disappears with the ship and is feared dead. The crew then starts seeing his ghost. Apparently he was half caught in a transporter beam, and at the next interphase in space when the *Defiant* again becomes visible, they beam him back on board. Meanwhile, the Tholians are disturbed by the ship's presence and begin building a web around the ship because it will not leave. Of note: Barbara Babcock's voice is used for the Tholians.

Tholian Web

web spun around the *Enterprise* by the Tholians to capture them in Classic episode "The Tholian

Web." This special effect was created by Mike Minor.

Tholians

Kyle Riker is the only survivor of an attack by the Tholians in TNG. Kirk first encountered them in TNG episode "The Tholian Web." They are an unfriendly, territorial race who will kill to keep people away from them. The leader, who shows himself to Kirk, is named Loskene. He looks as if he's made of crystal and light. Tholians supposedly live on a hot planet, and are possibly hive-minded.

THOLL, KOVA

Mizarian who is held captive with Picard, Esoqq and Mitena Haro in TNG episode "Allegiance." He is played by Stephen Markle.

THOMAS, CRAIG

played a Klingon in "Star Trek: The Motion Picture." He also appears in the 1983 movie "Spring Fever."

THOMAS, SHARON

played the waitress in "The Search For Spock." She also appears in the 1982 movie "Portrait of a Showgirl."

Thomas Paine, U.S.S.

Captain Rixx commands this frigate in TNG episode "Conspiracy."

THOMPSON, BRIAN

played Klag in TNG episode "A Matter Of Honor."

THOMPSON, GARLAND

played the second crewman in Classic Trek episode "Charlie X" and Technician

Wilson in "The Enemy Within."

THOMPSON, SCOTT

played DaiMon Goss in TNG episode "The Price."

THOMPSON, SUSANNA

played Varel in TNG episodes "The Next Phase" and "Frame of Mind."

THOMPSON, YEOMAN LESLIE

Enterprise junior officer who is killed by the Kelvans in Classic episode "By Any Other Name." She is played by Julie Cobb.

THORLEY, KEN

played Mot in TNG episode "Ensign Ro" and Seaman in TNG episode "Time's Arrow Part I."

THORNE, DYANNE

played Girl #1 in Classic Trek episode "A Piece Of The Action."

THORNE, WORLEY

scriptwriter of TNG episode "Justice." He has written scripts for "Paper Chase," "Sesame Street," "Barnaby Jones," "Cannon," "Apple's Way," "Dallas," "Fantasy Island" and "The Adventures of Grizzly Adams." He currently writes film scripts.

THORNE, ENSIGN

an *Enterprise* junior officer in TNG episode "In Theory." She was played by Pamela Winslow.

THORNTON, COLLEEN
THORNTON, MAUREEN

twin actresses who played the "Barbara" series in

Classic Trek episode "I, Mudd."

THORNTON, NOLEY
played Clara in TNG episode "Imaginary Friend."

THORSON, LYNDA
appeared in TNG episode "The Chase."

THRETT, MAGGIE
played Ruth Bonaventure in Classic Trek episode "Mudd's Women."

THRONE, MALACHI
played Commodore Mendez in Classic Trek episode "The Menagerie." He also played Pardek in TNG episode "Unification Part I and II." TV credits include "Iron Horse," "Lost In Space" and "Voyage To The Bottom Of The Sea," as well as a regular role in "It Takes A Thief." Film credits include "The Doomsday Flight," "Assault On The Wayne" (with Leonard Nimoy) and "The Sex Symbol."

Tian An Men, U.S.S.
ship which took part in the blockade between the Klingons and Romulans in TNG episode "Redemption."

Tibella Minor
Dr. Crusher recommends this world to Nurse Ogawa as a nice place to vacation in TNG episode "The Icarus Factor."

Tiburon
mentioned as Dr. Sevrin's home world in Classic episode "The Way To Eden." This world is also mentioned as the site of

Zora's horrible experiments on native tribes in "The Savage Curtain."

TIERNEY, LAWRENCE
played Cyrus Redblock in TNG episode "The Big Goodbye."

TIFFE, ANGELO
played the electronic technician in "The Voyage Home." He also appeared in the 1984 film "The Dollmaker."

TIGAR, KENNETH
played Ornaran Leader in TNG episode "Symbiosis."

Tilonus Institute for Mental Disorders, Ward 47
where Riker finds himself confined in TNG episode "Frame of Mind."

Tilonus IV
the government of this world collapses into anarchy while a Starfleet team is on the planet. The team hides and Riker poses as a merchant to find them but is abducted and hallucinates that he is confined in the asylum located on this planet.

TIME SQUARED
second season TNG episode written by Kurt Michael Bensmiller and Maurice Hurley and directed by Joseph L. Scanlan. One of the *Enterprise*'s own shuttlepods with a twin Captain Picard on board is encountered. It comes from six hours in the future, a future in which the *Enterprise* is destroyed. Guest star: Colm Meaney.

TIME TRAP
written by Joyce Perry, this animated Classic Trek episode aired 11/24/73. In a triangle of space where ships have disappeared, the *Enterprise* meets up with the Klingon ship *Klothos*. They enter an alternate universe where all the other ships that vanished previously now drift. The place is called Elysia and is inhabited by the Elysians, the people of all races from the other ships who have made a peaceful society for themselves. They tell Kirk and the Klingon captain that there is no way out. The two ships must work together to escape.

TIME'S ARROW, PART I
fifth season TNG episode written by Joe Menosky and Michael Piller and directed by Les Landau. Data's head is discovered in a cave on Earth, a clue that aliens are going into Earth's past and killing people. Guest stars: Whoopi Goldberg, Jerry Hardin, Michael Aron, Barry Kiven, Ken Thorley, Sheldon Peters Wolfchild, John M. Murdock, Marc Alaimo, Milt Tarver and Michael Hungerford.

TIME'S ARROW, PART II
sixth season TNG episode written by Joe Menosky and Jeri Taylor and directed by Les Landau. Picard and his crew are stranded in Earth's past in San Francisco, where Picard meets a woman who looks exactly like Guinan. Meanwhile, aliens are feeding off human life forces. Guest stars: Whoopi

Goldberg, Jerry Hardin, Alexander Enberg, Van Epperson, Pamela Kosh, Michael Aron, James Gleason, Bill Cho Lee, William Boyett and Mary Stein.

TIMESCAPE
sixth season TNG episode written by Brannon Braga and directed by Adam Nimoy. While Picard, Geordi, Data and Troi are en route to the *Enterprise* via a shuttle, they start experiencing periodic time freezes, and discover the *Enterprise* is frozen in space in the midst of a Romulan attack. Time has stopped, and they must figure out a way to start it again without allowing their ship destroyed by the frozen phaser beams directed at it.

TIMICIN, DR.
a Kaelon astrophysicist specializing in research aimed at re-energizing dying stars. His theory fails on the star Praxillus but he wants to try again. However, his death is scheduled for his 60th birthday, an involuntary ritual he cannot refuse to carry out. Lwaxana Troi becomes briefly involved with him in TNG episode "Half A Life." Dr. Timicin is played by David Ogden Stiers.

TIMOTHY
friend of Kirk's who gives him the cold shoulder on Starbase 11 in Classic episode "Court Martial." He is played by Winston DeLugo.

Tin Man

organic creature born in space, also known as a Gomtuu in TNG episode "The Tin Man." It is actually a live spaceship which can be run telepathically by a crew. It had been alone, without a crew, for thousands of years.

TIN MAN

third season TNG episode written by Dennis Putman and David Bischoff and directed by Robert Scheerer. A Betazoid named Tam Elbrun and a corporeal entity, which is actually also a space vessel, come together in this story of loneliness and telepathy. Guest stars: Harry Groener, Michael Cavanaugh, Peter Vogt and Colm Meaney.

TIPPO, PATTI

played Temple in TNG episode "Transfigurations."

Tirellia

world mentioned in conversation to Data by Commander Hutchinson as being one of three inhabited worlds without a magnetic pole. Data says five Tirellians serve aboard the *Enterprise*. It is also one of seven inhabited worlds with no atmosphere. All this trivia is discussed in TNG episode "Starship Mine."

Titus IV

O'Brien got his pet tarantula Christina from this world as mentioned in TNG episode "Realm of Fear."

TOBIN, MARC

played Joaquin in Classic Trek episode "Space Seed" and a Klingon in "Day of the Dove."

TOCHI, BRIAN

played the child, Ray, in Classic Trek episode "And The Children Shall Lead." He also played the helmsman Kenny Lin in TNG episode "Night Terrors." He had regular roles in the series "Anna And The King," "Renegades" and "Space Academy." He also appeared in the 1981 film "We're Fighting Back."

TODD, HALLIE

played Data's daughter Lal in TNG episode "The Offspring." She is best known for her recurring role on the sitcom "Brothers."

TODD, TONY

played Kurn in TNG episodes "Sins Of The Father" and "Redemption Part I and II."

TOFF, PALOR

alien with three nostrils who is Kivas Fajo's rival. He appears in TNG episode "The Most Toys" and is played by Nehemiah Persoff.

TOG, DaiMON

Ferengi captain of the *Krayton* who falls for Lwaxana and kidnaps her along with Deanna and Riker in TNG episode "Menage A Troi." He is played by Frank Corsentino.

TOKATH, COMMANDER

commands the Romulan prison colony on Carraya IV in TNG episode "Birthright." He married a Klingon, Gi'ral, and fathered a half Romulan, half Klingon daughter, Ba'el.

Tokyo Base

in TNG episode "The Icarus Factor," Kyle Riker worked on Ferengi tactics here.

TOLAKA, CAPTAIN L.

captain of the *Lantree* who rapidly ages in TNG episode "Unnatural Selection."

Tolstoy, U.S.S.

one of the ships destroyed by the Borg at Wolf 359 according to Shelby in TNG episode "Best of Both Worlds."

TOM, SEBASTIAN

played the samurai in Classic Trek episode "Shore Leave."

TOMALAK

commander of the Neutral Zone security force for the Romulans in TNG episodes "The Enemy" and "The Defector." He is played by Andreas Katsulas.

TOMAR

Scotty drinks this Kelvan literally under the table with his "green" drink in Classic episode "By Any Other Name." He is played by Robert Fortier.

Tomid Incident

the last encounter with the Romulans, 53 years, 7 months, 18 days before

TNG episode "The Neutral Zone."

TOMLINSON, SPECIALIST ROBERT

he marries Angela Martine in Classic episode "Balance of Terror." He worked in the phaser room where he was killed by phaser coolant fumes which leaked during a Romulan attack. He was played by Stephen Mines.

TOMORROW IS YESTERDAY

written by D.C. Fontana and directed by Michael O'Herlihy, this first season Classic Trek episode aired 1/26/67. The Enterprise is thrown back in time to the year 1969 where they are mistaken for a UFO. They must erase evidence of their presence before they can leave, but Kirk gets captured by Air Force personnel. Guest stars: Roger Perry, Sherry Townsend, Hal Lynch, Ed Peck, John Winston and Mark Dempsey. Of note: This episode introduces the sling shot time travel effect, and shows food processors in the transporter room.

TOMPKINS, PAUL

played Breville in TNG episode "Identity Crisis."

TONDRO, ANINA

widow of General Tondro, who was killed on Klystron IV before Dax became Jadzia Dax. Curzon Dax was best friends with the man, and in DS9 episode "Dax" Jadzia is accused of killing the general. Dax, however, is in the clear because he was the general's widow's lover and with her at the time of the murder. It is Tondro's son, who did not know of this fact, who pursues Dax to avenge his father's murder.

TOO SHORT A SEASON
first season TNG episode written by Michael Michaelian and Dorothy Fontana and directed by Rob Bowman. The *Enterprise* brings aboard an admiral who is taking a youth serum that is killing him. They are headed to Mordan IV to negotiate a hostage situation. Guest stars: Clayton Rohner, Marsha Hunt and Michael Pataki.

Topaline
mineral used in life support systems on sealed colony worlds as mentioned in Classic episode "Friday's Child."

TOQ
a young Klingon in the prison colony on Carraya in TNG episode "Birthright." He wants Worf to teach him how to become Klingon.

TORAK, GOVERNOR
Klingon official who oversees the region of space near Subspace Relay Station 47 where Aquiel is stationed in TNG episode "Aquiel."

TORAL
Klingon boy and Duras' bastard son whose aunts, Lursa and B'Etor, intend to help him claim the title of the Head of the High Council in TNG episode "Redemption." He was played by J.D. Cullum.

TORETH, COMMANDER
commands the Romulan warbird *Khazara* in TNG episode "Face of the Enemy." She hates the Tal Shiar because she believes they killed her father. Troi relieves her of command once she convinces her Troi is Major Rakal of the Tal Shiar.

TORG
second in command under Kruge, this Klingon is killed when he boards the *Enterprise* in "The Search For Spock." He is played by Stephen Liska.

TORME, TRACY
scriptwriter of TNG episodes "Haven," "The Big Goodbye," "Conspiracy" and "The Schizoid Man." He was also the creative consultant on the show.

TORMOLEN, JOE
this *Enterprise* crewman is the first to catch the Psi 2000 virus when he beams down to the station with Spock in Classic episode "The Naked Time." He stabs himself in the rec room and later dies in Sickbay, though not of the wound itself, but of "despair" according to McCoy. He is played by Stewart Moss.

Torona IV
planet located in the Jarada sector with whom Picard establishes diplomatic relations in TNG episode "The Big Goodbye."

TORRES
an *Enterprise* ensign frozen by Q in TNG episode "Encounter At Farpoint."

He is played by Jimmy Ortega.

TORSEK, DIERK
played Dr. Bernard in TNG episode "When The Bough Breaks."

TOSK
in DS9 episode "Captive Pursuit," Tosk is an alien from the Gamma Quadrant who was raised to be prey in a deadly hunt.

TOUSSAINT, BETH
played Ishara Yar in TNG episode "Legacy."

Tovin III
according to Gul Madred, this is the closest neutral world to Seltris III in TNG episode "Chain of Command."

TOWERS, ROBERT
played Rata in TNG episode "The Battle."

TOWLES
Enterprise security officer stationed at the command post on the world which the now aggressive Borg command in TNG episode "Descent."

TOWNES, HARRY
played Reger in Classic Trek episode "The Return of the Archons." TV credits include "Rawhide," "Voyagers!" and "Planet of the Apes." He also appeared in the 1959 film "Cry Tough" and the 1983 film "Agent of H.E.A.T."

TOWNSEND, BARBARA
played Admiral Rossa in TNG episode "Suddenly Human."

TOWNSEND, SHERRI
played a crewmember in Classic Trek episode "Tomorrow Is Yesterday."

Tox Uthat
device which can halt nuclear reaction in a star. It was invented by Kal Dano in the 27th century and resembles a small crystal cube. It is hidden on Risa in the past, when Picard and Vash, with people from the future, are drawn into the intrigue in relocating it in TNG episode "Captain's Holiday."

TOYA
Alexandra's mother in TNG episode "When The Bough Breaks." She was played by Connie Danese.

TOYOTA, VIC
stunt double for Sulu in Classic Trek episode "Catspaw."

Tra'nusah
Klingon world mentioned in TNG episode "A Matter of Honor."

TRACEY, CAPTAIN RONALD
captain of the *Exeter* in Classic episode "The Omega Glory." His crew dies of a terrible disease they caught on Omega but Tracey survives when he stays on Omega, because the planet's atmosphere provides a natural immunity to the plague. He ends up breaking the Prime Directive and interfering with the planet's natural progression because he thinks he has found the answer to immortality

since the Omegans live for centuries. He tries to kill Spock and Kirk when he discovers they won't help him discover the planet's properties or keep his secret about breaking the Prime Directive. He is played by Morgan Woodward.

TRACY, LIEUTENANT KAREN
an *Enterprise* officer who beams down to Argelius to give Scotty tests in Classic episode "Wolf In The Fold." She is killed by the Jack the Ripper entity. She was played by Virginia Aldridge.

Trager
name of Gul Macet's Cardassian Galor class warship in TNG episode "The Wounded."

TRAINOR, SAXON
played Larson in TNG episode "The Nth Degree."

Tralesta Clan
clan massacred by their enemy, the Lornacks of Acamar III, in TNG episode "The Vengeance Factor." Five of the Tralestas survive. In the episode, Yuta, the last survivor, tries to kill Chorgon, the last of the Lornacks.

Transceiver
long range communication device found on Thelev, the Orion spy, in Classic episode "Journey To Babel."

TRANSFIGURATIONS
third season TNG episode written by Rene Echevarria and directed by Tom Benko. The only survivor of a wrecked ship is aided

by the *Enterprise*. His amnesia hinders him from relating his experience but some very strange qualities, such as an ability to heal very rapidly, make him appear not quite human. He is really a Zalkonian evolving into a higher being who is being pursued by his own people who fear this transfiguration of their species. Guest stars: Mark La Mura, Charles Dennis, Julie Warner, Patti Tippo and Colm Meaney.

Transmuter
device which amplifies Sylvia and Korob's power in Classic episode "Catspaw."

Transparent Aluminium
Scotty gives the matrix for this unique man-made substance to the head of a polymer factory in "The Voyage Home." It is apparently a very strong, clear substance that can be used in space, underwater, etc.

Transporter
a matter/enery conversion device on the *Enterprise* that can move people and objects by scrambling matter and then rematerializing it at its destination. In TNG, intership beaming is common, whereas during Classic Trek time, it was considered very dangerous. A transporter cannot be used when the shields of the ship are up. Biofilters in transporters automatically screen out harmful bacteria from alien worlds. Scotty survives into the 24th century because his pattern is

held in statis in a transporter beam.

Transporter Code 14
in TNG episode "Captain's Holiday," Picard gives Riker this code with which Riker then transports the Tox Uthat into space where it is disintegrated.

Transtater
device on which much of Federation technology is based including the transporters, phasers, and communicators as mentioned in Classic episode "A Piece of the Action."

Tranya
drink offered to Kirk, Spock, McCoy and Bailey by Balok in Classic episode "The Corbomite Maneuver."

TRAVELER, The
appears in TNG episode "Time Squared." In "Where No One Has Gone Before," he was played by Eric Menyuk. He travels through time using his mind power.

TRAVERS, COMMODORE
mentioned as the leader of the Earth colony on Cestus III that is attacked by the Gorns in Classic episode "Arena."

Treaty of Algeron
treaty which ended the Romulan war 200 years before. It forbids any ships from either side to enter the Neutral Zone as mentioned in TNG episode "The Defector."

Treaty of Armens
treaty which established peace between the Federation and the Sheliaks as mentioned in TNG episode "The Ensigns of Command." The treaty took 372 experts to negotiate and is more than 500,000 words long. The humans on Tau Cygna V are in violation of the treaty and the Sheliak want them off the world.

Treaty of Sirius
treaty which forbids the Kzin to possess any weapons beyond police vessels in animated episode "The Slaver Weapon."

TREFAYNE
clairvoyant member of the Organian Council in Classic episode "Errand of Mercy." He is played by David Hillary Hughes.

TRELANE
an omnipotent energy being who acts like a spoiled brat and plays deadly games with the *Enterprise* in Classic episode "The Squire of Gothos." He appears in human form to toy with them (much like Q in TNG) until his parents show up, also energy beings, and make him stop. He is played by William Campbell.

TRENT
Beate's servant on Angel One in TNG episode "Angel One." He is played by Leonard John Crofoot.

Triox compound
McCoy says he's giving this to Kirk during his fight with Spock in Classic

episode "Amok Time" so Kirk can breathe easier in the thin atmosphere. He actually slips him a neural paralyzer to simulate death and save his life.

Triacus

located in Epsilon Indi, the Starnes expedition runs into the Gorgon on this planet in Classic episode "And The Children Shall Lead." Spock says that according to legend Triacus was the site of a band of marauders who made war throughout Epsilon Indi and were themselves destroyed in the war. However the evil power that caused these marauders to war still waits on Triacus for a catalyst which will set the evil in motion throughout the galaxy again. The Gorgon of Triacus is possibly the last of these marauders who survived.

Triangulum System

mentioned in TNG episode "The Survivors." Renegade Andorians hid a ship here by dismantling it.

Tribble

a ball of fur that purrs. Thousands are seen in Classic episode "The Trouble With Tribbles" and the animated "More Tribbles, More Troubles." If they eat too much, they get pregnant and have more tribbles. Their breeding gets out of control on the *Enterprise*. In the animated episode, it is learned the Glommer is the tribble's natural predator.

Tricobalt Satellite Explosion

in Classic episode "A Taste of Armageddon," Anan 7 tells Kirk the Enterprise has been destroyed by a tricobalt satellite explosion.

Tricorder

device that is both a computer, sensor unit and recorder which is taken on landing parties. It is a small box on a strap. In TNG, tricorders are smaller and fit in the palm of the hand featuring a little screen.

Tricordrazine

Pulaski uses this on Riker to slow the absorption of the microbes in his system in TNG episode "Shades of Gray." Probably related to cordrazine (see entry.) It is also mentioned in "Yesterday's Enterprise" and "Who Watches The Watchers."

Tricyanate

element which has contaminated the water on Beta Agni II in TNG episode "The Most Toys." Fajo used this on the water deliberately to lure the *Enterprise*. Hytritium is the only known substance that can negate tricyanate poisoning.

Trieste, U.S.S.

ship closest to Starbase 74 when the Bynars steal the *Enterprise* in TNG episode "11001001."

Trilaser Connector

medical device McCoy uses during surgery to restore Spock's brain to his body in Classic episode "Spock's Brain."

Trilithium

substance a team of thieves is trying to steal from the *Enterprise* in TNG episode "Starship Mine."

Trill

symbiot race first encountered in TNG episode "The Host." Not all Trills receive symbiots. Jadzia of DS9 trained all her life for the opportunity to be chosen to host a symbiot. Jadzia's symbiot is Dax whose previous host was Curzon. Trills who are symbiots can remember their previous body's memories because, though the humaniod bodies wear out from old age, the symbiot's life span lasts hundreds of years. Therefore, a symbiot Trill can draw on the experiences of several lifetimes, as does Jadzia Dax. Trills in "The Host" have a kind of ridge structure on their foreheads and the bridge of their noses. This look was changed for Jadzia in DS9 who has very human features. Her only physical differences include small horseshoe-shaped markings like light freckles that cover the sides of her forehead, her temple curve against her ears to her neck and disappear under her uniform down her back. They are barely noticeable except when Jadzia is filmed in a close up shot. If she wore her hair down, they would not be seen at all.

Trillium 323

in TNG episode "The Price," a Caldonian mineral for which Riker tries to make trade agreements in

order to offer it to the Barzans during the wormhole negotiations. In Classic episode "Errand of Mercy," Spock pretends to be a Vulcan merchant selling Kivas and Trillium. Trillium is never defined.

Trimagnesite

fuel used in the satellites that create the light flares which destroy the parasites in Classic episode "Operation Annihilate!" It was also called trivium.

Triolic Waves

form of radiation harmful to humans that Geordi can see with his visor. These waves are produced by the power source used by the aliens who historically preyed upon humans in TNG episode "Time's Arrow."

Trioma System

in this system, Keith Rocha was absorbed by a coalescent organisim according to Dr. Crusher in TNG episode "Aquiel."

TRION, GOVERNOR LEKA

she is the one who asked Ambassador Odan to mediate a dispute between her world's two moons, Alpha and Beta in TNG episode "The Host." She is the leader of the world Peliar Zel.

Tripoli, U.S.S.

ship that found Data on Omicron Theta IV in TNG episode "Datalore."

Tripolymer Composites

Data is composed mostly of this as mentioned in

TNG episode "The Most Toys."

Trisec

time unit used on Triskelion in Classic episode "The Gamesters of Triskelion."

Triskelion

planet with a trinary sun called M24 Alpha to which Kirk, Chekov and Uhura are taken when they are kidnapped by a powerful transport beam in Classic episode "The Gamesters of Triskelion." The Providers live here, enslaving the people they have kidnapped and forcing them to participate in deadly games for the Providers' entertainment. The Providers gamble on the outcome of the games.

Tritanium

alloy which the weapons of Minos can melt because they are so powerful as mentioned in TNG episode "The Arsenal of Freedom." It can be found on Argus X as mentioned in Classic episode "Obsession."

Trititanium

element used on the hulls of starships as mentioned in Classic episode "Journey To Babel."

TRIVERS, BARRY

scriptwriter of Classic Trek episode "The Conscience of the King."

Trivium

see entry for Trimagnesite.

Troglytes

the blue collar workers and miners on Ardana who are basically slaves to the upper class citizens of Stratos in Classic episode "The Cloud Minders."

TROI, IAN ANDREW

Deanna's human father whom Deanna named her son Ian Andrew after in TNG episode "The Child."

TROI, LT. COMMANDER DEANNA

regular in "The Next Generation," played by Marina Sirtis. She is the ship's counsellor, a half-human, half-Betazoid with empathic powers that allow her to read the emotions of others (except for Ferengi.) She has full telepathy with her Betazoid mother, Lwaxana Troi, who is an eccentric aristocrat of Betazed's fifth house, one of the oldest and richest families on the planet, and holder of the sacred chalice of Riix. Lwaxana is a woman steeped in tradition, outspoken and somewhat of an embarrassment to her daughter, but who loves Deanna very much. Deanna's father was a Starfleet officer named Ian Andrew who died when she was a baby. In the seventh season of TNG it is discovered that Deanna had an older sister who drowned on a picnic at about the age of seven. Deanna was too young to remember her. Deanna and Will Riker knew each other before either one was posted to the *Enterprise*. They had a love affair and almost married, but Riker was called away by his career. She still refers to him as her "imzadi" (see entry.) She once gave birth to an alien child, whose conception was mysterious and whose life was very brief. She named him Ian Andrew after her father. She now helps Worf care for his son, Alexander, and as a result she and Worf have become very close friends. In alternature universes, (seen in the TNG seventh season episode "Parallels,") Deanna and Worf are married and have children. Deanna loves chocolate more than any other food.

TROI, LWAXANA

Deanna Troi's mother who has made several appearances on TNG and one on DS9. She is played by Majel Barrett. She is a Betazed aristocrat of the fifth house, the holder of the sacred chalice of Riix, heir to the holy rings of Betazed. She was married to Ian Andrew, Deanna's father, and they had another daughter who drowned at age seven when Deanna was a baby.

TROSE, KALIN

a representative from the moon Alpha, orbiting Peliar Zel, in TNG episode "The Host." He stopped Ambassador Odan from being killed in an assassination plot 30 years before. Trose is played by Franc Luz.

TROST, SCOTT

played a Bajoran officer in DS9 episode "A Man Alone," and an ensign in TNG episode "Unnatural Selection."

TROUBLE WITH TRIBBLES, The

written by now noted science fiction author David Gerrold and directed by Joseph Pevney, this second season Classic Trek episode aired 12/29/67. Tribbles, little purring balls of fur that multiply if you feed them too much, become a pest problem for the Enterprise and the Space Station K 7. Klingons are another problem, especially for Scotty when they insult his ship. Guest stars: William Schallert, William Campbell, Stanley Adams, Whit Bissel, Michael Pataki, Charlie Brill, Ed Reimers and Guy Raymond. Of note: David Gerrold penned an entire book called *The Trouble With Tribbles* which narrates the autobiographical story of the creation of this episode. Also, a sequel to this was made into an animated episode, "More Tribbles, More Troubles." It is said David Gerrold patterned his tribbles after Robert Heinlein's Martian flat cats. This episode was nominated for the Hugo Award for Best Dramatic Presentation of 1967 but placed second.

TROUPE, TOM

played Lt. Harold in Classic Trek episode "Arena." TV credits include "Griff" and "The Young Rebels." He also appeared in the 1959 film "The Big Fisherman" and the 1973 film "The Alpha Caper."

Trova

drink offered to Kirk by Anan 7 on Eminiar in

Classic episode "A Taste of Armageddon."

TROY, DAVID
played Lt. Matson in Classic Trek episode "The Conscience of the King."

Troyius
located in the Tellun star system (see entry) on the border of Klingon space. The monarch of this world is to be married to Elaan of Elas in Classic episode "Elaan of Troyius." Troyius has been at war with Elas for centuries. The marriage is supposed to bring peace.

TRUE Q
sixth season TNG episode written by Rene Echevarria and directed by Robert Scherrer. An eighteen year old girl joins the *Enterprise* crew as an intern as the result of a student competition she won. It is soon discovered she has incredible mental powers that she has been hiding from everyone because she doesn't want to be seen as different. Then Q arrives, dropping the bombshell that she is not really human, but a Q herself, born of a Q couple who left the Continuum to be human. The couple was killed for their "treason" and Amanda was adopted by human parents. Q gives her the opportunity to be a part of her true race but Amanda has other aspirations for her life. Guest stars: Olivia D'Abo and John deLancie.

TRUMBLE, DOUG
special photographic effects supervisor on "Star Trek: The Motion Picture."

He has also worked on the films "Close Encounters of the Third Kind" and "2001: A Space Odyssey." He also directed the movies "Silent Running" and "Brainstorm."

Tsingtao, Ray
one of the children of the Starnes party rescued from Triacus in Classic episode "And The Children Shall Lead." He is played by Brian Tochi (who also had a small role in a TNG episode. See entry for Tochi.)

Tsiolkovsky, U.S.S.
a freighter, Grissom class, infected by the Psi 2000 virus from TNG episode "The Naked Now." Its crew committed suicide.

TSU, TAN
a survivor of the *Arcos* in TNG episode "Legacy." He is played by Vladimir Velasco.

TUBERT, MARCELO
played Jared Acost in TNG episode "Devil's Due."

TULA
Reger's daughter in Classic episode "The Return of the Archons." She was attacked by Bilar during the Festival. She is played by Brioni Farrell.

TUMEN, MARION
script supervisor on "The Final Frontier."

Turbolift
elevator on the ship that transports people to the various levels and moves sideways as well as up and down. They are verbally

commanded to their destinations.

Turing Test of Sentient Ability
test given to Data by Starfleet which he passed.

Turkana IV
Tasha Yar's world where the society is split into two factions, the Alliance and the Coalition. They fight constantly as seen in TNG episode "Legacy." The planet no longer belongs to the Federation (as of 15 years ago.)

TURNABOUT INTRUDER
written by Arthur H. Singer and Gene Roddenberry and directed by Herb Wallerstein, this last third season Classic Trek episode aired 6/3/69. Kirk's old friend Janice Lester discovers a device that allows her to switch bodies with him. Now she is Captain Kirk, and he is Janice, and no one will believe him except Spock (who can tell with a mind meld who is who.) Guest stars: Sandra Smith, Harry Landers, Barbara Baldavin and Roger Halloway. Of note: While filming this episode, William Shatner had the flu which weakened him, and when he was required to pick up Janice Lester (Sandra Smith) and place her on the bed, he dropped her several times before he got the shot right. This episode has some of the best acting ever seen in the series.

Twenty first Street Mission
where Edith Keeler works to feed the homeless in Classic episode "The City On The Edge Of Forever." It is located in New York City in 1930.

Tycho IV
where the vampire cloud attacked the *Farragut* eleven years before the *Enterprise* encounters it. It has returned there to breed when the *Enterprise* destroys it.

Tyken's Rift
a rift or rupture in space that traps the *Enterprise* and another ship in TNG episode "Night Terrors."

TYLER, JOSE
also called Joe, he is Pike's navigator in Classic episode "The Menagerie" and"The Cage" and is played by Peter Duryea.

Typerias
mentioned in Classic episode "A Private Little War" as a world where coagulating sand can be found which can be used ot stop the flow of blood.

Typhon Expanse
in TNG episode "Cause and Effect," the *Enterprise* is the first to explore this region of space.

TYREE
Kirk's friend on Neural whose wife, Nona, is a Kanutu woman. He is the head of the hill people and met Kirk 13 years before when Kirk was a lieutenant on a landing party studying Neural. He does not

know Kirk is an alien until, on their second meeting when Kirk is in command of the *Enterprise* it is discovered the Klingons are interfering with the world's natural progression.

Tyrus VIIA

a mining station orbits this world, directed by Dr. Farralon, who is experimenting with a particle fountain for excavationing in TNG episode "The Quality of Life."

Ugly Bags of Mostly Water

phrase the microbrains of Velara III use to refer to humans in TNG episode "Home Soil."

UHNARI, LIEUTENANT AQUIEL

a young lieutenant assigned with Lt. Keith Rocha to Subspace Relay Station 47 in TNG episode "Aquiel." She is a Hahliian, and has a sister, Sheana, to whom she often sends messages. Rocha went crazy and attacked her, then killed himself but Aquiel is suspected of murdering him. She also falls for Geordi, who is one of the only people who believes she's innocent. She has a dog, Maura. Aquiel is played by Renee Jones.

UHURA, LIEUTENANT

a regular on "Star Trek," the animated series and the films, she is played by Nichelle Nichols. Uhura, the communications officer on the *Enterprise*, eventually rises in rank to "commander" in the movies. Uhura has been a role

model for women everywhere, proving to the 1960's audience (and on into the 90's) that women can be as effective as men in their careers. She was born in the United States of Africa as mentioned in the animated "Counter Clock Incident." She is Bantu and speaks Swahili fluently (which has become the main language in the United States of Africa.) Uhura means "freedom" in Swahili. She is a talented singer, musician and dancer, performs often in the rec room to entertain others and has played duets with Spock. She also knows how to play the Vulcan lyre. Uhura loves animals, as seen in "The Trouble With Tribbles." She buys a tribble to take back to the ship, not knowing it is already pregnant (from eating too much.) In "The Final Frontier," it appears that Uhura and Scotty have, after many years, discovered a mutual affection for each other that could lead to more. Uhura and Sulu also appear to be very good friends. Uhura has one of the best scenes in "The Search For Spock" when she locks "Mr. Adventure" in the closet. Another priceless moment in Trek is when she and Chekov are looking for nuclear "wessels" in San Francisco in "The Voyage Home." She also performs an erotic dance in "The Final Frontier" to distract some men away from their camp and horses. Uhura has no trouble melding both her feminine, softer side with the strict regimen

of a Starfleet career. She can be tough while retaining her grace, beauty and charm.

ULETTA

name of Isak's fiancee, who was shot down in the streets where she lay for five hours before dying in Classic episode "Patterns of Force."

Ullians

telepathic race of people, three of whom board the *Enterprise* to go to Kaldra IV in TNG episode "Violations." They all have white hair and indentions at their temples.

ULTIMATE COMPUTER, The

written by D.C. Fontana and Lawrence N. Wolfe and directed by John Meredyth Lucas, this second season Classic Trek episode aired 3/8/68. The Enterprise is equipped with a new computer that can not only run the ship on a skeleton crew, but can replace the captain by making all necessary decisions. Guest stars: William Marshall, Barry Russo and Sean Morgan. Of note: The M 5 computer voice is performed by James Doohan.

Ultrasonics

sound weapon used by Dr. Sevrin to try to kill the *Enterprise* crew in Classic episode "The Way To Eden."

Ultretie Pae

an explosive which lines the Antedians robes in TNG episode "Manhunt."

Ultritium

an explosive substance. Traces of it are found in the wreck of a Romulan vessel in TNG episode "The Enemy."

Undari

means "coward" in the Narsicaan language from TNG episode "Tapestry."

UNIFICATION, PART I AND II

fifth season TNG episode written by Rick Berman, Michael Piller and Jeri Taylor and directed by Les Landau (part I) and Cliff Bole (part II.) The Federation suspects that Ambassador Spock, who has been working closely with the Romulans, has defected. Picard is sent to find out what is going on, meets with a dying Sarek in the process, then heads into Romulan space with Data. In part II, we learn Sarek has died from Bendii Syndrome while Picard and Data meet with Spock, who is a member of the Romulan underground on Romulus. Sela gets involved to undermine it all. Guest stars: Leonard Nimoy, Denise Crosby, Malachi Throne, Norman Large, Stephen Root, William Batiani, Susan Fallender, Vidal Peterson, Daniel Roebuck and Harriet Leider. Of note: After Data neck pinches Sela, you can see a camera man chewing gum in the glass pyramid on the table.

Uniform Code of Justice

Picard cites this in TNG episode "The Drumhead."

Chapter Four, Article 12 gives him the right to make a statement before being questioned by Admiral Satie.

Uniforms

in Classic Trek, the uniforms consist of black pants, boots, and tunics in gold, red and blue. Gold is for command personnel, blue for science, red for security and engineering. (At times Kirk has been known to wear a variation of the gold shirt which is green. He has two styles of green command shirts.) The women have an option of wearing pants or dresses in "Where No Man Has Gone Before," however, they wear short mini dresses throughout the rest of the series. Dress uniforms involve simply a change of tunic which are made of a shiny, satin material. All uniforms have the ship's insignia sewn above the left breast. Gold braid on the sleeve denotes rank, depending on how many rows or broken rows there are. One row is Lt. One and half rows equal Lt. Commander. Two rows denote the rank of commander. Two and a half rows rank Captain. Three rows equal Commodore. Four rows stand for Admiral.

Unit XY 75847

a unit of ships exploring the Organian system for Klingon ships mentioned in Classic episode "Errand of Mercy."

United Earth Space Probe Agency

term used in Classic episode "Tomorrow Is Yesterday." Kirk tells Christopher the *Enterprise* is part of this organization in the future.

United Federation of Planets

also known as UFP, it is a large organization to which many alien worlds in the galaxy belong. Starfleet is under the jurisdiction of the Federation. The UFP symbol is a circle with star systems within it, and on the outside of the circle are the silhouetted partial profiles of a human male and a female. There is a constitution called "The Articles of the Federation." Their ultimate goal is peace in the galaxy. (The entire "Articles" is published in *The Starfleet Technical Manual* by Franz Joseph.) The main currency in the Federation is the credit. The Federation came into being in 2161. The capital of the Federation is San Francisco on Earth, which is also the home of Starfleet Command and Starfleet Academy.

United Nations

mentioned has having been dissolved in 2079 in TNG episode "Encounter At Farpoint."

United States of Africa

Uhura's birthplace as mentioned in animated episode "The Counter Clock Incident." Swahili is the main language.

Universal Gravitational Constant

Q refers to altering this as a way of solving the problem of Bre'el's moon in TNG episode "Deja Q" but Geordi and Data don't understand him.

Universal Translator

this device is seen in Classic episode "Metamorphosis." Spock uses a hand held version to talk to the "Companion," the cloud entity who has befriended Cochrane. It can translate unknown alien language into Federation Standard. This device is equipped in all ships' computers. By the time of TNG and DS9 it appears to be a device that works in conjunction with each person's brain or thought waves.

UNNATURAL SELECTION

second season TNG episode written by John Mason and Mike Gray and directed by Paul Lynch. A genetic experiment goes awry and the entire crew of the *Lantree* dies from accelerated aging. Pulaski is affected when she tries to help the children on a station who are afflicted. Guest stars: Patricia Smith, J. Patrick McNamara, Scott Trost, George Baxter and Colm Meaney.

UP THE LONG LADDER

second season TNG episode written by Melinda M. Snodgrass and directed by Winrich Kolbe. The *Enterprise* encounters a dying race of clones when they rescue a colony in the Ficus Sector from solar flares. Guest stars: Rosalyn

Landor, Barrie Ingham, Jon de Vries and Colm Meaney. Of note: While Picard is looking at a list of ships, one appears on the list by the name of *Buckaroo Banzai* captained by John Whorfin and built by Yoyodyne Propulsions.

Ursulian Neopoppy

mentioned in Classic episode "A Private Little War" as a plant with anti-hallucination pollen.

Utopia Planitia

shipyards on Mars where the *Enterprise* was built in orbit about Mars. This is mentioned in TNG episode "Booby Trap."

Uttaberries

Deanna, Lwaxana and Riker are kidnapped when Homn leaves them while he picks these berries in TNG episode "Menage A Troi."

Ux Mal Ux

Mal prisoners on the moon of Mab Bu IV take over Troi, Data and O'Brien in TNG episode "Power Play." They are noncorporeal beings.

UXBRIDGE, KEVIN

a Douwd, an immortal being, who disguises himself as the human Kevin Uxbridge. His wife is Rishon, a human woman to whom he has been married for 53 years. Kevin uses his mental powers to destroy all Husnocks everywhere because some of them invaded and killed all the people in the colony in which he lived in TNG episode "The Survivor." An

action which killed billions of people. He is played by John Anderson.

UXBRIDGE, RISHON
Kevin's human wife of 53 years. She is 82, a botanist, a composer and she has lived with Kevin on Rana IV in the colony for the past five years. She was killed when the Husnocks attacked the colony. She is played by Anne Haney.

V'SAL
played Shelly Desai in TNG episode "Data's Day."

VAAL
a computer-like "god" that rules the people of Gamma Trianguli VI in Classic episode "The Apple." The Vaal temple looks like a giant cave formed like the mouth of an animal with red eyes on the side of the cave. The mouth has fangs.

VAGH, GOVERNOR
leader of the Klingon colony Kreos in TNG episode "The Mind's Eye." LaForge, who is brainwashed, almost kills him. He is played by Edward Wiley.

Vagra II
located in the Zed Lapis sector, this is the world on which Armus lived. He killed Tasha Yar in TNG episode "Skin of Evil."

VALENZA, TASIA
played T'Shanik in TNG episode "Coming Of Age."

VALERIS, LT.
Vulcan protege of Spock's seen in "The Undiscovered Country." She is a traitor who is in league with Chang to keep the Klingons from making peace with the Federation. She is mind raped by Spock because she will not give much needed information to save the Federation president's life. She is played by Kim Cattrall.

Valiant, U.S.S.
this ship's recorder was retrieved by the *Enterprise* in Classic episode "Where No Man Has Gone Before." It had encountered the galactic energy barrier 200 years before and one of the crew became so dangerous with his accelerated psi powers that the captain destroyed the ship to keep the galaxy safe. Another ship named the *Valiant* was the first to contact the planet Eminiar in "A Taste Of Armageddon" fifty years before the *Enterprise* came along. That *Valiant* was never heard from again.

VALKRIS
Klingon agent used by Kruge in "The Search For Spock" to get information on the Genesis device. Kruge kills her when he gets the information from her. She is played by Cathie Sherriff.

VALLIS, ELIZABETH
Wilson Granger's chief aide and chief of starr on Mariposa in TNG episode "Up The Long Ladder."

VALLONE, JOHN
art director on "Star Trek: The Motion Picture." He also worked on the movies "Southern Comfort," "48 Hours" and "Brainstorm."

Valo System
Ensign Ro introduces Picard to the rebel leader Orta on the third moon of this system in TNG episode "Ensign Ro."

Valt Minor
in TNG episode "The Perfect Mate," this planet has long been in a long conflict with Krios.

Vampire Cloud
in Classic episode "Obsession," this is what the cloud entity that feeds off red blood cells is called. Its home is the planet Tycho IV. It can travel through space using gravitational fields to move. Kirk met up with this creature once when he was a Lt. on the *Farragut*, and it killed his captain, Garrovick. He meets it again on Argus X.

VAN DER VEER, FRANK
creator of the special optical effect in the Classic Trek episode "The Immunity Syndrome."

VAN GELDER, DR. SIMON
assistant director to Dr. Tristan Adams of the Tantalus Penal Colony in Classic episode "Dagger of the Mind." He has been subjected to a device called the neural neutralizer which has drained his will and his brain of knowledge because Dr. Adams doesn't want him telling people he is using this device at the colony. Spock uses the Vulcan mind meld on him to get information the man cannot communicate by speech. This is the first time the mind meld is seen in Trek. Van Gelder was played by Morgan Woodward.

VAN HISE, DELLA
author of Classic Trek novel *Killing Time*. This novel was pulled off the shelf in its first edition for reediting, since the unedited manuscript inadvertantly went to the typesetter. The changes in the final edition were minor, but the mistake makes the first edition a collector's item.

VAN HISE, JAMES
author of many non-fiction works about Trek and other areas of popular culture. First publisher and editor of *Enterprise Incidents*, the pioneer Trek fan publication.

VAN MEYTER, LIEUTENANT
in TNG episode "In Theory," she is an *Enterprise* officer who is killed when she falls into a partially dematerialized deck up to her waist.

VAN ZANDT, BILLY
played the alien ensign in "Star Trek: The Motion Picture." He also appeared in the 1981 film "Taps."

VANDENBERG, CHIEF ENGINEER
the administrative head of the mining colony on Janus VI in Classic episode "The Devil In The Dark." He learns to work with the Horta and its babies by the end of the episode. He is played by Ken Lynch.

Vandor IV

one planetoid in a binary star system which has B-class giant star and a pulsar. Dr. Paul Manheim experiments with time here in TNG episode "We'll Always Have Paris."

VANESSA

young woman helped out by Texas and Data in TNG episode "The Royale." She is played by Jill Jacobsen.

VANNA

Troglyte woman who has been educated to serve Plasus in Stratos, though she is still considered to belong to a lesser class in Classic episode "The Cloud Minders." Vanna heads an underground movement called the Disruptors (like terrorists.) It is actually the zienite gas that makes her fellow Troglytes less intelligent, as Vanna realizes when she is removed from the influences of the gas to live on Stratos. Exposure to the gas makes a person sluggish and slow, but it is not a permanent condition if they are removed from exposure. Vanna is played by Charlene Polite.

VANTAKAR

prisoner who comes to DS9 with a guard in DS9 episode "The Passenger." He is a scientist who kills to prolong his own life and is very dangerous but Bashir enters his cell anyway. Vantakar appears to be dead, but he has really transferred his consciousness into Bashir.

VARDEMAN, ROBERT E.

author of Classic Trek novels *The Klingon Gambit* and *Mutiny On The Enterprise.*

VARGAS, JOHN

played Jedda in "The Wrath of Khan." His TV credits include a regular role on "At Ease," and he has appeared in the films "Only When I Laugh," "Emergency Room" and "My Tutor."

VARLEY, CAPTAIN DONALD

commander of the *U.S.S. Yamato* in TNG episode "Contagion." He is killed when the *Yamato* self-destructs. He is played by Thalmus Rasulala.

Varon T Disruptor

Kivas Fajo owns four of these banned weapons in TNG episode "The Most Toys." He kills his aide, Varria, with one. It disrupts the body from inside out and is an extremely painful way to die.

VARRIA

Zibalian who is Kivas Fajo's aid in TNG episode "The Most Toys." Fajo kills her. She is played by Jane Daly.

VASH

a woman Picard meets in TNG episode "Captain's Holiday." She is passionate about archeology and she and Picard immediately discover a mutual rapport which leads to an affair. She appears in future episodes, and ends up in "Q Pid" traveling into the Gamma Quadrant with Q, who is very fond of her. She shows up in DS9 in "Q Less." Vash

is played by Jennifer Hetrick.

VASSEY, LIZ

played Kristin in TNG episode "Conundrum."

VAUGHN, NED

appeared in TNG episode "Tapestry."

VAUGHN, REESE

played Latimer in Classic Trek episode "The Galileo Seven." TV credits include "Dan August."

Vault of Tomorrow

what the Horta calls her nest of eggs in Classic episode "The Devil In The Dark." She also calls the nest The Chamber of the Ages.

Vaytan

the name of the star where Dr. Reyga's experiment is tested successfully in TNG episode "Suspicions."

Vedala

a cat-like creature and a member of the oldest spacefaring race seen in animated episode "Jihad." They live on an asteriod within a globe or dome.

Vega IX

destination of the *Enteprise* in Classic episode "The Menagerie" before it is called to Talos IV.

Vega IX Probe

probe of this sort is sent to the Beta Stromgren system in TNG episode "Tin Man."

Vega Omicron Sector

the *Ares* is patrolling this sector as stated in TNG episode "The Icarus Factor."

Intelligent life has been reported here.

Vegan Choriomeningitus

an inflammation of the brain tissues that causes fever. Kirk had this a long time ago, and is still a carrier of the microorganisms which are used by the Gideons to infect Odona in Classic episode "Mark of Gideon."

VEJAR, MICHAEL

director of TNG episode "Coming Of Age."

Vejur

what the cloud being in "The Motion Picture" calls itself. It is actually a variation of the word "Voyager." Vejur is actually part of the Voyager VI which was launched by NASA in the 20th century. The machine passed into an alternate machine universe, was changed and then sent back into the galaxy of its origin to seek out all knowledge and its creator. Decker and Ilia merge with Vejur at the end of the film in order to help it rise to a higher level of being where it destroys itself.

VEKMA

Klingon officer who taunts Riker on the *Pagh* in TNG episode "A Matter of Honor." She is played by Laura Drake.

Velara III

planet being terraformed in TNG episode "Home Soil." It is home to the microbrain, a life form that is intelligent but was undiscovered until it killed a per

son on the terraforming project to make itself known.

VELASCO, VLADIMIR
played Tan Tsu in TNG episode "Legacy."

Veltan Sex Idol
in TNG episode "The Most Toys," Fajo says he has four of these rare items with pearls intact.

VENDER
he gave Picard a free newspaper in TNG episode "The Big Goodbye." He is played by Dick Miller.

Vendikar
the planet that has been at war for 500 years with Eminiar in Classic episode "A Taste of Armageddon." They fight their war by computer since it is a cleaner and cheaper method.

Vendorian
they are a race who can rearrange their molecular structures into anything with the same mass as themselves. Carter Winston's form is actually a Vendorian in animated episode "The Survivor."

Vendurite
Ferengi renegades mine this mineral found on Ligos VII in TNG episode "Rascals."

VENGEANCE FACTOR, The
third season TNG episode written by Sam Rolfe and directed by Timothy Bond. The Acamarians and the Gatherers have had a long standing dispute, and the *Enterprise* steps in to assist

in keeping the cease fire. There are people, however, who don't want to see peace. Guest stars: Lisa Wilcox, Joey Aresco, Nancy Parsons, Stephen Lee, Marc Lawrence and Elkanah J. Burns.

Ventanin
in TNG episode "The Perfect Mate," Kamala recognizes one of Picard's artifacts as being from this world.

Ventax II
in TNG episode "Devil's Due," this world struck a bargain with a being named Ardra, who is equivalent to the devil, in exchange for a thousand years of peace and prosperity. The deadline, however, is up and Ardra returns.

VENTON, HARLEY
played Collins in TNG episode "Ensign Ro."

Venturi Chamber
power is rerouted through this channel to the main engines on the *Mondor* in TNG episode "Samaritan Snare."

Venus Drug
drug Harry Mudd gives to the three women he is travelling with in Classic episode "Mudd's Women." It makes women more curvaceous and gives them more allure, or "more of what they already have." Given to men, it makes them more masculine, stronger and more handsome. It is a highly illegal substance.

Verdanis
the planet to which the *Enterprise* relocates the Terratins in animated episode "The Terratin Incident."

Verul
Romulan word for an uncultured or rude person used by Riker in TNG episode "The Defector."

Verustin Infection
in TNG episode "The Bonding," it is mentioned that Jeremy Aster's father died of this five years before.

VETO, RON
played an Eminiar technician in Classic Trek episode "A Taste Of Armageddon" and a security guard in "The Alternative Factor."

Vians
humanoid race who are from one of the worlds of Minara. They are testing Gem's empathic people to see if they are worth saving. The Minara sun is going nova and the Vians have the power to save only one race from one planet in the fully inhabited system. They tortured the science team which preceded the *Enterprise*, killing them, and then torture Kirk, Spock and McCoy in Classic episode "The Empath."

VICKERY, JOHN
played Hagan in TNG episode "Night Terrors."

Vico, U.S.S.
Grissom class research ship lost while investigating the Black Cluster in TNG episode "Hero Worship."

Timothy is the only survivor.

VICTOR, TERESA E.
played an usher in "The Voyage Home." She is also the bridge voice in "The Wrath of Khan," and the Enterprise computer voice in "The Search For Spock." She was the assistant to Leonard Nimoy for over 20 years, from the early days of Trek in the 1960's through the fourth movie. She currently lives in Los Angeles with her husband.

Victory, U.S.S.
ship of the Constellation class which the *Enterprise* is to meet in TNG episode "Elementary, Dear Data."

VIGNON, JEAN PAUL
played Edouard in TNG episode "We'll Always Have Paris."

VIGO
Stargazer weapons officer in TNG episode "The Battle."

Vilmoran System
a system with seven worlds. It does not belong to the Federation, but it is thought that this world holds the final clue to Professor Galen's micropaleontology mystery in TNG episode "The Chase."

VINA
the only survivor of a crash on Talos IV, she was rescued by the Talosians and put back together wrong so that she looks horribly deformed. She lives in a fantasy world of illusion they have created for her, in which she

remains forever young and beautiful in Classic episode "The Menagerie." Spock ends up bringing the injured Captain Pike back to stay with her. She is played by Susan Oliver.

VINCI, FRANK
played a stunt double in Classic Trek episode "The Galileo Seven," an Eminiar technician in "A Taste of Armageddon" and a Vulcan banner carrier in "Amok Time." He was also the stunt double for Spock in "Catspaw."

VIOLATIONS
fifth season TNG episode written by Shari Goodhartz, T. Michael Gray, Pamela Gray and Jeri Taylor and directed by Robert Wiemer. The *Enterprise* escorts the highly telepathic Ullians to Kaldra IV, but in the process Troi, Riker and Beverly experience a form of mind rape, a crime the Ullians abhor.Picard must discover who the culprit is at the risk of offending these people. Guest stars: Ben Lemon, Eve Brenner, David Sage, Rosalind Chao, Doug Wert, Rick Fitts and Craig Benton.

VIRGO, PETER JR.
played Lumo in Classic Trek episode "The Paradise Syndrome."

VISITOR, NANA
stars as Major Kira Nerys on "Deep Space Nine." Raised in New York, she has studied dance since the age of seven. Her stage career began after high school when she appeared in many Broadway produc-

tions before landing regular roles on the soap operas "One Life To Live" and "Ryan's Hope." She was also in the 1977 movie "The Sentinel" and has guest starred on such TV shows as "Jake and the Fatman," "Baby Talk," "Murder, She Wrote," "L.A. Law," "Empty Nest," "In The Heat Of The Night," "Matlock" and "Thirtysomething." She also had a regular role on the TV series "Working Girl." Nana is a "Star Trek" fan who watched the show regularly in reruns and is thrilled to now have a place in its chronicles.

V.I.S.O.R.
Geordi wears one of these to "see." It looks like a silver headband worn about the eyes and fits into red blinking nodes at Geordi's temples. It allows him to access visual information better than a human, but he still cannot "see" as a human. The word is an acronym for Visual Instrument and Sensory Organ Replacement and it covers the spectrum from 1 hertz to 1 terahertz, which covers radio, microwave and infrared requencies. It is supposedly constantly painful for the wearer.

Visor
used by Spock when he deals with the Medusan, Ambassador Kollos, in Classic episode "Is There In Truth No Beauty?" The visor is silver with a transparent red stripe around it which allows the wearer to see.

Visual Acuity Transmitter
attached to Geordi's Visor in TNG episode "Heart of Glory." It allows the bridge crew to see objects as Geordi sees them. They are able to see the Battress and Data's aura.

Vitalizer Beam
this is a medical "field" of energy used to keep the patient from using more blood in Classic episode "A Private Little War."

VOGT, PETER
actor in DS9 episode "A Man Alone." He also played the Romulan commander in TNG episode "Tin Man."

VOLLAERTS, RIK
scriptwriter of Classic Trek episode "For The World Is Hollow And I Have Touched The Sky." His TV writing credits include "Voyage To The Bottom Of The Sea."

VOLNOTH
a member of the Lornack species who is killed when Yuta transmits a microvirus into him. He is one of the last Lornacks alive in TNG episode "The Vengeance Factor." He is played by Marc Lawrence.

Voltera Nebula
the *Enterprise* is to study this "stellar nursery" in TNG episode "The Chase."

VON PUTTKAMER, JESCO
special NASA advisor on "Star Trek: The Motion Picture." He also wrote an introduction to one of the

stories appearing in the book *The New Voyages*.

Vorgons
a race from the future, the 27th century, who come to Risa to find the Tox Uthat in TNG episode "Captain's Holiday." They are actually criminals whom the inventor of the device feared would get hold of it. He hid it in the past hoping they would never find it.

VORNHOLT, JOHN
author of TNG novels *Masks, Contamination, War Drums*, and Classic Trek novel *Sanctuary*.

Vortex
in DS9 episode "Vortex," this is an area where Crodon tells Odo he found a colony of changelings.

VORTEX
first season DS9 episode written by Sam Rolfe and directed by Winrich Kolbe Miradorns, who are twin beings, are chasing a man visiting DS9 named Crodon. He attacks them and kills one leaving his twin alone, but pleads self defense. Odo arrests him but while en route to Miradorn to deliver the criminal, he learns the truth about the man's life and helps him rescue his daughter and escape. He also comes a step closer to learning about his own heritage as Crodon gives him a device that, though inanimate, has the same metamorph properties as Odo himself. Guest stars: Cliff DeYoung, Randy Oglesby Max Grodenchik, Kathleen

Garrett, Leslie Engelberg and Gordon Clapp.

Vortis
a Klingon ship in TNG episode "The Defector."

Vulcan
class M planet that is a member of the Federation. It has a sister planet, T'Khut, but no moon. It is a desert world with thin air, red skies and a very bright sun. Spock grew up on this world in the city of ShiKahr. Vulcan is seen in Classic episode "Amok Time" and in "The Motion Picture," "The Search For Spock" and "The Voyage Home." Picard visits Vulcan briefly in TNG episode "Unification."

Vulcan
a native of the planet Vulcan. They revere logic and are very unemotional because they believe logic is the answer to the philosophy of life. They have green, copper-based blood, pointed ears and resemble Romulans. They have low blood pressure, a high pulse and respiration and a body temperature higher than humans. Their heart is where the human liver is located. They can heal themselves mentally when they enter a Vulcan healing trance. Vulcans are vegetarians and have an inner eyelid to protect them from the harsh glare of the Vulcan sun. Every seven years, the Vulcan male goes into pon farr during which he must mate or die. There is no indication that that is the only time a Vulcan mates, however. They are

touch telepaths, but can sometimes sense thoughts over a distance if the sender is strong. In Classic episode "Where No Man Has Gone Before," the obsolete term Vulcanian is used for "Vulcan." 5000 years ago, Vulcans were a barbaric race with warrior clans who constantly fought until Surak, the father of logic, came along and introduced order. The Vulcans have a quasi-religious ritual called Kolinahr which is used by Vulcans to purge all emotion from their minds. Very few people who attempt it succeed. Spock tries and fails.

Vulcan Academy of Sciences
Sarek wanted Spock to attend school here and eventually teach, but Spock chose a career in Starfleet, a decision which created a rift between father and son for 17 years as mentioned in Classic episode "Journey To Babel." The director of the Vulcan Science Academy visits the *Enterprise* in TNG episode "Suspicions." Her name is T'Pan and she is married to a human.

Vulcan Death Grip
Spock uses this on Kirk to kill him in Classic episode "The Enterprise Incident." There is really no such thing, Kirk simply fakes unconsciousness, but the Romulans buy it. Vulcans do have a form of a death grip, however, called Tal Shaya. It snaps the neck very quickly. Gav the Tellarite in "Journey To Babel" is killed this way.

Vulcan Kiss
also a Vulcan embrace. Two people extend their first two fingers, and place them against each other. Romulans kiss this way as seen in "The Enterprise Incident," as do Sarek and Amanda in Classic episode "Journey To Babel."

Vulcan Mind Meld
also called the Vulcan mind fusion (ultimate joining) or mind touch (a light joining,) or mind link, it involves joining two minds together mentally with a telepathic touch. Spock proves he can do this over short distances in Classic episode "By Any Other Name" when he influences a Kelvan to believe they have escaped their prison. He uses the meld many times throughout the series. It is first introduced when he uses it on Dr. Van Gelder to open his mind in "Dagger of the Mind." The mind "fusion" is used by Spock on Kirk in "The Paradise Syndrome" to bring Kirk's memories back. He also uses a mind touch on Kirk to help him forget his grief over Reena in "Requiem For Methuselah." He melds several more times with Kirk, once while he is in the body of Janice Lester in "Turnabout Intruder" and once in "Spectre of the Gun." (In that episode he also melds with Scotty and McCoy.) Spock melds with the Horta in "Devil in the Dark" and with Nomad in "The Changeling." His empathic powers also allow him to feel the deaths of 400 Vulcans

when the *Intrepid* is destroyed in "The Immunity Syndrome." Spock also melds with Vejur in "The Motion Picture," which nearly kills him. Spock uses the mind touch on McCoy in "Mirror, Mirror" and "The Wrath of Khan" (to pass his katra on to him.) He also uses the mind touch on the humpback whale Gracie in "The Voyage Home," learning she is pregnant. Saavik uses the mind touch on a teenage Spock in "The Search For Spock" to calm him when he goes into his first pon farr. Sarek uses a mind touch on Kirk in "The Search For Spock" to see if he carries Spock's katra. Sarek also uses it on Picard to help Sarek maintain control of his emotions in TNG episode "Sarek." The mind touch is an ultimately personal thing, and Vulcans rarely use it unless it is an emergency. It can be forced on an individual, as Spock does to Valeris in "The Undiscovered Country," but it is considered akin to rape and hurts the attacker as much as the victim. Sybok uses it to control his subjects by forcing them face their fears and griefs in "The Final Frontier." He also uses the mind touch on Spock to give him his katra toward the end of that movie.

Vulcan Mind Touch and Vulcan Mind Fusion
see entry for Vulcan mind meld.

Vulcan Neck Pinch

invented by William Shatner and Leonard Nimoy in Classic episode "The Enemy Within," it involves placing the fingers on the side of the neck, thumb on one side, fingers on the other, and pressing. It knocks a person out. Spock uses it often and has tried to teach it to Kirk, but Kirk still can't do it. It is also called the Vulcan nerve pinch. Spock teaches Data this technique in TNG episode "Unification," and Data performs it flawlessly.

Vulcan Salute

the right hand is raised with the fingers spread only between ring finger and middle finger. Thumb is extended outward. It is accompanied with the words "Live long and prosper" or "Peace and long life."

Vulcana Regar

Vulcan colony world where T'Shalik is from in TNG episode "Coming of Age."

Waddi

beings who come aboard Deep Space 9 in DS9 episode "Move Along Home." They introduce Quark to a new game, in which the players are actually the crew of DS9. It puts them in seemingly real danger, forcing them to play out extremely dangerous scenarios without realizing it is only a game.

WAGNER, LOU

appeared in DS9 episode "The Nagus."

WAGNER, MICHAEL

scriptwriter of TNG episodes "Evolution," "The Survivors" and "Booby Trap."

WAGNOR

Angosian pilot in TNG episode "The Hunted." He is played by Andrew Bickell.

WALBERG, GARY

played Commander Hansen in Classic Trek episode "Balance of Terror." He had a regular role on "The Odd Couple" and "Quincy." Film credits include "The Challenge," "Man on the Outside" and "Rage."

WALKER, ROBERT JR.

played Charlie Evans in Classic Trek episode "Charlie X." Born April 15, 1940 in New York, his film credits include "Ensign Pulver," "Easy Rider" and "The Passover Plot." His parents are Robert Walker and Jennifer Jones.

WALKING BEAR, ENSIGN DAWSON

an *Enterprise* helmsman in animated episode "How Sharper Than A Serpent's Tooth." He is a Comanche Indian.

WALLACE, ART

scriptwriter of Classic Trek episodes "Obsession" and "Assignment: Earth." His other writing credits include "Dark Shadows," "Planet of the Apes" and the films "Dr. Cook's Garden," "She Waits" and "Charlie and the Great Balloon Race."

WALLACE, BASIL

played a Klingon guard in TNG episode "Reunion."

WALLACE, GEORGE D.

played an admiral in TNG episode "Man Of The People."

WALLACE, WILLIAM A.

played the adult Wesley in TNG episode "Hide and Q."

WALLACE, DR. JANET

an endocrinologist who is aboard the *Enterprise* when the radiation that makes people rapidly age hits Kirk, Spock, McCoy and others of the landing party on Gamma Hydra IV in Classic episode "The Deadly Years." She is an old girlfriend of Kirk's who married Dr. Theodore Wallace who died pror to the episode. She was played by Sarah Marshall.

WALLER, PHILLIP N.

played Harry in TNG episode "When The Bough Breaks."

WALLERSTEIN, HERB

director of Classic Trek episodes "Whom Gods Destroy," "The Tholian Web," "That Which Survives" and "Turnabout Intruder." His other credits include assistant director of "Father Knows Best" and the films "The Tingler" and "Snowbeast," and unit production manager of "Iron Horse." His other directing credits include "Petrocelli."

WALSH, GWYNYTH

actress in DS9 episode "Past Prologue." She also played B'Etor in TNG episode "Redemption Part I and II."

WALSH, LEO FRANCIS

Harry Mudd's alias in Classic episode "Mudd's Women." Walsh was once a spaceship captain, now deceased, and Harry goes about impersonating him. Harry is played by Roger C. Carmel.

WALSTON, RAY

played Boothby in TNG episode "The First Duty." He is best known for his role as Uncle Martin in the series "My Favorite Martian."

WALTER, TRACY

played Kayron in TNG episode "The Last Outpost."

WARBURTON, JOHN

played the centurion in Classic Trek episode "Balance of Terror." Born in Ireland in 1903, he died on October 27, 1981. His credits include the films "A Study In Scarlet," "Tarzan and the Huntress" and "City Beneath The Sea" as well as many TV appearances.

WARE, HERTA

played Picard's mother in TNG episode "Where No One Has Gone Before."

WARHIT, DOUG

played Kazago in TNG episode "The Battle."

WARNER, DAVID

played St. John Talbot in "The Final Frontier" and Chancellor Gorkon in "The Undiscovered Country." He is a British born actor whose many credits include "The French Lieutenant's Woman," "Holocaust," "Time Bandits" and "The Omen."

He also appeared in TNG episode "Chain of Command."

WARNER, JULIE
played Christy Henshaw in TNG episodes "Booby Trap" and "Transfigurations."

Warp Core
vital mechanism of the warp drive in which matter and antimatter are combined. A warp core breach can destroy an entire ship. According to TNG episode "Booby Trap" it is mentioned that the dilithium crystal chamber on the *Enterprise* was designed at Outpost Seran T One.

Warp Drive
drive on a starship that bends space so ships can travel faster than the speed of light. Every starship is equipped with warp drive. The warp engines run on dilithium crystals and the propulsion is a matter/antimatter mix of delicate proportions. The ships theoretically cannot exceed warp ten, but under special circumstances some have. Usually a ship travelling past warp 10 will break up.

WARREN, DR. MARY
scientist injured in the Mintaka station explosion in TNG episode "Who Watches The Watchers." She later dies. She was played by Lois Hall.

Warrior/ADONIS
a member of Riva's chorus who is also the romantic representing passion and lust. He talks alone with Troi. He is killed by a Solari

gunman in TNG episode "Loud As A Whisper." He is played by Leo Damian.

WASHBURN, BEVERLY
played Lt. Arlene Galway in Classic Trek episode "The Deadly Years." TV credits include regular roles in "Professional Father" and "The New Loretta Young Show" as well as a guest star role in "Adventures of Superman."

WASHBURN
an *Enterprise* engineer who beams aboard the *Constellation* with the landing party in Classic episode "The Doomsday Machine." He is played by Richard Compton.

WASHINGTON, KENNETH
played John B. Watkins in Classic Trek episode "That Which Survives." TV credits include a regular role in "Hogan's Heroes." He was also in the TV movies "Climb An Angry Mountain," "Cry Rape!" and "Money On The Side."

WASSON, SUZANNE
played Lethe in Classic Trek episode "Dagger of the Mind."

WATKINS, JAMES LOUIS
played Hagon in TNG episode "Code of Honor."

WATKINS, JOHN B.
Enterprise engineer who is killed on the ship by Losira when she appears out of thin air and starts asking him questions about the ship in Classic episode "That Which Survives." He

was played by Kenneth Washington.

WATSON, BRUCE
played Crewman Green in Classic Trek episode "The Man Trap." His TV movies include "Dragnet," "Judge Horton and the Scottsboro Boys" and "Billy: Portrait of a Street Kid."

WATSON, TECHNICIAN
Enterprise engineer who discovers sabotage and tries to prevent Kryton from transmitting a message to the Klingon ship in Classic episode "Elaan of Troyius." Kryton kills him. He was played by Victor Brandt.

WAY TO EDEN, The
written by Arthur Heinemann and Michael Richards and directed by David Alexander, this third season Classic Trek episode aired 2/21/69. A group of young, rebel adults comes aboard the *Enterprise* when their shuttle, the *Aurora*, explodes. They are led by an insane alien named Dr. Sevrin and are looking for the mythical planet Eden. When Spock finds a planet that might fit the description, they steal a shuttle to go there. As they leave, Sevrin sets up a trap to murder the entire crew of the ship. Guest stars: Skip Homeier, Mary-Linda Rapelye, Victor Brandt, Charles Napler, Deborah Downey, Phyllis Douglas and Elizabeth Rogers. Of note: Spock plays a musical duet with a young woman playing an instrument that looks like a bicycle wheel.

WE'LL ALWAYS HAVE PARIS
first season TNG episode written by Deborah Dean David and Hannah Louise Shearer and directed by Robert Becker. A scientist named Dr. Manheim, who married an old girlfriend of Picard's, set the universe into a time loop with one of his experiments and Picard and Janice Manheim must correct the problem. Guest stars: Michelle Phillips, Rod Loomis, Isabelle Lorca, Dan Kern, Jean Paul Vignon, Kelly Ashmore and Lance Spellerberg.

Weather Modification Net
device which regularizes Earth's weather patterns as mentioned in TNG episode "True Q." Since Amanda's parents were killed in a freak tornado, Picard suspects the Q continuum actually had something to do with their deaths.

WEBB, RICHARD
played Lt. Commander Benjamin Finney in Classic Trek episode "Court Martial." TV credits include "Voyage To The Bottom Of The Sea" and "The Guns of Will Sonnett." He also appeared in the 1959 film "On The Beach." He played Captain Midnight in the series of the same name.

WEBB, TECHNICIAN
one of the Air Force personnel who sights the *Enterprise* over the Omaha Air Base in Classic episode "Tomorrow Is Yesterday." He is played by Richard Merrifield.

WEBBER, BARBARA
played the young woman in Classic Trek episode "The Return of the Archons."

WEBER, PAUL
played one of the Vulcan masters in "Star Trek: The Motion Picture."

WEBSTER, JOAN
played a nurse in Classic Trek episode "Space Seed."

Weeper
plant Sulu keeps in the botany room in Classic episode "The Man Trap." It must be hand fed.

WEINSTEIN, HOWARD
scriptwriter of the animated episode "The Pirates of Orion." Born in 1954, this script was his first professional sale. He is the author of the TNG novels *Power Hungry, Exiles, Perchance To Dream* and Classic Trek novels *The Covenant of the Crown* and *Deep Domain* as well as three novels based on the series "V."

WEISS, ERICK
played a crewman in TNG episode "Conundrum" and Kane in "Relics."

Wellington, U.S.S.
the Bynars worked on this ship before coming to work on the *Enterprise* in TNG episode "11001001."

WELLMAN, JAMES
played Professor Starnes in Classic Trek episode "And The Children Shall Lead."

WERNTZ, GARY
appeared in TNG episode "Frame of Mind."

WERT, DOUG
played Jack Crusher in TNG episodes "Family" and "Violations."

WESLEY, COMMODORE ROBERT
appearing in Classic episode "The Ultimate Computer," Wesley commands the *U.S.S. Lexington*. He leads the war game attack, which becomes a real attack, against the *Enterprise* which has Dr. Daystrom's M 5 computer on board. He mentions he has a daughter named Katie in animated episode "One Of Our Planets Is Missing." He and Kirk are old friends which explains why Wesley senses that Kirk lowers his shields as a message that the computer has been put out of commission and holds his fire, thus saving the *Enterprise* and the skeleton crew aboard her. Wesley is played by Barry Russo.

WESLEY, KATIE
Commodore Robert Wesley's eleven year old daughter mentioned in animated episode "One Of Our Planets Is Missing."

WESTERFIELD, KAREN
make up artist on TNG and DS9. She was part of the team that won an Emmy for make up on TNG. She now does Quark's make up on DS9.

WESTERVLIET, ADMIRAL
Starfleet officer who forbids the *Enterprise* to plot a parallel course with the spaceship world Yonada in Classic episode "For The World Is Hollow And I Have Touched The Sky." He is played by Byron Morrow.

WESTMORE, MICHAEL
make up design supervisor on DS9.

WESTON, BRAD
played Ed Appel in Classic Trek episode "The Devil In The Dark."

WEYLAND, PHIL
stand-in on "The Search For Spock."

WHALEN
the *Enterprise* historian almost killed by Felix Leech in TNG episode "The Big Goodbye." He is played by David Selburg.

WHAT ARE LITTLE GIRLS MADE OF?
written by horror writer Robert Block and directed by James Goldstone, this first season Classic Trek episode aired 10/20/66. The story involves Christine Chapel and her fiancee Dr. Roger Korby, who has been missing for some time. On Exo III, Korby has discovered a way to transplant the human mind into android bodies a discovery which offers virtual immortality. Guest stars: Michael Strong, Sherry Jackson and Ted Cassidy.

WHEATON, WIL
starred as Wesley Crusher in "The Next Generation" on the first 83 episodes, then in recurring episodes thereafter. He is most famous for his theatrical film roles, including the award winning "Stand By Me," and "Toy Soldiers." His first break was a Jello pudding commercial with Bill Cosby when he was just seven years old. He also appeared in the TV movie "A Long Way Home" and the afterschool special "The Shooting." Other feature length films include: "The Buddy System," "The Curse," "Hambone and Hillie," "The Last Starfighter" and "The Secret of N.I.M.H." (in which he was the voice of the rat Martin.) He has also guest starred on the TV shows "Family Ties," "St Elsewhere" and "Highway To Heaven." Since starring in TNG, he's appeared in the movies "Young Harry Houdini," "The Last Prostitute" and "A Deadly Secret." He left the show during its fourth season in order to pursue more theatrical film roles and to attend college. He has a younger sister named Amy who is also into acting. He likes to surf, is an avid Star Trek fan, and dreams of one day owning a Malibu beach house.

WHEELER, JOHN
played Gav in Classic Trek episode "Journey To Babel." Film credits include "Rescue From Gilligan's Island" and "The Wild Wild West Revisited."

WHELPLEY, JOHN
scriptwriter of TNG episode "Suddenly Human." He also worked on the shows "Trapper John, M.D." "Kay O'Brian" and "The Wizard," and as producer/writer of "MacGyver." He currently

has feature film screenplays making the rounds.

WHEN THE BOUGH BREAKS

this first season TNG episode was written by Hannah Louise Shearer and directed by Kim Manners. *Enterprise* children are kidnapped by beings on the planet Aldea in an attempt to repopulate their dying world. Guest stars: Dierk Torsek, Michele Marsh, Dan Mason, Philip N. Waller, Connie Danese, Jessica and Vanessa Bova, Jerry Hardin, Brenda Strong, Jandi Swanson, Paul Lambert and Ivy Bethune.

WHERE NO MAN HAS GONE BEFORE

aired during first season 9/22/66, this was the second pilot for the original Star Trek series, and has a slightly unfinished look and feel compared to other first season episodes, mainly because the uniforms are different (Spock wears a gold shirt) and the props are cruder. Written by Samuel A. Peeples and directed by James Goldstone, the story deals with extra sensory perception powers in humans and how that power, expanded, creates a monster out of Kirk's friend and first officer, Gary Mitchell. Dr. McCoy had not yet been conceived in the Star Trek bible during the filming of this episode. Instead, a Dr. Piper, played by Paul Fix, appears. Guest stars: Gary Lockwood, Sally Kellerman, Paul Carr and Lloyd Haynes. Of note: In this episode, Mitchell quotes from a futuristic

poem called "Nightengale Woman," Kirk and Spock play tri d chess, and the newly discovered energy barrier around the galaxy sets a standard for future Trek episodes.

WHERE NO ONE HAS GONE BEFORE

this first season TNG episode was written by Diane Duane and Michael Reaves. Directed by Rob Bowman, this episode introduces the character of the Traveler who enhances the ship's engines and sends them hurtling into an alternate reality where thought becomes reality. Guest stars: Eric Menyuk, Stanley Kamel, Herta Ware, Biff Yeager, Charles Dayton and Victoria Dillard.

WHERE SILENCE HAS LEASE

this second season TNG episode was written by Jack B. Sowards and directed by Winrich Kolbe. The *Enterprise* is trapped in a black void by an advanced life form who is studying them. Then the alien sentences half the crew to death, to everyone's shock and outrage. Guest stars: Earl Boen, Charles Douglass and Colm Meaney.

Whip

Ferengi energy weapon seen in TNG episode "The Last Outpost."

WHITE, CALLAN

played Krite in TNG episode "The Outcast."

WHITE, DIZ

played the prostitute in TNG episode "Elementary, Dear Data."

White Rabbit

this creature from *Alice In Wonderland* is the first strange apparition/sighting McCoy sees on the recreational planet in Classic episode "Shore Leave." The rabbit is followed by a young girl with blonde hair.

WHITING, ARCH

played an engineering assistant in Classic Trek episode "The Alternative Factor." He played Sparks on "Voyage To The Bottom Of The Sea" and has also guest starred on "Cannon" and "Barnaby Jones."

WHITMAN, PARKER

played a Cardassian officer in DS9 episode "Emissary."

WHITNEY, GRACE LEE

starred as Yeoman Janice Rand during the first half of "Star Trek's" first season. She also reprised her role as Rand in "Star Trek: The Motion Picture" (she played the transporter chief,) "The Search For Spock," "The Voyage Home" and "The Undiscovered Country" (in which she was Commander Rand under Captain Sulu on the ship *Excelsior*.) Born in Detroit, MI on April 1, 1930, her first role was as the mermaid in the Chicken of the Sea commercials. She appeared in the 1959 film "Some Like It Hot" and guest starred in "The Twilight Zone," "Batman" and "One Step Beyond." She is a singer and has recorded some singles, a couple of which have Star Trek themes. She is a recovered alcoholic and gives lectures in women's prisons to inspire people who have similar problems.

WHITNEY, MICHAEL

played Tyree in Classic Trek episode "A Private Little War." His TV credits include "Cannon" and "Iron Horse."

WHO MOURNS FOR ADONAIS?

written by Gilbert Ralston and Gene L. Coon and directed by Marc Daniels, this second season Classic Trek episode aired 9/22/67. The *Enterprise* encounters a powerful alien being who claims to be Apollo and demands the crew beam down to his world to worship him. Guest stars: Michael Forest, Leslie Parrish and John Winston.

WHO WATCHES THE WATCHERS

third season TNG episode written by Richard Manning and Hans Beimler and directed by Richard Wiemer. Riker and Troi disguise themselves as Vulcans to infiltrate a somewhat primitive Vulcan colony in order to search for a missing Federation anthropologist. Guest stars: Kathryn Leigh Scott, Ray Wise, James Greene, Pamela Segall, John McLiam, Lois Hall and James McIntyre.

WHOM GODS DESTROY

written by Lee Erwin and Jerry Sohl and directed by Herb Wallerstein, this third season Classic Trek episode aired 1/3/69. On Elba II, a penal colony for the criminally insane, inmate Garth of Izar, a once famous starship captain, takes over and uses his morphing powers to try to trick Kirk and

Spock into giving him access to the Enterprise. Guest stars: Steve Inhat, Yvonne Craig, Keye Luke, Richard Geary and Tony Downey.

Widen Dairy
company name printed on the side of the horse drawn buggy in New York in the 1920's in Classic episode "The City On The Edge Of Forever."

WIEDLIN, JANE
played the alien communications officer in "The Voyage Home." She is a singer in the group "The Bangles."

WIEMER, ROBERT
director of TNG episodes "Who Watches The Watchers," "Data's Day," "Violations," "Schisms" and "Lessons."

WILBER, CAREY
scriptwriter of Classic Trek episode "Space Seed." His other writing credits include "Lost In Space," "Bonanza" and "The Wackiest Ship In The Army."

WILCOX, LISA
played Yuta in TNG "The Vengeance Factor."

WILDER, GLENN R.
stunt coordinator on "The Final Frontier."

WILDERSON, RONALD
scriptwriter of TNG episode "Imaginary Friend."

WILEY, EDWARD
played Governor Vagh in TNG episode "The Mind's Eye."

WILKERSON, RONALD
scriptwriter of TNG episodes "Lessons" and "Schisms."

WILKINS, PROFESSOR
one of the first archeologists to find and explore the Gorgon's cave before the Starnes expedition showed up on Triacus in Classic episode "And The Children Shall Lead."

WILLIAMS, R.J.
played Ian in TNG episode "The Child."

WILLIAMS, ENSIGN
a member of Picard's art class in TNG episode "A Matter of Perspective." According to Data, his style of painting is influenced by geometric constructivism.

WILLIAMS, MICHAEL
character in Data's Henry V holo simulation in TNG episode "The Defector." The cameo role is played by Patrick Stewart.

WILLIAMSON, FRED
Anka in Classic Trek episode "The Cloud Minders."

WILLINGHAM, NOBLE
played Texas in TNG episode "The Royale."

WILLIS, MIRRON E.
played a Klingon guard in TNG episode "Reunion."

WILLRICH, RUDOLPH
played Reittan Grax in TNG episode "Menage A Troi."

WILLS, RALPH
scriptwriter of TNG episode "Justice."

WILSON, STARR AND TAMARA
twin actress who played the "Maisie" series in Classic Trek episode "I, Mudd."

WILSON, TECHNICIAN
transporter technician on duty when two Kirks beam up in Classic episode "The Enemy Within." The evil Kirk beats him up and steals his phaser. He is played by Garland Thompson.

WILSON
on the *I.S.S. Enterprise* in Classic episode "Mirror, Mirror," he saves Kirk's life when Chekov tries to assassinate Kirk in the hopes he'll get on the captain's good side. Kirk punches him in the mouth for it. Wilson is played by Garth Pillsbury.

WINCELBERG, SHIMON
scriptwriter of Classic Trek episodes "Dagger of the Mind" and "The Galileo Seven." He also writes under the pen name S. Bar David (see entry.) He wrote the pilot for "Lost In Space," as well as episodes of "Voyage To The Bottom Of The Sea" and "Planet of the Apes."

Wind Dancer
in TNG episode "Cost of Living," the wind dancer is the Parallax colony's sentinel who challenges all who wish to enter. He has a clown face and is balloon-like.

WINDOM, WILLIAM
played Commodore Matt Decker in Classic Trek episode "The Doomsday

Machine." Born in New York on Sept. 28, 1923, his TV credits include "The Feather and Father Gang," "Iron Horse" and "The Bionic Woman." He starred in the series "The Farmer's Daughter," "My World And Welcome To It," (for which he won an Emmy,) "The Girl With Something Extra" and "Brothers and Sisters." He appeared in the 1962 movie "The Kill A Mockingbird" and the 1978 film "Mean Dog Blues."

WINFIELD, PAUL
played Captain Terrell in "The Wrath of Khan." He also played Captain Dathon in TNG episode "Darmok." Born in Los Angeles in 1940, Winfield's films include "Damnation Alley" and "The Terminator." He has had many TV appearances, including a regular stint on "Wiseguy" during a series of episodes about a record company. He is a UCLA alumni.

WINGREEN, JASON
played Dr. Linke in Classic Trek episode "The Empath." TV credits include "The Man From U.N.C.L.E.," "Voyage To The Bottom Of The Sea" and "The Guns of Will Sonnett." He also had regular roles in the series "The Rounders" and "All In The Family."

WINK OF AN EYE
written by Arthur Heinemann and Lee Cronin and directed by Jud Taylor, this third season Classic Trek episode aired 11/29/68. Beings who exist

in a different time frame (in the wink of an eye) use a potion to accelerate Kirk and another crewman to their speed of existence, where Kirk finds out they plan to take over his ship and put his crew into deep freeze storage. Guest stars: Kathie Brown, Geoffrey Binney, Eric Holland and Jason Evers.

WINSLOW, PAMELA
played an ensign in TNG episodes "Clues" and "In Theory."

WINSTON, JOHN
played Transporter Chief Kyle in Classic Trek episodes "Tomorrow Is Yesterday," "Space Seed," "The City On The Edge Of Forever," "Who Mourns For Adonais?" "Mirror, Mirror" (in which he also played the voice of the mirror universe computer,) "The Apple," "The Doomsday Machine," "Catspaw," "Wolf In The Fold" (in which he played the bartender,) "The Immunity Syndrome," "The Lights of Zetar," and in the movie "The Wrath of Khan." His other TV appearances include "The Man From U.N.C.L.E." and "The Young Rebels."

WINSTON, CARTER
in animated episode "The Survivor," he is a famous space trader who was engaged to *Enterprise* security officer Anne Nored but mysteriously disappeared. The *Enterprise* finds him after five years, but is not who he seems to be. He is actually a Vendorian shape changer who has taken

Winston's form. The real Winston died on Vendor, despite the Vendorians attempts to to save his life. His voice is played by Ted Knight.

WINTER, RALPH
associate producer of "The Search For Spock," and executive producer of "The Voyage Home."

WINTERS, TIME
played Gen Daro in TNG episode "The Wounded."

WINTERSOLE, WILLIAM
played Abrom in Classic Trek episode "Patterns of Force." His TV credits include "The Young Rebels" as well as a regular role on "Sara." Film credits include "Pray For The Wildcats" (with William Shatner,) "Son Rise: A Miracle of Love" and "The Day the Bubble Burst."

WIRT, KATHLEEN
played an aphasia victim in DS9 episode "A Man Alone."

WISE, DAVID
scriptwriter of the animated episode "How Sharper Than A Serpent's Tooth."

WISE, DOUG
second assistant director on "Star Trek: The Motion Picture" and first assistant director on "The Voyage Home," "The Final Frontier" and "The Undiscovered Country." He was also an assistant director on the 1981 film "Private Eyes."

WISE, RAY
played Liko in TNG episode "Who Watches The Watchers." He is most famous for his role as Leland Palmer on "Twin Peaks" and in the film "Twin Peaks: Fire Walk With Me."

WISE, ROBERT
director of "Star Trek: The Motion Picture." Born September 10, 1914, he was a film editor for "Citizan Kane" and "The Magnficent Ambersons." His first directorial debut was "Curse Of The Cat People." He went on to direct "The Day The Earth Stood Still," "West Side Appearances," "The Haunting," "The Sound of Music" and "The Andromeda Strain," among others.

WISTROM, BILL
sound editing supervisor on DS9.

Witches
there are three witches encountered by the landing party on Pyris VII in Classic episode "Catspaw." They are like the three witches in *Macbeth*, and try to warn the *Enterprise* away. They are played by Rhodie Cogan, Gail Bonney and Maryesther Denver.

Woden
this unmanned, automated freighter is destroyed by the M 5 computer against orders in Classic episode "The Ultimate Computer."

WOLF, VENITA
played Yeoman Teresa Ross in Classic Trek episode "The Squire of Gothos."

Wolf 359
the battle of Wolf 359 is where many Federation Starfleet vessels were destroyed by the Borg, including the *Saratoga*, Benjamin Sisko's ship on which he served as first officer. Nearly 11,000 people were killed in the battle including Sisko's wife, Jennifer. The battle is shown briefly at the beginning of DS9 episode "Emissary." This was the battle in which Locutus/Picard, who was part of the Borg hive mind at that point, led the Borg in TNG episode "The Best of Both Worlds."

WOLF IN THE FOLD
written by horror writer Robert Bloch and directed by Joseph Pevney, this second season Classic Trek episode aired 12/22/67. A rewrite of the old Jack the Ripper tale, Kirk and crew must find the identity of a brutal killer on Argelius II. Guest stars: John Fiedler, Charles Macaulay, Pilar Seurat, Joseph Bernard, Charles Dierkop, Judy McConnell, Virginia Aldridge, Judi Sherven and Tania Lemani.

WOLFCHILD, SHELDON PETERS
played an Indian in TNG episode "Time's Arrow Part I and II."

WOLFE, IAN
played Septimus in Classic Trek episode "Bread and

Circuses" and Mr. Atoz in "All Our Yesterdays." Born in Canton, IL in 1896, his films include "The Scarlet Claw," "The Lost World" and "The Terminal Man." He had guest appearances in the TV series "The Feather and Father Gang" and had a regular role in "Wizards and Warriors."

WOLFE, LAWRENCE N.
scriptwriter of Classic Trek episode "The Ultimate Computer."

WOLFE, ROBERT HEWITT
scriptwriter of DS9 episodes "Q Less" and "The Passenger" and TNG episode "A Fistful of Datas."

WOLVINGTON, JIM
sound effects supervisor on DS9.

Woman
part of Riva's chorus, she represents harmony, balance and wisdom. She is killed by Solari gunmen in TNG episode "Loud As A Whisper." She is played by Marnie Mosiman.

WONG, NANCY
played the personnel officer in Classic Trek episode "Court Martial."

WONG, LIEUTENANT
Enterprise officer mentioned in TNG episode "Angel One." She repairs climate control systems.

WOOD, EUGENE
assistant editor of DS9.

WOOD, LAURA
played the old lady in Classic Trek episode

"Charlie X" and Elaine Johnson in "The Deadly Years."

WOODS, BARBARA ALYN
played Kareen Brianon in TNG episode "The Schizoid Man."

WOODS, BETH
scriptwriter of TNG episode "Contagion."

WOODS, GRANT
played Lt. Commander Kelowitz in Classic Trek episodes "The Galileo Seven," "Arena" and "This Side Of Paradise." His TV credits include a regular role on the show "Custer" as well as guest spots on "The Wackiest Ship In The Army" and "The Man From U.N.C.L.E."

WOODVILLE, KATE
Natira in Classic Trek episode "For The World Is Hollow And I Have Touched The Sky." Her TV credits include "The Avengers." (She was married to star Patrick MacNee at the time.) She moved to the U.S. from England where she appeared in the films "Fear No Evil," "Widow" and "Keefer" and she guest starred on "Kolchak: The Night Stalker."

WOODWARD, MORGAN
played Dr. Simon Van Gelder in Classic Trek episode "Dagger of the Mind" and Captain Ronald Tracey in "The Omega Glory." He had regular roles on "The Life and Legend of Wyatt Earp" and "Dallas" as well as guest appearances

on the shows "Iron Horse," "Planet of the Apes" and many others. He appeared in the films "Yuma," "The Last Day" and "A Last Cry For Help."

WORF, COLONEL
this character is supposedly the grandfather of TNG Worf, and is played by Michael Dorn in the film "The Undiscovered Country." He is the defense attorney for Kirk and McCoy when they are tried in the Klingon courts for high treason and murder. He defends them honorably, but loses.

WORF
a regular on "The Next Generation" and played by Michael Dorn. He is the *Enterprise*'s resident Klingon and chief of security (after Yar's death), raised by human, Russian parents on the farming colony Gault from a very early age, along with a foster brother. His Klingon father, Mogh, and mother were killed in the Khitomer massacre. His brother, Kurn, is alive because he was not present at Khitomer. He was an infant when their parents died and Worf was about six. Worf was the first Klingon to attend Starfleet Academy. He has a young son, Alexander, by K'Ehleyr. Worf makes up for his lack of a true Klingon upbringing by trying to be a super Klingon, but has mellowed out some as the series progresses, showing a deep loyalty for Riker and Picard, and an ability to be a good friend, especially to Troi who is

like a godmother to Alexander. Lwaxana Troi often calls Worf 'Woof'. He likes prune juice, calling it a "warrior's drink." His quarters are on Deck 7, Section 25 Baker.

World War III
mentioned by Spock as occurring in the late 20th century on Earth. Mentioned by Q as a war that happened in the middle of the 21st century and nearly destroyed Earth.

WORONICZ, HENRY
played J'Ddan in TNG episode "The Drumhead."

Wortham Units
unit of power of a ship's engines or on a phaser mentioned in Classic episode "The Apple."

WOUNDED, The
fourth season TNG episode written by Stuart Charno, Sara Charno, Cy Chermak and Jeri Taylor and directed by Chip Chalmers. The *Enterprise* engages a Cardassian ship in mutual fire, only to learn that a Federation ship destroyed a Cardassian vessel against orders and Picard must investigate the matter. Guest stars: Bob Gunton, Rosalind Chao, Marc Alaimo, Time Winters, John Hancock and Marco Rodriguez.

WRENN
leader of the last of the Tarellia in TNG episode "Haven." he is played by Raye Birk.

WRIGHT, GARY
played a Vulcan litterbearer in Classic Trek episode "Amok Time."

WRIGHT, HERBERT J.
scriptwriter of TNG episodes "The Last Outpost," "The Battle," "Heart of Glory" and "Power Play." He is also a producer.

WRIGHT, LIEUTENANT
officer who is in Picard's art class in TNG episode "A Matter of Perspective." According to Data, her art suffuses surrealism with Dadaism.

WU
one of the Kohm leaders in Classic episode "The Omega Glory." He has seen 42 years of the redbird, which only make an appearance once every eleven years. This makes him 462 years old, a fact which convinces Tracey that he has discovered a world with the answer to immortality. In reality, it's just natural for the Omegans to live long lives. Wu is played by Lloyd Kino.

WYATT, JANE
played Amanda, Spock's mother, in Classic Trek episode "Journey To Babel." She reprised the role in "The Voyage Home." Born August 12, 1911 in Campgaw, NJ, her film credits include "Lost Horizon" and "Gentleman's Agreement." She also starred in, and won three Emmy awards for her role in "Father Knows Best," which lasted nine years. Her TV credits include guest appearances in

"Wagon Train," "Going My Way," "Alcoa Premiere," "The Virginian," "Alfred Hitchcock Hour: The Monkey's Paw," "Love, American Style," "Here Come The Brides," "Men From Shiloh," "Alias Smith And Jones," "Marcus Welby, M.D.," "Medical Center," "Fantasy Island," "Quincy" and many others. She has done dozens of TV movies, including "Tom Sawyer," "Emelia Earhart," "Superdome," "The Nativity," "The Millionaire" and "Missing Children: A Mother's Story." She is married to Edgar Ward and has a passion for poodles.

WYATT, ENSIGN
an *Enterprise* transporter technician killed by Losira in Classic episode "That Which Survives." He is played by Brad Forrest.

WYLLIE, MEG
played the Keeper in Classic Trek pilot "The Cage" and "The Menagerie." TV credits include regular roles in "Hennesey" and "The Travels of Jaime McPheeters." She also appeared in the TV movies "Death Sentence," "Elvis" and "The Thorn Birds." Guest star spots include "Perry Mason," "The Man From U.N.C.L.E." and "Alias Smith and Jones."

Xanthras System
the *Enterprise's* destination at the end of TNG episode "Menage A Troi."

XELO
mentioned as a previous valet to Lwaxana Troi who

had pornographic thoughts of her. She dismissed him for it as mentioned in TNG episode "Haven."

Xenopolycythemia
disease McCoy is dying from in Classic episode "For The World Is Hollow And I Have Touched The Sky." It is characterized by too many red blood cells in the blood stream. Before the Fabrini knowledge cures him, McCoy figures he has about a year to live.

Xerxes VII
on this world, the Neinmann civilization simply disappeared, much like Atlantis, in Classic episode "When the Bough Breaks."

Xylo Eggs
Data paints these in TNG episode "11001001."

YACOBIAN BRAD
first assistant director of TNG.

YALE, MIRASTA
minister of science on Malcoria III with whom the *Enterprise* makes first contact, via Picard and Troi, in TNG episode "First Contact." Though Chancellor Durken decides his world is not ready to know of alien life, Mirasta has permission to leave the world and travel with the *Enterprise* among the stars, as she's always dreamed of doing. She is played by Carolyn Seymour.

Yamato, U.S.S.
Galaxy class sister ship to the *Enterprise* with the call letters NCC 1305 E and is commanded by Captain

Donald Varley. It is destroyed by a transmitted computer virus in TNG episode "Contagion."

YANAR
daughter of Debin of Atlek in TNG episode "The Outrageous Okona." She is pregnant and believes Captain Okona is the father but is supposed to marry Benzan of Streleb. She is played by Rosalind Ingledew.

Yang Tse K'ien
runabout from Deep Space 9 in DS9 episode "Emissary."

Yangs
group of people fighting the Kohms in Classic episode "The Omega Glory." They are a human species, with a culture so parallel to Earth's they could actually be Earth descendents.

YAR, ISHARA
sister of Tasha Yar whom the *Enterprise* meets in TNG episode "Legacy." She is a soldier of the Coalition faction on Turkana IV, and uses the *Enterprise* without their knowledge to get close to her enemy, the Alliance, in order to fatally attack them. She is played by Beth Toussaint.

YAR, LT. TASHA (Natasha)
a series regular in the first season of "The Next Generation." Yar is played by Denise Crosby, and was the *Enterprise's* security chief at the young age of 28. She and Data have a very close relationship, in

fact, she seduced Data successfully in "The Naked Now." She dies on Vagra II in "Skin of Evil," murdered for no apparent reason by a slimey-looking creature named Armus. Data has a holo-image of her, and remembers her always with fondness. Yar grew up in hostile conditions in an Earth colony, Turkana IV, that deteriorated into anarchy. The colony no longer belongs to the Federation. She left her colony to attend Starfleet Academy, leaving behind one sister, Ishara. Yar reappears in "Yesterday's Enterprise," still living in the altered timeline. The timelines merge in the past, and Yar goes to the *Enterprise* C where she will survive in the past and ends up having a half Romulan daughter, Sela, who shows up in "Redemption" at the same age Yar would have been if she had not escaped into the past. She is a high ranking Romulan official who tries to outwit Picard.

YAREENA

in TNG episode "Code of Honor," she challenges Tasha to a death duel. She is the wife of Lutan of Ligon and the former First One. She is played by Karole Selmon.

YARI

a Mintakan in TNG episode "Who Watches The Watchers."

Yarnek

name of the rock creature encountered on Excalbia in Classic episode "The Savage Curtain." He is a master of illusion, creating a place on his boiling, burning planet where humans can survive and breath. The creature itself is portrayed by Janos Prohaska, and its voice is played by Bart LaRue.

YARNELL, CELESTE

played Yeoman Martha Landon in Classic Trek episode "The Apple." Film credits include "In Name Only," "Ransom For A Dead Man" and "The Judge and Jake Wyler." TV credits include "The Man From U.N.C.L.E."

YASHIMA, MOMO

played a bridge crewwoman in "Star Trek: The Motion Picture." Film credits include "Charlie Chan and The Curse of the Dragon Queen," "V" and "The Return of Marcus Welby, M.D." She also had a regular role in "Behind the Screen."

YASUTAKE, PATTI

played Nurse Ogawa in TNG episodes "Future Imperfect," "Identity Crisis," "The Host," "Ethics," "Imaginary Friend," "The Inner Light" and "Realm of Fear."

YEAGER, BIFF

played Argyle in TNG episodes "Where No One Has Gone Before" and "Datalore."

Yellow Alert

a standby alert. The ship could be in danger, and all hands should be ready move if this is so.

YEP, LAURENCE

author of the Classic Trek novel *Shadow Lord.*

YESTERDAY'S ENTERPRISE

third season TNG episode written by Trent Christopher Ganino, Eric Stillwell, Ira Stephen Behr, Hans Beimler, Richard Manning and Ronald D. Moore and directed by David Carson. A rare phenomenon, a temporal rift, causes timelines to shift. In the new timeline, Yar is still alive and the Federation is at war with the Klingon Empire. Guest stars: Denise Crosby, Christopher McDonald, Tricia O'Neil and Whoopi Goldberg.

YESTERYEAR

written by D.C. Fontana, this animated Classic Trek episode aired 9/15/73. On the planet of the Guardian of Forever, somehow Vulcan timelines have changed and no one recognizes Spock. An android first officer works on the Enterprise, and Spock must go back in time and find out what went wrong. He visits hís home city of ShiKahr and meets himself at seven years of age. Guest voices: Mark Lenard (Sarek), Majel Barrett (Amanda), Billy Simpson (young Spock) and James Doohan (The Healer, Thelin the Andorian, Guardian of Forever.)

Yonada

spaceship world travelling off its course and endangering the inhabitants of Daran V. The people on Yonada do not know they are on a manufactured vessel in Classic episode "For The World Is Hollow And I Have Touched The Sky." It is constructed to look like an asteroid, 200 miles in diameter. It was built by the Fabrini, whose sun went nova, and is run by an Oracle. Priestess Natira rules the world.

Yorktown, U.S.S.

the *Enterprise* is supposed to rendezvous with this ship in Classic episode "Obsession." They are delayed by the vampire cloud.

Yosemite, U.S.S.

in TNG episode "Realm of Fear," the *Yosemite* is found badly damaged with its crew of five missing. In "Frame of Mind," when Riker is in the Tilonus Institute for Mental Disorders, he meets a woman who says she is Commander Bloom of the *Yosemite.* She claims two other inmates are also from the *Yosemite.*

YOUNG, DEY

played Hannah Bates in TNG episode "The Masterpiece Society."

YOUNG, TONY

played Kryton in Classic Trek episode "Elaan of Troyius." TV credits include "Iron Horse," "Get Christie Love!" and "Barnaby Jones." He was also a regular in "Gunslinger." He was in the 1963 movie "He Rides Tall" and the 1969 film "Charro."

YOUNGBLOOD, ENSIGN
an *Enterprise* officer and science specialist, seen in several TNG episodes. He is played by James Becker.

Yridian
in TNG episode "Birthright," a Yridian named Jaglom Shrek tells Worf he knows where his father Mogh is. Yridians are blue with large ears and no thumbs. In "The Chase," Professor Galen's shuttle is destroyed by a Yridian ship.

YURICICH, RICHARD
special effects producer of Star Trek: The Motion Picture." He also did work on the film "Brainstorm."

YUTA
the last survivor of the Tralesta Clan in TNG episode "The Vengeance Factor." She is the chef and taster for Sovereign Marouk of Acamar III. She is also the chosen assassin, whose cells have been restructured to age slowly, to destroy the last Lornack, Chorgon, but Riker kills her to prevent her from doing so. She is played by Lisa Wilcox.

YUTAN
one of Tyree's men, a hill person from Classic episode "A Private Little War." He is played by Gary Pillar.

Z Particles
according to Geordi, these particles jump every time Armus uses his powers in TNG episode "Skin of Evil."

ZABO
a hood who works for Krako and captures Kirk in Classic episode "A Piece of the Action." He is played by Steve Marlo.

ZAHEVA, CAPTAIN CHANTAL R.
captain of the *U.S.S. Brattain* in TNG episode "Night Terrors." She is played by Deborah Taylor.

Zakdorns
master strategists mentioned in TNG episodes "Unification," "Peak Performance" and "Menage A Troi." They have wavey lines on their cheeks but apparently no sense of humor.

Zaldan
the humanoids of this world are insulted by courtesy and have webbed hands as seen in TNG episode "Coming Of Age."

Zalkon
John Doe's homeworld in TNG episode "Transfigurations." Located in the Zeta Gelis Cluster. The Zalkonian ship is equivalent in speed and armaments to the *Enterprise*.

Zalkonian Weapon
an invisible device that chokes the crew on the *Enterprise* in TNG episode "Transfigurations."

ZAMBRANO, JACQUELINE
scriptwriter of TNG episode "Loud As A Whisper."

Zan Periculi
species of the Ferengi flower Periculus, indigenous to Lappa IV. Tog gives one to Lwaxana in TNG episode "Menage A Troi."

Zanza Men's Dance Palace
in TNG episode "We'll Always Have Paris," this place is mentioned as located right across from the Blue Parrot Cafe.

Zapata, U.S.S.
the *Enterprise* is to rendezvous with this ship when it leaves Betazed in TNG episode "Menage A Troi."

ZARABETH
a young woman, trapped in the past on Sarpeidon, who lives a lonely life in that planet's ice age in Classic episode "All Our Yesterdays." She lives in a cave and was sent there as punishment by a leader named Zor Kahn. Spock and McCoy run into her and because she wants them for companions she lies to them, telling them they will die if they ever try to return to the future. She is played by Mariette Hartley.

ZASLOW, MICHAEL
played Darnell in Classic Trek episode "The Man Trap" and Ensign Jordan in "I, Mudd."

Zatteral Emerald
in TNG episode "Devil's Due," Picard tells Ardra he knows where to find the fabled Zatteral Emerald lost among the Ruins of Ligilium.

ZATUCKE, DONALD W.
played first Lt. USMC in "The Voyage Home."

ZAYNOR
Prime Minister Nayrok's aide in TNG episode "The Hunted." He is played by J. Michael Flynn.

Zed Lapis Sector
Vagra II is located here in TNG episode "Skin of Evil."

Zedak IV
an *Enterprise* boy named Harry Bernard used to live on this world as mentioned in TNG episode "When The Bough Breaks." It is made up of mostly oceans.

ZEGOV
a Klingon female on board the *Pagh* in TNG episode "A Matter of Honor."

ZEK
the Ferengi Grand Nagus in DS9 episode "The Nagus." He is an ancient ruler who has hair growing out of his ears, which his aides comb. Disgusting and crude, he is motivated by profit and is played by Wallace Shawn.

ZEMBATA, CAPTAIN
mentioned in TNG episode "Elementary, Dear Data" as the captain of Geordi's old ship, the *Victory*. Geordi served under him as an ensign.

ZENA
she is chosen to be Alexandra's mother on Aldea in TNG episode "When The Bough Breaks."

Zendi Sabu System
it is in this system that the *Enterprise* encounters the lost *Stargazer* and DaiMon Bok's ship in TNG episode "The Battle."

ZENGA, BO

played Asoth in DS9 episode "Babel."

Zeon

a neighboring world to Ekos and involved in a war with that world. Zeon's star is M43 Alpha. The Zeons are peaceful people who were first attacked by the Ekosians who want to dominate and rule them in Classic episode "Patterns of Force."

Zera IV

in TNG episode "Realm of Fear," O'Brien mentions he was on a Starbase here that was infested by Talarian hook spiders. He still shivers when he thinks about cleaning them out.

ZERBST, BRAD

played a nurse in TNG episodes "Heart of Glory" and "Skin of Evil."

Zeta Alpha II

where the *Lalo* disembarked to fight the Borg in TNG episode "The Best of Both Worlds."

Zeta Gelis Cluster

place where the *Enterprise* finds John Doe's ship in TNG episode "Transfigurations." It contains several pulsars and G-type stars.

Zetar

a whirlwind of lights calling themselve the "lights of Zetar" appear in Classic episode "The Lights of Zetar." They speak through Mira Romaine and try to take over her body. They destroy the files and all personnel on Memory Alpha.

They say they are what is left of the desires, hopes and dreams of the Zetars whose world was destroyed long before and that they have searched for a body to take over ever since. Their morality ignores murder so they are deemed insane by the *Enterprise* crew, who must kill the Zetars to survive.

Zhukov, U.S.S.

ship on which Barclay previously served, commanded by Captain Gleason and mentioned in TNG episode "Hollow Pursuits."

Zibalia

Kivas Fajo of TNG episode "The Most Toys" is from this world.

ZICREE, MARK SCOTT

scriptwriter of TNG episode "First Contact."

Zienite

substance mined by the Troglytes on Ardana in Classic episode "The Cloud Minders." It produces an invisible gas that temporarily effects a person's thinking and retards their brain functions.

ZIMMERMAN, HERMAN

production designer of DS9 and set designer of TNG.

ZOR KAHN THE TYRANT

the tyrant in Sarpeidon's past who exiled Zarabeth to that world's ice age in Classic episode "All Our Yesterdays." Her punishment is to live alone. He apparently killed all her family except for her as

some sort of revenge against a plot to overthrow him. The ice age in which she lives is 6000 years in the past from the time when the *Enterprise* discovers Sarpeidon.

ZORA

an infamous scientist of a previous age who experimented with body chemistry on Tiburon tribes and is brought back into being to face off against Kirk, Spock, McCoy, Lincoln and Surak in Classic episode "The Save Curtain." She is played by Carol Daniels Dement.

ZORN, GROPPLER

leader of the Bandi on Deneb IV in TNG episode "Encounter At Farpoint." He held an alien entity hostage. He is played by Michael Bell.

ZUCKERMAN, ED

scriptwriter of TNG episode "A Matter of Perspective."

ZUCKERT, BILL

played Johnny Behan in Classic Trek episode "Spectre of the Gun."

ZWELLER, ENSIGN COREY

one of Picard's two best friends from the Academy, along with Marta Batanides, seen in TNG episode "Tapestry." He got revenge on a Narsicaan who cheated him in a game of Dom jot. He is eventually posted to the *U.S.S. Ajax.*

Zytchin III

mentioned in TNG episode "Captain's Holiday" as a place where Picard spent four lovely days. He says he lied about enjoying those four days however.